LANGUAGE

AND

ACTION

A STRUCTURAL MODEL OF BEHAVIOUR

INTERNATIONAL SERIES IN EXPERIMENTAL SOCIAL PSYCHOLOGY

Series Editor: Michael Argyle, University of Oxford

Vol. 1. BOCHNER
         Cultures in Contact

Vol. 2. HOWITT
         The Mass Media and Social Problems

Vol. 3. PEARCE
         The Social Psychology of Tourist Behaviour

Vol. 4. COLMAN
         Game Theory and Experimental Games

Vol. 5. ALBERT
         Genius and Eminence

Vol. 6. SMITHSON, AMATO and PEARCE
         Dimensions of Helping Behaviour

Vol. 7. CLARKE
         Language and Action: A Structural Model of Behaviour

A Related Pergamon Journal

LANGUAGE & COMMUNICATION*

An Interdisciplinary Journal
Editor: Roy Harris, University of Oxford

The primary aim of the journal is to fill the need for a publicational forum devoted to the discussion of topics and issues in communication which are of interdisciplinary significance. It will publish contributions from researchers in all fields relevant to the study of verbal and non-verbal communication.

Emphasis will be placed on the implications of current research for establishing common theoretical frameworks within which findings from different areas of study may be accommodated and interrelated.

By focusing attention on the many ways in which language is integrated with other forms of communicational activity and interactional behaviour it is intended to explore ways of developing a science of communication which is not restricted by existing disciplinary boundaries.

*Free specimen copy available on request.

NOTICE TO READERS

Dear Reader

An invitation to Publish in and Recommend the Placing of a Standing Order to Volumes Published in this Valuable Series.

If your library is not already a standing/continuation order customer to this series, may we recommend that you place a standing/continuation order to receive immediately upon publication all new volumes. Should you find that these volumes no longer serve your needs, your order can be cancelled at any time without notice.

The Editors and the Publisher will be glad to receive suggestions or outlines of suitable titles, reviews or symposia for editorial consideration: if found acceptable, rapid publication is guaranteed.

ROBERT MAXWELL
Publisher at Pergamon Press

LANGUAGE

AND

ACTION

A STRUCTURAL MODEL OF BEHAVIOUR

by

DAVID D. CLARKE
Department of Experimental Psychology,
University of Oxford

PERGAMON PRESS
OXFORD · NEW YORK · TORONTO · SYDNEY · PARIS · FRANKFURT

U.K.	Pergamon Press Ltd., Headington Hill Hall, Oxford OX3 0BW, England
U.S.A.	Pergamon Press Inc., Maxwell House, Fairview Park, Elmsford, New York 10523, U.S.A.
CANADA	Pergamon Press Canada Ltd., Suite 104, 150 Consumers Rd., Willowdale, Ontario M2J 1P9, Canada
AUSTRALIA	Pergamon Press (Aust.) Pty. Ltd., P.O. Box 544, Potts Point, N.S.W. 2011, Australia
FRANCE	Pergamon Press SARL, 24 rue des Ecoles, 75240 Paris, Cedex 05, France
FEDERAL REPUBLIC OF GERMANY	Pergamon Press GmbH, Hammerweg 6, D-6242 Kronberg-Taunus, Federal Republic of Germany

First edition 1983

Library of Congress Cataloging in Publication Data
Clarke, David D.
Language & Action
(International series in experimental social psychology; v.7)
Bibliography: p. 291
1. Conversation.   2. Discourse analysis.   3. Inter-
personal relations.   4. Human behavior.
I. Title.   II. Series.
P95.45.C58   1983   401'.41   83-4204

British Library Cataloguing in Publication Data
Clarke, David D.
Language & Action
1. Interpersonal communication.
I. Title
302.4   BF637.C45

ISBN 0-08-026090-X

Printed and bound in Great Britain by
William Clowes Limited, Beccles and London

TO MY PARENTS

'Of all the truths relating to phenomena, the most valuable to us are those which relate to the order of their succession. On a knowledge of these is founded every reasonable anticipation of future facts, and whatever power we possess of influencing those facts to our advantage.'

Mill, 1851: 335

PREFACE

THIS book contains a series of studies I have been doing to look for better ways of describing the structure of human action, the relation between key decisions and outcomes, and the forces that give shape to events. I would like to think that the results could be applied to a variety of activity systems, particularly those which are especially problematic, such as interpersonal and intergroup conflict. For the most part, however, I will confine my examples to one single activity, which is in itself a 'test-case' for many others — conversation. This presents a degree of complexity which challenges orthodox methodology, but is sufficiently common and recordable to be a good introduction to the greater difficulties which lie beyond.

Although my intention is to use conversation analysis as a means to an end, the material may also be of some interest to those who study talk in its own right. The book does not set out to offer a comprehensive review of the field of discourse analysis, or to do justice to opinions and appraisals other than my own, but it does provide a context for its main studies and issues by citing certain key works from the literature of linguistics, the philosophy of language, ethnomethodology, machine intelligence, cybernetics, operations research and general systems theory.

I would, of course, like to thank friends and relations too numerous to mention, for their help and support, but in particular Dr. John Breaux who has influenced my thinking more than anyone else; the SSRC for financial support; St. John's and Wolfson Colleges, Oxford, of which I was a member while carrying out this research; the Department of Experimental Psychology, Oxford, in which it was done; and Dr. Michael Argyle without whose help as graduate supervisor, senior grant-holder, series editor and friend this book would never have been written. Many thanks are also due to Ann McKendry for typing the various drafts, and to research assistants who helped enormously with the running and analysis of experiments, particularly Christine Smith, and also Peter McPhail, Dr. Anne Campbell, Peter Hancock and John Collins. Special thanks are due to Jill Crossland and Giovanni Carnibella for their assistance with proof reading and the preparation of indexes.

CONTENTS

Introduction to the Series   xi

List of Illustrations   xiii

1. Introduction and Overview   1

2. Experiments   44

3. The Linguistic Analogy   106

4. Breaking the Code   133

5. Theories and Models of Structure   169

6. The Human Aspect   196

7. Applications   240

8. Conclusions   260

Appendix A   Glossary   276

Appendix B   Example Dialogue — Experiments 1 and 2   279

Appendix C   Example Dialogue — Experiment 5   281

Appendix D   Dictionary of Speech-act Categories   285

Appendix E   Experimental Speech-act Sequences   288

Appendix F   Key to Classroom Study   289

Bibliography   291

Author Index   301

Subject Index   305

INTRODUCTION TO THE SERIES

MICHAEL ARGYLE

SOCIAL psychology is in a very interesting period, and one of rapid development. It has survived a number of 'crises', there is increased concern with external validity and relevance to the real world, the repertoire of research methods and statistical procedures has been greatly extended, and a number of exciting new ideas and approaches are being tried out.

The books in this series present some of these new developments; each volume contains a balance of new material and a critical review of the relevant literature. The new material consists of empirical research, procedures, theoretical formulations, or a combination of these. Authors have been asked to review and evaluate the often very extensive past literature, and to explain their new findings, methods or theories clearly.

The authors are from all over the world, and have been very carefully chosen, mainly on the basis of their previous published work, showing the importance and originality of their contribution, and their ability to present it clearly. Some of these books report a programme of research by one individual or a team, some are based on doctoral theses, others on conferences.

Social psychologists have moved into an increasing number of applied fields, and a growing number of practitioners have made use of our work. All the books in this series have been of some practical application, some will be on topics of wide popular interest, as well as adding to scientific knowledge. The books in the series are designed for advanced undergraduates, graduate students and relevant practitioners, and in some cases for a rather broader public.

We do not know how social psychology will develop, and it takes quite a variety of forms already. However, it is a great pleasure to be associated with books by some of those social psychologists who are developing the subject in such interesting ways.

LIST OF ILLUSTRATIONS

Figure 1   The skill model of social interaction   5
Figure 2   A model of dyadic interaction   6
Figure 3   The relation between well-formed and observed sequences   19
Figure 4   Histogram of scores from resequencing task (Dialogue One)   48
Figure 5   Mean ratings given to nine dialogue types of different orders
            of approximation   71
Figure 6   Experimental layout for condition in which interlocutor
            records expectations   77
Figure 7   Example trace from condition in which speaker expectations
            were recorded   79
Figure 8   Aggregate trace produced by speakers   80
Figure 9   Aggregate trace produced by interlocutors   80
Figure 10   Aggregate trace for speakers — the last 10 seconds sampled
            at 2.5-second intervals   81
Figure 11   Aggregate trace for interlocutors — the last 10 seconds at
            2.5-second intervals   81
Figure 12   Dialogue structures   86
Figure 13   Mean ratings on seven-point scale of three dialogue structures   89
Figure 14   Pure dialogue structures   91
Figure 15   Showing the numbers of subjects who identified relations
            between pairs of utterances in different structures   94
Figure 16   Tree structures in sentences and discourse   105
Figure 17   The meta-structure of classifications. (After Collett 1975)   142
Figure 18   Taxonomy experiment — response form   148
Figure 19   Dendrogram of speech-act types   151
Figure 20   'Zipf's Law' plot of frequencies of item use   164
Figure 21   Log survivor function. Distribution of run lengths between topic
            delimiters (excluding runs containing conversation delimiter)   164
Figure 22   Log survivor function. Distribution of run lengths between
            conversation delimiters (excluding runs containing script
            delimiter)   165
Figure 23   Dendrogram of speech-act types   166
Figure 24   Network map of transitions between utterances   167

Figure 25   State-space diagram   175
Figure 26   Proactive rule matrix   181
Figure 27   Matrix of reactive rules   182
Figure 28   Mean rating of three dialogue types on seven-point scale   184
Figure 29   Cluster analysis   186
Figure 30   Question and answer simulation   194
Figure 31   *A priori* tree-diagram for dispute between neighbours   223
Figure 32   Transformed surface structure   224
Figure 33   Minimum, maximum and mean displacement values   227
Figure 34   Role of models – first version   229
Figure 35   Role of models – second version   230
Figure 36   Goal map for Jo(e)   235
Figure 37   Goal map for Pat   235
Figure 38   Composite goal map for Jo(e) and Pat   236
Figure 39   First four nodes of a conflict situation taken from a role-
             playing enactment of two scenarios   245
Figure 40   Transition map for all teacher and pupil acts, where observed
             frequency (O) and 'chance' frequency (E) were different
             according to the criterion $\frac{(O-E)^2}{E} > 3.83$ 249
Figure 41   Main recycling groups and their interrelations   249
Figure 42   Internal structure of recycling groups   250
Figure 43   Derivation of vector field from deviations in trajectory   255
Figure 44   Anatomy of a sequence model   267
Figure 45   Surface-linked sequence models   267
Figure 46   Theory-linked sequence models   268
Figure 47   Sets of known and unknown phenomena and processes   269
Figure 48   Cog-wheel analogy for action, conscious experience and
             psychological processes   271

1

INTRODUCTION AND OVERVIEW

IT USED to be the case, until quite recently, that the greatest threats to people's
health and happiness came from the natural environment. The quality and length
of their lives depended principally on their resources for resisting infectious
diseases, starvation, exposure and other bio-physical hazards. Now the problems
have changed. The technologies of medicine, agriculture, building, navigation
and the like have made the natural world in itself into a relatively safe and
manageable place. We have the means to cure disease, grow food and provide
housing and welfare for the world more effectively than ever before; and yet
people still starve. They die of diseases for which simple cures exist, and in many
other ways they kill and maim one another by indifference or design. 'Structural
violence' as it is called claims huge numbers of lives. Each year, 10–20 million
people starve to death, according to Köhler and Alcock (1976), in a world that
could support twice its present population without making further improvements in agriculture or technology (Cribbin and Marstrand, 1978).

The world of human action is now the place where the greatest dangers
originate, where the effects of deliberate malevolence, unfair distribution of
world resources and the horrible efficiency of military technology can combine
to put our species as a whole in jeopardy. The future, if there is to be one at
all, depends on an intricate mechanism of human judgement and decision,
whereby policies are formulated and complex social systems set in motion, often
along paths that no one individual can foresee or control.

The mental processes which evolved with the species, enabling us to deal
with a simple environment, to hunt and farm in groups, to bring up children in
an organised family structure, generally to appraise our circumstances and choose
a suitable course of action, these same processes which once must have seemed
so puny compared with the forces of nature, are now in charge of our collective
destiny. They have the tools of modern science at their disposal, and yet are
themselves little better understood than in the dark ages.

We know a great deal, admittedly, about the biology of the brain as an organ
of the body, and we are beginning to unravel the 'software' or program structure
which enables us to see, to remember, and to control patterns of movement;
but we are still a very long way from an understanding of the principles of
thought and decision which shape long 'behavioural episodes' such as a career,

a relationship, or a national policy. Unless we learn very quickly how human plans and decisions guide our actions over time, how they form the process that generates the future, there may well be no future left for us to make plans for.

In setting about this, however, we face a dilemma. There are two schools of thought, each containing a good deal of truth, which are very hard to reconcile. On one hand there are those who argue that we need a science of human action if we are to attack the problem systematically and successfully. They see present-day attempts to resolve conflicts and to govern wisely as being like the attempts of early physicians to cure disease, without the aid of medical science. Planners, politicians and managers are no doubt well meaning, and experienced with the problems at hand, but experience and intuition alone are no substitute for a coherent body of well-tried knowledge about the underlying structures and processes at work.

On the other hand, there are those who point out that much of contemporary social science compares poorly as a practical tool with natural science (in its rather different sphere of application) and with the experience and judgement of people who deal with human problems in traditional ways, without trying to make a science of them. Lawyers, historians, and for that matter the man in the street, often seem to talk so much more sense than the supposedly rigorous social scientists.

If I had to choose between those views I think I would say this: the richest and most useful picture of human nature and action currently available is to be found outside the rigorous social sciences. The humanities, the helping professions, and the theory of action embodied in natural language, with its vocabulary of intention, feeling and thought, all subscribe to much the same picture of how people work. This is sometimes called the anthropomorphic model of man (Hampshire, 1965). I believe that is the foundation on which we should build, and that for many practical purposes it represents the present state of knowledge. However, while this humanistic baseline may be *necessary* for the programme I want to outline, it is far from *sufficient*. It has several crucial shortcomings. It is comparatively static: there seems to be no prospect of a break-through or even a steady advance towards new levels of insight. It has no effective procedure for detecting and discarding the inaccuracies it undoubtedly contains. It is uncatalogued and hard to access systematically. It uses implicit rather than explicit forms of reasoning, which are hard to follow and check. It is difficult to pass on, and so, rather than being cumulative like a science, tends to be a lifetime's saving of personal wisdom, which must die with its owner.

What I want to suggest, then, is an approach to social science-making, that takes our knowledge of people, and tries to distil it into some more rigorous form, as opposed to the commoner practice of taking a knowledge of scientific procedure and applying it to human affairs (usually setting aside all common-sense knowledge in the process, in order to build on some 'objective' fragment of mechanism, modelled as often as not on the idea of a reflex arc or more abstractly a stimulus and response pair, as the fundamental unit of neuro-anatomy and hence human action).

My examples, for the most part, will be from the study of conversation structure, which provides a conveniently circumscribed 'test-case' for a more general theory of action. What follows can be read either as an attempt to build an account of discourse structure for its own sake, or as a preamble to that more general theory of action, using conversations as the empirical material. In the latter case the processes governing what we say may be taken as a (possible) model for the more general process governing what we do.

The status of conversation as a topic of study is ambiguous. As an example of action theory it belongs to a largely uncharted area, but as a natural language construction it belongs to a world of linguistic enquiry, which is already highly structured and richly endowed with concepts and analytical tools. This inter-disciplinary status is further emphasised by the prominence in linguistic prag-matics and conversation theory of speech act theory (Austin, 1962; Searle, 1969) which seems to play quite deliberately on this ambiguity by treating locutions as social acts, and at the same time, perhaps pre-figuring the growing fashion for treating social action as an appropriate corpus or text on which to perform (quasi-)linguistic analyses; or as Harré puts it, language is both an *instance* and an *analogue* of social action.

Later on I shall develop the ideas of language as a form of action, and more particularly action as a form of language, to the extent of suggesting that there is a *syntax of action* which can be constructed as the canonical form of descrip-tion for regularities in the social world. That will involve the parsing (or dis-section) of action segments and the search for code-breaking methods and 'grammatical' structures in addition to the more orthodox considerations of cause and effect.

In outline then, the aim is to explore a different kind of social science, humanistic in spirit but rigorously formatted, which could provide the policy *science* to underpin the burgeoning *technologies* of policy such as operations research, decision theory, game theory, futures research and systems dynamics. In this the role of language is crucial, both as a form of action on which to develop and test new methods, and as a source of linguistic techniques from which those methods will be derived in many instances. In looking towards a general science of action, or a morphology of complex events, there can be few precedents more attractive than the similarly motivated and very successful attempts of general linguists to describe the architecture of natural language.

To justify this unusual and apparently arbitrary view of social-science methodology we shall need to go back to the beginning of the story, and consider in outline the present state of play in natural and behavioural science, asking just why the scientific study of social behaviour is so often viewed as a pale imitation of the exact sciences, although at this stage it will be sufficient to introduce issues and concepts in a tentative and general form, leaving more detailed and careful statements until later.

The last century was a time of great success for natural scientists. The work of physicists and biologists enlarged our understanding of the physical environment, and gave us the power to control large parts of it. Engineering and medicine flourished in the wake of pure scientific discovery, and a number of changes were brought about which have been (arguably) for the general good. The same cannot be said of the social and behavioural sciences. They have not produced anything like the coherent picture of their subject matter which is available in chemistry or astronomy, for example. The discoveries which have been made are often hard to integrate, and whole areas remain unexplained. Some people would argue that this is inevitable, since the nature of human behaviour is quite unlike the phenomena of the natural world; others would go to the other extreme and claim that the domains of matter and energy on the one hand, and meaning on the other, are so similar that the experimental method which has proved so successful in physics can be applied without modification to psychology. The answer probably lies somewhere in between. We can approach social psychology as a physical scientist would, provided we are prepared to modify the logic of discovery at certain points.

The general problem, of course, is to explain the behaviour of the social actor by relating it to some enduring qualities or processes of mind. To do that one might first try to discover those regularities of behaviour which testify to an orderly generative process, and then infer from such behaviour patterns the nature of a device that could produce them. One could then complete the hypothetico-deductive argument by postulating the existence of some such device, predicting further regularities of behaviour, and doing experiments to look for them. This course of events is surprisingly rare in social psychology. There is often no mental structure or process postulated, and the outcome of an experiment only demonstrates a relation between dependent and independent variables. As no reference is made to the source of that relation no enduring property of mind is discovered. Consequently such studies, which are really micro-sociological or ethological rather than social-psychological, are often hard to integrate and the various behaviour patterns which are observed have to be viewed as isolated phenomena, rather than the different manifestations of the same process or processes. The first methodological point, then, is one which has been generally appreciated in the natural sciences, but has often been overlooked in the behavioural sciences, as a by-product of the effort to avoid the pitfalls of introspective mentalism: a respectable scientific account can include hypothetical objects or forces in addition to those which are observed directly. Were it not for the postulation of lines of magnetic force, imaginary numbers, invisible particles, and even the concept of causality itself, the data of physics would be as hard to integrate as the data of social psychology.

This preoccupation with superficial observations at the expense of underlying processes was neatly challenged by Chomsky (1963: 328), in the taunt:

> As general designation for psychology, behavioural science is about as apt as 'meter reading science' would be for physics. . . .

The argument that the principles of logical positivism are unsuited to social psychology is presented in detail in Harré and Secord (1972). They go on to argue that a truly scientific study of social behaviour must incorporate a new model of social man, as a self-regulating rule-following agent, and not an object driven blindly by outside forces. They advocate a 'new paradigm' for research in which the capacity of the actor to monitor his behaviour and provide *accounts* of his actions is of central importance. A number of the features of this new paradigm will be discussed and adopted later.

One starting-point is to find some pattern in the actor's behaviour which will indicate how it was produced. Social behaviour is patterned in all kinds of ways. The probability that a particular item of behaviour will be produced in a specified interval of time is influenced by a number of factors, each forming the focus of a particular school of psychological thought. The probable form of behaviour changes from one actor to another and from one situation to another. A large part of the variance can only be accounted for by unique combinations of actor and situation (Argyle and Little, 1972; Mischel, 1973). The greatest observable influence on the efflux of motor information from the individual's brain (and hence on his behaviour) is the influx of stimulus information. It is the central theme of experimental psychology that responses are related primarily to each other and to the past history of stimulation, assuming the nature of the brain itself to be a constant. In its unelaborated form this is the stimulus-response view of psychology.

The important relation between stimulus and response is emphasised by the motor skill model of social interaction (Argyle, 1967) and supplemented by the addition of a motivational component. This is shown diagrammatically in Figure 1.

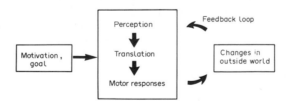

FIG. 1   The skill model of social interaction.

When the motor skill model of psychology deals with the actor's behaviour in relation to the physical world, the 'feedback loop' of mutual influence passes through one physical system and one behavioural one. If the diagram is redrawn to represent social behaviour in a dyad, the picture changes, and the previously distinct events of input and output become equivalent for the outside observer, since each event constitutes an output for one actor while at the same time providing an input for the other (provided each actor is attending to the other's behaviour). This feedback loop does not behave as a *closed system* (Beishon, 1971) as each actor will produce some behaviour which escapes the other's attention, and will attend to some events which do not arise from the other's behaviour. The dyadic picture (Figure 2) is very like Saussure's (1916: 29) notion of a 'speaking circuit'.

As an approximation to dyadic behaviour, it is acceptable to regard the system as closed, and bounded by the dotted line in Figure 2. This means that only those events are considered which are responses by one party to the dyad and stimuli for the other.

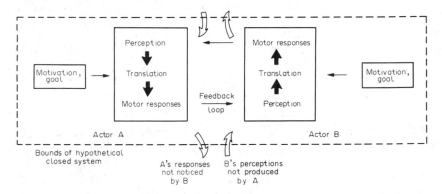

FIG. 2   A model of dyadic interaction.

The elements of the systems which have received most attention from psychologists are the perception and response processes of each individual, often referred to as the encoding and decoding processes. The encoding and decoding of non-verbal communication (NVC) has been extensively studied by such authors as Ekman & Friesen (1969), Argyle (1972), and Mehrabian (1972). The verbal counterpart of these studies is to be found in linguistics (e.g. Chomsky, 1957, 1965) and more specifically in semantics (e.g. Katz and Fodor, 1963; Fillmore, 1968; Chomsky, 1971). The concern of linguists with the encoding and decoding of language is emphasised by their use of the term 'speaker/ hearer' for the language-user. The experimental investigation of language production and comprehension has fallen to psycholinguists (e.g. Miller, 1951; Miller and McNeil, 1968; and Greene, 1972) while the effect of sociological variables on the use of specific speech codes has been the central issue in sociolinguistics (e.g. Brown and Gilman, 1960; Brown and Ford, 1961; Bernstein, 1962; Lawton, 1968; and Labov, 1970).

This concern with the means of encoding and decoding messages, verbal and non-verbal, has overshadowed the study of the process called *translation* in the

Summer Program: Fast Track To Progress

Brainworks' summer programs offer students an unique opportunity to combine rapid academic progress and skill-building with friendship and fun in a lively, positive setting. The fundamental elements of the regular fall and spring sessions remain the same. However, the summer program expands the scope to include training in social skills and motivation, and its compact curriculum contributes to the development of students who not only learn independently, but who take pleasure from doing so.

The quick-pace of the summer classes often results in dramatic improvements. The lessons, designed to meet the needs of each individual, are monitored on a constant basis by licensed professional educators. Feedback on student achievement, takes the form of written tutor reports on each of the activities (which number up to 16 per day), conferences with parents, and post-testing at the program's end.

Unfortunately, for students who *don't* participate in a Brainworks' summer program, summer might be nothing more than a few hot weeks of mindless tanning or staring at daytime television. As for the students who *do* participate, the summer could be memorable as a time when "learning to learn" actually became fun!

ADD QUICK TIPS

**Practical Ways to Manage
Attention Deficit Disorder Successfully**

Carla Crutsinger & Debra Moore

Structured on a question/answer format, this handbook provides parents, educators, and ADD students with a quick reference resource for dealing with many of the problem areas associated with the condition. The book focuses on practical approaches to resolve "real-life" situations, and these suggestions offered by the staff of Brainworks have been drawn from over sixteen years of experience working with ADD children and adults. The information is divided into four topic areas, and an additional section offers tips for ADDers in grades K–6.

- Organization Options
- Time Tips
- Study Strategies
- Personal Pointers

SUMMER PROGRAM

June 9 - 27   **July 7 - 25**

Students K–12

5 days a week in 2-hour blocks

$85 per hour

Registration and Deposit (25%) due May 1

Balance due on first session

Deposits not refundable after May 15 for June program or June 27 for July program

Adults

2-hour sessions available daily

June 2 - August 29

$95 per hour

CALL BRAINWORKS (972) 416-9410 for details

Current SOI (Structure of Intellect) scores must be on file by May 15 social skills model, in which the semantic representation (or decoded form) of an incoming message affects the semantic representation of outgoing messages. This means that a lot is known about how people make sense of their circumstances, and also about how they manage to plan and carry out their actions. What is less well understood, at least when dealing with other people, is how their appraisal of their circumstances *affects* what they decide to do, and that is crucial. In terms of the analogy which is often drawn between human psychology and the workings of a computer program, these studies have sought to discover the routines of the *compiler* which convert FORTRAN and ALGOL into binary machine code, while neglecting the *algorithm in core* which governs the form of the computation which is carried out, and hence the relation between input and output. The logical extension of this is to investigate the translation process by describing the input/output relations of the individual — the *transfer function* — in certain aspects of social interaction. However, as Figure 2 shows, a third party observing a dyad sees the sensory input to actor A as equivalent to the response output of actor B (while the assumptions of the closed system hold). Working from this perspective the observer is justified in transforming the problem so as to treat the relationship between an output by A and the previous inputs to A as equivalent to the relationship between the output from A and the previous outputs from B. Similarly B's responses may now be viewed in relation to A's previous actions, so the whole issue of input/output relations, translation processes, or transfer functions for each actor, appears to the outside observer as the issue of how each new item of behaviour relates to the past behavioural sequence produced jointly by the two actors, or more generally, of what are the regular and predictable properties of sequences of interactive behaviour (such as conversations). This perspective also allows us to appreciate the interplay of factors external and internal to the individual in determining behaviour, since external influences show up in the relation between a person's actions and previous actions of the other, while internal factors such as the 'momentum' which carries through a plan once initiated in spite of changing circumstances, can be seen in the relation between an act and previous actions by the *same* person. From now on these issues will be discussed mostly in terms of behaviour sequences, but it should be kept in mind that they are also *de facto* transfer characteristics of the human social actor.

By focusing on behaviour sequences in this way, we can describe any simple S–R relations in social behaviour, in addition to the more complex patterns which may arise. The behaviour stream would only be suitable for a simple S–R analysis, if it was constituted in a particular way. It would have to consist of a sequence of events, each of which occurred with a probability determined only by the nature of the immediately preceding event. Such a series is called a Markov chain (Kemeny and Snell, 1960). A Markov chain may be uniquely described by a matrix of transitional probabilities, giving for each possible pair of antecedent event and sequitur, the conditional probability of a transition occurring to give rise to that sequitur, given that that antecedent has occurred. The Markov chain is the simplest of a family of mathematically specified sequences known as stochastic series. The higher-order members of the family may also be uniquely described by matrices of transitional probability provided they show the probability of any item occurring after a specified arrangement of several previous items, rather than just the immediate antecedent.

Needless to say, the stream of human social behaviour may not have the stochastic properties which would make it suitable for Markov analysis (a point which is elaborated later). The analysis of behaviour sequences may be extended to overcome the limitations of the simple S–R or Markov model. One necessary modification is to study each item of the actor's behaviour in relation to the preceding item of his own behaviour, as well as in relation to the preceding item of the other's behaviour. To return briefly from the perspective of the outside observer to that of the individual actor, this means that response–response contingencies are now included, in addition to the stimulus–response contingencies of output upon input. Bales (1953) acknowledged the importance of both these influences upon the production of social behaviour by presenting his analysis of small group problem-solving as a table of *reactive tendencies* (the individual's S–R contingencies), and a table of *proactive tendencies* (R–R contingencies). The terms reactive and proactive (from Murray, 1951) will be used to distinguish between items of behaviour as they relate to previous behaviour of another actor, and items of behaviour as they relate to the earlier behaviour of the same actor.

To capture the likely form of social interactions this picture should be extended further to relate each item of behaviour to more than one preceding item of behaviour by the same person and the other. This raises the general question of how each item of social behaviour that goes to make up an interaction is related to the recent history of events in that interaction. Does social interaction operate as a kind of chain-reaction, and if so, what constrains the form that the chain of events may take?

One aspect of the search for a systematic relationship between items of social behaviour, and the past history of the interaction in which they occur, has to do with the ongoing structure of the actor's own behaviour. The events of a social interaction need not be subject to social influences alone. Many items of behaviour will be fashioned to fit the framework of the actor's plans, in the hope of carrying him or her towards chosen goals. This aspect of the structure of behaviour was discussed at length by Miller, Galanter and Pribram (1960), who reject the idea of the simple S–R schools of thought in favour of a model in which behaviour is seen in relation to the actor's mental image of the world, and his plans for dealing with it.

> What an organism does depends on what happens around it. As to the way in which this dependency should be described, however, there are, as in most matters of modern psychology, two schools of thought. On the one hand are the optimists,

who claim to find the dependency simple and straightforward. . . .

Arrayed against the reflex theories are the pessimists, who think that living organisms are complicated, devious, poorly designed for research purposes, and so on. They maintain that the effect an event will have upon behaviour depends on how the event is represented in the organism's picture of itself and its universe.

Miller, Galanter and Pribram (1960: 6)

The 'pessimists' seem to have the more realistic view, but some of the cause for pessimism may be dispelled by the study of behaviour sequences, if we are able to discern in them the effect of the plans, rules, strategies, and so on, which direct the actor in the maze of the internal cognitive world. Of course the effects of simpler mechanisms like response matching, social learning, and reinforcement should not be ignored, but their influence will also be imprinted upon the behaviour stream, where they can be recognised during a sequence analysis for whatever part they play in shaping behaviour.

It has been assumed that interaction consists of a number of discrete behavioural events, produced by the actors in perfect alternation. This is an approximation which corresponds to some kinds of social behaviour better than others. On the whole it is hard to apply to NVC, while fitting the verbal aspects of interaction quite well. For this reason, among others, *conversation structure* is to be the main source of examples here. A model of social interaction based on conversation has a number of attractions, as speech is a central aspect of social behaviour. It may also help to redress an imbalance in our understanding of social behaviour, which stems from the greater attention paid in the past to NVC by students of interaction, and bring us nearer to the synthesis of verbal and non-verbal studies which is essential if interaction as an integrated process is ever to be fully understood. As Argyle (1969) pointed out:

Human social behaviour consists primarily of the exchange of verbal utterances, but until recently there has been little contact between the work of social psychologists and linguists. Social psychologists have overlooked the detailed content and organisation of utterances, as causes and effects of behaviour. Linguists on the other hand have considered speech in isolation from its interpersonal setting, and have paid little attention to whether utterances are intended to convey information, produce action or express feelings, or to differences due to the method of communication, e.g. face-to-face, telephone, writing. . . .

It also turns out, as we shall see later, that the structure of action and the structure of language share a number of rather technical features, and so it is particularly fitting that the middle ground between the two, in the form of conversation structure, should be the point of departure for an analysis of collective action whose precedents are largely in linguistics.

Another approximation has been made, in assuming that dyadic interaction is representative of the behaviour of groups of all sizes. In some ways this is reasonable. The principles of conversation structure are likely to be invariant whether they are studied in dyads or larger groups. Some problems, such as coalition formation, or the choice of next speaker from a group of listeners, do not arise in dyads. They are, however, relatively minor issues, and can be left out of the account for now.

So now the task and the reasons for choosing it should be clear: the study of dyadic conversation as a rule governed sequence of contributions from the two participants, bearing in mind possible extensions of this simple model to include some aspects of non-verbal behaviour and the interactions of larger groups. This in turn would serve as a platform on which to build an applied science of action and policy.

Models

There have not been all that many studies of behaviour sequences in social psychology, so it is useful to examine first the methods and concepts developed in other disciplines which do usually deal with sequences and structures. The universe of discourse is always a set of elements whose arrangements in space or time or some logical array are governed by rules or laws. Moreover, these arrangements, configurations or structures are often essential for the understanding of the system, since each structure can behave differently if its constituent elements are rearranged. The essence of such a system cannot be captured by an account which only deals in the presence or absence of elements. The distinction is sometimes drawn between those structures which do not involve the deployment of elements over time (*synchronic structures*) and those which do (*diachronic structures*), such as the arrangement of paint spots on a finished canvas as opposed to the pattern of musical notes which form a melody (Saussure, 1916). (The terms synchronic and diachronic were introduced originally to distinguish between the form of a language at a given time, and the process of historical change. Here they will be used to distinguish any static and time-based structures. Note that to call a structure diachronic is to say more than that it changes. Indeed diachronic structures do not usually have a structure at any given instant that could change. Rather it is to say that time is the dimension in which the parts are arranged to form a structure.) Sometimes the same structure can have synchronic and diachronic aspects, like an embryo for example. The organs of the embryo may be studied as they fit together at a particular stage of development (a synchronic structure), or the changes in embryonic anatomy with the passage of time may be charted (a mixture of synchronic and diachronic structures). A similar combination of spatial and temporal patterns may be expected in social interaction. Certain aspects of behaviour, features on the actor's face, individuals in a crowd, limb positions or population densities, are all part of social synchronic structures, but they change with time to give us a moving, diachronic picture of social reality.

The following sections are only intended to introduce a few of the most useful analogies. They will be explored in more detail later when they are used to illustrate particular aspects of the structure of conversation and action.

Language

The best models for the arrangement of speech acts in sequences to form conversation comes from another level of linguistic description, namely the arrangement of morphemes in sequences to form sentences. This analogy (insofar as it is appropriate) suggests that we should look for a structure described by generative rules rather than physical laws; that the rules may be known, potentially at least, by competent native users of the system; and that rules of sequence exist which operate on classes of elements (such as noun, verb, adverb and adjective) rather than on particular elements (such as 'run', 'table', 'blue' and 'slowly'). Similar analogies may be drawn with codes, computer languages and programs, and systems of symbolic logic. The latter in particular suggest the *well-formed formula* as an object of study, and illustrates how an abstract formal descriptive system can reveal structural isomorphisms which would not be apparent with a more superficial and (seemingly more complete) description. For instance, the equivalence of form between syllogisms only becomes clear when the content of their individual propositions is omitted. The same may be true of social behaviour. There may be a temporal pattern in conversation which only appears when the dialogue is represented as a string of comparatively abstract event classes.

The importance of sequential structure as a feature of language was recognised by Miller and Selfridge (1950). Their comments only need a few changes to the units of description to be equally fitting as an account of conversation structure.

> Communicative behaviour, perhaps more than any of man's other activities, depends upon patterning for its significance and usefulness. An accidental inversion of letters or words or sounds can produce grotesque alterations of a sentence, and to scramble the elements at random is to turn a sensible message into gibberish. . . .
>
> We can dependably produce and distinguish only a small number of different letters or speech sounds. We must use these few elements to talk about millions of different things and situations. To stretch these few elements to cover these many needs, we are forced to combine elements into patterns and to assign a different significance to each pattern.
>
> Miller and Selfridge (1950: 176)

Temporal pattern is such a fundamental feature of interaction, and particularly of conversation, that it is hard to imagine what the disordered counterpart of a normal conversation would be like. Some indication of the meaningless and unfamiliar nature of such a conversation can be found in Laffal's (1965: 85) example of schizophrenic discourse:

> A: What is your name?
> B: Well, let's say you might have thought you had something from before, but you haven't got it any more.
> A: I'm going to call you Dean.

Interestingly each of the utterances in this passage is acceptable in itself. Even the comment of the schizophrenic patient (B) could be seen as quite normal in other contexts. Its only anomaly lies in its use after A's question. Clearly a conversation where intrinsically sensible remarks are offered in random sequence is no conversation at all.

Not all aspects of the structure of sentences corresponds exactly to their counterparts in the study of conversation. The sub-components of a sentence, phonemes, morphemes or words recur (with certain acoustic variations) and are used again and again in different contexts. In contrast it is most unusual for speech acts to recur. The pattern of their use depends on their identification with particular categories or classes of act. In this way we might regard 'Hi', 'Hello' and 'How are you?' as recurring instances of the act *greeting*, in the same way that we regard the use of 'table', 'chair' and 'spoon' as instances of the class *noun* when they appear in sentences. The use of complex behavioural sequences does not arise in conversation simply so as to make the system more economical as Miller and Selfridge suggest for sentences. Indeed it would be possible to envisage a language which did not use sequences, if the speaker/hearer were willing to use a new symbol for each message, as is the case in some simple codes and signalling systems. The same cannot be said of social interaction, since by definition it requires the contribution of more than one actor, and hence more than one act. It is only when several contributions are made to an ongoing behaviour stream by two or more actors that social interaction may be said to occur. Therefore the issue of arrangements or sequences is *always* present.

Games

The structure of a conversation is also similar to the structure of a game. Very often in a game the participants make their moves in some kind of alternating sequence, and again the effect of a move upon the game depends upon the sequence of prior events, the *state of play*, which the move follows. In chess, the move of Bishop to Queen's Knight 4 will win the game on some occasions and lose it on others. So too with a conversation, the same utterance may be polite or rude, absurd or wise, arrogant or humble depending on the occasion of its use. In conversations, as in games, the interpretation of an event may depend on its context. It is also useful to borrow from the world of games the distinction between rules (which allow the players to avoid sanctions or misunderstandings), strategies (which allow the players to achieve their personal goals within the framework of the rules) and conventions (which embody the habitual patterns of play). Of course games differ from interactions in being mainly competitive and having highly formalised rules.

This analogy between games and interpersonal encounters is quite different from *game theory* (or exchange theory as economists sometimes call it) which is a mathematical tool for understanding and optimising decisions taken under uncertainty by considering the pay-offs (advantages and disadvantages) to each player of each combination of strategies the players may adopt. A game in this sense may be played against another person or group, in which case both sides make strategic choices in the light of their expected pay-offs, or against nature when one 'player' is making strategic choices and the other following 'laws' which are unaffected by the pay-off structure of the game. To give a simple example, a person going out for the day plays a game against nature in deciding whether to take a raincoat. He can make one of two moves: to take it or not. Nature can make one of two moves: to rain on him or not. If he could predict nature he would take his mack on the days it will rain and not otherwise. However, he cannot completely predict rain and must sometimes tolerate the inconvenience (negative pay-off) of getting caught in the rain without a mack, or carrying a mack on a dry day. If he cannot even estimate the likelihood of rain, then the relative inconvenience of these two things will determine his optimum strategy, that is the strategy causing him the least inconvenience in the long run. Since nature's tendency to rain is unaffected by his likelihood of carrying a mack, or the inconvenience of his doing so, it is a rather one-sided game. Furthermore, it follows that his best bet on one occasion is always his best bet, and he can adopt a 'pure strategy' by always making the same move. Playing against a malevolent human opponent, however, he would have to contend with an opposing strategy which *was* influenced by what he did, and so he could no longer afford to be that predictable. Different optimising principles would apply.

A strategy can involve a number of behavioural stages provided it lays down an unequivocal rule dictating what each party's behaviour would be in each class of circumstance, so that the course of events and eventual pay-off to each player were specified by any given combination of strategies the players chose. In practice, though, this gives us very little help with the analysis of conversation and similarly structured systems as the current problem is our inability to characterise realistic strategies. One could say that game theory provides the second stage of an analytic procedure which· is currently stuck on the first, or rather that the full potential of game theory will not be realised until we have a better scheme for describing and reasoning about strategies.

Chemistry

The analogy between conversation structure and molecular structure is a little more obscure, since it likens a synchronic physical structure to a diachronic behavioural one. However, the principles are much the same. Again there is a set of elements, whose possible combinations are constrained (in this case by the laws of chemical bond formation). The structure of a molecule illustrates nicely two important properties of such a system. First, there is the use of element classes (the families of the periodic tables of elements, Mendeleev, 1879). It is on the basis of class or family membership that the behaviour of elements may be predicted. (This is also a basic property of syntax as we shall see later.) It is true that there are differences of a kind within each family, atomic weight, atomic number and possible radioactive properties vary from one element to another, but their essential structural feature, *the combinations which they can form with other elements*, remains the same for all family members. The same may occur with speech-acts. Certain categories may emerge which are homogeneous with respect to their combinatorial properties, but heterogeneous in other respects, such as the syntax and semantics of their constituent sentences.

The second point to emerge from the chemical analogy is the importance of accounting for structure, as well as simply the *composition* of molecules (or social episodes). For instance, the early studies of protein chemistry were hampered by a lack of techniques to investigate the arrangement of atoms in space. The best picture available came from studies where the molecule was destroyed, and its composition reported as being so many % carbon, a certain % hydrogen, and so on. This is useful in the early days as an approximate characterisation of the objects of study, and gives a crude means of discriminating between one 'molecule' and another, but it is a travesty of the delicate architecture that gives the protein its most vital biological properties. This aspect of the analogy also suggests reasonable features for the study of conversation or social interaction structures. Here too it is possible and perhaps useful to smash the 'molecules' of social life, to report that interaction X consisted of certain percentages of time spent in gaze, mutual gaze, talking, looking while talking, and so on, but it hardly does justice to the intricacies of interaction, nor would such an account enable the observer to follow a plot, to attribute motives, attitudes or beliefs to an actor, or to perform any of the usual interpretive tasks which are possible given the fully structured behaviour stream.

Systems Theory and Cybernetics

These disciplines abound in rich analogies for the study of social behaviour. The S—R model of psychology with which this discussion began, embodies the control theory notions of *feedback loops*, and *transfer functions*. The distinction in systems theory between open and closed systems has already been mentioned.

These are not the only analogies which point to features we should look for in so beautifully structured a system as human conversation. The synchronic structures of the other sciences: genetics, anatomy, topology, geology; or the diachronic structures of music, poetry, physics and astronomy are all potential sources of theory.

The detailed implications of these ideas for a structural analysis of conversation will be explored later as a model develops. For the present, it is enough to know that these models are potential sources of theory and methodology, and to appreciate the main points of equivalence between them.

The similarities which exist between conversation sequences and other objects of scientific study have not come about by accident. The point is not simply to show that there are a few examples dotted about the literature of natural science which can be used to illustrate the arguments of linguistic structuralism, although that would be useful in itself. The real point is that the analysis of *structure* has come to be a dominant pre-occupation of scientists in recent times, and the search for structure in language and behaviour is part of this move towards a structural description of the world.

> The fact of the matter is that our conception of science now, towards the end of the twentieth century, has changed radically. Now we see science as a description and explanation of the underlying structures of nature; and words like *structure, pattern, plan, arrangement, architecture* constantly occur in every description that we try to make.
>
> Bronowski (1973: 112)

Methods

This project uses a synthetic, generative method rather than a simple analytical one. One of the great successes of structural methods in all branches of science has been their application to the synthesis of new forms. Just as the chemist is able to create new substances by virtue of his knowledge of elements and bonds, or the computer programmer new routines from his knowledge of PASCAL symbols and syntax, the psychologist may be able to realise the potential for new behavioural configurations, new ceremonial forms, new strategies for the resolution of conflict, if he uses communicative *competence* as his material, with its emphasis on possible rather than naturally occurring structures, instead of the more restricted domain of observed performance.

> The notion of an underlying order in matter is man's basic concept for exploring nature. The architecture of things reveals a structure below the surface, a hidden grain which, when it is laid bare, makes it possible to take natural formations apart and assemble them in new arrangements. For me this is the step in the ascent of man at which theoretical science begins. And it is as native to the way man conceives his own communities as it is to his conception of nature.
>
> Bronowski (1973: 95)

According to Aristotle four kinds of explanation or cause would be needed to complete this picture: efficient causes (or causes in the familiar modern sense); final causes (dealing with reasons, purposes and intentions); material causes (having to do with the properties of things which enable them to display particular characteristics, so a brick can have momentum because it has mass, whereas a concept cannot); and lastly formal causes or structuring principles. This last type of cause or explanation will play a large part in the theory of conversation and action and is worth distinguishing from efficient causes. Suppose that I suddenly turn on my friend and accuse him of treachery. Efficient causes may have triggered this event, such as my discovery that he has stolen and published my research findings, but the *form* of the accusation is a different matter. There are ways of accusing people in our culture, certain things which are held to count as legitimate parts of a properly performed accusation, and it is on a knowledge of these 'formal' considerations that the design of my accusation will rest, quite apart from the initiating circumstance.

We must also consider the goal which the theory seeks to attain. If it is merely to be observational adequacy then the task is relatively straightforward. If, however, we are to consider the semantics of behaviour, the tendency for one sequence of behaviour to lead us to one set of inferences about the actors, while another behaviour sequence leads us to another, we shall have to consider the possible relations between the observed behaviour stream and the *semantic representation* which the observer erects from it. There may be a *deep structure* to social behaviour in the same way as there is said to be a deep structure to a sentence (Chomsky, 1965). With this possibility in mind, it is desirable to use methods which might bring such a structure to light.

The relative merits of emic methods versus etics; competence versus performance; holism versus atomism, and so on, all raise further issues. In practice, however, these aspects of research policy tend to align themselves with one of two major perspectives. On one hand, there is the 'experimental psychological' approach associated with atomism, etics, experimentation, additivity, performance, mechanism, positivism and determinism; and on the other hand, is the 'linguistic' approach typified by holism, emics, discovery procedures, relativity, competence, rules, mentalism and agency. Either approach would be impoverished by a complete ignorance of the other. The ideal solution would be found in the reconciliation of the two, trying to combine the virtues of both. Such a union of social psychological perspectives might be modelled upon the marriage which has been taking place between theoretical linguistics, and experimental psycholinguistics. Theoretical work must precede empirical tests. So at this early stage of conversational analysis there is most need for those methods which produce quasi-linguistic theories, not because they are superior, but because they represent an earlier stage in the natural history of the subject. At a later stage the validity of models can be tested against the intuitions and observed behaviour of the real social actor.

The methods which are used in the following studies are chosen and modified from the repertoire of linguistic and psychological techniques so as to allow for the following likely properties of the discourse system.

(1) There is an arbitrary relationship between symbol and meaning which prevents the use of data recording physical stimulus properties and contingencies as the basis for an analysis of meaning. Harré and Secord (1972) refer to this as the 'act/action' structure of behaviour, which relates specific patterns of sound or movement (movements) to their socially meaningful counterparts (actions), and thence to large meaningful units (acts).

Inferences about the nature of acts from observations of action can only be made for simple behaviour in instrumental systems, where the outcome depends on physical laws. The behavioural 'meaning' of an oyster-catcher's onslaught on the shell of its prey is easy to discern because the outcome depends on the laws of physics. That being the case, there will only be certain velocities, angles, torques and frequencies which prove successful, and two behaviours which are similar in these respects, may be seen as being functionally similar, and reliably assigned to the same category. If, however, the outcome rested on the tacit agreement between bird and shell-fish as to their conventions and rules for the use of symbols, it would no longer be reasonable to assume that behaviours of similar form carried similar meaning, or even that behaviours of dissimilar form were dissimilar in meaning. When the whole exchange is conducted symbolically as in the case of conversation, the assumption made by some ethno-methodologists (e.g. Garfinkel, 1967) that the meaning or propriety of a symbolic act may be inferred from its symbolic response, is open to criticism. In the technique which has come to be known as 'Garfinkelling', for example, the investigator breaks what he takes to be a social rule, and then observes the consequences. A sanction applied by other actors will indicate when a rule has been broken. This is strange reasoning since an investigator who knew acceptable behaviour when he saw it would not need the procedure, and one who did not would be unable to distinguish between correctly and incorrectly applied sanctions, and in alien cultures may be unable even to recognise the sanctions themselves.

Nonetheless the idea is most intriguing that language can be analysed, not by direct scrutiny of the 'text', but by the reaction it invokes in the people to whom it is addressed. Then the procedures could be sought whereby listeners are able to extract relevant features of other people's talk and display their comprehension or lack of it, in what they go on to say.

(2) The elements of the discourse system fall into classes whose members stand in *paradigmatic* relation to each other and *syntagmatic* relation to the members of other classes. This is to say, that members of the same category share the relation of exchanging for each other in certain contexts, while members of different categories share the relation of combining together to form a well-formed string, or a sequence meeting some criterion of structural integrity. This is the criterion of commutability. Consequently, each new instance is to be evaluated by some categorical rather than dimensional scheme. The phenomenon of categorical perception (for instance as it occurs in phonology, Liberman *et al.*, 1957) makes it advisable to use the category boundaries which are apparent to the actor, even though the stimuli are continuously distributed on their physical dimensions. It may also prove useful to recognise some dimensional variation, such as intensity, within each category or paradigm, just as Katz and Fodor (1963) use *distinguishers* which can represent comparative or dimensional information in their semantic theory, in addition to categorical *markers.*

(3) The system is creative. Accounts must be provided for an infinite variety of well-formed strings which may be generated and interpreted.

(4) The discourse system may be regarded as an object of study in its own

right, abstracted like the notion 'the language L' from the observed behaviour of actual speakers or actors.

(5) The system is highly configurative and relativistic. The probability of use, and propriety of interpretation associated with any element in the structure of an ongoing conversation, is highly dependent on the configuration it forms with other items.

(6) The most obvious experimental procedure, that of presenting a subject with an utterance as if it were an independent variable, and observing the response, cannot be used. The stimulus utterance would only have experimentally controlled and invariant properties if it could stand in controlled and invariant relations to its context. But the subject generates part of the context, and his behaviour cannot be controlled as an aspect of the independent variable. Somehow, the relationship of each item of behaviour to its whole context must be studied.

(7) The discourse system, like a language, has syntactic rules, because some combination of elements (speech acts) form permissible well-formed structures in the system, while others do not. This is unlike the rules for forming, for instance, all possible integers from the arabic numerals 0 to 9. In that system there is a set of structural semantic relations, but no syntax. That is to say that any digit string is permissible and meaningful, but that each different combination of digits represents a different quantity or conveys a different meaning. Language and conversation rules are more complex. They allow only certain configurations of elements (defined by *syntactic rules*) and different members of the permissible set carry different meanings (defined by *semantic rules*).

One can imagine four basic types of code or representational system. In the first, which might be called a *unit code*, units of the code correspond to units of meaning. Several code units carry their several meaning units regardless of combinations. In some respects the naval flag code works in this way. Secondly, there is the *sequence code* in which different arrangements of the same units mean different things, but all arrangements are legal, as in the case of digit sequences. Thirdly, a *surface semantic code* carries meaning according to the sequence *and grouping* of items. So 'They were frying steaks' has two meanings depending on whether 'frying' is grouped with 'were' or 'steaks'. Lastly there is a *deep structure code* where semantic varieties of a message exist with no counterparts in the order or grouping of symbols. This is only to say that the distinction made by Chomsky (1965) between surface and deep structure in language may provide at least a taxonomic framework for other semiological (or sign and meaning) systems.

There is here a methodological problem in that only some strings are 'grammatical', and these are the only ones from which the grammar may be correctly inferred, but to say which they are may be circular, since it rests on the formulation of grammaticality to be tested. The problem is confounded because syntactic rules are imperfectly applied in everyday life, so the set of structurally permissible strings does not correspond with the sets of strings to be observed in use. Nor is one a sub-set of the other. A confusing distinction exists. On the one hand, there are permissible strings which lie outside the set of observed use. These are of particular practical interest since they represent the possible domain of the synthetic use of the system, to form new but naturally comprehensible ceremonial or behavioural modes to overcome existing problems. And on the other hand, there may be members of the set of observed usages which lie outside the domain of comprehensible rule-governed sequences. These would also be of interest, since they would provide a population of misunderstandings for structural analysis and classification. It should be emphasised that unless there is an explicit statement to the contrary, the terms permissible, well-formed, proper and the like refer to the limits of *semiotic competence*, not *moral competence*. The behaviours which are referred to as ill-formed, impermissible or improper are those which disobey the rules for the clear use of signals and are prone to misinterpretation, not those which are rude or immoral. Of course there will be certain sub-groups in the population who also understand codes and jargons which are meaningless to everyone else. For the time being the distinction will only be used of widely shared non-technical language. The problem for etic methodology is to describe set A, from observations of set B (below), when there is no available information on the extent or nature of the overlap.

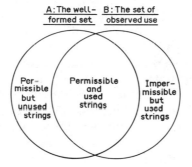

FIG. 3   The relation between well-formed and observed sequences.

Given that the aim is to study the discourse system DCS as an abstraction like the language L, there are two overwhelming reasons for choosing emically based methods. First is the need to discriminate between items of behaviour lying inside and outside the system. This distinction rests on criteria of propriety and well-formedness which are only available from the native actor, who has (potential) knowledge of the rules. Secondly, the system has to be analysed in terms of its sub-components, and these are defined by the discontinuities of meaning among the population of elements, not by discontinuities in the distribution of their observable physical properties.

Once this was under way and some overview was available of the units of discourse and the kinds of relations which could exist between them, an etic study of those behaviours which actually did occur would become much more feasible. The same could be said of the various branches of linguistic analysis, where emic studies of idealised data have tended to provide the necessary concepts and units for the later etic study of regional variations, individual differences and frequency distributions.

Before turning to the main task of proposing an analytic framework for systems of social action based largely on linguistic concepts, it will be useful to look briefly at the 'state of the art' in the sciences of conversation and action as it was when the present series of studies was beginning, although this is not the place and I am not the person to attempt a comprehensive review, such as that presented by Coulthard (1977), and the readings edited by Freedle (1977). A more popularised overview is also to be found in Farb (1974). The following examples will serve, however, to illustrate the diversity that exists in even a small sample of the conceptual schemes available for the analysis of sequential patterns in talk and action.

Until recently, the interface between language and social behaviour has attracted surprisingly little attention. A number of studies have tried to locate language within the rhetoric of social phenomena using concepts like *class*, *role*, *environmental deprivation* and so on, but it is only comparatively rarely outside the French 'Structuralist' school that any attempt has been made to reverse the process, and to fit the events of the social world into the scheme of language and language-like processes.

Studies of conversation sequences have been carried out in a number of disciplines using different methods and with varying success. Some of the major studies will be described below under the five methodological headings of naturalistic observation and recording; linguistic analysis; interaction process analysis; simulation; and experimentation. These categories represent a rough continuum running from those methods which seem to provide face validity at the expense of analytical rigour, to those which tend to do the reverse.

In addition to this literature which deals explicitly with language and social interaction, there is a more varied and technical literature which deals with behaviour grammars, automata theories and other mathematical models, which will be introduced in later chapters, as the need for more powerful analytical tools emerges.

Other aspects of the relation between language and social behaviour should be borne in mind, but they cannot be given any detailed treatment here. These include the effects of the speakers' situation, role and class on verbal style; the use of non-verbal signals in conversation; detailed studies of verbal content; and the role of language in elaborate communication networks and systems like large organisations.

Natural Observation and Recording

The best known example of this approach to conversation analysis was to be found in the work of the late Harvey Sacks' group at the University of California, Los Angeles. Their interest began with Sacks' Ph.D. thesis on the strategies which people use to obtain help in times of crisis, using as 'data' the transcriptions of telephone calls made to an American police department. The early work is for the most part unpublished, but a detailed account was available from duplicated class notes from Sacks' courses at U.C.L.A., and from manuscripts circulated by the group. Their aim (Schegloff and Sacks, 1973) was to

> . . . explore the possibility of achieving a naturistic observational discipline that could deal with the details of social action(s) rigorously, empirically and formally.
>
> Schegloff and Sacks (1973: 289)

As they point out in the same article:

> . . . two basic features of conversation are proposed to be (1) at least, and no more than, one party speaks at a time in a single conversation; and (2) speaker change recurs.
>
> Schegloff and Sacks (1973: 293)

This is the point of departure for one of their principal lines of analysis, which has to do with the organisation of speaker turns, and the selection of a next speaker, as each speaker turn is completed. The taking of turns is organised by a *turn constructional component*, which embodies the content of the turn until a *transition relevance place* is reached. This is the point in the turn where the speaker may be seen to have finished, and at which the *turn allocation component* is used. These form two groups. Group (a) contains those in which the next turn is allocated by the present speaker, and group (b) consists of those techniques by which the next speaker selects himself, principally by simply starting to speak. Often they assume that the semantic content of successive turns at talking may be disregarded when conversations are viewed as a rule-governed sequence of speech acts.

Having found that procedures exist whereby one speaker may, on completion of his turn, appoint the next speaker, Sacks *et al.* turned their attention to one such device: the adjacency pair (Schegloff and Sacks, 1973). The adjacency pair is distinguished by five features:

1. They consist of two utterances, which
2. are adjacent in the conversation, and
3. produced by different speakers.
4. They have a particular relative ordering of parts (the *first pair part* preceding the *second pair part*).
5. They have 'discriminative relations'. ('. . . the pair type of which the first pair part is a member is relevant to the selection among second pair parts.')

This fifth feature implies that in using a particular first pair part, the speaker not only gives the addressee the right and obligation to be next speaker, but also constrains the responses he may make. Examples of adjacency pairs include Greeting–Greeting, Question–Answer, 'Goodbye–Goodbye', Complaint–Excuse, Offer–Accept/Refuse, Request–Accept/Reject and Compliment–Acceptance. Very often the use of a first pair part leaves the next speaker with several alternative types from which to choose his second pair part, so the chain reaction which is established is one which branches in an indeterminate way.

Special uses of adjacency pairs are also discussed. The routine of 'opening up closings', whereby the normal chain reaction is broken, employs an adjacency pair which allows consecutive speakers to offer and accept an end to the conversation.

Of course conversations contain longer sequences than the adjacency pair. Some, like the riddle sequence of question, counter-question, response, or the introductory sequences of greeting, introduction, orientation are standard set pieces having more than two components. Others are constructed from the basic adjacency pair, using such devices as the *insertion sequences* (Jefferson, 1972). The insertion sequence operates like the embedded or nested sequences which occur in sentences, in which the ongoing connected chain of events is interrupted by a new sequence and then resumed. The 'not hearing' sequence is a good example:

> 1A: What is the time?
> 2B: What did you say?
> 3A: I asked you what the time was.
> 4B: It's three o'clock.*

Sacks discussed even more complex insertion sequences like 'Can I borrow your car?', 'When?', 'This afternoon', 'For how long?', 'A couple of hours', 'Okay', which has the form (Q (q.a.) (q.a.) A). The importance of side sequences is greater than may be apparent at first sight. They are commonplace and their existence requires little proof. The fact that they do exist seems to invalidate any *linear stochastic model* of conversation sequences (that is any model attempting to describe or explain the occurrence of certain sequences of states or behaviours, by reference to a set of *transformational probabilities* governing the likelihood of any act following immediately after another specified act or group of acts).

Another way in which utterance pairs or chains may be linked to form larger units is by the use of tying rules. These establish the continuity of the discussion, demonstrate that the new speaker has understood what went before, and provide him with an elliptical code in which new points may be made. For example, the

---

*This notation is used for my own examples of conversation, SPEECH–ACT–NUMBER SPEAKER–NAME: UTTERANCE. In quotations from the other authors the original notation is used.

exchange 'What happened last night?', 'John and Lisa went to the movies', 'What did they see?' begins with an adjacency pair (of question and answer) while the third utterance is tied to the first two by syntactic and semantic links: the use of 'they' for John and Lisa; 'did . . . see' in reference to 'last night'; and so on. Such links are produced by tying rules.

An even longer-range link back to a previous item may be established by the use of constructions like 'I still say though . . .' or 'As you were saying the other day . . .'. Such utterances have important implications for the conception of discourse structure to be developed here.

One of the most striking features of conversation described in Sacks' class notes is something which I will call a *context sensitive constitutive rule*:

> . . . for some sorts of things, the very recognition of what the item *is* turns on its placement. That is to say, for example, for the category 'answers', that something is an 'answer' turns on it placing after a recognisable question; where answers do not have, by and large, the sorts of form that permit their de-contexted recognition. Various sorts of things, like 'I went to the movies', are seeable as 'answers' via their placement.

This context-dependent identification process, the use of 'chameleon categories', is seen in its most extreme form in the interpretation of inactivity or silence. If an item is expected in a given context, an omission is seen as a failure to produce that particular item. Such items, which may be seen to occur when they do occur, and seen to have been omitted when they do not, are referred to as *observably oriented to* features.

Sacks' analysis is based on a concept of social rules which may be detected in various ways. The breaking of rules is noticed by participants, and gives rise to the use of *sanctions* and *remedial sequences*.

Utterance completion was found to occur on occasions when one speaker faltered, or left his turn at a point where the sentence could be continued, and reference to persons was found to employ terms allowing *minimisation* and *recipient design*.

Much of this early ethnomethodological work on conversation analysis is summarised in Sacks, Schegloff and Jefferson (1974), and in Wootton (1975). The notion of adjacency pairs is taken up and modified in Goffman (1981). One of Sacks' early colleagues, Emmanuel Schegloff, has published many studies of conversation structure using the same methodology. Best known is his (1968) treatment of the beginnings of telephone conversations. Looking for a mechanism by which the regular alternation of speakers was established, he investigated the choice of first speaker in a number of tape-recorded telephone conversations. The first hypothesis (called the *distribution rule*) suggested that the recipient of the call spoke first, followed by the caller. This was found to be true in all but one deviant case. Then, instead of treating this as a deviant case, which would not invalidate a rule defined according to some notion of shared propriety, Schegloff amended his rule so as to account for all observed cases, arriving at the *summons–answer sequence*. This says that the call is initiated when one party issues a summons which the other answers, which is as much as to say that the alternation of speaking is established by the strategy of one party speaking first and the other responding. The strange concept of a rule which is used here produces two problems. First, it runs counter to the spirit of work on social competence, rules, proprieties and sanctions; and second, in so doing it sets itself an inductive problem. The usual treatment of rules would allow the one deviant case to be ignored, while suggesting that further deviant cases at large in the unsampled population of possible telephone calls posed no great problem. If, however, the rule is to encompass all observations, one must concede that other deviant cases might occur in a larger sample, leading to the conclusion that two-party phone calls may exist where one or other or neither or both parties takes the role of the first speaker!

More recent studies by ethnomethodologists have turned from general constructional features of conversation, like the adjacency pair, to the analysis of specific routines like repairs and requests for information.

Often the criticism applies that the analysis is speculative, and the result (apparently) obvious. It would seem perfectly logical to claim either that conversation is a complicated thing requiring the use of special discovery techniques, and the attention of a trained sociologist; or that it is relatively transparent, revealing its structure to any interested observer, without specialist help; but the illogical implication of the studies discussed so far seems to be that trained social scientists are required to draw to our attention features of the world so conspicuous that *they* can identify them at first glance.

Cicourel's (1973) study of cognitive sociology draws upon conversational materials to illustrate the use of rules and interpretive procedures to generate a cognitive representation of the social order. A number of linguistic concepts are used as well, to point out an interesting parallel between the processes of interpreting language and those for understanding the social world. In both cases a 'normative consensus' is required, and both rule systems employ a kind of *deep structure* to embody the semantic representation suggested by directly observable *surface structure* features. The use in ethnomethodology of shared understandings about the nature of everyday life is likened to the linguistic use of the native speaker's intuitions, when describing linguistic competence.

Goffman (1972) examined the way in which utterances may be linked in conversation using the following constructions:

1. The initiator of one interchange also initiates the next:
    A^1 : 'Where have you been?'
    B^1 : 'The bookstore.'
    A^2 : 'Get anything?'
    B^2 : 'No.'
2. The terminator of one interchange initiates the next:
    A^1 : 'Where have you been?'
    B^1/B^2 : 'The bookstore./Did you fix the tap?'
    A^2 : 'No.'

3. Two exchanges are initiated by one speaker, and then both are completed by the next:
    A^1/A^2: 'Hi./Say, I owe you five bucks. Here.'
    B^1/B^2: 'Hi./I'd forgotten.'
4. One exchange is embedded within another.
    A^1: 'What'll ya have?'
    B^1: 'Ya got those almond things?'
    A^2: 'Not today, honey.'
    B^2: 'Black coffee and a toasted muffin.'

Goffman, 1972: 179

Coulthard (1973) studied classroom conversations between teachers and pupils, using transcribed tape recordings of the proceedings. The aim was to produce a performance grammar for the observation of 'typics'. This might seem strange, since it implies that the observational basis of a performance model is to be combined with an idealisation of the data more often used in studies of competence. Certain words were found to mark transaction boundaries like 'Well', 'Right', 'Now' and 'O.K.' which are similar in form and function to the devices reported in Schegloff and Sacks (1973) for 'opening up closings'. The 'unitary exchange' between teacher and pupil, which is the structural building block of longer transactions, was found to be a Teacher–Pupil–Teacher triadic sequence, rather than the dyadic Teacher–Pupil exchange which was expected (cf. Sacks on adjacency pairs). A five-part sequence was observed for the teachers' questions to the class, consisting of:

1. *The question*, which the teacher puts to the class at large.
2. *Bids*, which the pupils make, for example by raising their hands, to show they feel able and willing to answer.
3. *Nomination*, by the teacher, of a pupil to attempt the answer.
4. *The answer*.
5. *Evaluation* of the answer by the teacher.

This is a nice example of a well-structured sequence of conversation, although it is not entirely spontaneous. This routine for dealing with questions is often deliberately suggested to the teachers during their training, and enforced as a teaching method in the classroom. It has the effect of compelling all the children to prepare an answer, which is not the case when the more obvious sequence of nomination, question, answer, evaluation is used. Two rules were used by teachers to transform commands to their pupils into a 'softened' form:

1. Any declarative or interrogative concerned with a forbidden activity in the classroom is used to mean STOP that activity.
2. Any interrogative, with the subject 'you', and the verb 'can', 'could', 'will' or 'would' and a feasible action is used to mean CARRY OUT that action.

In their later book Sinclair and Coulthart (1975) report in further detail on their studies of classroom interaction. They developed a descriptive system for classroom events, intended to satisfy four criteria: it should have a finite number of terms; clear rules for assigning events to categories; the capacity to represent all the data; at least one impermissible sequence. Their coding system is hierarchical with *lessons* containing *transactions* containing *exchanges* containing *moves* containing *acts*. The acts are marker, starter, elicitation, check, directive, informative, prompt, clue, cue, bid, nomination, acknowledge, reply, react, comment, accept, evaluate, silent stress, meta-statement, conclusion, loop, aside. These are clearly attuned to the classroom situation. A category scheme for general discourse analysis would need other categories like blame, apologise, insult and so on, while placing less emphasis on the elicitation of information.

A large number of studies of classroom interaction have been carried out in America (e.g. Bellack *et al.*, 1966; Amidon and Hough, 1967; Flanders, 1970). These studies are all confined to classroom situations and events, which limits their relevance to a more general model of interaction. They use a stochastic analysis of sequences, the limitations of which will be examined in later chapters.

One problem with the study of conversation is always the collection of suitable materials for analysis, by means which do not invade the subjects' privacy. Soskin and John (1963) found a novel solution to the problem by using young married couples as volunteers, who were sent to the natural and varied setting of a holiday camp, wearing small radio transmitters which relayed their conversation to the investigators, as the couple moved freely about the camp. With the exception of a period at night, the recording was continuous, taking in a number of activities and interaction settings. Their view of verbal behaviour, like that of most authors who consider language in its social context, includes the central role of conversation in controlling the social world, as opposed to the narrower view of language as a code for transmitting information, which is often taken by pure linguists.

> A record of one person's talk over a long period of time is a record of the means by which that person tries to achieve, maintain, relieve or avoid certain intrapsychic states through the verbal management of his relations with his social environment.
>
> Soskin and John (1963: 229)

Utterances were classified by assignment to one of six functional classes:

1. *Expressive*, such as 'Ouch', 'Wow'.
2. *Excogitative*, in which the subject's thoughts are verbalised, for example, 'What have I done wrong here?'
3. *Signones*, which report subjective states of the speaker such as 'I'm cold'.
4. *Metrones*, expressing value and obligation, for example 'Yours is the best one here'.
5. *Regnones*, which give commands, permission, requests.
6. *Structones*, which convey information.

These categories are used in the subsequent analysis of the corpus of transcribed conversation. The ecological analysis relates episodes of talk to their environmental setting; the structural analysis deals with times spent talking by each participant; and the functional analysis records the proportion of utterances belonging to each of the six categories above. There was also a dynamic analysis employing a six-point scale of affect, and a phase analysis showing how the use of each functional class fluctuates from one phase of interaction to another. The scheme of six functional categories permits analysis of a conversation according to the role of the speakers. For example, the use by 'Roz' and 'Jock' of utterances from the six categories was significantly different; Roz used more expressive utterances, while Jock used more regnones and structones.

Some of the best treatments of discourse structure in recent years have come from American sociolinguist William Labov. He gives some rules for discourse analysis (Labov, 1970), such as:

1. If A utters a question of the form $Q-S_1$, and B responds with an existential E (including 'yes', 'no', 'probably', 'maybe', etc.), then B is heard as answering A with the statement $E-S_1$.
   For example:

   A: Are you going to work tomorrow?
   B: Yes.

B's reply is seen as equivalent to 'Yes I am going to work tomorrow'.

2. If A makes a statement about a B event, it is seen as a request for confirmation.
   For example:

   A: You live on 115th St.
   B: No. I live on 116th St.

3. If A requests B to perform an action X at time T, A's utterance will be heard as a valid command only if the following preconditions hold: B believes that A believes (it is an AB event that)
   (a) X should be done for a purpose Y,
   (b) B has the ability to do X,
   (c) B has the obligation to do X,
   (d) A has the right to tell B to do X.
   For example, the following commands do not satisfy these pre-conditions, and are therefore seen as joking, insulting or otherwise invalid as normal commands:

   Drop dead.
   Go jump in the lake.
   Get this dissertation finished by the time I get back from lunch.

4. If A makes a request of B about whether an action X has been performed, or at what time T X will be performed, and the four pre-conditions (as for

commands) hold, then A will be heard as using an underlying form *B: do X!*

5. If A has made a request, and B responds with a request for information, A reinstates the original request by supplying that information.

Labov also introduces the useful notion of a two-stage rule scheme for the analysis of discourse. One set of rules (for interpretation and production) relate particular utterances to their functions; and the other set of rules (rules of sequence) relate one function to the next.

> There are no simple one-to-one relations between actions and utterances; rules of interpretation (and their nearly symmetrical rules of production) are extremely complex and relate several hierarchical levels of 'actions' to each other and to utterances. Sequencing rules do not operate between utterances, but between the notions performed with those utterances.
>
> Labov (1970: 80)

Unfortunately Labov's diagram which makes this point even more clearly, is set out in a way which implies that the successive action/utterance units form a Markov chain, which is not the case, and is almost certainly not Labov's intended meaning.

In a later paper (Labov, 1972), further rules for the analysis of discourse are presented, some of which apply to the game of 'sounding' or 'playing the dozens' in which ritual insults are exchanged by Negro adolescents.

1. If A makes a request for information $Q-S_1$, and B makes a statement S_2 in response that cannot be expanded by the rules of ellipsis to the form XS_1Y, then S_2 is heard as an assertion that there exists a proposition P known to both A and B:

If S_2, then $(E) S_1$

where E is an existential operator, and from this proposition there is inferred an answer to A's request:

$(E) S_1.$

For example:
    A: Are you going to work tomorrow?
    B: I'm on jury duty.

2. A rule for ritual sounding. The sound has the structure

T(B) is so X that P

where T is the target of the sound, X is the attribute of T which is focused upon, and P is a proposition that is coupled with the attribute by the quantifier *so . . . that* to express the degree to which T has X.

For example, 'Your mother is so ugly that she looks like Flipper', often rendered in elliptical form as 'Your mother looks like Flipper'. The rule for the identification and interpretation of a sound may be summarised:

If A makes an utterance S in the presence of B and an audience C, which includes reference to a target related to B, $T(B)$, in a proposition P, and

> (a) B believes that A believes that P is not true and
> (b) B believes that A believes that B knows that P is not true . . .
> then S is a *sound*, heard as $T(B)$ is so X that P

where X is a pejorative attribute, and A is said to have sounded on B.

As with all of Labov's work the treatment is elegant and scholarly, and if only we had a similar understanding of other kinds of verbal exchange perhaps Labov would not have had to begin his article with the comment:

> Linguists have not made very much progress in the study of discourse. By and large, they are still confined by the boundaries of a sentence. If *discourse analysis* is not a virgin field, it is at least technically so in that no serious penetration of the fundamental areas has yet been made.
>
> Labov (1972: 120)

One of the most useful things to emerge from the observational studies of conversation is a consensus about the nature of the task, and the sort of selectional process which is involved when a speaker chooses his next utterance. This is summarised by ethnographers Frake (1964: 127):

> If messages were perfectly predictable from a knowledge of the culture there would be little point in saying anything. But when a person selects a message, he does so from a set of appropriate alternatives. The task of the ethnographer of speaking is to specify what the appropriate alternatives are in a given situation and what the consequences are of selecting one alternative over another.

and Basso (1972: 68):

> These studies may be viewed as taking the now familiar position that verbal communication is fundamentally a decision-making process in which, initially, a speaker, having elected to speak, selects from among a repertoire of available codes that which is most appropriately suited to the situation at hand. Once a code has been selected, the speaker chooses a suitable channel of transmission and then, finally, from a set of referentially equivalent expressions within the code. The intelligibility of the expression he chooses will, of course, be subject to grammatical constraints.
>
> But its acceptability will not. Rules for the selection of linguistic alternates operate on features of the social environment and are commensurate with the rules governing the conduct of face-to-face interaction. As such, they are properly conceptualised as lying outside the structure of language itself.

Anthropological work on particular forms of discourse in particular cultures has an important part to play here, such as Brown and Levinson's (1978) detailed analysis of the strategies for threatening and saving 'face' that go to make up the devices for polite or rude exchange in English, Tamil and Tzeltal. Special settings in our own culture have also been widely studied, such as court proceedings (Atkinson and Drew, 1979) and research interviews (Brenner, 1978).

Observational studies of conversation suggest the following conclusions. The natural use of language in conversation is varied and complicated, as Rommetveit (1968) has emphasised. It is also very familiar to us all as it occurs in our own culture, so it seems unlikely that very much will be gained by direct observation alone which is not already common knowledge. Categorisation of events poses a great problem, particularly as studies of inter-observer reliability alone cannot demonstrate that a particular system is valid. Observational techniques as they exist at present lend themselves best to the observation of the association between contiguous events, whereas real conversational structures may require more elaborate description.

Linguistic Analysis

This section will include some studies of discourse analysis, in so far as they have a bearing on the analysis of conversation, and several studies which are similar to those described above, except that they take their origins from theoretical and quasi-linguistic issues, rather than observations of actual verbal performance.

Foremost in this category are the studies of prose texts by Harris (1952) who suggested that the techniques which linguists have evolved for studying sentence structure could be applied to larger units of analysis.

> The first problem arises because descriptive linguistics generally stops at sentence boundaries. This is not due to any prior decision. The techniques of linguistics were constructed to study any stretch of speech of whatever length. But in every language it turns out that almost all the results lie within a relatively short stretch, which we may call a sentence. That is, when we can state a restriction on the occurrence of element A in respect of the occurrence of element B, it will almost always be the case that A and B are regarded as occurring within the same sentence.
>
> Harris (1952: 1)

Harris emphasises the importance of capturing the *paradigmatic relations* between elements of the discourse system by casting them into equivalence classes. When this is done associated pairs of items may be tabulated in a two-dimensional array, showing the sequence of occurrence (syntagmatic relations) along the rows, and the equivalence classes (paradigmatic relations) down the columns. In this way the structure of the passage may be formalised and certain inferences made about its logical implications. For instance, if the following subject predicate pairs were found in a text

$$AB:AC:ZB$$

we might deduce

$$A = Z$$

and, therefore,

$$ZC.$$

In a later book (1963) Harris elaborates these ideas to produce a scheme for the analysis of a passage of technical jargon.

As a basis for a conversational analysis method this has two drawbacks. The first, and minor, difficulty is that Harris' scheme deals with short (roughly clause length) units in the structure of monologue, according to semantic content of the units. A scheme for conversation analysis would have to deal with larger units (of speech act or sentence length) in the structure of multi-party conversation, according to the social function of the utterances. So Harris' scheme would not be directly applicable without modification. The second problem is more serious. He suggests that units are assigned to the same equivalence class if, and only if, they are found in equivalent (verbal contextual) environments. But that only transfers the problem from the search for equivalent units to the search for equivalent environments; it does not solve it. It is true of both, that exact recurrences are rare, and intuitive judgements of functional equivalence, suspect.

Gunter (1966) attempted to identify classes of utterance, and inter-utterance relations with particular prosodic contours. He said 'A given variety of a sentence signals its own particular kind of relevance to its context', and, furthermore, that the signalling was done largely by the pattern of stress on the sentences. For example, if

     1A: John went to town.

were to be followed by

     2B: WHY did he GO?

or by

     2B: Why did HE go?

it would be heard as calling into question the reason for a visit in the first case, and the choice of John as visitor in the second. Using such considerations, categories like recapitulation, replacement and addition are derived for the stages of a discourse, each with its distinctive prosodic features.

Hymes (1967) proposed a model to integrate a number of aspects of language in its social context. He points to the importance of a number of aspects of situated language use which may be grouped into *S*ettings, *P*articipants, *E*nds, *A*ct sequences, *K*eys, *I*nstrumentalities, *N*orms and *G*enres, which for mnemonic convenience spell *SPEAKING*. The concept of communicative competence is used as the more inclusive counterpart to linguistic competence, embodying rules of presentation, relevance and so on. He advocates the use of certain features of linguistic methodology in the study of sociolinguistics including the context-sensitive rewriting rule notation for the representation of sequential structure.

Searle (1965) analysed promises, using the kind of rules which Labov adopted later to describe sounding. Searle suggested the following defining characteristics of promises.

Given that a speaker S utters a sentence T in the presence of a hearer H, then, in the utterance of T, S sincerely (and non-defectively) promises that p to H if and only if:

1. Normal input and output conditions obtain.
2. S expresses that p in the utterance of T.
3. In expressing that p, S predicates a future act A of S.
4. H would prefer S's doing A to his not doing A, and S believes H would prefer his doing A to his not doing A.
5. It is not obvious to both S and H that S will do A in the normal course of events.
6. S intends to do A.
7. S intends that the utterance of T will place him under an obligation to A.
8. S intends that the utterance of T will produce in H a belief that conditions (6) and (7) obtain by means of the recognition of the intention to produce that belief, and he intends this recognition to be achieved by means of the recognition of the sentence as one conventionally used to produce such beliefs.
9. The semantic rules of the dialect spoken by S and H are such that T is correctly and sincerely uttered if and only if conditions 1–8 obtain.

There follow five rules for the use of the *function indicating device* 'promise'.

RULE 1. *Propositional content rule. P* is to be uttered only in the context of a sentence (or larger stretch of discourse) the utterance of which predicates some future act A of the speaker S.

RULE 2. A *preparatory rule. P* is to be uttered only if the hearer H, would prefer S's doing A to his not doing A, and S believes H would prefer S's doing A to his not doing A.

RULE 3. Another *preparatory rule. P* is to be uttered only if it is not obvious to both S and H that S will do A in the normal course of events.

RULE 4. *Sincerity rule. P* is to be uttered only if S intends to do A.

RULE 5. *Essential rule.* The utterance of P counts as the undertaking of an obligation to do A.

This is an interesting analysis. It clearly embodies the features which we, as users of such devices, associate with promising, including the all important intention of S to do A. It is particularly interesting to note the close correspondence between the features which are used to define a promise, and the rules for its use. This appears to contradict the spirit of the earlier part of the same article in which the *constitutive rules* (which define units), and the *regulative rules* which provide for their correct use, are seen as quite independent.

Having arrived at such a perspicuous analysis by the use of native intuition, it would be reassuring if it could be put to an empirical test. But it is hard to see what predictions may be derived from this which are objectively falsifiable.

The content of the rules concerns the propriety of using and interpreting promises in certain ways, so the most direct prediction would be that a larger sample of native actors would agree that any instance of a promise they were shown, which conformed to the rules, was properly conducted and interpreted. They should also form the converse judgement that any promise which did not follow the rules was ill-formed. This kind of prediction is useful, particularly in combination with other rules, in building up a picture of how social discourse *may be* meaningfully carried on, provided that the naïve assumption is not made that such rules relate in any simple way to the lines of demarcation between the kinds of speech act which are observed to occur, and those which are not.

Ervin-Tripp (1969) provides a rule scheme, in which a number of influences on language production may be integrated under the headings of *alternation, sequencing,* and *co-occurrence rules.* These are rules which provide, respectively, for paradigmatic relations, syntagmatic relations and stylistic consistency between utterances.

Since linguistics includes linguistic pragmatics, and that in turn includes discourse analysis, there is a sense in which all approaches to the analysis of conversation belong within a linguistic framework, and this is reflected in the fact that a number of the reviews of discourse and pragmatics coming from linguists and from departments of linguistics have spanned most of my five categories of approach outlined here, such as Coulthard' (1977) and Allwood (1976). Other aspects of the analysis of conversation fitting broadly into the 'linguistic' category are the study of language games (Wittgenstein, 1953, and Rommetveit, 1972); the analysis of conversational semantics (Grice 1957 and 1968); developmental studies of discourse rules (Nelson, 1973); and the analysis of psychotherapeutic talk (Labov and Fanshel, 1977).

Rule models of discourse (Pearce, 1976a, and Cicourel, 1978) are specially relevant here, and more particularly so are generative 'grammatical' models of discourse structure (e.g. Frentz, 1975), to which a later chapter will be devoted.

The linguistic analyses of conversation structure seem to offer a much richer potential for the exploration of complex forms than does the observational technique described earlier. The linguistic analysis does need some empirical support, though, from observational or experimental studies, in order to show that it is not merely an inaccurate speculation on the conduct of discourse.

Interaction Process Analysis in the Laboratory

This group of studies used laboratory settings, and procedures which include careful coding and recording of interaction events, but no experimental intervention in the course of the behaviour. Foremost in this category are the studies by Robert Bales (e.g. 1953) of *Interaction Process Analysis.* The method was devised for the study of problem-solving groups, but has since been used in a number of contexts including the investigation of doctor-patient interactions (Korsch and Negrete, 1972) and the interaction of people at conferences (Bales, 1955). Bales' procedure employs a twelve-category system for coding each item of verbal behaviour and some non-verbal ones, during a group discussion task, typically involving two to ten people. The twelve categories come from Bales' observations, theories about the crucial elements of group problem solving, and studies of coder reliability. They do not appear to be equivalence classes, constituted so as to embody the paradigmatic relations which exist between utterance types. This is a disadvantage of the method which may account in part for its limited power. The twelve categories of act are:

1. *Shows solidarity*, raises other's status, gives help, reward.
2. *Shows tension release*, jokes, laughs, shows satisfaction.
3. *Agrees*, shows passive acceptance, understands, concurs.
4. *Gives suggestion*, direction, implying autonomy for other.
5. *Gives opinion*, evaluation, analysis, expresses feeling, wish.
6. *Gives orientation*, information, repeats, clarifies, confirms.
7. *Asks for orientation*, information, repetition, confirmation.
8. *Asks for opinion*, evaluation, analysis, expression of feeling.
9. *Asks for suggestions*, direction, possible ways of action.
10. *Disagrees*, shows passive rejection, formality, withholds help.
11. *Shows tension*, asks for help, withdraws 'Out of Field'.
12. *Shows antagonism*, deflates other's status, defends or asserts self.

The interaction, thus coded, may be represented in a number of ways. Comparison of the numbers of each event type may be made within or between interactions, giving an indication of the style and emotional tone of discussion. For instance, in one study, a discussion which was rated by members as satisfactory, was found to consist of acts in the proportions *Agrees* 24.9%, *Disagrees* 4.0%; while another discussion rated as unsatisfactory consisted of *Agrees* 9.6%, *Disagrees* 12.4%. This is a relatively crude analysis, since it disregards the structure of the interaction, rather like the early studies of protein chemistry which had to destroy the molecular structure in order to report on its composition. A more sophisticated representation is to be found in Bales' transitional frequency matrices, which show the frequency with which one of the twelve act categories follows each of its twelve possible antecedent types. The terms *reactive* and *proactive* are used to distinguish between transitions from the last act of one speaker to the next act by a *new* speaker, and the transitions from act to act within the talk of the *same* speaker. It is here that other shortcomings of the category scheme become evident. The categories are very broad, leaving out a number of subtle distinctions between utterance types and functions. Consequently the frequencies in the transition matrices are relatively low. Even a transition one would expect very often, like *asks for suggestion* leading to *gives suggestion*, only occurs on 35.8% of occasions on which suggestions are sought. The highest transitional frequency of 73.7% is for *asks for orientation* leading to *gives orientation.* One virtue of Bales' category scheme is that it embodies an elegant symmetry. The first six categories are positive, while the last six are their negative counterparts. Items 1–3 and 10–12 are concerned with the task, while 4–9 deal with the socio-emotional state of the group. So four groups of three items are formed, being respectively positive-social, positive-task-related, negative-task-related and negative-social.

Bales also found that if group members were rank-ordered according to the number of acts they produced, the number of remarks addressed to each man preserved the same rank order. So the man who says most, has most said to him; the man who says second most, has second most said to him, and so on. This applies wherever the speaker stands in the rank ordering.

These findings were incorporated in a kind of simulation of group discussion, the 'T$_5$ Model', which used ranges of random numbers to represent the probabilities from the tables of reactive and proactive tendency.

Bales has also used this system to show how the characteristic use of his twelve act types varies from role to role in the group, and from phase to phase of a long debate.

Bales' work should not be underestimated. It is one of the best precedents so far for studies of conversation structure. However, it does have its limitations, of which some have already been mentioned. A particularly serious handicap arises from the presentation of the sequence analyses in the form of transitional frequency tables. It implies a kind of simple Markov structure which is inadequate in two respects. Firstly it does not account for enough past information in estimating the probability of a next act being drawn from a particular one of the twelve categories. A representation which relates each act to the previous two, three, or four would account for more of the variance and enable reactive and proactive influences to be represented together in one table. At present the combination of reaction and proaction to give a uniform impression is difficult.

The main problem is that tabulations of two-unit interchanges cannot be used to build up a picture of larger sequences. As was pointed out earlier in the discussion of interactive effects, there is certainly *no justification* for assuming that transitions between verbal events are independent and that the probability P of seeing category string XYZ, given X, or

$$P(XYZ|X)$$

is

$$P(XY|X) \times P(YZ|Y).$$

Unless the assumption of independence is justified (which it is not), there is *no inference* which may validly be drawn about the sequence XYZ from the study of XY and YZ. It is perfectly possible to envisage a system where X leads to Y

with monotonous regularity, and Y most commonly leads to Z, but XYZ is *never* observed because the generative rule is Y leads to Z except after X. For instance, in written English *ci* is common, *ie* is common, but *cie* is prohibited.

This introduces the second objection to transitional frequency analysis. Even if a longer string of past events is accounted for, so that the matrix shows $P(WXYZ|WXY)$, say, rather than simply $P(YZ|Y)$, the model is still inadequate because it assumes an even regular progression of influence along the chain of events, with each element being strongly influenced by those which are nearest to it. But as the description of side sequences by Jefferson, Goffman and others has shown, one very plausible structure for conversation is the nested or self-embedded sequence. Here, the most intimate structural relations are found between items which are some way apart in the string, while adjacent items may be unconnected. Some means must be found of analysing longer strings of acts, without making assumptions of independence, or linearity.

Bjerg (1968) made a number of 'clandestine recordings' of couples, which he later discussed and interpreted with them. (Harré and Secord (1972) use the term *negotiation of accounts* for the process whereby actors and investigators arrive at agreed reports of their activities.) Bjerg decided that the interactions could be seen as exchanges of messages, goods or moves (according to the linguistic, economic or game models). He described and labelled a number of discrete activities which he called *agons*. The list is very exhaustive and includes agons relating to the exchange of information or goods, the expression of power, esteem, love and justice, and the activities of hurting, blaming and consoling. Bjerg's agons will be discussed further in the section on categorisation of events. Bjerg's analysis is a further illustration of the richness and complexity of the procedures and routines of social life, but his results only take the form of descriptions and examples so there are no precise predictions to be tested.

Ferrara (1973) developed a method of recording verbal interaction, by using the segments of a circular chart to represent actor, recipient of act, category of act, and time. Categories are left largely to the discretion of the user although four (*positive, negative, raises problems, solves problems*) are suggested. These correspond roughly to the four main blocks of three categories in Bales' system. Apart from the convenience which this particular chart offers, the method has no particular advantages over Interaction Process Analysis.

Usually the most crucial stage of any statistical inductive sequence analysis is the formulation of a coding scheme of descriptive categories for the events. Extensive work on category schemes, with special reference to classroom observation, is found in Dunkin and Biddle (1974) and Simon and Boyer (1974).

Statistical analysis of behaviour sequences and chains is becoming increasingly popular, especially with ethologists, and is used with reference to generalised behaviour sequences (Bakeman and Dabbs, 1976) and specialised sequences such as speech (Burke and Schiavetti, 1976), peer interaction in children (Raush, 1965) and psychotherapy dyads (Hertel, 1972). Nowhere is the potential of sequence analysis better explained and illustrated than in Gottman's (1979) treatment of social interaction in married couples.

Sequence analysis of real behaviour seems to have a special appeal, although both laboratory and field observations of interaction events and sequences tend to show certain common limitations. The categories are rather arbitrary, the sequences are assumed to be too simple, and the studies are analytic rather than synthetic. Consequently they may suffer the same limitations as corpus-based linguistic analyses. There is an additional problem with laboratory situations: the discussions are nearly always between strangers, and are contrived by the investigator. They may well be unrepresentative and unrealistic, and provide the subjects with less information and motivation than they would have when talking spontaneously.

Simulation

A number of natural language computer simulations have attempted to preserve the response tendencies of the human speaker/hearer to the extent that utterances which are input to the program elicit plausible replies, in addition to receiving other syntactic and semantic treatments. This has entailed a certain effort to produce a simulation of discourse structure, albeit incidental to the primary purposes of the simulations.

Weizenbaum's (1966) ELIZA and (1967) DOCTOR programs produced responses rather like those of a non-directive therapist. This is a simple discourse structure in which the usual responses are those of calling into question the previous assertion of the 'patient', reflecting emotion and encouraging the 'patient' to describe problems in greater detail.

Winograd's (1972) simulation is altogether more sophisticated. Its principal concern is with syntax and semantics (which as one of the main innovations of the system are treated together). The discourse structures involved are still (intentionally) simple, but they contain some points of interest. The program uses a computer display screen, showing geometrical figures, as its universe of discourse. The dialogue between program and operator concerns the movement of these figures, and is typified by the following extract in which the operator will be called 'A' and the program 'B'.

> 1A: Pick up a big red block.
> 2B: O.K.
> 3A: Grasp the pyramid.
> 4B: I don't understand which pyramid you mean.
> 5A: Find a block which is taller than the one you are holding and put it into the box.
> 6B: By 'it' I assume you mean the block which is taller than the one I am holding.
> 7A: . . . .

As a feat of natural language programming this is a tremendous achievement, but as a discourse it is still primitive. The exchanges are only two units in length, and the connection between units is formed at the level of propositional content rather than a wide variety of performative types. Three utterance classes are used *question, declarative* and *imperative*, although subtle distinctions like reports on action, and requests for confirmation, may be seen in the above material. In producing a coherent discourse structure the program had to account for three levels of context dependency. Local discourse dependency governs the interpretation of elliptical forms, so a question like 'Why?' or 'Where is it?' can only be properly answered when interpreted in the light of (at least) one previous utterance. Overall discourse dependency governs the interpretation of common phrases in the light of the topic of conversation, so 'the board' will figure differently in discussion of company policy, and carpentry. There is also a context dependency in the interpretation of items which requires a knowledge of the world in addition to a knowledge of the language. In the sentences

> The boy fell off his bike because it was faulty.

and

> The boy fell off his bike because it was raining.

the different referents for 'it' cannot be detected from linguistic features alone.

In so far as this program deals with the structure of discourse, it only has to do with the propositional content of utterances and the *logical* relations between them, which is a relatively minor consideration for the student of social behaviour. The same is true of the Simmons and Slocum (1972) study of discourse simulation, which employs a semantic net of concepts and relations. The narrative structure of monologue may be preserved, but the subtleties of dialogue are largely unrepresented.

In a similar way work on story-understanding systems, scripts and frames has shown a great deal about our dependence on stored expectations of sequence when understanding brief or incomplete stories (see Schank and Abelson, 1977; Wason and Johnson-Laird, 1972; and Boden, 1977). How else would we make sense of a sentence like 'John saw the black clouds looming and was furious to find the umbrella-stand empty'. This requires in the reader a 'script' like:

1. Sky darkens
2. Rain begins
3. People search for protective clothing
4. Fail to find it
5. Anticipate a soaking
6. Become annoyed.

as a plausible course of events in memory, so that given 1, 3, 4 and 6 they see the implicit connection of 2 and 5 and can produce these 'stages' by way of explanation for what happened.

For the present purpose, however, the present state of development of script analysis does not solve the immediate problem, namely how the common diagnostic features of a set of apparently different sequences are to be discovered and stated. Given this problem, script analysis appears to offer no more help than would an example sentence and a footnote that variations are possible in writing the grammar of a language.

The idea that discourse structures can be modelled, or 'analysed by synthesis' does not necessarily involve computer simulation. A variety of mathematical descriptions of interaction sequences and processes have been produced with or without computer realisation, and based on differential equation representations of complex physical systems (Simon, 1952); matrix games (Huesman and Levinger, 1976); information theory (Shannon, 1948, and Altman, 1965) and Recursive Augmented Transition Network procedures for sentence parsing (Woods, 1970).

The work of the mathematician and philosopher Turing (1950) is often cited in the context of simulation studies, although his contribution was not in the production of simulations *per se*. He discussed the objective criteria which might be used in deciding whether a device was or was not 'intelligent', suggesting as one such criterion the 'imitation game'. This requires the device to pass for an intelligent being (namely a human) when the performances of the two are compared. For example, subjects might be asked to conduct a verbal interaction over a teletype link with a respondent who was either human or a computer. If the subject cannot decide the nature of his partner with better than chance accuracy, as a result of this conversation, then the simulation may be said to behave like a thinking being. The argument was introduced as an example to clarify our conception of what it is to attribute intelligence to a person or thing, but has since been used as an experimental procedure for the evaluation of simulations, and will be used here to evaluate artificial rule systems.

The study of conversation by simulation offers exciting possibilities of complex models of discourse structure which are generative and creative, and whose predictions (output) may be tested by comparison with real corpora of speech. However, in putting this idea into practice, a dilemma arises in that simulations whose output is in the form of simple speech act descriptions lose many of the subtleties of real talk, while simulations in which full-blown utterances are the medium of input and output require enormously complex models of the syntax and semantics of natural language, quite apart from discourse conventions, like Winograd's (*op. cit.*) SHRDLU. Later on a compromise will be described which goes some way towards giving the best of both worlds: computational simplicity, and a rich enough description of discourse patterns to model interesting structures.

Experimentation

This section includes those studies in which detailed observations and measurements of conversation were made by means other than an interaction process analysis.

Experiments on the conduct of conversation have been rare, partly because of the difficulties outlined earlier, and those which have been performed have tended to avoid the central issue of what people say and when, in order to concentrate on the 'battle for the floor', and the signals used to negotiate the roles of speaker and listener. Kendon (1967) found that the non-verbal signal of looking at another person in the region of his eyes, variously known as *gaze* or *Looking* when performed by only one actor, and *mutual gaze* or *eye-contact* when performed simultaneously by both members of a dyad, was used to effect a smooth exchange of the roles of speaker and listener. Typically the speaker looks slightly less than the listener, during a long utterance. Then during the last few seconds of his utterance the speaker's probability of Looking rises from about 55% to about 75%, while the listener's probability of Looking falls by 65% to about 25%. If this signal is not used the exchange of speakers may be impaired by long pauses between utterances.

Speech amplitude serves as a signal to resolve battles for the floor (Meltzer *et al.*, 1971). When interruptions or simultaneous speaking occur, the outcome may be predicted from (a) the change in the interruptee's vocal amplitude from before to during the interruption and (b) the difference between the interruptee's and interrupter's amplitude during simultaneous speech. It is not surprising to learn that one way of winning a contest for the floor is to 'shout down' the opposition, and the claim made in the article that it heralds an age of 'social psychophysics' seems unwarranted. The idea that social behaviour may be viewed as a simple function of a few physical variables would not generalise far beyond this level of description. Morris (1971) also deals with the outcome of periods of simultaneous speech, but by rather more elaborate means. The members of his subject pairs sat in different rooms, conversing over an audio link like a domestic telephone. The signals were passed though an attenuator controlled by an on-line computer, so that boosts in the transmitted amplitude of a speaker's voice could be simulated by temporary reductions in attenuation. The computer was programmed to detect bouts of simultaneous speech, and insert amplitude boosts on certain trials. The relationship was recorded between amplitude boosts, and interruption outcomes, and three conclusions reached.

1. Amplitude is causally related to interruption outcomes.
2. Amplitude increments are only effective if made by the 'defender' of the floor.
3. Subjects whose attempts are continually thwarted 'retaliate' by boosting their own vocal amplitude when in the role of defender.

Duncan's analyses (1972, 1973 and with Fiske, 1977) of turn-taking in conversation encompass a greater variety of signals and ploys. He finds that turn-yielding signals include the use of middle intonation; a drawl on the final syllable; termination of a hand gesture; sociometric sequences such as 'but uh', and 'or something'; a drop in pitch or loudness with drawl; and completion of a grammatical clause. The use of continued gesture acted as a signal to suppress bids for the floor, and the present speaker could be encouraged to continue by the listener's use of *back-channel communications* like nods of the head, brief requests for clarification, and brief summaries of the speaker's recent points.

The opportunities for speaker change are also governed by the content of speaking turns, and by the syntactic structure of their component utterances. Argyle and McCallin (1981) presented subjects with tape-recorded examples of interruption, and asked them to judge to what degree each interruption violated the rules of polite conversation. The tapes included interruptions at different points in the structure of the first speaker's sentence, and the perceived propriety of interruption was found to vary accordingly. Interruptions at the end of a sentence were viewed as most acceptable, followed by those at the end of a clause. Interruptions in mid-clause were least acceptable. The length of the interrupted utterance made no difference. This provides experimental confirmation for Sacks' theory that the speaker turn contains *transition relevance places* at which bids for the floor may legitimately be made. The various studies of speaker change are hard to integrate, since their authors place such different emphasis on the factors involved. Meltzer *et al.* consider the role of non-verbal cues in effecting speaker change, while Argyle reports the effects of message structure, and Sacks the influence of message content. A fourth school of thought seeks to relate the distribution of speech and silence in the dyad simply to the immediate history of speech and silence. Jaffe, Feldstein and Cassota (1967) find that the probability of an individual speaking in a 300-msec interval of time may be predicted from the state of talk in the previous 300-msec interval, as represented by the four possibilities of A speaks, B speaks, both speak, neither speak. Thus the distribution of talking seems to adhere closely to Markovian principles, with little additional power being added to the prediction by the consideration of longer interaction histories. They also find that the predictions of an 'independent decision' model hold good. That is to say that each speaker seems to take the decision to speak independently, with the result that simultaneous speech occurs with a probability equal to the product of the probabilities that A speaks, and B speaks.

In a later elaboration of this approach, Feldstein (1972) investigated other temporal features of the pattern of speech and silence. His method involves a complex computer analysis and an analog/digital converter to record the occurrence of speech and pauses. Many of the findings seem disappointingly obvious, given the care that was used in producing them. For example, his matrix of correlations between vocalisation, pauses, switching pauses and simultaneous speech shows amongst other things that his two categories of vocalisation correlate positively, the two categories of silence correlate positively, and each kind of vocalisation correlates negatively with each kind of silence. This seems rather like saying that in a finite interval of time, the more one talks, the less one keeps silent — an observation we can have little reason to doubt. His recursive model of sound and silence, which is presented in the form of an argument in the predicate calculus, allows the periods of vocalisation, pausing, simultaneous speech and switching pauses to be defined and correlated, but it is hard to see what predictions such a model could produce which would be of much practical or theoretical importance.

The difficulties of performing experiments on conversation are exemplified by Webb's (1972) study of speech rate in interviews. He tried to control for variations in interviewer performance which might disrupt the experimental investigation of interviewee performance. In order to achieve this degree of control the interviewer was replaced by a prerecorded audio-tape playing from another room, which Webb called an 'automated standard interview'. In practice the procedure seems to restrict the experimental paradigm, since all visual cues are omitted, which may have interacted in important ways with speech rate; the essential contingency between utterances which characterise any conversation is lost; the interviewer is confined to vague de-contextualised utterances such as

> Would you like to carry that on a bit further and round it out a bit? Perhaps you could tell me something about some of the other things that you know or have heard about!

A more realistic control would be to use interviewer utterances in each experimental condition which stand in a constant relation to their verbal context, rather than simply using the same utterances. This, however, would require a knowledge of utterance types and conversation rules which is well beyond our present capability.

Those rare studies which have dealt with the content of conversational components, and their interrelations, have often employed the model of exchange theory as their theoretical base. Using such a framework Heller (1972) reports that subjects responded to challenging interview conditions with attempts to meet and overcome the challenge. Also subjects whose defensive style allows them to be more open in admitting personal concerns do so more frequently in moderately stressful interview conditions than in more subjectively pleasant and less threatening conditions. Similarly Foa and Foa (1972) analyse dyadic interaction as an exchange of interpersonal resources, but this approach leads to even higher levels of abstraction, operating over longer periods of time, than are required for sequence analysis in conversation.

The effect of context on utterance processing has been studied experimentally by Rommetveit et al. (1971) who found that 'content' was extracted and registered rather than the exact syntactic form of utterances. Pearce (1976b) was able to find an experimental way to investigate sequences of speech-act types in discourse, which so many authors had neglected or found too elusive. He gave speech-act names to subjects on cards to be shuffled into appropriate sequences, providing convenient if somewhat unrealistic data for subsequent sequence analysis. The reordering of utterances on cards had previously been the basis of an early study by the present author (1975) described in the next chapter.

One of the main centres of experimental work on conversation structure has been the psychology department of the University of Gothenburg, where Brenner and Hjelmquist (1974 a, b and c, and 1975), Brenner (1975) and Hjelmquist (1975) have been tracing the interdependence between various interaction process variables, content variables and personality variables in social interaction.

Experimental work on conversation sequences is reviewed more extensively than is possible here in Clarke and Argyle (1982).

On the whole, laboratory studies of conversation structure are difficult to perform by the obvious means of manipulating the performance of one speaker (as an independent variable) and observing the effect on the speech of the other (the dependent variable). Two major problems arise. If the confederate is to be fully controlled he cannot react to the subject, so one aspect of the sequence is distorted; and if each response by the subject is to be set in a predetermined context, then his own proaction will have to be restricted. The difficulty is overcome to some extent in studies of verbal conditioning and ingratiation by the use of very general stimulus and response categories.

The studies which can be successfully carried out using conventional experiments concern behaviour at a much lower level of description than the speech-act sequence, and they shed rather little light on the issue here.

Finally, it is worth repeating that this is by no means a general review of work in conversational analysis (for which see, for example, Coulthard, 1977), let alone of the other fields that bear upon this problem. It is merely intended to set the scene and provide some orientation to the historical context in which the following studies were carried out.

2

EXPERIMENTS

THE BRIEF review of the literature in Chapter 1 showed that relatively little social psychological work has been done on the structure of conversation, and those studies which do exist have addressed a number of disparate topics, without reference to any single unifying theoretical framework. Furthermore, some of the results have been speculative, and unsupported by empirical findings. In short the field is still rather open, leaving a number of basic principles to be firmly established. The first and most fundamental issue in the study of conversation structure has to do with the very existence of a structure — the *sine qua non* for this project. The idea of a structure implies that the object of study (in this case conversation, in its broadest sense including dispute — negotiation, argument, and so on) is a thing of many parts (which correspond roughly to the individual utterances, 'lines' or 'turns-at-talking' of different speakers), and that the arrangement of parts to form the whole is not a haphazard matter, but a complex process in which some configurations may be allowed to occur, while others are not. Also some of the permissible arrangements may be found to occur more frequently than others. The former constraint belongs to the realm of communicative competence, and the latter to the domain of performance.

Experiment 1: Demonstration of Sequential Patterns

Introduction

This experiment is orientated towards observed performance, and seeks to demonstrate that spontaneous dyadic conversation between individuals employs utterances in a patterned, predictable sequence, implying the existence of a conversation structure worthy of further investigation.

It may seem strange to begin the enquiry with a demonstration that structures exist, when they cannot be described or give rise to behavioural predictions until much later. What is it to say of a system that it is structured when there is not even a single feature of the structure which can be identified? The question is best met with an analogy. Suppose the claim were made that a computer program was available which turned English prose into some esoteric language,

L. There are sceptics who would like to test this claim, but who do not speak L. They submit passages of English to the device for translation, but are unable to recognise in the output the internal consistencies which would be apparent to the fluent speaker of L. Nor can they detect the lawful dependencies of output upon input which would impress the bilingual user of English and L. In desperation they decide to ignore the properties of L itself, in order to concentrate on the simpler issue of whether or not the device produces an output which stands in any predictable relation to the input. This they are able to do by using the facility for translation from L to English to recover the English form of one of their original passages. For this test to work three things must be true,

1. The English–L translation must follow some pattern.
2. The L–English translation must follow some pattern.
3. A certain reciprocity must exist between the English–L, and the L–English procedures.

Then, the inference may validly be made that the output of 'L' is patterned, and that it stands in a predictable relationship to the English input, without there being any aspect of the pattern of 'L' which is apparent to the observer.

A similar argument is used in this experiment. The systematic 'translation' to be detected is not from one language to another, but the input/output translation of the human speaker/hearer which appeared in the motor skill model in Chapter 1. If the speaker normally translates the past history of a conversation into a set of systematic constraints on the form and content of his next utterance then it may be possible to employ a reverse translation to retrieve the history of events from the nature of the individual utterances. It should be possible, therefore, to reconstitute the correct sequence of such a conversation, when given its component utterances in the wrong order. That was the essence of this experiment. As with the example of computer translation quoted above, the experiment would only work if three assumptions about the nature of conversation and conversationalists are *all* true.

1. Spontaneous conversation employs utterances in non-random sequences, which is to say that each utterance has characteristics which relate systematically to those of previous utterances.
2. The native user of the discourse system has an understanding of these patterns, which may be called upon in making judgements about the speech of others.
3. The native speaker's beliefs about conversation patterns are largely correct.

These are tested simultaneously in the experimental hypothesis that subjects can reassemble an unfamiliar dialogue with greater than chance accuracy when presented with its component utterances in random order.

The essence of this study was to scramble some real conversations to form strings of randomly ordered utterances, and then show that people could recover the original sequence (to a large extent) without prior knowledge of it, purely on the basis of their knowledge of conversational patterns *in general.*

Method

The experiment itself was conducted in two parts, the first to produce a set of spontaneous dialogues; and the second to assess their sequential structure, by the reassembly of utterance sequences. Four pairs of subjects took part in the dialogue-generation stage, all students or junior research staff of Oxford University. Each pair was shown into a waiting room to await the arrival of a (fictitious) third subject. Their conversation while waiting was tape recorded, using concealed microphones and recording equipment in an adjacent room. Subjects were then debriefed and told the true nature and purpose of the experiment and the reason for the originally misleading instructions. In all cases they gave their permission for their conversation to be transcribed and used in the later stages of the experiment. The subjects' anonymity was preserved throughout, and the few proper names and places which occurred in the conversations were replaced by fictional equivalents.

Twenty consecutive lines of each dialogue were used, starting with the introduction of a major topic after a steady state had been reached. Each utterance was typed on a separate $4 \times 6''$ file card, bearing no other information as to the original speaker or the nature of the sequence, which later subjects could use. On the back of each card was a code letter relating to a key from which the correct sequence could be checked by the experimenter.

Interruption and simultaneous speech were represented on the cards by quoting any interruption in parenthesis at the start of the interrupter's next utterance card: for example,

(Why . . .?/Bill probably said . . .) Why was that?

would represent the case in which the person who said

'Why was that?'

had interrupted the other's previous utterance with

'Why . . .?' and 'Bill probably said . . .'.

This notation was chosen as it allows all the speech of both actors to be represented, without introducing stray cues to the overall sequence, as could have been the case if interruptions were placed on the card of the interrupted speaker.

In the resequencing stage of the study, ten student subjects were asked to rearrange each of the four dialogues into what they took to be its original form, given 10 minutes for each. The order of presentation of the twenty cards in each set and the four sets in the experiment was randomised. The subjects had a 10-minute practice with a similar set of cards before the experiment proper began.

The sequences produced by these subjects were scored in three ways:

1. *Slot scores*: a count of the number of occurrences of card number n in nth position in the series.
2. *Reactive scores*: a count of the number of occurrences of card n, followed immediately by card $(n+1)$.
3. *Proactive scores*: the occurrence of card n followed by any other followed by $(n+2)$.

Each such occurrence constitutes a correct 'item'. The data were expressed as the number of subjects correct on each item, rather than the number of items correctly identified by each subject. In this way a profile of the points of greatest and least structural integrity within each dialogue was obtained. Also the recognition of one item by several subjects may be regarded as independent events, making the data more amenable to statistical treatments. This assumption does not apply to the recognition of several items by the same subject.

The probability of achieving a given score under the null hypothesis that subjects were performing at chance, was estimated as follows:

Slot scores. Under the null hypothesis, each card may be placed with equal likelihood in any of the 20 positions, thus having a probability of 0.05 of assignment to the one correct place. A single item could be combined in 19! ways with the 18 remaining cards, giving 19! occurrences of each item in 20! possible assortments, and again a 0.05 probability of correct identification.

Proactive scores. There were 18 proactive pairs in each set of cards (1—3, 2—4, . . ., 18—20) and each may have one of 18 other cards in its middle position. This group of three may combine in any one of 18! ways with the remaining 17 cards, to give a probability of identifying any pair of

$$\frac{18 \times 18!}{20!} \text{ or } 0.047.$$

Interestingly the apparently simpler argument that each of the 18 proactive pairs combines with the remaining 18 cards in one of 19! possible ways, giving a probability of detection of 0.05, is incorrect, as may be seen if a similar argument is applied to the assortment of a small number of items, whose combinations can be tabulated in full.

Thus the likelihood of m out of 10 subjects recognising a given sequence by chance is

$$\frac{10!}{(10-m)!m!}(p)^m(1-p)^{10-m}$$

where p is the probability of correct sequencing of a single item on each score quoted above (by the Binomial Test, Siegel, 1956: 36—42).

Results

An example dialogue may be found in Appendix B. Figure 4 shows histograms for the same dialogue of the subjects' performance on the three indices as a function of the original (correct) order of items. (Items consisting of two cards are identified by the number of the second.)

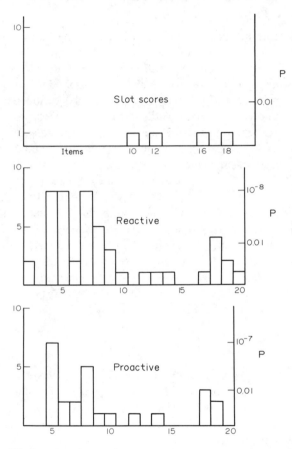

FIG. 4   Histogram   of   scores   from   resequencing   task
(Dialogue One)

All three indices of correct sequencing (slot, reactive and proactive scores) produced a number of items placed with greater than chance accuracy. On the slot scores 9 out of 80 items (11%) were placed correctly by 4 or more subjects (for each, $p < 0.01$). On the reactive scores 26 out of 76 (34%) of items were placed correctly by 4 or more subjects ($p < 0.01$), and on proactive scores 19 out of 72 (26%) were placed correctly by 3 or more subjects ($p < 0.01$). There were three reactive pairs which were identified correctly by 9 out of 10 subjects ($p < 10^{-10}$).

TABLE 1   *Number of utterances assigned to correct slot by* m *out of 10 subjects, total = 20*

	m and probabilities of occurrence under null hypothesis										
	0 ns	1 ns	2 ns	3 0.05	4 0.01	5 10^{-4}	6 10^{-5}	7 10^{-7}	8 10^{-8}	9 10^{-10}	10 10^{-11}
Dialogue 1	16	4	0	0	0	0	0	0	0	0	0
Dialogue 2	8	6	3	0	1	0	2	0	0	0	0
Dialogue 3	1	8	4	1	3	1	1	1	0	0	0
Dialogue 4	14	4	2	0	0	0	0	0	0	0	0

Number of reactive pairs correctly identified by m *out of 10 subjects, total = 19*

	m and probabilities of occurrence under null hypothesis										
	0 ns	1 ns	2 ns	3 0.05	4 0.01	5 10^{-4}	6 10^{-5}	7 10^{-7}	8 10^{-8}	9 10^{-10}	10 10^{-11}
Dialogue 1	4	6	3	1	1	1	0	0	3	0	0
Dialogue 2	3	3	1	5	4	1	1	0	0	1	0
Dialogue 3	1	2	1	4	4	2	1	1	1	2	0
Dialogue 4	6	4	1	5	1	0	1	0	0	0	1

Number of proactive pairs correctly identified by m *out of 10 subjects, total = 18*

	m and probabilities of occurrence under null hypothesis										
	0 ns	1 ns	2 ns	3 0.01	4 10^{-3}	5 10^{-4}	6 10^{-5}	7 10^{-7}	8 10^{-8}	9 10^{-10}	10 10^{-12}
Dialogue 1	8	4	3	1	0	1	0	1	0	0	0
Dialogue 2	5	4	5	2	2	0	0	0	0	0	0
Dialogue 3	2	4	2	3	4	2	1	0	0	0	0
Dialogue 4	6	8	2	0	2	0	0	0	0	0	0

This study is also reported in greater detail in Clarke (1975 a and b).

Discussion

The hypothesis is supported by the results. Subjects were able to reassemble the conversations with greater than chance accuracy, reaching significance levels of 10^{-10} and 10^{-11} on a few items. This suggests that the original dialogues did embody some systematic relationship between verbal context and the nature of each utterance; that the pattern is one on which the native speaker can pass judgement from his own knowledge of the speech community, and that a consensus may be reached by the judges which is reasonably accurate. In the terms of Chapter 1 these findings indicate that communicative performance has a temporal pattern; that descriptive competence is shared by native speakers; and it is largely accurate.

As to the nature of the sequences which were used, further inferences could be drawn. The histograms for each dialogue may be compared with the transcript to give an idea of the location of the strongly and weakly sequenced strings, and of the kind of sequential constraints which are operative. In the linguistic analogy this corresponds to a *parsing* operation which indicates the *surface structure* of the dialogue. The derivation of a *phrase structure* for the dialogues in the form of a plot of the probability of associating pairs of items is similar to the technique used in Johnson's (1965) psycholinguistic experiment. He gave subjects eight sentences to learn, and, upon recall, plotted the probability of any word being wrong given that the previous word was right. These *transitional error probabilities* were greatest at grammatical phrase boundaries, indicating that the subjects' cognition of the sentences had been structured in accordance with the predictions of the grammar. Here, there is no formal grammar, but a similar argument could be invoked in support of this procedure as a possible means of discovering episode boundaries.

In making such judgements two things should be considered. Firstly, the reactive and proactive scores are not independent indices, and a subject who produces a string of items in correct sequence will necessarily contribute to both reactive and proactive scores. This is how the measures were meant to function. Their purpose was not to distinguish between the influences which are 'purely reactive' and those which are 'purely proactive', it would be impossible to do so. The three different scores were included so that they might detect between them a structure which as yet defies explicit description. The one interscore comparison which can be made is between slot scores and the other two. The slot scores are much lower (11% of slot scores were significant at $p < 0.01$; as opposed to 26% of the proactive scores, and 34% of the reactive scores). This confirms that the structural rules, such as they are, are relative rather than absolute. With the exception of procedures like greeting and leave-taking, the rules relate utterances to each other, rather than to fixed positions like '14th utterance'.

Secondly, the probability of a particular sequence being recognised is not only a function of the intrinsic properties of that sequence, but also of the number of other items in the card set which might be mistakenly substituted for its members. Thus a dialogue with a number of similar items will be easily confusable, and will show an apparently weak sequence even though it may have been subject to strong sequential constraints during its production.

Since this experiment deals with typewritten transcripts of dialogue it points to effects within the verbal aspects of the interaction. In the face-to-face situation, where there is an interplay of verbal and non-verbal information, the scope for examining complex sequences would be still greater.

It seems that there is a sequential structure in conversation, which is hardly surprising. Unless our normal view of interaction were grossly distorted by some *post hoc* rationalisation, it could hardly be otherwise. What is more interesting, however, is the strength of the sequence effect. In this experiment, most of the factors which are thought to regulate social interaction were omitted, and yet the subjects realised what was going on, and were able to re-create an accurate representation of a conversation they had never seen before. Clearly the effect of verbal context on future verbalisation is very strong. Why, then, is it not stronger still? The subjects did make a number of errors. This testifies to the very principle of entropy which is the essence of communication. If the course of a sentence, message, or interaction were perfectly predictable from the outset, it would carry no information. The structural perspective suggests not perfect predictability, but bounded uncertainty: a range of alternatives whose selection carries information.

It should also be noted that the pattern which emerges in this experiment is not necessarily the product of a syntax. We have simply observed that some patterns of use are more common, and known to be more common than others. That is true of most things whether rule-governed or not. The question of a syntax of conversation will arise if rules of semiotic competence emerge, which show that only some of the possible sequences of speech-acts are meaningful.

An utterance is a thing of many parts, and it has many levels of description. As yet it is impossible to say which of these is moulded by conversation structure, and which cues the experimental subject recognises in performing this kind of task. That issue will be investigated in the next experiment.

Experiment 2: Semantic Sequences

Introduction

The kind of conversation structure which is of interest governs what people say under given circumstances, not how they say it. It has been pointed out (A. Treisman, personal communication) that the results of the previous experiment could arise from the effect of conversation structure on the syntactic form of utterances, without there being any effect on the other levels of description. In that case the present project would cease to be feasible. There is some evidence that utterance form is modified by conversation structure, and a simple example may be found in the first transcript in Appendix B. There is a tendency for utterances to get longer as the conversations progress – a cue to sequence which could be employed even by non-speakers of the language.

Fries (1952) documented three utterance forms which are dependent on conversation structure. The 'situation sentences' which can begin an exchange; the 'sequence sentences' with which the same speaker might continue; and the 'response sentences' with which a new speaker may reply, vary considerably in the degree to which *ellipsis* (an incomplete or abbreviated construction) is allowed. For example:

1 A: I shall be in town this afternoon (Situation sentence).

2A: Got to get some shopping (Sequence sentence).

3B: Suppose so (Response sentence).

Osgood (1971) found the linguistic presuppositions implied by certain question forms, led subjects to formulate their replies differently. This kind of phenomenon could account for the findings of Experiment 1, if subjects were only sensitive to syntactic variations, or if the material only contained syntactic variations.

If, on the other hand, there is a systematic effect of conversation structure on utterance *content*, then speakers who are obliged to use a very monotonous syntactic form should nevertheless invest their utterances with sufficient semantic variation as to make the conversation reproducible by the procedure of Experiment 1.

The hypothesis for Experiment 2 was that subjects can reassemble with greater than chance accuracy, the original sequence of a passage of unfamiliar dialogue generated from a grammar devoid of syntactic cues to the sequence of utterances.

Method

In many respects this experiment was similar to Experiment 1. The procedure will only be described in detail where the two techniques differ. Again the experiment was in two parts: to generate a set of dialogues; and to assess their structure by the reassembly of sequences.

Four pairs of student subjects took part in the dialogue-generating stage. Each pair produced one twenty-line dialogue, writing alternate lines on a script which was passed back and forth. They were asked to use complete, well-formed sentences as far as possible, but avoiding third person pronouns, all articles, and all relative clauses. Each utterance had to be a statement or question in the present tense and active voice, and had to be comprehensible in itself without reference to other utterances in the dialogue. Furthermore, utterances could not start with 'Yes', 'No', 'Well', 'And', or 'But', or refer to previously mentioned matters except in the terms of their first introduction. These rules were explained to subjects in detail, and checked as each new utterance was added to the 'script'.

The rules were chosen so as to eliminate the more obvious cues to sequence, arising particularly from the progressive use of ellipses, pronominalisation, relegation of attributes to subordinate clauses, and so on.

The dialogues were again transferred to 6 X 4″ file cards, and reassembled from random sequences by ten subjects, just as in the first experiment.

Results

An example of this type of rather 'telegraphic' dialogue is given in Appendix B.

Histograms are not presented as there is little point in trying to parse or look for particular structures in these artificial and very unusual dialogues.

The results are similar to those of the first experiment. On the slot scores 17 out of 80 items (21%) were placed correctly by 4 or more subjects ($p < 0.01$). The reactive scores showed 49 out of 76 items (64%) correctly paired by 4 or more subjects ($p < 0.01$), and on the proactive scores 39 out of 72 pairs (54%) were identified by 3 or more subjects ($p < 0.01$). Nine reactive pairs were correctly identified by all 10 subjects ($p < 10^{-11}$), and 3 proactive pairs were recognised by all 10 subjects ($p < 10^{-12}$).

TABLE 2　*Number of utterances assigned to correct slot by m out of 10 subjects, total = 20*

	\(m\) and probabilities of occurrence under null hypothesis										
	0 ns	1 ns	2 ns	3 0.05	4 0.01	5 10^{-4}	6 10^{-5}	7 10^{-7}	8 10^{-8}	9 10^{-10}	10 10^{-11}
Dialogue 1	11	4	1	3	0	1	0	0	0	0	0
Dialogue 2	0	2	6	9	2	1	0	0	0	0	0
Dialogue 3	8	5	6	1	0	0	0	0	0	0	0
Dialogue 4	4	3	0	0	1	10	1	0	1	0	0

Number of reactive pairs correctly identified by m out of 10 subjects, total = 19

	\(m\) and probabilities of occurrence under null hypothesis										
	0 ns	1 ns	2 ns	3 0.05	4 0.01	5 10^{-4}	6 10^{-5}	7 10^{-7}	8 10^{-8}	9 10^{-10}	10 10^{-11}
Dialogue 1	5	1	0	2	3	1	2	1	1	1	2
Dialogue 2	0	3	2	2	4	0	0	1	0	6	1
Dialogue 3	0	2	2	1	0	0	3	1	1	5	4
Dialogue 4	1	1	3	2	0	0	1	2	3	4	2

Number of proactive pairs correctly identified by m out of 10 subjects, total = 18

	\(m\) and probabilities of occurrence under null hypothesis										
	0 ns	1 ns	2 ns	3 0.01	4 10^{-3}	5 10^{-4}	6 10^{-5}	7 10^{-7}	8 10^{-8}	9 10^{-10}	10 10^{-11}
Dialogue 1	8	0	1	3	3	0	1	1	0	1	0
Dialogue 2	0	2	6	4	1	0	0	0	3	2	0
Dialogue 3	1	1	5	1	1	0	3	1	0	4	1
Dialogue 4	2	4	3	0	0	0	2	1	2	2	2

Discussion

The hypothesis is supported. The great reduction in syntactic variation brought about by the grammatical constraints used in this experiment did not result in any reduction in subjects' performance. On the contrary, performance on all indices was improved, so the ability to recognise sequential structure in dialogue does not seem to depend on syntactic information alone. There must be other properties of the utterances which vary systematically with verbal context. Perhaps semantic content is the crucial factor, or the performative quality of the utterances. Experiment 3 will be concerned with the attempt to distinguish these two possibilities.

The utterance resequencing technique developed for these experiments has since been used by Shapiro (e.g. 1976) in studies of empathy in psychotherapy dyads.

Experiment 3: Speech-act Sequences

Introduction

The structure of discourse may affect all levels of description in the hierarchy of language. Successive utterances are liable to have related syntactic forms, as we have seen. They are also likely to have related semantic content, but even this is not the level at which the pattern of social behaviour emerges. It should be possible to show that there are patterns and regular sequences in the structure of conversation even when the information conveyed by variations in syntax and semantics has been removed. These would be patterns of utterance use, having to do with the related functions of successive utterances in requesting and supplying information, expressing emotions, issuing instructions, and so on. In later chapters the idea of the 'social function' of utterances will be elaborated, and identified with Austin's (1962) theory of *performative utterances*, or *speech-acts* as they are often called. For the time being suffice it to say that the utterance properties of greatest interest in this study lie at an even higher level of abstraction than the semantic representation, and are therefore inadequately demonstrated in Experiment 2, which could conceivably have drawn upon semantics alone, in the absence of any syntactic cues. It would be possible, for example, for a dialogue to contain only two references to a particular person, place, object or topic. Any subject who assumed correctly that these two utterances should be contiguous would have a 0.5 probability of making the correct reactive pair instead of the 0.05 specified in the null hypothesis. In this way high scores could be achieved even under those circumstances in which the performative structure of the dialogue played no part. Unequivocal demonstration of a performative structure can only come from an experiment in which syntactic and semantic information has been removed from the component utterances.

This raises the methodological problem of conveying to a group of subjects the properties of a set of utterances, whose syntactic form and semantic content are to remain unknown. Some scheme of functional categories has to be used, together with a description of the way these categories occur in sequences. The Bales (1953) 12-category system, and table of reactive tendencies shown in Table 3, were used for this purpose.

TABLE 3 *Matrix of Reactive tendencies: Output probabilities for a given input. 16 meetings of 5-man groups*

Category of prior act (input type)	Category of following act (output)												Total per-cent
	1	2	3	4	5	6	7	8	9	10	11	12	
1 SHOWS SOLIDARITY, raises other's status, gives help, reward:	28.4	11.9	3.0	13.4	14.9	11.9	4.5	4.5	–	3.0	1.5	3.0	100.0
2 SHOWS TENSION RELEASE, jokes, laughs, shows satisfaction:	0.7	68.2	3.2	3.1	10.2	6.7	2.2	1.5	0.3	1.7	0.6	1.5	99.9
3 AGREES, shows passive acceptance, understands, concurs:	0.6	2.7	15.9	8.5	40.8	21.4	2.3	3.0	0.9	2.7	1.0	0.2	100.0
4 GIVES SUGGESTION, direction, implying autonomy for other:	1.3	6.7	46.0	8.6	9.2	8.8	2.3	1.5	1.5	12.4	1.3	0.4	100.0
5 GIVES OPINION, evaluation, analysis, expresses feeling, wish:	0.6	4.3	48.9	2.2	19.2	6.3	2.3	2.8	0.3	11.8	0.6	0.6	99.9
6 GIVES ORIENTATION, information, repeats, clarifies, confirms:	0.6	5.8	35.0	3.6	15.2	24.0	5.6	1.3	0.4	5.7	1.1	1.7	100.0
7 ASKS FOR ORIENTATION, information, repetition, confirmation:	–	1.0	5.6	0.7	10.0	73.7	5.6	1.0	0.3	1.6	–	0.7	100.2
8 ASKS FOR OPINION, evaluation, analysis, expression of feeling:	1.5	5.4	9.2	2.4	45.9	13.2	10.7	3.0	0.5	4.4	2.0	2.0	100.2
9 ASKS FOR SUGGESTION, direction, possible ways of action:	–	13.2	–	35.8	28.3	9.4	1.9	1.9	–	3.8	3.8	1.9	100.0
10 DISAGREES, shows passive rejection, formality, withholds help:	0.3	6.6	12.4	5.2	25.0	13.5	3.6	2.0	0.3	24.2	3.9	3.0	100.0
11 SHOWS TENSION, asks for help, withdraws 'Out of Field':	4.1	7.2	5.2	2.1	39.2	22.7	2.1	4.1	–	4.1	9.3	–	100.1
12 SHOWS ANTAGONISM, deflates other's status, defends or asserts self:	1.0	18.1	4.8	3.8	12.4	11.4	1.0	3.8	–	5.7	1.9	36.2	100.1

(From Bales, 1953). Reprinted with permission of Macmillan Publishing Company from *Working Papers in the Theory of Action* edited by T. Parsons, R. F. Bales, E. A. Shils. Copyright 1953 by The Free Press, a Corporation.

The principle is similar to those of Experiments 1 and 2. Again there are three postulates to be tested, which must all be true if the predicted outcome is to occur. The structure of conversation as represented by transitional probabilities between utterance classes must be non-random; subjects must be able to give some account of their beliefs about its non-randomness; and their judgements must be accurate, in that they are seen to correspond to the objective data on conversation structures. These three necessary conditions were tested by asking subjects to judge accurately the relative cell values in the Bales matrix of reactive tendencies.

Bales' data plays the role in this experiment of the transcribed dialogues in Experiments 1 and 2. Similarly the attempts by the subjects to reproduce an observed pattern by supplying cell values for a transitional probability matrix are equivalent to their card-sorting task in the earlier experiments.

The hypothesis was: subjects can provide estimated cell values for a transitional probability matrix of utterance types, which correlate with observed values.

Method

Eight female occupational therapy students aged 18 to 25 were the subjects for this experiment. They met as a group in the laboratory, and were briefed on the nature and purpose of the study. Each subject was given a response sheet showing a 12 X 12-celled blank matrix, with a brief description of Bales' 12 categories labelling the rows and columns. The subjects were asked to attend first to column 1, treating the description at its head 'shows solidarity, raises other's status, gives help, reward' as an event in a hypothetical interaction. They were to indicate the relative probability of the 12 possible sequiturs by placing the 12 cells of that column in rank order, entering the rank as an integer in each cell. So, for example, a subject who thought the most likely response to category 1 was category 7, would enter a 1 in column 1 row 7, and so on. The subjects were spaced throughout the room and each worked independently, ranking the cells in column 1, from 1 to 12, and then going on to treat each of the subsequent columns as a separate interaction event, receiving a new set of ranks from 1 to 12. The subjects were told that they should consider only those occasions on which the first utterance came from one speaker, and the second from another, in other words the reactive contingencies. They were also asked to provide the judgements which they thought would correspond most accurately to the structure of conversation in groups of the following kind:

> Experimental groups containing three to six members, who were usually unknown to each other before the first meeting. Each group met four times to discuss a 'human relations case'. The group members, who were male Harvard undergraduates, were given a 5-page summary of facts

about someone in an administrative setting, having difficulty with the men under him, and a supervisor pressing him to get a certain job done. Each subject had a separate case summary, and was left uncertain as to whether the others had the same information. The summary was removed before discussion began. The subjects were asked to regard themselves as members of the administrative staff of the central character, meeting to decide why the people in the case were behaving in that way, and the best course of action. Each discussion lasted 40 minutes, and had no appointed leader. The experimenter left the room before the start of the discussion, which was tape recorded and observed through a one-way screen.

The above is a brief description of the circumstances under which Bales' data were obtained, so that my subjects could base their judgements on an accurate conception of the setting for the behaviour sequences they were to reproduce.

Results

The data were pooled over subjects by summing the cells across subjects and entering in each column the rank order of the summed ranks. This procedure is advocated by Kendall (1948: 101) for giving the best estimate of the true order of items from a number of concordant rank orderings. The resulting data formed a 12×12-celled matrix, still having antecedent utterance types characterising the columns, and rank orders of perceived transitional probability in the rows.

In processing the data from the eight individual subjects it was found that on 9 out of 96 possible occasions the instructions had been misapplied in that a column of ranks contained one value twice, while another value was missing. This is an easy mistake to make in a task of this kind and did not seem to indicate a gross misunderstanding of the experiment by the subjects concerned. It was, however, a distortion of the data, which would have caused column totals in the matrix to assume unequal values. It was not the subjects' intention to use tied ranks, so the repeated values were not given equal values in the corrected data. Nor could the two items receiving the same rank be given that rank and the missing one by random allocation, as one of the items would have received a very different value from that entered by the subject. In fact the following correction was applied. All ranks between the repeated value and the missing value were displaced one rank towards the missing value, thus removing the omission. The two items which had been given the same rank were then randomly assigned to that rank or the adjacent rank which was now vacant. For example, the ranking

$$3 \quad 6 \quad 12 \quad 4 \quad 5 \quad 7 \quad 9 \quad 2 \quad 1 \quad 8 \quad 7 \quad 10$$

(with two items at rank 7 and none at 11) would become

or
$$\begin{array}{cccccccccccc} 3 & 6 & 12 & 4 & 5 & 8 & 10 & 2 & 1 & 9 & 7 & 11 \\ 3 & 6 & 12 & 4 & 5 & 7 & 10 & 2 & 1 & 9 & 8 & 11 \end{array}$$

at random. This correction was applied to the data from individual subjects before applying tests of concordance, and subsequent statistical treatments. The correction produces a perfect rank ordering, similar to the imperfect ranking provided by the subject, but containing a slight and random distortion. This can only have the effect of militating against the hypothesis of regular and accurate perception.

Response bias

The subjects can respond to the task in two ways so as to produce an accurate correspondence between their judgements and the objective Bales data. On the one hand, they can attend simply to the properties of the second utterance in each pair, since some utterances are more commonly used than others and are therefore likely to follow an antecedent *whatever* the antecedent is. In Bales' data, for example, category 12 (shows antagonism, deflates other's status, defends or asserts self) very rarely occurs. Consequently any subject who gave category 12 the rank 12 in all cases would produce an accurate performance without demonstrating any sensitivity to the differing probabilities of finding that response after the different classes of antecedent. This effect will be called the response bias, and is a source of variance in the data matrix which gives rise to differences between rows but not differences between cell values along each row. (The terms row and column refer throughout to the organisation of my data matrix, in which, for the convenience of subjects, the antecedent classes defined the columns, and the sequitur classes the rows. This convention is also used in my description of the Bales matrix although Bales himself used rows and columns the other way round.)

The effect of this response bias may be seen by calculating the concordance between columns of the matrix. That is the extent to which subjects gave the same rank ordering to each column, in spite of the differences in preceding utterance type. The following results were obtained: Kendall's $W = 0.20$; $r_{s_{av}} = 0.12$; $\chi^2 = 26.00$; d$f = 11$; $p < 0.01$.

The tendency to give consistent responses across columns is not necessarily a source of error, as the objective data also have the property that some rows contain higher mean values than others. That is, the objective data are also partly a product of the tendency for some utterances to occur more frequently than others, regardless of the nature of the antecedent. Bales' matrix converted to ranks has a concordance of 0.63 between columns ($r_{s_{av}} = 0.59$; $\chi^2 = 82.5$; d$f = 11$; $p < 0.001$). The ability of subjects to reproduce this feature of the Bales data may be assessed by calculating the rank order correlation between the row means from the two matrices. $R_s = 0.30$; $t = 0.978$; d$f = 10$, n.s. one-tailed (Kendall, 1948; Siegel, 1956).

Reactive contingency

The second, and for our purpose more interesting, way in which the judgemental data from the subjects can correspond to the objective data matrix is by reproducing the variations in probability of a given utterance occurring as a function of its different possible antecedents. This may be regarded as a residual source of systematic variance in the matrix which emerges when the effect of response bias is removed. To remove the response bias or between row variance the matrices of subjective and objective data were recalculated, replacing each cell value with the difference between observed cell value and row mean. Thus x_{ij} was replaced by

$$\frac{x_{ij} - \sum_{i=1}^{12} x_{ij}}{12} \quad ,$$

for all values of i and j. Now each cell of the matrices shows how much more or less probable than usual (the mean) a particular sequitur becomes, by virtue of its following a particular antecedent. This is in contrast to the previous form of the matrices in which each cell showed how much more or less probable a particular sequitur is than the other possible sequiturs, given that particular antecedent. There should now be a cell-by-cell correlation between the new version of the subjects' matrix and the new version of Bales' matrix, if subjects were accurate on this aspect of the task. The corresponding cells from the two matrices were treated as paired items, and correlated using the Pearson product-moment correlation coefficient. $r = 0.32$, $z = 3.51$, $p < 0.00025$, one-tailed (Bruning and Kintz, 1968). This procedure is legitimate even though one of the matrices is derived from a set of ordinal data. The unequivocal result could not arise from the relatively small distortion introduced by treating ordinal data to product-moment correlation. In calculating the significance of this result, it must be remembered that both matrices now have rows and columns summing to zero, so the 144 pairs of observations only have 120 degrees of freedom instead of the 143 which might otherwise be expected.

Discussion

The concordance between subjects was significant: $(p < 0.001)$ for three out of twelve utterance classes, $(p < 0.02)$ for one class, $(p < 0.05)$ for another and a trend $(p < 0.1)$ for two more. There can be little doubt from these results that significant agreement existed between subjects on the task as a whole. However, these levels of significance cannot be combined as independent results to give a summary value for the whole task, as the twelve sub-tasks are not entirely independent. In so far as the subjects were describing the 'response bias' in the conversation sequences, they were producing twelve judgements of the same order of probability, not judgements of twelve completely different orders. Therefore the combination of results as if they were independent would only be a false inflation of their true significance. One of the results having $p<0.001$ would in itself be sufficiently unlikely in twelve trials to suggest that significant concordance exists over the task as a whole.

The level of concordance is very variable, which may be a reflection of the properties of different utterance types. Categories 4 (gives suggestion . . .), 6 (gives orientation . . .), 10 (disagrees . . .) and 11 (shows tension . . .) were those which failed to produce concordant responses at even the 0.1 level.

The concordance between columns of the 12×12 matrix, summed across subjects, indicates that they are indeed giving similar judgements of sequitur probability in spite of differences in antecedent type. The correspondence between the overall response probabilities for the subjective and objective data was indicated by a rank order correlation (Spearman's r_s of 0.30; Siegel, 1956). This is insignificant with only 12 pairs of observations available, but it is interesting to note that the correlation is approximately equal to that obtained for the revised matrices of reactive contingency (which is very significant because of the large number of observations). This result far from proves, but is quite consistent with, the idea that subjects can express accurately the differences in absolute likelihood of occurrence between utterances of different types.

The issue of greatest interest as part of a scheme of sequence analysis is the subjects' ability to express the effect of antecedent type on sequitur probabilities. This appears in the revised matrices of cell value minus row mean, and their correlation. This was significant ($p<0.00025$) suggesting that subjects can give accurate accounts of different transitional probabilities as a function of differences in antecedent type, even when working with abstract utterance classes. This supports the belief that a sequence analysis of the use of speech-acts in conversation is feasible, since the result is only likely to occur if the production of conversation (performance) has a predictable temporal structure which is accurately reflected in the beliefs (descriptive competence) of the native actor.

The task was made particularly difficult for the subjects by the requirement that they reproduce a conversation pattern from another speech community, in another culture, recorded approximately 25 years earlier. Furthermore, they were subject to the limitations of an imperfect category scheme, and a Markov model of sequential structure, which may have obscured their real capacity to give complex veridical judgements of the pattern of discourse. It is to be hoped that refined category schemes and structural models will give us access to areas of communicative competence at least as rich and possibly more accurate than those achieved in this experiment.

The correspondence between subjective and objective data in these studies, and the great advantages of flexibility and semantic sensitivity offered by emic methodology, suggest that we should look for the pattern of conversation first in communicative competence, before examining its counterpart in the more difficult realm of observed performance.

Experiment 4: Collective Knowledge of Speech-Act Sequences

Introduction

It seems from Experiment 3 that the judgements of individual subjects may be pooled to give an accurate picture of certain aspects of conversation structure, and therefore that such behavioural 'accounts' might serve as a legitimate source of data in future experiments. The final overview of the subjects' beliefs which constitute the data may be obtained from their individual beliefs in different ways. In Experiment 3, each subject reported independently, and the experimenter produced a mathematical summary statement, from their individual responses. Harré and Secord (1972) propose that accounts be arrived at by *negotiation* between actors, and judgements be made on the basis of group discussion.

Experiment 4 used much the same paradigm as Experiment 3, except that judgements were made after discussion in a group of judges, who had not taken part in the interactions but who were required to negotiate a common report on the basis of their shared knowledge of the social world. The purpose was not to make a controlled comparison between the two approaches, but rather to establish the viability of each, in case other methodological considerations should make it the more desirable alternative for particular studies. Consequently no attempt was made to match the two groups. On the contrary this experiment provided an opportunity to explore the generality of the effect by using a different and more heterogeneous subject group. In many respects the procedure was exactly as for Experiment 3. These aspects of the experiment will not be described again in detail.

The hypothesis was: subjects in group discussion can provide cell values for a transitional probability matrix of utterance types, which correlate with observed values.

Method

Subjects

Eight subjects took part in the experiment, five males and three females. Six were students reading subjects other than psychology, one was a photographer and one a retired biochemist. Five were in the age range 18–25, one was 27, one 32 and one 66.

Procedure

The procedure was the same as Experiment 3, except that the blank matrix was presented to the subjects on a large 'white-board' at the front of the group, and the experimenter filled in a single rank for each cell after suggestions and discussion from the group had given rise to a consensus of opinion. Care was taken by the experimenter not to reinforce suggested values by the use of verbal or non-verbal cues, and the experiment was conducted blind, in that the experimenter was unaware of the cell values in the Bales matrix at the time, as a further precaution against the unwitting but accurate direction of subjects' responses by the experimenter's behaviour.

Results

Concordance between subjects

Because of the way the experiment was conducted this issue does not arise as it did in the previous study. In all other respects the two experiments received identical statistical treatment.

No formal measures were taken of the degree to which each group member participated in discussion. However, the contributions from all members appeared to be approximately equal, with most cell values finding unanimous support after very brief discussion.

Response bias

The concordance between the twelve columns of ranks in the results table was calculated using Kendall's W. This indicates the extent to which the subjects gave similar ranks to the probability of an utterance type occurring, regardless of the nature of its antecedent. $W = 0.084$, which corresponds to a mean rank-order correlation $r_{s_{av}}$ between pairs of columns of 0.00, which is of course insignificant.

The rank order of row totals was again compared with its counterpart from the Bales matrix to see if subjects had accurately represented the different frequencies with which the twelve categories are used. $r_s = 0.30$, $t = 0.99$; $df = 10$. The correlation between the two sets of ranks was not significant (one-tailed test).

Reactive contingency

The subjective and objective data matrices were transformed as in Experiment 3, to give two 12×12 matrices whose cell values represented the increases and decreases in sequitur probability which resulted from variations in antecedent type. Values of the corresponding cells in the two matrices were used to calculate Pearson's product-moment correlation coefficient (r),

$r = 0.26, z = 2.86, p < 0.0025$, one-tailed.

(The value of r obtained by this procedure is given as positive in both Experiments 3 and 4, to indicate that the underlying variables were directly rather than inversely related. Those utterance transitions which were found to be most common in the objective data, were believed to be most common in the subjective case. However, one data matrix is derived from percentage frequencies using high numbers to represent the more frequent events; and the other is derived from ranks in which low numbers represent the most frequent events, so the arithmetic value of the correlations *as calculated* was *negative*.)

Discussion

The effect of 'response bias' is completely absent, with zero correlation occurring among the different columns of ranks. The subjects in this experiment underestimated the similarity of the columns even more than the subjects in Experiment 3, who produced twelve columns of ranks which were significantly concordant ($W = 0.20$; $r_{s_{av}} = 0.12$; df = 11; $p < 0.01$). The concordance between columns in the objective data matrix which Bales provides was found to be 0.63 ($\chi^2 = 82.5$; $r_{s_{av}} = 0.59$; df = 11; $p < 0.001$), when each column was converted to a set of twelve ranks.

Experiment 4 gives further evidence that subjects can accurately reproduce the transitional probabilities of a conversation sequence. The data matrix when transformed to show changes in the probability of a sequitur occurring as a function of the different possible antecedent types, correlated significantly with the equivalent transform of Bales data. It also correlated with the equivalent matrix in Experiment 3, $r = 0.31$; $z = 3.35$; $p < 0.00025$, one-tailed, from which one may calculate that the difference between the correlations obtained in Experiments 3 and 4 is insignificant ($t = 0.59$; df = 118; n.s. two-tailed).

A comparison of Experiments 3 and 4 does not suggest that either technique is superior, but rather that essentially similar and significant results may be obtained under different circumstances and with different kinds of subjects. This supports the idea that the native actor has a descriptive competence which enables him to give an accurate account of the social world, and which is a legitimate source of data for the behavioural scientist.

The accuracy of subjects' judgements is sufficient to produce highly significant correlations with the objective criterion, but when viewed in other ways it is not all that striking. The correlations involved are after all only of the order of 0.3, leaving 91% of the variance unaccounted for. This may seem like a hopelessly noisy source of data to use in future studies, unless the following favourable factors are taken into account:

1. A discrepancy between subjective and objective accounts does not necessarily mean that the fault lies entirely with the subjective data. A number of

factors were operating to reduce the correlations which reflect no discredit upon the subjects' ability to judge contemporary scenarios. They were trying to reproduce behaviour patterns from another time and another culture. The Bales category scheme is an imperfect representation of our perception of utterance types, and the use of transitional probabilities an oversimplification of interaction structures. All these limitations can be reduced in future studies by the appropriate use of judgemental data.

2. Interaction structure is an abstraction from observed reality. It may only be studied if information is available on such things as the functional equivalence of dissimilar utterances, meaning, and the relations between utterances. None of these are directly observable, so judgemental data becomes a necessity for at least a part of the analysis.

3. Part of the interest in interaction structure centres on competence rather than performance. The limits of possible or permissible interaction should be studied as well as the limits on what is observed to occur. Again judgemental data are a necessity.

4. The results of different kinds of judgement may be cross-checked, so as to discriminate between ubiquitous beliefs and random errors of judgement. *Systematic* errors of judgement, of course, cannot be detected in this way, but they may be discovered when the model of descriptive competence is compared with performance.

It is just possible that results like those of Experiments 3 and 4 could be derived from a discourse system which had no sequential patterns in its production, but strong sequence effects on its perception. For example, if utterances of type B were no more or less common than usual when following utterances of type A, but the judgement that an utterance *was* of type B was more readily given after a type A, then Experiments 3 and 4 could be explained away as an artefact of the way in which Bales' coders interpreted the original conversations. It does not seem likely that the effect is entirely due to a strange quirk of Bales' judges, and even if this were part of the explanation we should still be left with an account of social reality as we perceive it. We all believe that answers (amongst other things) follow questions, but whether this is because special kinds of utterances called answers are produced after special kinds of utterances called questions; or whether any utterance is more likely to be seen as an answer after another has been seen as a question, it is difficult, and perhaps unnecessary, to decide. The implications of this problem will become apparent when utterance typologies are discussed later on.

Experiment 5: Orders of Approximation

Introduction

The results presented so far indicate that speech acts are produced in a regular predictable sequence, so that the recent history of an interaction may be used in making inferences about its likely future course or, conversely, each item in the sequence may be explained and understood by reference to the recent past. The next step of this analysis is to attempt a description of the various relations which may exist between a speech-act and its predecessors, by focusing attention on particular speech-acts and the predecessors which influenced them. This immediately raises the question of the number of past speech-acts which are likely to be involved, or the amount of historical context to be reviewed before there is no further detectable *direct influence* on the present. That is the subject of the next experiment.

The concept of direct influence is worth elaborating. In any temporally structured system the present is influenced by past events, arguably by all past events, since if the past had been different in any respect, the present would probably have been different as well. For a system which progressed with perfect predictability from state A to state B, and from state B to state C, any passage into state A would give rise to the sequence ABC. So one could argue A influences C in that C has occurred by virtue of the passage of the system into state A. However, A influences C only by taking the system into the intervening state B, and any other state which led to B would have exactly the same effect as A. Therefore state B has the same prospect as the history AB, and the knowledge of A is redundant. One would say in this case that the direct influence of C extended back to B, but no further. Of course there may be systems in which AB has one outcome and XB another, in which case the direct influence on events may be said to encompass two items from the historical record.

The same point is made more succinctly in the language of finite automata theory (Minsky, 1972). A simple system or machine will produce a next response (R_{t+1}) which is a function of its history of input up to the present (H_t), and its present input or stimulus (S_t). That is

$$R_{t+1} = f(H_t, S_t).$$

However, f cannot be stated since H_t cannot be pinned down, consisting as it does of indefinitely many possible permutations of past events. However, if the machine or system only has a finite number of internal states (Q), then there will only be that many different histories which it can distinguish and register in different forms with different implications for the future. Now the characteristics of the machine may be described by a 'next-response function' employing present state instead of history up to the present

$$R_{t+1} = f(Q_t, S_t)$$

and of course a 'next-state function' describing the laws by which it passes from state to state

$$Q_{t+1} = g(Q_t, S_t).$$

Note that 'state' here is an abstraction which may or may not correspond to a known arrangement of the machine's internal constituents. By definition each state is a set of histories with identical behavioural implications for the future.

Now we can distinguish the two types of example more clearly: in the first any history culminating in B is a state, as they all behave identically in future; whereas in the second case histories ending in B have different futures depending on earlier items in the historical record, and so the states require more elaborate definition. The former is called a first-order sequence, and the latter a higher-order sequence, including, for instance, the category of second-order sequences where two previous items bear upon the selection of the next.

Most studies of interaction sequences have examined strings of events which were short, and whose length was not varied as part of the investigation. Bales related each act to the preceding act of the same actor (proactive tendency) or another actor (reactive tendency). Jones and Gerard (1967) elaborated this classification, adding asymmetrical contingency and mutual contingency. In asymmetrical contingency one actor behaves reactively and the other proactively. Examples of this arise in formal interviews if the candidate reacts to each of the interviewer's questions, but the interviewer follows a rigidly preordained plan. In mutual contingency each item of behaviour by each actor is related simultaneously to his own ongoing behaviour stream, and to the last act of the other. The Jones and Gerard scheme retains reactive and proactive tendencies under the names of reactive and pseudo-contingency, giving four kinds of behavioural structure in all. This exhausts the possible relations between an item of dyadic behaviour and the preceding act of each party (with the exception of 'non-contingency'), but it takes no account of the more complex structures which could exist in longer strings of behaviour. Nor does it tell us whether the previous acts of self and other are all the sources of direct influence on the current act which need to be considered.

There have been a large number of studies using essentially Markovian analysis. Sacks' adjacency pair is a form of reactive structure as is Schegloff's (1968) summons–answer sequence. Even van Hooff's (1973) elaborate flow chart of 'within-animal transitions' (in other words proactive tendencies), during chimpanzee social behaviour has to be interpreted as an essentially Markovian analysis as it provides no indication of the effects of events two items ago in the behaviour stream. For instance, the flow chart shows that both *crouch* and *flight* are commonly followed by *bared-teeth scream*, and that *bared-teeth scream* is often followed by *bared-teeth yelp*. However, it does not indicate whether exit from the state *bared-teeth scream* into *bared-teeth yelp* is more common when entry was from *crouch* or from *flight*.

Other authors have described longer behaviour sequences for the most part assuming rather than demonstrating that this was desirable (e.g. Goffman, 1972; Laffal, 1965). Labov has employed both forms of analysis on different occasions. In a diagram of the structure of dialogue (Labov, 1970: 81) relating actions to each other and to the utterances which embody them, he makes the structure look like a perfect Markov chain. However, in another paper (Labov, 1972) he considers longer passages of discourse and assigns to them a much more language-like structure. Altman (1965) compared zero-, first-, second-, third- and fourth-order models of the communicative behaviour of rhesus monkeys, and found an increasing accuracy of prediction up to the fourth order.

So which approach is correct? Should the study of conversation sequences allow for long and complex structures, and if so how long need they be to capture the most important influences of speech-acts upon speech-acts, and meanings upon meanings? In order to answer this question an experiment was performed on a number of *statistical approximations* to English dialogue. The idea was that a number of artificial dialogues constructed so as to allow each utterance to relate to different numbers of their antecedents should resemble genuine spontaneous dialogue only when a sufficient amount of history had been considered in their construction. The technique was a modification of that used by Miller and Selfridge (1950) for the investigation of sentence structures. They wanted to know whether the greater memorability of sentences than random word strings was due to the meaning of the sentence, or to its use of words in likely, although not necessarily meaningful, sequences. They produced a series of word strings, which they called *statistical approximations* to English, in which each word was chosen so as to form a plausible part of a unit of varying size. In the 'zero-order approximation' each word was chosen with no unit in mind, that is completely at random. In the 'first-order approximation' each word was chosen so as to form part of a likely one-word unit. So, words were chosen in proportion to their likelihood of occurring in an English sentence, but were deployed in random order. In the 'second-order approximation' each word was chosen so as to form part of a common two-word unit (hence second order), which meant that each word was chosen for its likelihood of following the one immediately preceding it. In the case of the 'third-order approximation' each word was chosen for its probability of following the previous two, thus forming a three-word unit and so on. Such statistical approximations may be formed by studying large passages of English and tabulating the transitional probabilities between word strings and their sequiturs. This is extremely tedious for the higher-order approximations, and Miller and Selfridge used a simpler method. To construct an approximation of the nth order, they showed $(n-1)$ words to a subject and asked for a likely sequitur, to give a string n words long. The first word was then deleted and the most recent $(n-1)$ shown to a new subject to obtain another sequitur and so on. In this way long strings of words may be obtained, each of which was chosen in the knowledge of the previous $(n-1)$. The results of such an exercise look like this:

Zero order

Combat callous irritability migrates depraved temporal prolix alas pillory nautical.

First order

Days to is for they have proposed I the it material of are its go studies the our of the following not over situation if the greater.

Second order

Goes down here is not large feet are the happy days and so what is dead weight that many were constructed the channel was.

Fourth order

We are going to see him is not correct to chuckle loudly and depart for home. (Miller, 1951).

This principle was scaled up by using whole utterances in place of words to produce approximations to dialogue instead of sentences, and the resemblance of each approximation to genuine dialogue was assessed by means of a 'Turing-like' criterion, making use of subjects' ability to distinguish poor simulations of dialogue from the real thing, but not good ones (Turing, 1950).

The hypotheses were:

1. Subjects agree on the relative plausibility of conversation sequences.
2. Higher orders of approximation to discourse are seen as more plausible.
3. At about 5th order, approximations approach a maximum standard.

Method

The experiment was in two parts: the first was to generate a series of thirty-six transcribed dialogues, each ten lines long, and the second to assess their similarity to 'genuine' conversation.

Genuine or control dialogues consisted of four ten-line extracts from real conversations recorded in a waiting-room situation for experiment 1. Zero-order artificial dialogues were produced by taking forty utterances from forty separate works of contemporary fiction (as there is no 'dictionary of utterances' from which to draw a random sample) and arranged randomly in four lists of ten lines each.

The remaining artificial dialogue (four each of 1st, 2nd, 3rd, 4th, 5th, 6th, and text orders of approximation) were produced by ten subjects, each of whom contributed one line to each of the twenty-eight extracts. There were seven female subjects and three males aged 18–26. Six were students in subjects other than psychology, one was unemployed, one an art student with a psychology degree, one a research assistant in psychology (but with no formal qualifications in psychology), and one an undergraduate psychologist.

In each case the experimenter read the appropriate number of lines from the incomplete transcript, which the subject could not see, and then recorded the next line suggested by the subject. The bundle of transcripts was thoroughly shuffled after each subject had completed the task, thus ensuring that each subject contributed to the twenty-eight dialogues in a different order and eradicating any order effect.

In cases where the first few subjects needed a longer leader than the experimental part of the dialogue, the appropriate lines from the following greeting were used:

1A: Hello.
2B: Hi.
3A: How are you?
4B: I'm fine thanks, and you?
5A: Fine, how nice to see you like this.

Again, the transcribed dialogues are a kind of 'data' in themselves, and they demonstrate clearly the effect on discourse structure of increasing order of approximation (see Appendix C for examples).

Additional assessment was provided by a panel of ten judges of whom six were female and four male. All were in the age range 18–26. There were six students of subjects other than psychology, two psychology students, a librarian and a photographer.

The judges filled in their ratings on a response sheet on which each dialogue was identified by a code number. These had been allocated to the different transcripts at random, and bore no systematic relation to the nature of the transcripts. The transcripts were shuffled before presentation to each new judge.

Results

Transcriptions

The dialogues used in this experiment are shown in Appendix C. The effect of varying the order of approximation on the structure of the dialogues is clearly apparent.

Judges' assessment

The seven-point ratings of the thirty-six dialogues by ten judges were subjected to a factorial analysis of variance, using the computer program BMD 8V (Dixon, 1973: 693–704). There were three factors: C(onditions), the various orders of approximation; E(xamples), the four different examples in each condition; and S(ubjects). C was specified as a fixed effect having nine levels, E as a random effect with four levels, nested in C, and S as a random effect with ten levels crossed with C and E. The results of this analysis are shown in Table 4.

The specification of E as a random effect, means that the F ratio for C is depressed in so far as E and C interact. A variance estimate for the interaction of E × C is added into the error term for C. Therefore any significant main effect of C which is found is more likely to have general validity.

TABLE 4   *Experiment 5: Analysis of variance*

Source	ss	df	MS
Mean	6342	1	6342
S	30.58	9	3.398
C	1067	8	133.3
E(C)	119.8	27	4.438
S × C	77.49	72	1.076
S × E(C)	226.4	243	0.9318

Parentheses indicate nesting relations. E(C) means E is nested in C. *F* ratios and levels of significance are not shown in this table as the peculiarities of the experimental design make an *F* ratio inappropriate. F' or F'' ratios may be used (Winer, 1962: 184 and 199).

An experimental design of this kind requires that the variance due to source C be evaluated by comparison with an error term that does not correspond to any single mean square value produced by the experiment. So a simple *F* ratio of two mean squares will not suffice. The variance due to C may be tested by using one of two *F*-prime ratios usually represented as F' and F'' respectively. Details are given in Clarke (1981). There was an F' ratio of 29.10 distributed approximately as *F* with 8 and 28 degrees of freedom. The critical value of *F* for $df = 8, 28, \alpha = 0.001$ is 4.69, so the main effect of C (the nine different orders of approximation) is significant at well beyond the 0.001 level.

$F'' = 24.35$ distributed approximately as *F* with $df = 8, 41$. The critical value of *F* for $df = 8, 41$ $\alpha = 0.001$ is 4.21, so again we can say that the main effect due to C is significant at well beyond the 0.001 level.

The only other effect to emerge from this analysis is the main effect E(C). (There is no interaction term for E and C as E is nested in C.) The effect of E(C), the difference between the four different examples of each dialogue type used in the experiment, may be evaluated using the simple *F* ratio. This gives an *F* value of 4.76; $df = 27, 243; p < 0.001$.

The mean ratings given to each of the nine dialogue types are plotted in Figure 5. The confidence interval of 0.98 shown for pairwise comparisons is the value of Fischer's LSD (least significant difference) multiple comparison test (Kirk, 1968: 87). In other words, any pair of mean ratings which differ by more than 0.98 are significantly different ($p < 0.05$, two-tailed).

Discussion

The results suggest a number of conclusions. They show yet again that subjects have a conception of what is likely and what is not in the sequential structure of conversation, that they agree with each other in such matters, and their judgements are accurate (in so far as the orders of approximation of the artificial

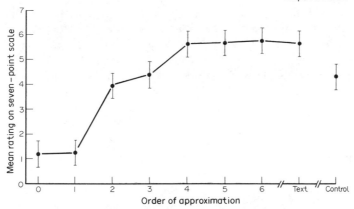

FIG. 5   Mean ratings given to 9 dialogue types of different
orders of approximation.

dialogues can be taken as a measure of their 'true' resemblance to real conversation).

Conversations become more or less realistic as the amount of history influencing each utterance choice is varied. There is a tendency for higher orders of approximation to be more realistic, culminating in the result that a fifth-order approximation can seem more like real dialogue than real dialogue itself. Perhaps the study of dialogue structure should take account of longer sequences than the usual item pairs. If so, an examination of ten item sequences would appear from these results to be more than adequate, and that is the convention which will be adopted in some of the later experiments.

It may seem that this experiment can only provide a very crude estimate of the number of utterances which have to be considered in accounting for the structure of discourse, but then the issue itself is rather vague. To ask how far the influence of an utterance extends is like asking how long is a piece of string. It is not in the nature of the question that its answer should be a precise quantity, or even a mean and standard deviation. It can take any value from no span to a lifetime. However, experiments such as this suggest that as a matter of research policy the search for structure somewhere in a ten-unit span should be fruitful, and sufficient to encompass a number of commonly found constructions.

By contrast the structure of a sentence does not present the same sort of problems. Here there is a definite delimitation of the span of influence by the boundaries of the sentence. Any syntactic influences which extend over larger spans are usually omitted from linguistic studies and are likely to be different in nature to the intra-sentence influences. In the analysis of discourse, where no such sentence-like units are evident, the analysis of structure must be guided by experiments like this, which direct attention to units of a particular size as being the most likely to embody the structural characteristics of the string.

Certain conclusions are not in order. The success of the higher-order approximations, does not mean that all dialogue has the properties of a fifth-order series or thereabouts. Nor does this experiment imply that the structure is linear, since other forms of structure, like for example a sentence-like tree, could also be captured by a simulation of this kind if the order of approximation were high enough to encompass the limits of the trees in the examples used.

Topics and the contents of individual utterances must be allowed to vary in an uncontrolled fashion from one dialogue to another, by the very nature of the experiment, which adds an unavoidable measure of noise to the data.

The possibility that the second-order approximation (alias Markov chain, or reactive contingency) is in some way special, will be considered in detail later.

After the pilot version of this experiment was carried out (not reported here), a similar study was published independently by Pease and Arnold (1973). Their conclusions are also compatible with the policy of looking for structures in strings of more than two items in length, and with an upper limit of five to ten items. They used much the same procedure, also inspired by the work of Miller and Selfridge, but a few important differences of technique should be mentioned. They generated zero, first, second and 'text' orders of approximation, but misapplied Miller's nomenclature by treating as second order those dialogues generated from a two-unit context (which should be called third order) and so on. To avoid confusion I shall describe their experiment in their terms with the numbering used by Miller and myself in parentheses. The 'text' order of approximation was generated by allowing subjects to see the whole of the dialogue so far. Subjects were given a description of the situation, roles of speakers, and topics in each case. Two different situations were used and one example of each order of approximation produced for each situation. The zero and text orders for the two situations were produced by two groups of subjects, and the first (second) and second (third) orders by two others. As a result of this part of the experiment, yet another group of subjects was used to produce a third (fourth) order approximation. The dialogues were ten lines long and produced in written form by the subjects.

A group of judges rank ordered approximations of zero, first (second), second (third), and text orders, and another group of judges ranked the third (fourth) order with the text order. As all the dialogues were artificial there was no measure of 'absolute plausibility' for any of them. An attempt was made to rectify this by having the dialogues rated as well on the assumption that a high plausibility rating would provide this absolute standard. The mean result for each subject's contribution at each level of approximation was calculated and sign tests performed between all possible pairs of orders of approximation. The only significant difference between adjacent orders of approximation was between first (second) and second (third), although there was a general tendency for perceived plausibility to increase with order of approximation throughout the series. The second (third) order approximation was not significantly worse than text order, and the third (fourth) order was better than the text order, but not significantly so. Judges were given detailed descriptions of the situations.

In general the outcome of this experiment was very similar to my Experiment 5. The fact that Pease and Arnold find that approximations get no better after the second (third) or third (fourth) order, rather than at the fifth order may be due to the extra information their subjects had from the description of the situations. In evaluating their results certain criticisms should be borne in mind.

1. The dialogue was generated in writing which makes the experiment less plausible as an investigation of natural dialogue production. Pease and Arnold admit this.

2. There was only one example of each combination of situation and order of approximation.

3. There were no natural dialogues against which to calibrate the judgements of plausibility. The argument that a five-point rating of plausibility will do instead is unconvincing.

4. The provision of information about the situation, speakers' roles and topics is a confounding factor, since a lot of this information would normally come from the dialogue itself, extending the span of influence of the utterances.

5. Different subjects were used to generate zero and text orders; first (second) and second (third) orders; and third (fourth) order of approximation, confounding intercondition differences with intersubject differences.

6. Different judges were used for the comparison of zero, first (second), second (third) and text orders of approximation; and third (fourth) and text orders of approximation.

These apparent shortcomings of the Pease and Arnold study came to light only after a pilot version of this study had been run, but in time for the version reported here to use a modified design which avoids all six difficulties.

The variance due to the nine different dialogue types, and due to the four examples of each type, are both large in comparison with their variation between subjects. This is shown by the significant values of the variance ratios. Increased orders of approximation are seen as more realistic, which shows again the importance of sequential influences in the generation of discourse, and the ratings approach an asymptotic maximum after about the fourth order of approximation.

The curve in Figure 5 has some interesting features. The zero- and first-order approximations are nearly identical. This may have been because of the following aspect of the experimental procedure. The first-order approximation was presented to the subjects as a limiting case of the higher orders. They were asked to provide an utterance which would fit well into an ongoing conversation, although they did not know what had preceded it. They were *not* told to produce the most common utterances they could think of. Therefore the first-order approximation consisted of utterances like

> Yes you can most certainly borrow it. I don't play it anymore. Though when Christopher becomes a little more proficient he will want to buy his own, and no doubt a better instrument than this.

which is very specific and perhaps a little implausible, when compared with the more obvious

> Hello.
> That's nice.
> Oh dear.

which formed the first-order approximation in the pilot study. In this respect the nature of the first and zero orders are more similar than might be expected otherwise.

The control dialogues were given a relatively low rating. They do not appear to be 'as good as' the text order of approximation for example. The reason for this is almost certainly the disfluency and situational specificity which is found in spontaneous dialogue and which confounds the comparison with the idealised artificial scripts.

The suggestion that future experiments should work with ten utterance spans might seem excessive in the light of this experiment showing that adequate simulation is achieved by fourth- and fifth-order approximations. However, the ten-item span will be used later on as a safeguard. The dialogues produced by this experiment are rather stilted and without clear motivation or ongoing themes. They do poor justice to the complexities which can emerge in conversation, and the finding that fourth-order approximations are as good as text order, would probably be modified if the greater complexities of the real-life situation had influenced the subjects' performance in generating the text-order approximations.

It is tempting to speculate further about the shape of the curve in Figure 5. It is roughly 'exponential' in form which is as one would expect. It departs from the shape of a perfectly smooth curve in having two abrupt increases in rating between first and second, and third and fourth orders of approximation. These are the points at which the last and penultimate contributions of *the other speaker* become known. The increments in rating between second and third, and fourth and fifth orders of approximation are much smaller. These are the points at which the last and penultimate contributions of *the same speaker* become known. This suggests that reactive structures are much more important for the production of realistic dialogue than proactive ones in this kind of conversation, and that the reactive contingencies may span more than two items in the sequence.

Experiment 6: The Future Machine

Introduction

   As the last experiment attempted to show, the recognisable structure of conversation depends on each utterance being chosen to suit the context established by the last few remarks. But that is not all there is to it. Our intuitions as conversationalists make it clear than anticipation as well as recollection is involved in this, as in most other orderly sequences of human activity. The speaker's problem is not only to follow sensibly what has gone before, but also to lead the conversation towards topics and points he would like to include, and away from possible pitfalls, undesirable revelations, and so on. If this is so, it is fair to ask about the span of a speaker's anticipation, as well as the span of past context bearing upon the choice of each utterance. How far ahead is a conversationalist able to look, in order to recognise the possible future opportunities or dangers that his present choices will lead to? The question may be unimportant in relation to casual or friendly encounters, but in the context of argument, negotiation or other forms of strategic behaviour it is likely to be a crucial determinant of successful or unsuccessful outcomes.

   The obvious way to study anticipation is to let a sequence of events or conversations proceed normally, and then take each participant back over the same ground, perhaps with the aid of recordings or transcripts, to ask what was anticipated and planned at each stage. This presents two problems. Time and further interaction will have intervened between the moment when an anticipation was formed or used, and the time when it comes to be reported, and memory may well have played false. Indeed this is all the more likely if, as is probable, such plans and anticipations are created, used and forgotten, in a systematic cycle as the sequence of events moves forward, so as to leave the mind free of unnecessary clutter, just as a shopping list is made with a view to being discarded once it has served its purpose. The second problem is the retrospective reinterpretation of events. Like a person who reads detective stories, but cheats by looking first to see who committed the crime, the plot takes on a quite different character once you know the outcome. In much the same way, the retrospective account of someone's former anticipations of events which have since become known, can only be suspect.

   What is really needed would seem to be a method which generates a record of people's anticipations *at the time*, but without undue disruption to the conversation or whatever other sequence is being studied in this way. Again there is an obvious but problematic solution, namely to fix a period of anticipation, say the next utterance, or the one after that, and leave it to the subject to indicate in the experimental situation just *what* is anticipated, by pressing one of an array of keys, for instance, to represent different categories of remark that were expected from the other speaker, or conversely which event-type the key-pressing subject expected to be able to use appropriately himself, at that point. The task, however, is over-elaborate, and likely to divert too much attention from the conversation. Instead the technique can profitably be turned around, so that the event or remark to be anticipated is fixed, and the subject's job is to say when it will occur. Now his fluctuating estimation of when the chosen event will arise is just a matter of giving a value on a simple scale to the time expected to elapse. This can be done quite easily while conversing, by turning a knob, or moving a calibrated pointer. The changing record of this variable 'time expected to elapse' with the passage of real time can be traced by connecting the subject's control to a chart recorder, which then produces a graph of subjective against objective time as the experiment proceeds. This was the basis of an apparatus that later acquired the nickname of 'the future machine' because of its role in measuring people's anticipations of future events.

When the target event does occur, the record can be so marked, and an 'ideal anticipation curve' constructed, showing what the subject's trace would have looked like, if, n seconds before the event, his estimate had also been n, and that was so for all values of n. With subjective time expected to elapse on the ordinate, and real time elapsed on the abscissa, this curve is a straight line with a slope of minus one, and an intercept with the abscissa at the moment the target event occurs, or $y = t_c - x$, where t_c is real time elapsed at the time of the event. For clarity the curves were later transformed to appear in the double-negative quadrant, as both time scales are best measured 'backwards' from t_o, when the event occurs. The ideal now becomes $y = x$ over the range $-\infty$ to 0.

The real trace obtained from a subject departs markedly from the ideal, of course, but as the event draws closer, there should be a point where it comes within range of the subjects' anticipation, and so thereafter, real and ideal curves should be approximately the same. That was the rationale for the experimental procedure to be reported, and the criterion by which the span of anticipation was to be measured.

Method

Subjects

There were twelve subjects, six male and six female, aged between 20 and 25, and all were university undergraduates or recent graduates.

Apparatus

The experiment was conducted in a laboratory with a one-way viewing screen separating two adjacent rooms. One room was used by an observer and contained no apparatus; the other contained two chairs, facing across a table on which there was a paper-chart recorder, the scale of which was visible from one side of the table and was calibrated in seconds from zero to ninety, with a further zone marked 'over 90 seconds'. The drive mechanism of the chart recorder, and the real time axis of the resulting charts was set to 0.1 inch/second. The chart recorder produced two traces at the same time. The first was controlled by the subject using a rotary potentiometer on a separate, uncalibrated unit, with the resultant deflection of the chart recorder pen over its scale as a guide to the amount of movement of the control required to produce a particular registration on the chart. The second trace was controlled by a simple push switch and was used to register a square pulse on the chart when the target event occurred.

Procedure

Subjects took part in groups of three. On each occasion, one became the *observer* and sat behind the one-way screen, while the other two held a 2-minute conversation in the other room, across the table with the chart recorder.

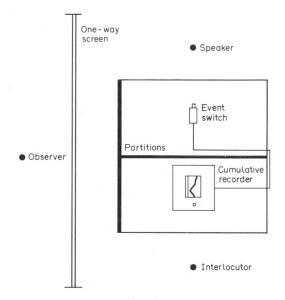

FIG. 6   Experimental layout for condition in which interlocutor records expectations.

The conversationalists were free to talk as they chose, except that one of them (called the *speaker*) was given a previously chosen utterance which had to be woven into the dialogue at the earliest appropriate point. The other conversationalist (the *interlocutor*) also knew what this 'target utterance' was, and was instructed to co-operate in making a suitable context for it. The observer did not know the target utterance, and his task was to try to find out which it was,

in which case it would be deemed to have been used unnaturally, and that particular trial abandoned, later to be re-run with a different target.

There were two conditions. In both, it was the speaker who operated the
push switch to signify the target event was beginning, but the other control
indicating the estimation of time to elapse before the event was worked by the
speaker in one condition, and the interlocutor in the other. Low partitions on
the table left the head and shoulders of speaker and interlocutor freely visible,
but hid the working of the chart-recorder controls.

After the target utterance had occurred the conversation continued until the
full 2 minutes had passed, when it was stopped by the experimenter. If the
target was not achieved within the first 2 minutes, the trial was abandoned
and re-run later. Each group of three people carried out twelve trials, rotating
each person through all combinations of three roles and two conditions.

In drawing up the list of target utterances, the following thirty-six speech
act categories were extracted from a larger taxonomy (Clarke, 1975b): prohibit,
request, question, advise, warn, permit, offer, promise, threaten, assert, justify,
accept, reject, comply, refuse, answer, agree, deny, continue, praise, defer, thank,
blame, accuse, confess, sympathise, boast, apologise, pardon, bid farewell,
pacify, terminate, attend, cheer, minimise and complain. A specific example of
each type was chosen, such as:

> 'Don't say that.'
> 'Could you move your head a bit so I can see.'
> 'What do we get paid for this experiment?'

which were the examples of *prohibit, request* and *question*, respectively. Before
each trial one of the list of thirty-six specific utterances, which had not yet
been used with that group of three subjects, was selected at random to be the
target.

Results

Figure 7 shows an example of a single trial, in which the trace was produced
by the speaker, and the target utterance was 'What do we get paid for this
experiment?' The conversation opened with 40 seconds of general discussion
and then moved abruptly to a more relevant topic, with a corresponding decrease
in the estimated time to elapse. Then there was something of a plateau while
the topic was consolidated until at $(t_0 - 61)$ seconds a much more specifically
appropriate series of remarks began, and the trace moved to a new and more ·
'optimistic' plateau. At $(t_0 - 34)$ the speaker confidently (but erroneously)
predicted that an opportunity to insert the target utterance was imminent.
Failing at the last moment, the speaker then indicated that a greater elapsed
time was anticipated once again, and the conversation returned to a more
general level. This pattern was quite a common occurrence in other traces,

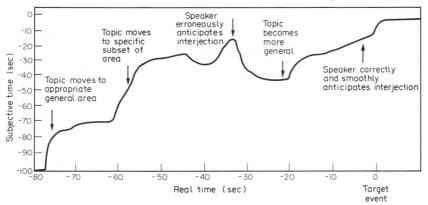

FIG. 7   Example trace from condition in which speaker
expectations were recorded.

and subjects reported frustration and a sense that a critical opportunity had been lost, which would be very hard to recover or re-create. Nonetheless the speaker could not afford to register this disappointment too clearly, or to force in the utterance unnaturally, as he knew the trial would be discarded if the observer in the other room were able to make out which was the target utterance. In this instance the conversation remained on the topic of the experimental participation for a short time and then from about $(t_o - 15)$ seconds the speaker foresaw and accurately predicted the approach of the target remark.

Each individual trace shows idiosyncrasies of the particular combination of conversationalists, topic, interactional skills and predictive ability, and consequently the variance between traces is considerable. Nonetheless a meaningful aggregate curve can be obtained by sampling each trace at the 10-second intervals and plotting the mean for each interval against real time.

Figures 8 and 9 show mean and standard deviation of expected time to elapse at 10-second intervals for 100 seconds before the target event, for speaker and interlocutor respectively. The last 10 seconds, which shows a pronounced improvement in anticipation in both conditions, and is likely to be of particular importance in selecting and preparing new utterances, is shown 'at higher magnification' in Figures 10 and 11, by sampling the real time base at 2.5-second intervals. Speaker expectations are plotted in Figure 10, while those for interlocutors appear in Figure 11.

Discussion

The aggregate curves show several interesting features. Both speakers and interlocutors show some awareness of the approaching target utterance, particularly in the last 10 seconds, although the accuracy of their expectations is

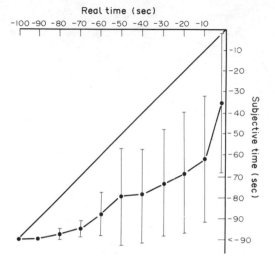

FIG. 8   Aggregate trace produced by speakers.

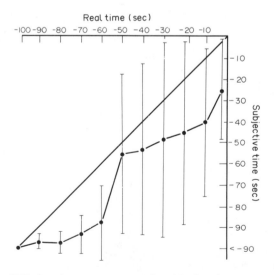

FIG. 9   Aggregate trace produced by interlocutors.

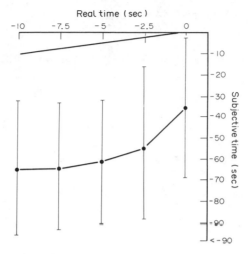

FIG. 10   Aggregate trace for speakers — the last 10 seconds
sampled at 2.5-second intervals.

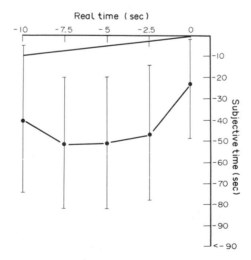

FIG. 11   Aggregate trace for interlocutors — the last 10
seconds at 2.5-second intervals.

generally poor, variable and short-lived. Some of their success may be put down to an awareness that as the 2-minute conversation rolled by the target event must have been increasingly imminent, regardless of what was happening at the time, or the validity with which it could be used as a basis for forecasting. Variation in estimates increased as time went by, probably because the early part of each run was very easy, the event was a long way off, and the subject's estimate fixed at 90 seconds or more. As the event approached, prediction began in earnest and the trace became more variable.

Throughout, the estimates of the interlocutor were more accurate than those of the speaker, which at first sight seems remarkable since it was the speaker's own voluntary behaviour that was being predicted. There may be two reasons for this. The interlocutor's task was probably easier. He only had to co-operate in creating a context for the target remark, rather than finding and using an opening for an utterance, which in the speaker's case he was also trying to remember verbatim. Consequently the interlocutor may have had more cognitive capacity to spare than the speaker, for the task of making and registering expectations. More interestingly for the understanding of real interaction processes, it is much more in the role of a listener to be monitoring talk for trends and openings than it is for the speaker, and it may be that the successful performance of the listener's role, with a view to becoming speaker at the next turn-relevance point (Sacks, class notes) depends on just this ability to make passive but accurate forecasts of the speaker's output. Both conditions produce a curve with a 'double scallop', more pronounced for interlocutors than speakers, in which the estimates of time to elapse showed a first down-swing at about $(t_0 - 50)$ seconds, as the appropriate topic was established, and another more pronounced one after $(t_0 - 10)$. The similarity of the two curves in this overall shape is all the more remarkable as they come from two different sets of trials. On no single occasion were speaker and interlocutor traces recorded together, which, had it been the case, might have produced similar kinks in both curves merely because idiosyncrasies of the conversations in question were recorded by both parties simultaneously.

Throughout, the time to elapse was over-estimated by speakers and interlocutors, meaning that their inaccuracy resulted from 'false negatives' or the failure to anticipate the approaching event, rather than 'false positives' or a tendency to foresee the event when it was not really imminent.

Turning to the magnified views of the last 10 seconds, some of the features of the long-term traces were reproduced in the short term. Interlocutors were more accurate than speakers, and accuracy increased most at the very end (in this case the last 2.5 seconds). Again this may reflect the interlocutor's natural role as forecaster, or the smaller demands made by competing aspects of his task.

Overall, the subjects' estimates of time were poor. This may have been due, not so much to their inability to anticipate events, as to their difficulty in reporting expectations in units of 'seconds' which correspond closely with the units of real time. If that is so, it is important here. It is the relative accuracy of expectations as an event approaches that matter, not the tendency for subjects to report in 'subjective seconds' which are roughly half the length of real seconds on the clock, which is another possible interpretation of their tendency to over-estimate times-to-elapse. Other sources of inaccuracy in the registration (but not estimation) of expected time to elapse are the reluctance of subjects to look often enough at the calibrated subjective-time scale against which their traces were accumulating, and the fineness of that scale ($0.35''/10$ seconds), which was necessary to fit a reasonable range of values into the width of the chart-recorder paper, but which cannot have helped the subjects to record accurately the exact time interval they had in mind.

As far as (tentative) conclusions are in order, it seems that anticipation is a feature of the participants' view of conversation, and should be included in process models of utterance selection or discourse generation, together with the more commonly considered constraints from past context. The effect of anticipation seems to work in two stages. One spanning about 50 seconds allows participants to appreciate the implications of topic changes, and the other extending only a few seconds into the future has to do with the planning and location of specific remarks.

On a more general level, the future is everybody's problem, and the extent and accuracy of our foresight has a lot to do with the success of plans, policies and strategies of all kinds. It may be that the procedures described here, with suitable modifications, may have more general application in mapping people's picture of the future, and understanding the processes by which these anticipations and hence the future itself are created. This is the kind of application of micro-research techniques to larger-scale problems which will be discussed in Chapter 7.

Experiment 7: Nested Sequences

Introduction

If, as the previous experiments suggest, the essence of dialogue structure is to be found in strings of a few utterances, the next issue will be to find the form of that structure. The results to date are compatible with either a linear stochastic series or a structure which allows the greatest influence to be exerted between events which are not contiguous in the observed order of events, such as the strings of morphemes which can be reproduced by tree-like rule schemes. In this experiment three kinds of structure will be compared, to see which of them should be included in a model of conversation.

The related items of behaviour which make up a predictable sequence or structure may be arranged in various ways. Some arrangements, called linear stochastic series, are relatively simple to describe, since the influence on each item of its antecedents operates in a linear fashion. (The notion and significance of linear structure were discussed earlier.) In essence it means that each element in the behaviour stream is influenced most strongly by its immediate predecessors. Once the influence has been traced back a few items into the history of the behaviour stream the bulk of the variance is accounted for, and the pattern may be adequately described by the matrix of transitional probabilities from each possible arrangement of the relevant number of preceding items to each possible class of sequitur. In the simplest case the transitional probability matrix gives a perfect description of the sequence when only one item of history is used — the defining property of the Markov chain.

However, not all patterned sequences are necessarily stochastic or linear. Some may have the property that the chain of related events may be interrupted and resumed, without destroying its structure, a possibility which has led to the present interest in non-linear or non-stochastic models.

The linear stochastic models have a number of advocates, partly because they may be treated by mathematical techniques which are simpler and better developed than those for many of the non-stochastic series, and a number of authors have found or assumed them to be quite adequate for the description of a variety of behaviour sequences. One source of the belief in stochastic or more specifically Markov models has been the application of control theory to behaviour. The central concept of the *feedback loop* suggests that each item of behaviour produces a change in the physical or social environment, which the organism perceives and uses to formulate or modify its next act (Leavitt and Mueller, 1951; Annett, 1969), giving the behaviour a stochastic structure. Bales (1953), Jones and Gerard (1967), and Shannon and Guerney (1973) all base their analyses of sequences on stochastic models of reactive and/or proactive structure. Jaffe *et al.* (1967), as we saw earlier, analysed the alternating pattern of speech and silence by speakers in a dialogue and found the Markov model suitable for the description of his data. The behaviour stream was found to be most predictable when segmented into 300-msec units. The possibility of speech occurring in a given interval could be predicted from the four possible states in the preceding interval of actor speaks, other speaks, both speak or neither speak; and the accuracy of prediction was not increased by considering more than one previous interval.

The advocates of non-stochastic models often base their argument on the ubiquity of non-stochastic sequences in human natural language, and the probability that the temporal patterns of speech and action are similar. For example, Lashley (1951) wrote:

> I have devoted so much time to discussion of the problem of syntax not only because language is one of the most important products of human cerebral action, but also because the problem raised by the organisation of language seems to me to be characteristic of almost all other cerebral activity. . . . Not only speech, but all skilled acts

seem to involve the same problems of serial ordering, even down to the temporal co-ordination of muscular contractions in such a movement as reaching and grasping.

Lashley (1951: 121)

More recent authors have based their descriptions of the similarly non-stochastic patterns in language and behaviour on the model of syntax originally advanced by Chomsky (1957). Miller, Galanter and Pribram (1960), Barker (1963), Marshall (1965), Ervin-Tripp (1969), Martin (1972) and Westman (1978) cover between them a variety of behaviours — human and animal, individual and social — all in the light of the tree-like temporal structure of English syntax.

A number of articles have appeared, analysing the arguments for and against linear stochastic models in some detail, and all concluding that the non-linear models are superior, if only because they are sufficiently flexible to describe either sort of behaviour sequence if the need should arise. The outline of the argument as presented by Chomsky (1957), Farrell (1970) and Hutt and Hutt (1970) is much the same. The simple Markov and higher-order stochastic theories are introduced, shown to be inadequate because of some kind of nesting (also called embedding, side sequences, insertion sequences) and replaced by a more flexible generative device based on tree rules, or perhaps feed-back loops with the added 'meta-organising feedforward' facilities suggested by MacKay (1972). The fact that sentences are not linear stochastic morpheme strings does not imply that they cannot be produced by a device with a finite number of states as Chomsky (1957) seems to have supposed. The distinction between tree and finite state generators has to do with 'top—down' as opposed to 'left-to-right' processing. The chapter in Hutt and Hutt on sequence analysis ends with the following evaluation of the 'phrase structure grammar model':

> The strength of the model lies in its ability to deal with a considerably greater behavioural repertoire and much longer sequences than can be treated by Markovian processes alone. An evaluation of the various models presented in this chapter awaits a study in which all three types are applied to the same behavioural data.
>
> Hutt and Hutt (1970: 184)

The purpose of the present experiment is to provide such an empirical comparison between models, for one aspect of discourse structure, namely the arrangement of related pairs of question and answer. These were chosen as the simplest units to identify and relate, so that the difficult problems of speech act taxonomy and sequence analysis could be left until a later stage. The question answer pairs Q1—A1 and Q2—A2 were used in the following structures:

1. *Linear*	Q1	A1	Q2	A2
2. *Nested*	Q1	Q2	A2	A1
3. *Cross-nested*	Q1	Q2	A1	A2

Their structure may be represented diagrammatically as in Figure 12. Two hypotheses were tested.

(1) Linear structure

1 a:	Question 1
2 b:	Answer 1
3 b:	Question 2
4 a:	Answer 2

(2) Nested structure

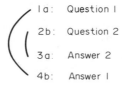

1 a:	Question 1
2 b:	Question 2
3 a:	Answer 2
4 b:	Answer 1

(3) Cross nested structure

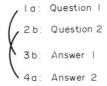

1 a:	Question 1
2 b:	Question 2
3 b:	Answer 1
4 a:	Answer 2

FIG. 12   Dialogue structures.

1. Linear and nested structures will seem equally acceptable to judges, but crossed structures will be perceived as significantly less likely to occur. This is in keeping with the predictions of the syntactic model, which does not generate cross-nested structures. Interestingly the structure of many computer languages allows the nesting of sub-routines in routines in a similar way, but forbids the use of cross-nesting (exit from and re-entry to a loop after an incomplete number of iterations), as this cannot be accomplished by 'push-down stack' storage devices.

2. Most of the variance will occur as a function of the experimental variation of structure, rather than as a function of the different topics presented as examples of each structure, or of the interaction of topic and structure. This is by way of a general vindication of a structural analysis, which requires that a particular structure have invariant effects despite the variety of different contents which it may contain.

Method

The questionnaire

This experiment, the one that follows it and three others not reported here, were all carried out by means of the same questionnaire.

Twenty-nine subjects completed the questionnaire: nineteen females and ten males. Twenty-six were aged 18–25, one was 26, one was 28 and one 32. There were twenty-one students (of subjects other than psychology), two psychology students, two photographers, one secretary, one research fellow (in zoology), one research assistant (in psychology) and one laboratory technician (in haematology).

Each questionnaire was self-explanatory and given to the subject to complete in his own time in the laboratory or at home.

Instructions were provided in a very explicit form, as subjects were to fill in the questionnaire on their own, without the opportunity to ask questions.

The instructions called for a judgement of probability of occurrence, so this is a test of descriptive not semiotic competence. The following pieces of dialogue were used in this experiment.

1. A   Do you have the time?
    B   It's three o'clock.
    B   Why do you want to know?
    A   I have a bus to catch.

2. A   Where are you off to?
    B   I'm going into town.
    B   Didn't I tell you this morning?
    A   No.

3. A   Did you forget Mike's birthday?
    B   I suppose I must have done.
    B   When was it?
    A   Three weeks ago tomorrow.

4. A   Where did you spring from?
    B   I was behind there.
    B   Did I make you jump?
    A   Nearly out of my skin.

5. A   Do you want to buy a second-hand camera?
    B   I'll think about it.
    B   How much do you want?
    A   Twenty-five quid.

Each of the five sets of sentences (henceforth called the *examples*) appeared on the questionnaire in each of the three arrangements shown in Figure 12 (henceforth called the *conditions*). Thus the experimental design became one of treatment-by-treatment-by-subjects or completely crossed factors, giving 5 (examples) × 3 (conditions) × 29 (subjects) = 435 data points. The order of presentation of items was derived by cycling both treatment dimensions simultaneously, starting:

Example 1 Condition 1
Example 2 Condition 2
Example 3 Condition 3
Example 4 Condition 1
Example 5 Condition 2
Example 1 Condition 3 . . . and so on.

In this way the experiment was controlled for order effects, and for differences arising from the properties of individual utterances rather than the structure in which they occurred.

Results

The subjects' ratings were subjected to a three-way analysis of variance, using the program BMD 08V (Dixon, 1973: 693). The results are given in Table 5.

TABLE 5   *Experiment 7: Analysis of variance*

Source of variance	ss	df	MS
Mean	9699	1	9699
Conditions	342.6	2	171.3
Examples	29.14	4	7.284
Subjects	129.9	28	4.638
Conditions × Examples	107.6	8	13.45
Conditions × Subjects	159.6	56	2.850
Examples × Subjects	231.0	112	2.062
Conditions × Examples × Subjects	453.4	224	2.024

Examples and subjects are treated as random effects, as in Experiment 5, so F' or F'' ratios have to be used for the main effect of conditions. Examples are not nested in conditions in Experiment 7, however, so there is a value for the variance due to the interaction between examples and conditions. Otherwise the calculation of F' and F'' is similar to that used for the nested design in Experiment 5 (Winer, 1962: 199).

F' Conditions $= 12.00$, $df = 2, 9; p < 0.005$,
F'' Conditions $= 10.63$; $df = 2, 12; p < 0.005$,
F Examples $= 3.53$, $df = 4, 112; p < 0.01$,
F Conditions × Examples $= 6.645$; $df = 8, 224; p < 0.001$.

In addition two *post hoc* tests were done on the data. Fisher's multiple comparison procedure, the LSD (Least Significant Difference) test (Kirk, 1968), was used to find which, if any, of the pairwise comparisons of the treatment means on the dimension *conditions* were significant. The least significant difference between means for conditions was found to be 1.44 points on the seven-point rating scale, $p<0.01$, two-tailed. This is shown as a confidence interval on a graph of rating against dialogue structure (Figure 13).

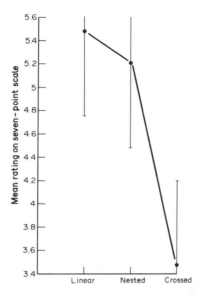

FIG. 13   Mean ratings on seven-point scale, of three dialogue
structures.

Both hypotheses are supported by the data. The experimental variation of structure gives rise to a significant main effect in the analysis of variance ($F' = 12.00$, $p<0.005$), and this is shown by Fisher's LSD test to be due to the low ratings given to the cross nested structure. If the criterion level of significance is set at 0.01, this test shows that the ratings given to linear and nested structures are not significantly different, but that the ratings for cross-nested structures are significantly worse than both.

An estimate of the variance component due to each of the main effects showed that the structure dimension accounts for about 18 times as much variance as the topic dimension. Arguably this was because topics were selected which were all of similar plausibility, and a different sample of topics would have led to greater topic variance. The original hypothesis is of the kind which may be falsified but not verified, so we can never be certain it is true, but the data *for this particular set of examples at least* fit the experimental prediction.

Looking at the unacceptable cross-nested structure, an obvious explanation for its unacceptability comes to mind. We see that from speaker B's view point the dialogue offers two binary choices.

1. After A has asked Q1, B may reply with A1 giving rise to the linear structure, or with Q2.

2. *If* he decides to counter Q1 with Q2 he has a further choice of waiting for it to be answered with A2 before providing A1, so producing the nested structure, or he may go straight on from Q2 to supply A1 giving the cross-nested structure.

If we now start attributing motives to B the issue becomes clear. He presumably either wants (or needs) the information from A2 to consider in giving A1, or alternatively does not. If he does he poses Q2 and waits for A2 before giving A1; and if he does not he provides A1 in response to Q1, before going on to explore his further interests in the matter with Q2. Both very plausible alternatives, but what could possibly lead B to pose Q2, and then supply A1 without waiting for A2? This may well have been the kind of puzzle which led subjects to give a low rating to the cross-nested structures, and it is a reminder that motives, attitudes and beliefs may have to be attributed to the speakers, which are not an explicit part of the behaviour stream, before the occurrence of certain items of behaviour in certain orders may be understood. The attributions made to speakers, on the basis of their speech, will be considered later.

Experiment 8. Perceived Embedding

Introduction

In the last experiment the nested version of the two pairs of question and answer Q1 Q2 A2 A1, was used to support the argument against linear-stochastic models of dialogue structure. It has a number of interesting properties as a construction, quite apart from its non-linear nature, which should be explored before passing on. The last utterance A1 has an ambiguous role. At the performative level of description it is an answer to Q1 and is related to the first utterance. This is how the structure comes to be one of nested relations. However, it also relates to the third utterance A2 at the constative or propositional level of description, in so far as the content of A1 is dependent on the content of A2. So when both levels of description are considered simultaneously, the utterances are seen to be linked by a chain of influence which splits and rejoins, passing through Q1 to A1 and through Q1 to Q2 and A2 at the performative level; and through Q1 to Q2, A2 and A1 at the propositional level in such a way as to produce a closed ring of linkages. For this reason the structure will be referred to as a *loop* when both levels of description are included in the analysis. The loop structure is illustrated in Figure 14.

The aim of this experiment was to justify the analysis given above as a legitimate part of the structure of discourse. Two aspects of the analysis seemed questionable: that the four-line extracts of dialogue used really had (or really

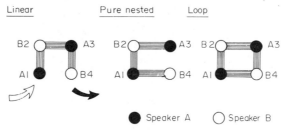

FIG. 14   Pure dialogue structures.

appeared to subjects to have) the loop structure; and that they were acceptable as examples of realistic dialogue.

Hypothesis 1   Subjects when asked to make judgements of the structure of 'loop' transcripts would take account of performative and constative levels of description, producing a structural description which shows the ring of inter-utterance relations.

Hypothesis 2   Subjects will be able to give ratings of plausibility to examples of the loop structure which are not significantly worse than those given to commonplace constructions from real dialogue.

Method

Subjects

The experiment was conducted on the same questionnaire as the previous experiment, so the subjects are as described in the last section.

Procedure

There were five items, each in the form of a four-line 'loop' dialogue, and five which were four-line exchanges from real conversations between pairs of students, as a control. These latter items came from unpublished transcripts obtained by Lalljee and Cook on non-verbal behaviour in newly introduced dyads. The ten items were arranged in random order on the questionnaire. The loop items were:

      1A: What are you having?
      2B: Do they have the new lager here?
      3A: No.
      4B: Pint of bitter then, please.

      1A: Are you going to the match?
      2B: Who's playing?

3A: City and Spurs.
4B: No, I don't think I'll bother.

1A: Who is that man over there?
2B: Which one?
3A: In the blue jacket.
4B: That's Simon, the one who won the scholarship.

1A: Where's Jake?
2B: I don't think I know him.
3A: You do – tall with gingery hair.
4B: Oh yes, he just went through there.

1A: Excuse me, could you tell me how I get to the station?
2B: Central or Northern?
3A: Central.
4B: It's down there, second right and then straight ahead.

The control items were:

1A: What are you reading?
2B: I'm doing English, what are you doing?
3A: Medicine, what college?
4B: I'm at Exeter.

1A: Where've you been, you were . . . you got here last night?
2B: I've been . . . yes, I've been in London working.
3A: Sorry, you've been where?
4B: I've been in London working.

1A: Do you belong to the film club?
2B: Yes.
3A: You have good stuff, don't you there?
4B: Yes.

1A: Have you travelled a lot round Europe?
2B: Europe – not much. I never went abroad 'till last year, I went
      to Greece last year. You?
3A: I've travelled a bit, went to Russia about three years ago.
4B: I'd like to go there.

1A: Where were you before you came to Oxford?
2B: Well, in a school in Kent.
3A: Yes, you come from Kent do you?
4B: No, Canada originally.

When subjects had provided plausibility ratings for these items they were then asked to indicate for each 'line', which previous line or lines it was derived from.

Results

The results are presented in Table 6 and Figure 15. The table shows the lower diagonal matrix formed from the results for each item by tabulating the number of subjects identifying a link between each pair of antecedent and sequitur. This is similar to the technique since described by Schlesinger (1972) except that in this version various degrees of relation between items are represented in the matrix in place of the zeros and ones which Schlesinger uses to represent relatedness or unrelatedness.

The figure presents the same results as a set of 'molecules'. Each circle represents a turn at talking, and the lines between them represent the number of subjects who judged them to be related.

TABLE 6   *Showing the numbers of subjects* (N = 29) *who identified relations between pairs of utterances in different structures. Columns show antecedents, rows are sequiturs.*

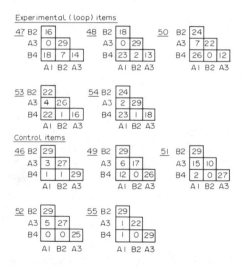

Key. In the following idealised examples the typical structure is represented by an X in the cells which have high entries.

Experimental (loop) items

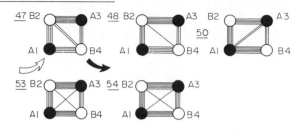

Control items

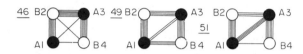

FIG. 15   Showing the numbers of subjects who identified relations between pairs of utterances in different structures. Where 1—4 subjects recognised the relation, 1 line is used, 5—9 subjects recognised the relation, 2 lines are used, 10—14 subjects recognised the relation, 3 lines are used, 15—19 subjects recognised the relation, 4 lines are used, 20—24 subjects recognised the relation, 5 lines are used, 25—29 subjects recognised the relation, 6 lines are used.

The seven-point ratings given by subjects to the different items were subjected to the analysis of variance procedure used in Experiment 6 (Dixon, 1973: 693). There were 2 C(onditions) of loop and control dialogues, 5 E(xamples) of each and 29 S(ubjects). C was treated as a fixed effect, E as a random effect nested in C, and S as a random effect fully crossed with C and E. The results are given in Table 7.

TABLE 7   *Experiment 8: Analysis of variance*

Source of variance	ss	df	MS
Mean	8861	1	8861
C	103.2	1	103.2
E(C)	74.87	8	9.359
S	177.0	28	6.321
C × S	58.50	28	2.089
E(C) × S	328.7	224	1.468

The mean rating for loop dialogues was 6.12, and for controls was 4.93.

$$F'_C = 10.34; \mathrm{d}f = 1, 9; p < 0.025,$$
$$F''_C = 9.143; \mathrm{d}f = 1, 12; p < 0.025,$$
$$F_{E(C)} = 6.375; \mathrm{d}f = 8, 224; p < 0.001.$$

Discussion

Both hypotheses find support in the data. It is clear from the tabulated judgements of structure that subjects' opinions confirm the loop or ring hypothesis for the experimental items but not for the control items which are predominantly linear in their structure. This detection of complex structures in agreement with the hypothesis is even more apparent in the molecular diagrams in Figure 15.

The analysis of variance shows that the experimental items were not given significantly lower ratings than the control items. On the contrary, the loop dialogues were seen as more plausible than the controls, $p < 0.025$. This could have been due to a number of factors. The experimental items were idealised, in that they contained no disfluencies, they covered a wider range of topics, and were not produced under the constraints (albeit minimal) of an experimental interaction. The issue is really one of sampling, which is difficult when dealing with corpora of discourse. The diversity of styles and functions represented in natural discourse cannot be adequately represented by a few excerpts. However, the comparison between these two sets of artificial loop structures and natural dialogue extracts favours the loops to such a degree that we may conclude with some confidence that this particular artificial construction is not one which strikes the native actor as completely unrecognisable, and alien to the discourse system as it is commonly understood.

It is reassuring to find that subjects presented with this task of structural judgement agree to a large extent on the nature of the structure. In the R-matrices for items 47, 48, 49, 51, 52, and 55 there are cell entries of 0 and 29, showing that subjects agreed unanimously that there was a relation between some pairs of items, and none between others. The subjects agree, not only with each other, but with the experimental hypotheses. This suggests that discourse structures of this kind do have some psychological reality, and are not a mere technical convenience embodying judgements which are only apparent to researchers. Perhaps the time will come when the procedures for identifying structure are sufficiently well established and validated against the judgements of the native actor, that they may be used on novel situations without the feeling that they may be misrepresenting the actor's view.

There have been attempts by psycholinguists to show that in a similar way, the structures which appear in the grammarians' theories of language may be recovered from the judgements of the native actor, but with limited success. Johnson (1965) suggested that subjects' parsing of surface structure agrees with the parsing produced by a Chomskian tree. He found that transitional error probabilities (the likelihood of being wrong on one word, given that the previous word was correct) in sentence recall were greatest at phrase boundaries. However, in Martin's (1970) study of subjective phrase structure, a discrepancy appeared between the judgements of the subjects and the dictates of the grammar. Subjects' estimates of the intimacy of relation between the components of sentences were cluster analysed to give a dendrogram equivalent to the tree structure of the sentence. This showed that in the subjects' estimation the two main components of the sentence were often a composite of subject and verb, and the object; whereas the usual linguistic analysis would make the subject one of the main units, and a verb-object composite (the predicate) the other.

In judging the loop structure subjects had to attend to two levels of description. The relation between items A1 and B4 is at the performative level, while that between A3 and B4 is constative. Both levels were taken into account, but more subjects identified the performative link than the constative one in all cases. This observation supports the conclusion drawn from Experiments 3 and 4, that structural analysis is feasible at the level of abstraction which has to do with the illocutionary force of speech acts, rather than their propositional content.

Experiment 9: Basis of Utterance Choice

Introduction

If we suppose on the basis of the previous studies that the essential process of dialogue generation is a succession of choices as to how to follow up the immediate past, is it possible to determine next, not *how much* of the past information, but *which aspects* of it will shape the future?

This study was developed from an idea of Richard Forsyth's, that I investigate the information necessary to select an appropriate next utterance, by asking subjects to choose a continuation for an unknown passage of dialogue, and allowing them to ask for any information about it, which would help their decision. The dependent variables would be (a) the questions the subjects asked, and (b) the order in which they asked them. For ease of interpretation and running, the procedure was modified, so that twenty factors were suggested to subjects who placed them in rank order of importance as cues to (a) the choice of a next line of dialogue and (b) the next five lines.

Method

Twenty subjects took part in this study, eleven females and nine males, aged 18 to 36. Each was presented with a form showing the following list of information types, in the following order:

What the speakers know about the topic . . . .
The speakers' political views . . . .
The mood of the conversation so far . . . .
The season of the year . . . .
The speakers' (long-term) ambitions in life . . . .
The sexes of the speakers . . . .
The personalities of the speakers . . . .
The last few 'lines' of the conversation . . . .
The marital statuses of the speakers . . . .
The sort of place (e.g. bar, classroom, railway carriage, etc.) . . . .
The speakers' religious views . . . .
The year . . . .
The topic of conversation . . . .
The speakers' occupations . . . .
The situation (e.g. a business meeting, a talk between friends, a therapy
    session, etc.) . . . .
The speakers' ages . . . .
The speakers' aims or motives in this conversation . . . .
The time of day . . . .
A summary of the speakers' previous conversations (if any) . . . .
The relationship between the speakers . . . .

Next to each item was a space in which subjects could write a number to indicate the rank importance of that type of information as a predictor of the next line of conversation to come up, and another space where each item could be ranked as a predictor of the next five-line span (on the assumption that short-term and medium-term anticipations may be based on different items of information).

Results

For the one-line condition the summed rank order was: the topic of conversation; what the speakers know about the topic; the last few lines of conversation; the mood of conversation so far; the situation (e.g. a business meeting, a talk between friends, a therapy session, etc.); the speakers' aims or motives in this conversation; the relationship between the speakers; a summary of speakers' previous conversations if any; the personalities of the speakers; the speakers' occupations; the sort of place (e.g. bar, classroom, railway carriage, etc.); the sexes of the speakers; the speakers' political views; the speakers' ages; the speakers' (long term) ambitions in life; the speakers' religious views; the marital status of the speakers; the time of day; the year and the season. There were no abrupt discontinuities in the summed ranks to suggest a dichotomous classification into relevant and irrelevant information. The ranking for the five-line case was different in that ambitions came four places higher; motives and personality three places higher; last lines and ages two places higher; knowledge of topic, sort of place and sexes three places lower and situation and relationship two places lower. Changes of one place in rank were disregarded. Concordance between subjects for the one-line condition was 0.66; $r_{s_{av}} = 0.64$; $\chi^2 = 250.99$; $df = 19$; $p < 0.001$, and for the five-line case 0.62; $r_{s_{av}}$ = 0.60; χ^2 = 236.74; df = 19; $p<0.001$. Correlation between one-line and five-line summed ranks was 0.94 (t = 11.63; df = 18, $p<0.001$).

Discussion

This study can only act as a rough guide to the kinds of events and factors in the history of a conversation that affect (and hence predict) its future course, since the subjects' intuitions about the relative merit of different items of information as predictors may have been inaccurate. In the next study the same subjects were put to the test, by trying to make predictions on the basis of different types of information so that the accuracy of predictions achieved could be related to the information that had been available to make them.

Experiment 10: Effects of Context

Introduction

It is a fair assumption that the variables from the past history of a course of events or conversation that have most to do with determining its future course will be those which it is most useful to know about in predicting the future. That principle was used in this study to investigate the relative importance of different classes of 'historical' information as predictors of (and hence possible causes of or constraints upon) the development of a pattern of conversation over time. More specifically the aim was to find out which aspects of the past course of a conversation (if any) would enable a subject to predict its future course as accurately as someone working from a complete transcription of the past discussion.

Method I

The twenty subjects described in the previous study also took part in this one.

The experiment was in four stages and a cyclic design allowed four groups of subjects to treat four dialogues to the four stages in turn, without repeating a stage or a dialogue. The four stages will be described for one dialogue passing through the hands of the four subject groups in succession. The material was real dialogue from candid recordings, and twenty-turn extracts were used in two separate parts, consisting of the first fifteen lines and the last five. In the first stage subjects saw the first fifteen lines only, and wrote a précis which was to be as brief as possible while being suitable for someone else to use it as a basis for predicting the last five lines. In effect subjects were asked what were, in their opinion, the most significant aspects of the first fifteen lines in shaping the likely course of the conversation.

The second group of subjects then took these summaries, but not the first fifteen lines, and made their written predictions of the last five lines. The third group of subjects predicted the last five lines from the first fifteen (but without seeing the summaries); and finally, the fourth group rated eleven versions of the last five lines, which were not identified but were in fact the *real* last five lines, five versions produced from summaries, and five versions produced from the first fifteen lines.

Results I

Mean rating for all 'real' continuations was 3.40 (on a seven-point scale), précis continuations 3.46, and script continuations 4.56. Having established that a précis can provide background information for continuing a dialogue as plausibly as the real actors, or as plausibly as other subjects working from the script itself (on some occasions), it only remained to be seen what information went into those summaries which subsequently produced the best continuations. This turned out to be much harder than expected, and clearly the question was not to be resolved by inspection alone, although one evident feature in many of the summaries, and particularly it seemed in those that had been the basis of highly rated continuations, was a reliance on reported speech. In order to look in more detail at the relationship between content of summaries and success of continuations, a second stage was added to the study.

Method II

For this stage, eighteen subjects took part, twelve females and six males, aged 19—45. They rated all of the summaries on a number of seven-point scales indicating the extent to which each of twenty-two different categories of information had been used. The twenty-two types were 'reported speech' and 'psychological speculation about states of mind or personality' for instance, together with the twenty categories of information used in the previous study. By now, each pair of a summary and the script continuation based upon it could be described in terms of the mean-rating given to the summary on each of twenty-two variables describing its *content* by the eighteen subjects in this phase of the study; and the mean-rating given to the *quality* of the script-continuation by the sub-group of five subjects out of twenty in the first phase of the experiment, who had rated that particular continuation together with the four others originating from the same script, five continuations produced directly from the script, and its 'real', original ending.

Next a quantitative relation could be sought between the content of summaries, and the quality of the continuations based upon them.

Results II

This was done in two ways. First a multiple step-wise regression of content variables onto 'quality' ratings was carried out. This showed that the combined multiple *r* of all independent variables with the dependent variable was 0.997. The variables with the highest single correlation with 'quality' of continuation were:

The speakers' occupations	−0.60
The speakers' religious views	0.51
The speakers' (long-term) ambitions in life	0.47

The next highest single correlation was 0.27. Negative correlations indicate that that feature was *absent* from the summaries with the 'best' continuations. Turning to the more satisfactory criterion of influence on the dependent variable, provided by standardised partial regression coefficients (beta coefficients), the most important predictor variables (if only by their absence as indicated by negative values) are

The personalities of the speakers	−4.53
The speakers' (long-term) ambitions in life	3.94
The speakers' occupations	−3.76
Extent of psychological speculation	3.30

(In order of unstandardised regression coefficients the principal variables are:

The speakers' (long-term) ambitions in life	13.24
The personalities of the speakers	−4.89
The speakers' religious views	−4.47
Extent of psychological speculation	3.95
The speakers' political views	2.83)

The relation between quality of continuation and individual variables depicting content of summaries creates a rather confusing picture, and tends to disagree with the rankings in the previous study. In order to identify a more global relations between types of summaries and the quality of the continuations based upon them a factor analysis was performed on the twenty-two ratings for each summary (averaged across judges) and the ratings of plausibility for the corresponding continuation. Varimax rotation was used and six factors emerged, the first three of which accounted for 69.0% of the variance.

Factor I was 'personal versus situational' descriptions; Factor II was called 'specific-acute-foreground versus general-chronic-background' as it differentiated ratings of such things as the emphasis given by the précis writers to the motives of the speakers and the last few lines of the transcript they were summarising, from the emphasis they gave to the speakers' religious and political views for example; Factor III concerned 'social versus task' aspects of the dialogue with the summary writers' emphasis on mood and personality and general psychological speculation loading on one pole and conversational history, goals and topic on the other. Factor IV, 'role versus individual variables', had religion, year, topic and time of day loading on one pole, and age, occupation and ambitions loading on the other. Factor V was called 'content versus setting' distinguishing knowledge of the topic and emphasis given to reported speech, for instance, from time of day, place, year, speakers' occupations and political views. Factor VI was dubbed 'platonic versus carnal' since marital status, sex, time of day and speakers' ages loaded on one pole, while the other was concerned with the year, the season, previous conversations, and the speakers' long-term ambitions in life.

If these six dimensions show the variety of summaries obtained, which factors were associated with the success of subsequent predictions? The ratings of continuations based on the summaries, loaded most on Factor IV where role as opposed to individual description produced a loading of 0.59. On Factor V there was a loading of 0.26 on content as opposed to setting and on Factor VI a loading of 0.11 appeared on social as opposed to task considerations.

Discussion

The results are suggestive but no more. By this time the data had passed through a long convoluted procedure, and it would be wise to reserve final judgement until there is corroboration, but they suggest that (for these dialogues at least) it is social roles and factual content which emerge from dialogue, as the best indicators of its future course.

Experiment 11: Stages of Utterance Choice

Introduction

Continuing for the time being with the view that treats conversation as a succession of choices of next utterance, constrained in some way by the immediate history of the talk, it might be argued that the speaker has two choices to make, and may well make them separately and in a definite order. On the one hand there is the choice of which of the possible past remarks to react to, and secondly which of several appropriate reactions to make. This study was carried out to test the hypothesis that speakers make those two decisions separately, and in that order, or at least with that priority.

The rationale was that subjects presented with certain kinds of transcribed conversation to continue, would have a choice of previous 'lines' to build upon, and for each a choice of possible continuations. If, having explored a number of these options, the various alternatives were rank ordered according to their plausibility, and if it is true that the choice of antecedent to build upon predominates over the choice of particular sequitur (rather like a nested experimental design), then it might be expected that all of the sequiturs to the 'best' antecedent would occupy adjacent positions at the top of the rank ordering, followed by a block or run of ranks allocated to all of the suggested sequiturs to the second best antecedent, and so on. This would imply that there were significantly more instances of sequiturs to the same antecedent occupying consecutive ranks (or runs of consecutive ranks) than chance alone would produce. Now if all blocks of utterances derived from the same antecedent and occupying adjacent ranks are called a 'run', including those that only have one element, the experimental hypothesis would be that the total number of such runs would be significantly *less* than predicted by chance, and it was this effect that the experiment set out to detect.

Method

This study was run together with Part II of the previous experiment, and the same subjects used in both cases. Each of the eighteen subjects was given an identical response booklet with three pages, each showing on the left-hand side a different, short passage of dialogue, written so as to leave a number of 'loose ends' from which it could be continued, and on the right, a wide column of fifteen spaces in which subjects were asked to write fifteen different versions of the next 'line' of talk. Beside each response space were two further spaces marked A and B which were not explained at the outset. When subjects had completed their list of fifteen alternatives they were asked to give them ranks in column A for their appropriateness, and when that was done, they were asked to indicate in column B which antecedent line each sequitur was most related to (for which purpose the antecedent lines had numbers typed against them). The particular continuations subjects had suggested could now be ignored as the data consisted of the ranks, and the antecedent number assigned to each. The experimental hypothesis could be tested against the relation between these two columns of figures.

There was quite a high proportion of incomplete or incorrectly executed responses, but sixteen complete response-book pages were obtained, each showing one of the eighteen subjects' work on one of the three conversations, and subsequent analysis was based on these sixteen instances.

Results

Clearly there are a very large number of ways of mapping antecedent labels to ranks in this task, and it is not even a straightforward combinatorial matter since the number of antecedent labels used by any subject, and the number of times each was used, was not fixed. The following argument was used (due in part to Peter Hancock, a former research assistant). Consider the combination of one 'page' of data consisting of fifteen ranks written beside some arrangement of L different labels or antecedent numbers used by that subject for that script. Then taking the items in order of their ranks, there are fourteen transitions between adjacently ranked items at which the label used could be the same as or different from that used for the previously ranked item. These two possibilities were called label preserving and non-preserving transitions respectively.

Taking the null hypothesis to be that for each rank a label was chosen independently of the previous rank, from the set L in use by that subject, each choice would have presented L alternatives only one of which was the same as that for the previously ranked item (thereby creating a 'preserving transition'), and $L - 1$ possibilities which, being different from the label of the previous item, would create a 'non-preserving transition'. Therefore the probability under the null hypothesis of any transition being non-preserving is

$$\frac{(L - 1)}{L}.$$

So the probability of a subject producing r runs (i.e. $r-1$ non-preserving transitions) is

$$^{14}C_{r-1} \times \frac{L-1}{L}^{r-1} \times \frac{1}{L}^{14-(r-1)}$$

from the general binomial expression for the likelihood of producing i occurrences of a binary event with probability p in n trials, which is

$$^{n}C_i \times p^i \times (1-p)^{n-i}.$$

This is because there are also $n-i$ occurrences of the binary counter-event whose probability is $1-p$. $^{n}C_i$ is the number of possible combinations (regardless of order) of i things from n, and is

$$\frac{n!}{i!\,(n-i)!}.$$

$n!$ is n factorial or $n \times (n-1) \times (n-2) \ldots \times 1$.

In this way values could be calculated for each data page, of the probability of that particular number of runs (r) occurring, and the probability of that number or less occurring, given the number of labels (L) used by that subject.

The sixteen values so obtained had a mean of 0.289 and ranged from 0.002 to 0.982, so individually at least they were unremarkable.

Next they had to be combined to give an overall probability value for the pattern of experimental results. However, the individual values were not simple probabilities as they did not apply to exclusively defined events, nor did they sum to a value of one. Rather they applied to overlapping segments of a range of events defined by a single value and all values below it. For this reason the usual procedure for combining independent probabilities could not be applied. An analogy may help to make this clearer. If a dice is thrown, no matter how loaded, or how many faces (n) it has, the probability of throwing a 1 ($p(1)$) plus $p(2)$ . . . $p(n) = 1$, and the probability of throwing a 1 and then a 2 in two throws is $p(1) \times p(2)$. That is the simple case. However, the equivalent of the present problem would be the probability of throwing a one ($p(<2)$) plus a two or less ($p(<3)$), plus $p(<4)$ . . . plus $p(<(n+1))$, all of which does not add up to one. Furthermore, the probability of throwing a 1 or less and then a 2 or less is not $p(<2) \times p(<3)$, since they are not exclusively defined events and the former is also an instance of the latter.

The values to be combined are not simple probabilities, but significance levels, and these may be combined using the expression:

$$2 \sum_{i=1}^{n} \log p_i = \chi^2 \text{, with } 2n \text{ degrees of freedom,}$$

where p_i is the ith significance level from a list of n independent trials (Fisher, 1970: 100). With the data from this study, that gives a χ^2 value of 64.8686 with 32 degrees of freedom ($p<0.001$). Consequently the null hypothesis can be rejected in favour of the alternative hypothesis that fewer runs are to be found in the data than chance alone would produce, or to put it another way, subjects did tend to give consecutive ranks to sequiturs based on the same antecedent remark. This is consistent with a two-stage selection procedure in which the conversational theme to continue is chosen before, and independently of the content of the continuation.

The values given here replace those based on preliminary calculations, which appeared in earlier research reports.

Discussion

This is the last experiment as such to be reported here, and signals a change in approach to conversation structure. While the experiments described may be sound enough in themselves, that is in their *internal* validity, they leave something to be desired according to the wider criterion of *external* validity. Indeed some would argue that by this stage they have become too artificial and sterile to bear much on the issues of real 'flesh and blood' interaction. They are also rather piecemeal in the hypotheses they can establish. Each experiment tests a different proposition of the form 'conversation in general has the property x', where x might be an order of approximation, a level of abstraction at which sequences are detectable, the presence of 'nested' sequences or various other things.

What this approach can never do is to show how in a given corpus or type of discourse all the relevant factors and features interlock to give a single coherent structure, and to describe the 'anatomy' of the structures so formed. In subsequent chapters that is what will be attempted, beginning with the consideration of discourse structure as a variant of sentence structure, with whole utterances or moves or 'turns-at-talking' being arranged with respect to one another, much as their component morphemes are arranged in sentences — an idea which is represented diagrammatically in Figure 16.

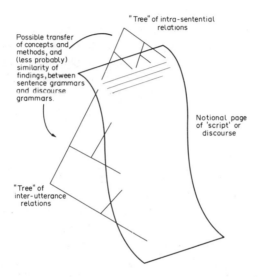

FIG. 16   Tree structures in sentences and discourse.

3

THE LINGUISTIC ANALOGY

THE TIME has come to turn from the general issues of whether or not there is a temporal pattern in dialogue, the level at which it might operate, the size of the structural units and the merits of linear and non-linear models, to the specific questions of which types of utterances are interrelated and in what way.

Generative Syntax

The Syntactic Analogy

So far the discussion of behaviour sequences has been open to various interpretations. It could be seen as an exercise in social psychology, human ethology or linguistics. However, the earlier discussion of methodological alternatives and the apparent need for distinctions like competence and performance, and deep and surface structure suggest that a linguistic analogy will be useful in studies of the detailed structure of conversation.

The problem can be redefined largely in linguistic terms. In this terminology the object is to write a generative grammar of social interaction (especially conversation) which describes the surface (and possibly also a deep) structure of the behaviour stream, explicating its syntactic and semantic properties.

This linguistic analogy may be viewed in two ways: firstly as a symmetrical double analogy, suggesting that language, discourse and interaction exist in separate domains, related by certain isomorphisms. Social interaction is like discourse and discourse is like language. More precisely the rules which will generate all and only the speech-act sequences which are sensible conversations are so like the rules which will generate all and only the morpheme strings which are well-formed sentences, that the study of the former may be assisted by the techniques for investigating the latter. Furthermore, the rules which will generate all and only the speech-act sequences which are sensible conversations are so like the rules which will generate all and only the sequences of social action which are acceptable, comprehensible episodes, that the study of the former may be expected to shed light upon the latter. So the analysis of discourse takes its methods from a lower level of description, and its purpose from a higher level, and demonstrates the isomorphism between all three.

The second way of viewing the analogy is to regard sentence structure and discourse structure as forming different levels in the hierarchy of the language itself. In this view the combination of speech acts to form a new kind of object, having new dimensions of meaning, is simply another instance of the phenomenon of linguistic multiple articulation. This means that at several levels of the linguistic hierarchy, the combination of sub-units creates a new kind of meaning, which is rather more than the sum of the semantic markers in those sub-units. Those linguists whose interests extend no further than the sentence unit speak of double articulation, referring to the combination of phonemes which do not carry referential meaning to form morphemes which do, and the combination of morphemes which do not carry propositional meaning to form sentences which do. The present analogy suggests that there is a tertiary articulation in which speech-acts which do not carry interactional meaning may combine to form conversations which do. The nature and representation of this 'interactional meaning', for want of a better term, will be discussed later on.

The idea that behaviour sequences could be studied by use of the grammarians' tools is certainly not new. Many eminent authors have made this suggestion, three of whom are cited below:

> The significance of Chomsky's work for disciplines other than linguistics derives primarily, then, from the acknowledged importance of language in all areas of human activity and from the peculiarly intimate relationship that is said to hold between the structure of language and the innate properties or operations of the mind. But language is not the only kind of complex 'behaviour' that human beings engage in; and there is at least a possibility that other forms of typically human activity (including perhaps certain aspects of what we call 'artistic creation') will also prove amenable to description within the framework of specially constructed mathematical systems analogous to, or even based upon, transformational grammar. There are many scholars working now in the social sciences who believe that this is so. For them, Chomsky's formalisation of grammatical theory serves as a model and a standard.
>
> Lyons (1970: 12)

> It is probably no accident that a theory of grammatical structure can be so readily and naturally generalized as a scheme for theories of other kinds of complicated human behaviour. An organism that is intricate and highly structured enough to perform the operations that we have seen to be involved in linguistic communication does not suddenly lose its intricacy and structure when it turns to nonlinguistic activities. In particular, such an organism can form verbal plans to guide many of its nonverbal acts. The verbal machinery turns out sentences – and, for civilised men, sentences have a compelling power to control both thought and action.
>
> Miller and Chomsky (1963: 488)

The particular points of resemblance between the grammar of natural language and the structure of other forms of behaviour which make this analogy so attractive are described below. Many of these points are clearly applicable to all symbolic aspects of interaction – language, NVC, ritual, and so on – but not to non-symbolic behaviours whose effects are determined by gross biological processes. That is to say, that the many varieties of signalling and communicating should fall within the scope of the analogy, but the varieties of killing, curing, feeding, giving birth, working with or working on another individual will probably require a different descriptive scheme to illuminate some, if not all, of their properties.

Structure

In social behaviour, just as in language, an orderly sequence of sounds or marks or gestures is used to convey information between the skilled users of that signalling system. In both cases, the signalling system is constructed in such a way that an enormous (potentially infinite) number of messages may be conveyed and acts performed, by the use of a finite repertoire of signals. This is made possible by the use of particular symbol *combinations* to convey information rather than the use of particular symbols. The importance of combinations to convey meaning is illustrated by the observation that the same set of symbols presented in a different order may convey a different meaning, whereas the substitution of symbol for symbol within the same structure can often leave the meaning unchanged.

Consider the sentences:

(a) Tom chased Mary.
(b) Mary chased Tom.
(c) Tom chased his sister.

(a) cannot mean the same as (b), although the same words are used; but (a) can mean the same as (c) although different words are used in similar constructions.

This is no rarity but a commonplace feature of sentence construction, and as such a grave problem for anyone who would seek to identify meaning with the presence or absence of symbols in a message. The importance of sequences or structures or patterns, whatever they are to be called, for the understanding of interaction, must result in a shift of attention from those studies which observe and count events, to those which study the nature of the events *and* the relations between them.

In language the patterns are diachronic: the sounds or marks which convey the message are produced and interpreted as a series of events in time. In social interaction some of the patterns are diachronic, while others like the arrangement of the facial features in a particular expression or the roles and relationships in an institution are synchronic. The diachronic patterns, including the structure of discourse, are those which fit the linguistic analogy best, although it has also been applied with some success to synchronic structures.

Since social meanings, like linguistic meanings, are conveyed largely by the way events are arranged in time, two obvious issues arise. Firstly, one would like to know whether all the possible arrangements of symbols can be used in a message or an interaction, and, if not, the distinctive properties of those which can. This might be termed the issue of syntax, or in the case of the 'grammar' of social behaviour, meta-syntax. Secondly, there is the relation between observable features of the symbol or event sequences and their meanings. This is the problem of semantics (or meta-semantics). In the early days of transformational linguistics the two issues were assumed to be separable. However, the claim by generative semanticists (e.g. Fillmore, 1968; Lakoff, 1968; McCawley, 1968) that the surface form of a sentence is inextricably bound up with its derivation from a semantic deep structure or logical form, has led subsequent workers to integrate syntactic and semantic considerations. One of the interesting features of Winograd's (1972) widely acclaimed natural language program, was the use of integrated syntactic and semantic components.

It may turn out to be the case that meta-syntax and meta-semantics have to be regarded as one in the analysis of discourse. However, that is an empirical issue which cannot be resolved until later. The assumption of separability is so convenient in the early stages of a structural analysis it will be made for the time being.

The nature of the diachronic patterns in language or interaction may be investigated according to two separate, although not wholly independent criteria. On the one hand, patterns may be described according to their probability of occurrence. This is a straightforward empirical approach as used in experimental social psychology. On the other hand, the patterns may be specified in such a way as to include all and only those sequences which the skilled users of the system regard as 'well-formed' (acceptable, meaningful, possessed of structural integrity, or some similar criterion). This definition tends to generate a larger set of possible strings, as it includes all those which would be acceptable if they were to occur, rather than just the ones which have been observed to occur. It also suggests the existence of some enduring quality of the language or the speakers which may be invoked to explain the observed patterns, and from which new but lawful strings may be derived to meet the demands of novel situations. Hence the latter approach leads to a system having synthetic as well as analytic powers, a feature which will be discussed further as it gives rise to some practical applications.

The distinction between linguistic analyses which depend on some postulated linguistic system which transcends the sum of observed usages, and those which do not, has become familiar in slightly different forms and under a variety of different names. Saussure (1916) distinguished *langue* — the abstract language system, and *parole* — observed language use. This is very similar to Chomsky's competence/performance distinction, and is reflected to some extent in Pike's (1967) methodological alternatives of emic and etic study.

The same choice is offered to the analyst of discourse. His analysis could be modelled on parole or performance, using etic methods; or by postulating some kind of discourse system (called DCS to distinguish it from the abbreviation DS which is usefully reserved for deep structure) which forms part of the actor's communicative competence, he could employ emic methods to study the equivalent of langue. One can either investigate the effects of structure on the probability of occurrence or the propriety of sequences. The next part of this book will deal with the latter since it provides a preferable starting-point in many ways. Competence is regarded as only one of several resources and limitations which shape performance, so it is simpler to study. It is also richer in that the competence model can encompass information about the equivalence and meaning of utterances or behaviours and the relations between them. It is assumed to be the same for all competent members, so a study of competence makes a simple binary distinction between permissible and impermissible strings which is useful, if only as an approximation; performance has to be described in terms of probability. Furthermore, the study of competence employs the notion of formal causality to explain the form of an observably structured object (a particular sequence of events) as a transformational product of some hidden structured object (the actor's knowledge of the DCS).

Miller and McNeil advance three arguments in support of the distinction between langue and parole (Miller and McNeil, 1968: 670):

> (a) Language is a social norm, a part of a culture, whereas speaking is an individual act that takes on significance only insofar as it conforms to the social practices of the language community.
> (b) Language is the cognitive component that a language user must know, as opposed to speaking, which is the behavioural component of a verbal communication event.
> (c) The description of a language is a hypothetical construct created by the theorist in order to account for empirical evidence provided by his observations of the speaking individual.

Argyle (1977) gives extensive discussion to alternative approaches to social psychology, with special reference to the problem of accounting for PXS inter-actions. He reviews the following models. There is the predictive model in which behaviour is seen as a mathematical function of personal and situational variables. This is criticised for taking insufficient account of the effect of actors on each other, and of the tendency for actors to select their situations to suit personal characteristics. The stimulus-response model is criticised for taking no account of proaction or embedding routines; and the social skill model for making schematic general predictions only, for paying too little attention to the effect of other actors, and for ignoring specific rules of situation. A system of descriptions is advocated which is based on the generative rules of language, with particular rules of situation included.

The study of social competence by the use of techniques similar to those found in linguistics also uses another of Chomsky's (1965) concepts, that of adequacy. A grammar is said to be *observationally adequate* when it will generate all and only the well-formed sentences of the language. It is *descriptively adequate* when it can also assign the correct structural descriptions to the strings it generates; and it is *explanatorily adequate* when it assigns structural descriptions which accord with the theory of linguistic universals.

The distinction between competence and performance is not universally accepted, particularly as applied to social behaviour. There seem to be two criticisms, both raised by those who believe that a psychological theory must ultimately describe performance if it is to have any value. Competence is sometimes said to be an insufficient condition for the understanding of performance. That seems reasonable, and quite compatible with the argument here. It does not seem reasonable, however, to make the second criticism that studies of competence are unnecessary for the understanding of performance. As has been argued above, the speaker has a knowledge of his language which influences the way he speaks, which is easily accessible and illuminating, and which allows for categorical, semantic and relational judgements which cannot be replaced by observations of performance, even when an understanding of performance is the ultimate goal.

Syntagmatic and paradigmatic relations

A second linguistic concept which is usefully applied to the study of social interaction is another Saussurian dichotomy, that between *syntagmatic* and *paradigmatic* relations (the latter term is now used in place of Saussure's original word 'associative'). According to Saussure these two relations are the two principal defining properties or axes of the linguistic system. Syntagmatic relations exist between the elements of a string, and paradigmatic relations between an element and the equivalents for which it might be substituted, or the other similar words with which it might be associated. For example in the sentences

    (a) The cat sat on the mat.
    (b) The dog stood on the table.

syntagmatic relations exist between cat, sat and mat; whereas paradigmatic relations exist between cat and dog, sat and stood, and mat and table. Since they were first distinguished by Saussure it has been assumed that syntagmatic and paradigmatic relations are interdependent, and the likelihood of the same proving true of relations in the DCS is a matter of very great importance. Students of interaction sequences have usually treated the assignment of utterances to equivalence classes, and the study of the sequences formed by successions of classified events, as independent issues. Consequently they classified the events according to characteristics which may have had no effect on their use in sequences, and then looked for sequential patterns existing between the elements so defined. Consequently the study of behaviour sequences has met with little success. A solution to this problem, also borrowed from linguistics, will be described in Chapter 4, as part of the study of surface structure of discourse. As with the langue/parole dichotomy, the distinction between syntagmatic and paradigmatic relations occurs in a number of different guises and under different names. Searle's (1965) distinction between the constitutive rules (which call into being new forms of social object) and regulative rules (which describe the proper use of such objects) is very similar to this. The idea of an act/action structure in social behaviour (Harré & Secord, 1972) again draws attention to the composition of meaningful signals from their sub-components, the kind of paradigmatic structure that might be embodied in constitutive rules.

In addition to the very significant observation by Saussure that syntagmatic and paradigmatic relations (or regulative and constitutive rules) are interdependent at any level of description, there is a tautological interdependence between the regulation of items at one level of description, and the constitution of those at the level above. It must surely be true of any hierarchical structure that the regulation of sub-units is the constitution of higher-order units.

Again the relevance for discourse and interaction analysis should be clear. Events in the behaviour stream have to be classified before their combinations can be studied, and the classification must be based on those properties which determine which combinations can occur. This principle is not confined to symbolic structures, but may be illustrated equally well by the analogy with structural chemistry, which was introduced earlier. Mendeleev's (1879) periodic classification of the chemical elements is based on assumptions similar to the interdependence of 'syntagmatic' and 'paradigmatic' relations. He categorised elements according to their chemical properties, such as their ability to substitute in crystal lattices without gross alterations of the structure, thus establishing families or groups of elements with similar combinatorial properties. His use of the property (which later turned out to be atomic number) which controlled the formation of interatomic bonds facilitated the study of molecular structures to a degree which would have been impossible if he had chosen a property which is independently detectable, such as colour, melting-point, solubility or density. And yet that is just the equivalent of much current practice in psychology: behavioural taxonomies are derived in isolation from any conception of sequential structure, and then applied (often unsuccessfully) to the study of behaviour sequences.

Types of sequence

The sequence of events in an interaction carries information just as it does in language, but in neither case is it always true that each element is bound to its immediate antecedents. This was demonstrated by Chomsky (1957) as part of his argument against finite state (or linear stochastic) models of language structure. Experiment 7 suggests that the linear stochastic model is also unsuitable for the analysis of discourse, and in both cases the rejection of the linear stochastic hypothesis poses something of a problem. Chomsky's answer was the rewriting of rule grammar, but there are other alternatives (Segal and Stacy,

1975). Clearly any model of discourse structure must account for the presence of each speech-act in a conversation by relating it to something else, from which it could have arisen or been derived. In the simplest case each speech-act is related to the one before it. This is the Markov chain. Like a number of these models the Markov chain is a kind of stochastic process. As we have seen, it is a sequence of events governed by transitional probabilities. In this discussion of different structural forms it is useful to enlarge that definition to include the limiting cases where probabilities are 0 or 1, and even cases where the transition is governed by a rule which says it is *permissible*, instead of a number which indicates whether it is *probable*. The term Markov chain will be used here for any sequence of events in which each item may be explained by reference to the one before. Similarly the term stochastic is used of any process governed by transitions between overt behavioural events, whether probabilistic or proscriptive.

If the Markov chain does not describe a particular structure adequately, the next recourse is to a higher order of linear stochastic model. That is any model in which each event may be accounted for by its relation with the few preceding events. The term linear is used to indicate that the only relevant transitions are those between adjacent events or strings.

The kind of problematic strings found in both language and social behaviour where a sequence of activity is diverted and then resumed cannot be explained by either the Markov model or the higher orders of linear stochastic model. Such a case would be the sentence

> The book which I bought last Tuesday, after taking the exams which marked the end of my first year at university, and which proved to be so difficult for some of my friends, especially those who had interrupted their revision to spend their time in the sunshine, was by Chomsky.

This kind of sequence could be generated by a device which worked on the transitions between surface items which are not adjacent events, which one might call a non-linear stochastic model. Alternatively it could be the product of a series of operations in which a number of elements, some of which are events appearing in the output (terminal elements) and others are not (non-terminal elements), are involved. By moving from one non-terminal element to one (or several) more and eventually to a string of terminal elements, sequences like the above sentence can be produced. This could involve rules which are either context-free or context-sensitive. Note that the final output string of events here is not produced by transition from one surface element to another. This is the form of a tree-like grammar used in Chomsky's language types 2, 1 and 0. (These are distinguished by context-free, context-sensitive and transformation rules respectively.) Such structures are best parsed from top to bottom, that is examined from their grossest units first, moving towards their finest, abiding as far as possible by Plato's recommendation that we try to cut nature at its joints.

One point should be noted in passing. Chomsky (1957) used the term finite state for those forms which are referred to here as linear stochastic series. This is misleading, since Chomsky's statement that the more elaborate languages cannot be produced by a finite-state device is only true if the device is confined to the use of terminal elements. The more elaborate strings may be produced by a looping finite-state device which only exists in one state at a time, or only stores one node of its structure at a time; or they can be produced by tree-like operations in which several nodes are stored simultaneously, provided non-terminal elements are employed in either case. The distinction is really between serial and parallel processing devices. At present, however, we are not concerned with the generative device, but only with a general characterisation of the output strings it produces. Consequently terms like stochastic and linear are used to describe the architecture of the behaviour stream as observed and not the real generative device in the head of the speaker.

Rules

Social interactions are very varied. The number of behaviour sequences which would be acceptable as an interaction is indeterminately large, if not infinite, so the obvious way of representing it by listing all the strings of speech-acts which could occur in the DCS would be rather impractical. Infinitely large books would be required to record the representations, and actors with infinitely large heads would be the only ones whose brain had sufficient capacity to use the system. Of course the same is true of language. It contains an infinite number of sentences, so the sentence structure which is common to the members of that infinite set must be represented by a finite set of rules, capable of storage and execution in a 'machine' of finite capacity. This is achieved in a generative grammar by the use of recursive rules. They give the grammar a generative capacity in that they may be employed to produce all and only the sentences of the language as opposed to testing the grammaticality of pre-formed strings. That does not imply that they represent in any way the processes of sentence production and comprehension in the speaker/hearer. They are best viewed as instrumentalist rather than realist descriptions of the source of grammaticality.

They are recursive in that they allow the same stage or node-type in the generative process to be revisited. Thus while there are rules which rewrite sentences to strings of sub-components, and noun phrases to strings of their sub-components, there are also rules which rewrite a sentence to another sentence plus additional items, or rewrite a noun phrase to another noun phrase plus additional items. These rules can be used an unlimited number of times, so a rule

$$S \rightarrow S + X$$

could be used once to create the theorem SX from the axiom S, and then again to produce $SXX, SXXX, SXXXX$ and so on. In fact that rule alone will produce an infinite set of strings of the form $S(X)^n$, for $n \geqslant 1$. It is also possible to organise non-recursive rules into recursive sets such as:

$$S \rightarrow A + B$$
$$A \rightarrow S + C$$

These are recursive rules from a top–down system like a generative grammar, but they could also be modified to fit a stochastic, or left-to-right, model without loss of their recursive properties.

Meanings

The meaning of a sentence or the meaning of an interaction is related to the symbols which articulate it in a complex way. There is no one-to-one mapping from symbol to meaning, because, as we have already seen, different combinations of the same symbols can carry different meanings. Nor is the meaning of any combination deducible from its form. Semantic relations are essentially arbitrary, arbitrary enough at least to necessitate some knowledge of subjective interpretation or response, before the meaning of an act may be determined. Again the basic methodology of generative linguistics offers a solution. Judgemental data from the native speaker are used to establish the similarities and differences in meaning between different signs or strings, from which the 'fundamental particles' of meaning or *semantic markers* may be inferred. This would appear to be a viable approach to the study of behavioural semantics, and particularly valuable if the system embodies categorical perception effects. In phonology, for example, it has been found that continuous variations in the physical nature of the acoustic object presented to subjects (phonetic units) produce a discontinuous or categorical distribution of subjective judgements (phonemic units), for speech and speech-like sounds (Liberman *et al.*, 1957). A set of artificial speech-like sounds, generated on a computer in such a way as to have physical properties ranging from those of a realistic /d/ to a realistic /g/, through a number of intervening mixtures of pitch and intensity, is heard by subjects as a set of perfect /d/s and a set of perfect /g/s, with a sharp discriminating boundary which has no complementary discontinuity in the physical attributes of the stimuli. (The original study found three distinct zones within the continuum from /b/ to /g/ through /d/.) The implication, of course, is that a discrimination between two phonemes, of great importance for the understanding of the language, is being determined by some cognitive procedure which can be inferred from judgemental data, but not from direct measurement of the speech sounds. In the analysis of social behaviour the problem is even more severe. The objective physical parameters of an item like a speech-act are too complex to use as the basis of a semantic representation. The 'objective' nature of the stimulus is so much more elaborate than a phoneme, that any suggestion of mapping it directly on to the illocutionary markers as a means of classifying utterances would seem impractical.

There is just a possibility that the complexities of the high-frequency signal could be ignored to give a simple mapping from *prosodic contour* to illocutionary status (Gunter, 1966). Even then some degree of subjectivity would be introduced by the need to validate categories of illocution. It seems much more feasible to use judgemental data throughout, using the competent speaker to judge what is said by the noises that are made, and what acts are performed by the things that are said.

Various kinds of behavioural meaning might be expected. Harré suggests four basic classes. There are the components of meaning based on the syntactic and paradigmatic relations of items. These are both *internalist* in that they provide meaning by reference to links within the system, rather like looking up a word in a mono-lingual dictionary only to find as the description of its 'meaning' a list of other words in the same language. In action there is also a kind of *externalist* referential meaning, often in the form of the symbolism in ritual or ceremonial, and a prescriptive meaning whereby an act renders certain future conduct proper or improper. Part of the 'meaning' of a marriage ceremony lies in the set of rights and duties which then attach to future behaviour.

Structure and meaning

This last section reiterates a language property that was touched upon earlier. Language and social behaviour sequences do not just convey meanings, they convey *structural* meanings. Saussure's dichotomy of substance and form draws attention to the importance of structure as well as content in the analysis of language. For Saussure, the notion of form was a simple matter of the succession of linguistic elements, but this has been elaborated considerably with the advent of the transformationalist schools. To a large extent, then, the parsimony and power of the structural method resides in its ability to discard the details of substance (content) in order to clarify those relations between sentences, or interaction sequences, or molecules or whatever, which depend on their form (structure).

The programme of research in which other forms of social action besides language are treated to the kind of analysis provided by linguistics, is what is referred to by one of the senses of the term structuralism. Like any hypothetico-deductive branch of research it provides explicit evaluation procedures by which theories may be tested, but no discovery procedures as such by which they may be arrived at. Its aim in dealing with behaviour grammars or similar formulations is not to describe sequences of behaviour and other events *per se*, since they are easily described by listing the things that happened in the order of their occurrence. That poses no problem. The problem arises with the characterisation of the *sets* of sequences that make up the sentences of a language or the examples of well-formed discourse, and for that purpose a canonical description may be required. This is a description which takes the form of a set of rules or prescriptions for the production of (descriptions of) the members of the set to be represented. It is important to note that the rules referred to here are employed by the *observer* of the system to generate *descriptions* of its behaviour, not by the system itself in *producing* the behaviour, just as a mathematical model of a bridge is used by the engineer to produce descriptions of deformations under load, but not used by the bridge in producing the deformations themselves.

This solves a problem that would otherwise arise with involuntary behaviour. A rule model should be comprehensive and reproduce all parts of a behaviour sequence. With voluntary behaviour it would make sense to talk either of the analyst's rules for representing behaviour or the actor's rules for producing it, but the latter kind of rule, interpreted as real rather than instrumental, would make a nonsense out of rules for emotion, feinting, uncontrollable rage, and so on. Used in the instrumental sense recommended here, the rules of a model could encompass all these things, and indeed more, since the environment with which the person interacts, whether animate or inanimate, could be represented by such rules. Another way of making the distinction is to say these rules would figure in the model but not in the theory.

Another problem with the 'grammatical' modelling of interaction is that two heads are more complicated than one. The grammar of sentences can often be taken in either the real or the instrumental sense, since all the generative operations go on inside one head, and *could* in principle (although probably do not in practice) take the form suggested by the grammar. With a grammar of conversation, it is hard to see how this could represent the real process unless it worked from left-to-right, or else was exclusively right-branching. Otherwise it would require one person to start executing terminal elements subtended by a node which had formed in the other person's generative system, but was not as yet represented in its output. The more acceptable solution again seems to be to reserve the grammar for describing the form of conversation but not the psychological processes of its production, which must presumably work separately in the heads of the participants (although not necessarily in identical form) and which must be coordinated solely by the exchange of remarks and signals, which for our purpose is their product.

In all fairness the list of similarities between the structural features of language and those of social behaviour should be accompanied by a list of probable dissimilarities. These are the features of the linguistic system which should not be assumed, for the time being at least, to have their counterparts in the DCS. They include many of the points from Chomsky's analysis which have been most severely criticised. Perhaps by discarding these features, explicitly, the criticism can be pre-empted that the model of discourse proposed here is based on an outmoded linguistic theory, which is no longer viable even in its own realm.

Of course the analogy with linguistics is not supposed to imply that the units of discourse analysis will correspond to morphemes, except in the role they play in the scheme as a whole. Nor is there any particular reason to suppose that the structural model which best describes language will be the best for discourse. In that respect the study of the DCS is not modelled on the peculiarities of Chomsky's theory, but on those general principles which are common to Chomsky, many of his followers, and the students of other structural systems. The structure of discourse is not thought necessarily to be innate, and the possible universality of its features will be a matter for later empirical enquiry, and not assumed here.

Opponents of the linguistic model have four main criticisms. Firstly, they see it as an unnecessary complication of a simple science. If the dependence of behaviour upon environment can be discovered by changing the environment and watching behaviour, then an elaborate methodology is unnecessary. The existence of complicated interactions between events, and the fact that response depends more on the meaning given to stimuli by the actor than on their physical properties, make this view untenable.

The second objection is that it is *unscientific*. Linguistic analysis is identified with introspection and mentalism, while the true course of scientific knowledge is thought to be served only by more positivistic methods. This too is untenable. The older sciences upon which psychology is supposed to be modelled abound with hypothetical constructs, imaginary particles, and forces which are an essential part of their descriptive system. No science can be successful for long if it confines its attention solely to observed patterns in the data. If we are to postulate some model to account for verbal behaviour, then what could be more scientifically respectable than something like a computer program which stores and processes information according to a set of formal operations, and whose nature can be discovered by testing hypotheses against observed patterns of judgement, or performance? This is the rather controversial use of competence as a *potential* model of performance.

The third criticism is that the linguistic model does not explain the minutiae of gaze shifts, pupil dilatation and so on, but then it does not claim to, as it is concerned with another level of description.

Fourthly it is criticised for oversimplifying the problem. A number of different speech practices are represented as a single language or DCS. It is an idealisation of the data of course, but then so is the 'anatomy of the dog' or 'the life-cycle of the seagull'. An idealised model, from which real cases vary slightly, has proved a useful construct in a number of sciences.

The suggestion that behaviour sequences, like languages, might have a syntax is not yet supported by the data. Experiments 1 to 4 showed that certain sequences of events occurred more frequently, and were thought to be more probable than others. As such they were investigations of performance and descriptive competence and the complementarity of the two. The existence of a syntax is a matter of semiotic competence. It hinges on whether the strings of events which are acceptable as valid instances of interaction form a sub-set of the universe of possible combinations.

Methodological Implications

Parametric and structural models

In the past the methods of social psychology have been modelled on the parametric sciences, and often rightly so. The quasi-linguistic properties of the DCS, however, suggest that the techniques of structural science are going to be more useful for this study. The parametric models used in physics, social psychology and econometrics, for example, imply that objects or systems have a number of continuously distributed properties which stand in lawful relation to one another (as in the relation between the temperature, pressure and volume of a fixed mass of an ideal gas, expressed by the gas laws). These qualities and their interrelations may be described by a regression equation, or similar procedures of correlation, factor analysis and analysis of variance. The structural models of linguistics, cognitive anthropology and chemistry describe a world made of discrete particles which form certain combinations having known properties, and capable of synthesis to form many structures with predictable properties. For this the mathematics of discontinuity is necessary: numerical taxonomy, group and set theory, automata theory and mathematical logic.

The parametric model provides a rich description of the infinite number of levels of each variable, but a relatively poor one of intervariable relations, and it works best when the various influences operating on some quality of the object are additive or non-interactive. In the structural model the reverse is true. Qualities are crudely defined as one of a finite number of classes, regardless of intra-class variations, but greater analytical resources are then freed for the complexities of class combinations. It is generally true to say that holistic analysis of relativistic systems is more feasible using structural than parametic models. Joos (1950: 702) made this distinction very forcefully:

> Ordinary mathematical techniques fall mostly into two classes, the continuous (e.g. the infinitesimal calculus) and the discrete or discontinuous (e.g. finite group theory). Now it will turn out that the mathematics called 'linguistics' belongs in the second class. It does not even make any compromise with continuity, as does statistics or infinite group theory. All continuity, all possibilities of infinitesimal graduation — are shoved outside of linguistics in one direction or the other.

One test of the suitability of a topic for structural or parametric analysis has to do with the way in which elements or qualities mix. Those attributes which would be subjected to parametric analysis are usually those which will blend. A hot gas mixes with a cold one to produce a lukewarm blend; a dense fluid and a light one form a moderately dense mixture. Both processes would be studied by parametric methods. (The term parametric is not being used here to distinguish parametric and non-parametric statistics.) Some things do not work like this, however. Red and white flowers do not cross to produce pink, but a set proportion of red and white (3 : 1 for the case where the parents are pure breeding with simple Mendelian characters). The word *carpet* in no sense combines the meanings of *car* and *pet* to produce an intermediate sense, like a domestic animal on wheels. Some aspects of interaction would seem to be miscible, like aspects of personality or attitude for example, while others combine configuratively such as the elements of languages, games, rituals, episodes, and institutional structures. Furthermore, the interrelation of each combination of classes is peculiar to that combination, and is not a simple constant that recurs across examples.

Competence and rules

The introduction of a competence/performance distinction to the study of the DCS and the preliminary investigation of competence are helpful steps even if the real goal is a picture of performance. The findings of a competence study may be used as a heuristic to guide work on performance. Suppose, for example, that a study of performance were undertaken directly on a signalling system which employed 50 different signals in 5-item strings (both figures are plausible estimates for the analysis of discourse). Each of the 50 items would have to be studied in relation to its 50^4 (6¼ million) antecedent strings, giving a data matrix of 312½ million cells to be filled! This is an example of the combinatorial explosion which has plagued the field of artificial intelligence, and led some authors to advocate a change from algorithmic to heuristic software. The problem is reduced in a competence study, by the use of judgemental data. The judgement, for example that two adjacent items were incompatible under all circumstances, would remove from the matrix their 125,000 possible sequitur triads 'at a stroke'.

Some rules may be elicited more directly than others as they are more explicitly transmitted and referred to, in the generation of behaviour. Taking the most conservative approach, the investigator would ask the actor only whether a given example was permissible or impermissible. In theory this is the linguists' approach, but since in practice investigator and informant are often two roles played by the same individual, it is often hard to decide how much of the analysis was present in the raw data provided by the informant and how much was inferred by the analyst. An alternative technique is the negotiation of accounts. In this case the informant may be called upon to provide an explicit report of a number of the rules which govern behaviour, as well as the distinction between valid and invalid instances. The analyst of discourse would be best advised to take a middle course between these extremes, using judgements which can be related directly to the acceptability of specific instances, while at the same time employing enough abstraction to provide the heuristic quality mentioned above. And still the 'rules' that are of interest are not 'realist' rules in the form of the actor's beliefs about what is proper and improper, which might be thought to guide the production of behaviour; they are the 'instrumentalist' rules, used like equations by the observer to reproduce observed patterns. This is a crucial and much-misunderstood distinction.

Another methodological distinction may be drawn by referring to the agonistic or game model of Chapter 1. Certain consistent features of play (performance) are derived from the rules (competence), and others from the goals and strategies of the players (a performance variable). These should be separated, and they can be if the subjects' judgements are considered. They are difficult to tell apart from the observed features of play. Consider the example of a stranger to the game of chess trying to learn the rules by observation. He might be struck by two regularities. Each turn consisted of one move, and each game began pawn to king four. The fact that one is governed by rule and the other by tactics is not apparent to the observer. The early ethnomethodologists' solution of entering the game so as to start pawn to queen four, and take several moves per turn, in the hope of eliciting sanctions when rules were broken is inappropriate. Needless to say, the difference may be gleaned from the players' reports of the rules, when questioned. The fact that a newcomer to the game would almost certainly learn the rules, before proceeding to the niceties of strategy, and would find the latter much easier to comprehend within the framework of the former, is another illustration of the point that competence makes an excellent heuristic for the study of performance. For more elaborate examples of formal and grammatical models of action structure see Pörn (1977) and Westman (1978).

Related Approaches

These were mentioned briefly in Chapter 1, and can only be given a very superficial summary here, but they do deserve at least some mention in this context. A full examination of the relevance of linguistics for research in social and behavioural science would take up an entire book in its own right.

In likening the problems of discourse analysis to those encountered in linguistics, it should be borne in mind that the structural approach is inter-disciplinary, and very similar assumptions are now to be found in many branches of social, behavioural and physical science.

The common principles of the structural method have been modified to suit the needs of a number of facets of behavioural science: social anthropology (e.g. Frake, 1964; Lévi-Strauss, 1968), developmental psychology (e.g. Piaget, 1971; Bruner, 1976), and social psychology (e.g. Barker, 1963; Harré and Secord, 1972; Cicourel, 1973). The relationship between linguistic structuralism and mathematics was pointed out by Gandy (1973), giving as examples the study in mathematics of morphisms like the 'Gödel-numbering' technique in which a simple numerical morphism may be used as a numerical model of a system of propositions for example. Grammatical models of plot-structure (story grammars) are now being used in cognitive science to analyse and model the properties of narrative (e.g. Thorndyke, 1977).

A Programme of Research

From the common features of all these structural models it is possible to infer the stages of analysis which would be required to produce a structural model of discourse, treating data-driven ethological methods and theory-driven grammatical approaches as related species of the genus of structural approaches, for the time being.

The meta-syntax of surface structure

This may be studied in three stages.

1. *Unitising the behaviour stream.* Behaviours which are produced as a continuous stream of movements and sounds are often perceived as discrete events. The process of categorical perception or perhaps analogue to digital conversion, produces behavioural 'particles', which in many respects elicit the responses due to an indivisible entity. It is important therefore to include in the formal analysis some means of re-expressing the behaviour stream as such a series of particles, and, furthermore, to place the interparticular boundaries in those places the native actor would choose in making his interpretation. This is not entirely unproblematic, as a stream of behaviour, like an acoustic object, may be partitioned in an infinite number of mutually exclusive ways, of which only some, maybe only one, has any psychological validity.

2. *The particles, units or elements formed in this way must then be classified.* The importance of this stage cannot be over-emphasised. It is absolutely crucial, and has usually been the failing of previous attempts at structural and ethological sequence analysis. The detection of temporal patterns depends on the recurrence of sequences of events. But in social interaction the events themselves seldom recur, much less the sequences. A meaningful event is a composite of the actor, his role, his action, situation and time. Some of these are unlikely to recur, others like time, by definition, cannot. So the whole analysis rests on an assertion of the kind '*XYZ* has been observed to occur *n* times', which can only have the force of an assertion like '*n* unique sequences of events have been assigned to the classification *XYZ*, because of similarities which seemed to be important, and in spite of differences which did not'. It is obviously *vital*, therefore, that the similarities which are noted, and the dissimilarities which are ignored when the equivalence classes (paradigmatic relations, or constitutive rules) are drawn up, are those which are recognised by the system. In other words, Saussure's doctrine of the interdependence of paradigmatic and syntagmatic relations must be incorporated at this stage. A fact which a number of sequence analysts (e.g. Bales, 1953; Sacks, class notes) seem to have overlooked.

3. *Sequence analysis.* Now a set of rules may be devised to express the regular relations which are found, not between the events, but between the classes of event generated in stage 2. A generative syntax, for example, does not have regulative rules relating morphemes like *table* and *chair*. Rather the items NP and N are used in conjunction with other rules (constitutive of the class N) which say

N → (table, chair, . . .).

This is known as *constitution by instantiation*. The technique by which *noun* can be identified as a part of speech, and *table*, and *chair* its tokens, will be discussed and used in the next chapter.

The semantic representation

A description of surface structure would provide a definition of the set of behaviour sequences which were social interactions. The next issue would be the nature of the mapping between the surface structures of the strings in that set, and the meanings, action implications and interpersonal judgements formed from them by the actor. If that should turn out to be an isomorph of surface structure then all well and good. If not, as in the case of the one-to-many, and many-to-one mappings found between English sentences and their meanings, then it may be necessary to postulate the existence of a behavioural deep structure which is distinct from the surface structure.

The model of performance

It has been said that the structures which are elicited in studies of competence may not be the same as those found in performance. On the other hand, though, they need not be very different. It will be an empirical matter to determine how closely the observed performance of the actor follows the picture of competence, and the extra operations which are needed to encompass both, particularly those embodying 'tactical' considerations. Some attention will be given in Chapter 7 to the practical applications of a model of performance.

The generative device

A competence model would contain generative rules, only in the sense that they may be used as a mathematical abstraction capable of deriving all and only the event strings which are interactions. As such they must represent some of the functional characteristics of any device which produced only the same set of outputs, but they do not necessarily embody the operations which it uses. Therefore the further characterisation of the generative process should be regarded as another phase of analysis, dealing with the nature of stores and recoding processes, information flow rates and the like.

This outline specification of a structural analysis of competence will form the plan for the next chapter. The characteristics of the generative device cannot really be studied successfully, until the other stages of the analysis have progressed much further.

It must be stressed yet again that if the DCS is a holistic, structurally integrated system, it must be described as a series of increasingly accurate overviews, rather than a definitive map of one area, leading on to the next. In moving from unitisation to categorisation, and from categorisation to sequence analysis, the aim is not to exhaust each topic so as to pass on to the next, but rather to jump ahead in search of even a crude picture of the later stages, to use in writing improved versions of the early ones. There will only be one iteration of this procedure reported here, although all the stages would need to be re-examined many times before a satisfactory understanding of conversation structure was achieved.

The problem is that discourse is a relativistic phenomenon and can only be described by a succession of global models of increasing specificity and accuracy. Any attempt to analyse it piece by piece would be foiled by the incalculable complexity of the relations between its parts.

Before beginning the structural analysis proper, there are two more pieces of theory that need to be described, the first of which is the basic unit of analysis, the *speech-act* which will be to this grammar of discourse as the morpheme is to the grammar of a sentence.

Speech-acts

In his William James lectures at Harvard in 1955, the late John Austin proposed an extension of the traditional view of semantics. (His lecture notes were edited after his death by Urmson, and later published: Austin, 1962.) Austin suggested that the idea of the sentence as a vehicle for propositional meaning, a constative utterance, asserting that certain states of nature exist and evaluated in terms of its truth or falsity, was incomplete. In addition to this aspect of semantics there is also the use of speech as action, exemplified by those utterances which do not so much report things as do them, such as promises, bets, threats, demands and so on. These he called *performative utterances*. At first they were put forward as a different class of utterance, so that a given sentence might be performative, if it paraphrased to an explicit *performative formula* such as 'I promise that . . .' or 'I threaten to . . .'; or constative, if it did not. In the later part of the argument, however, the distinction broke down as it became apparent that even the most constative of utterances had a performative aspect, as represented by the formula 'I assert that . . .', or 'I declare that . . .'. Furthermore, most truly performative utterances have a constative aspect since 'I promise that p' requires p to be a proposition as does 'I bet that p' or 'I envisage that p'. So in the end each utterance was agreed to have a constative content and a performative force. The performative aspects of the utterance were to be evaluated according to their *felicity* or *infelicity*, that is to say, their success or failure in achieving the speaker's intentions. Those conditions which had to be fulfilled before a performative was felicitous were called its *felicity conditions*. Since some of the felicity conditions for an utterance may be fulfilled by previous utterances in the sequence, it is easy to see how chain reactions of performatives may be formed, with each contributing to the felicity of those which follow.

Austin imposed two classifications upon the universe of performative utterances. The first, and best known, was a dichotomy between those utterances (*illocutions*) whose purpose was achieved inevitably *in* the saying of the utterance; and those (*perlocutions*) whose purpose might or might not be achieved *by* the saying of the utterance. A famous example is found in the distinction between urging and persuading. If A recommends to B that he do X, then by saying what he did A has urged B to do X. For B to be persuaded to do X, however, he has to hear, understand, agree and manage to do X, which may or may not happen. The necessity that the hearer recognises a performative for what the speaker intends is captured in the concept of *illocutionary uptake*.

Austin's second classification concerned the five performative classes of

Verdictives, by which judgement is given, e.g. to estimate, reckon or appraise.

Exercitives, using powers, e.g. voting, appointing, ordering and advising.

Commissives, which commit the speaker, e.g. promising, vowing and undertaking.

Behabitives, incorporating items of social behaviour, congratulating, apologising and condoling.

Expositives, which are meta-communicative, explaining the nature of one's action, e.g. 'I contend', 'I concede'.

It will be clear from these examples that the level of behavioural abstraction which they represent is rather like that used in the layman's description of behaviour, and most unlike an ethological or social psychological study of movements and noises. It places the analysis on the upper rather than the lower levels of the cognitive hierarchy of movements, actions and acts.

Searle (1965, 1969 and 1975) elaborated the notion of speech performatives, or *speech-acts*. He considered rules (*constitutive* and *regulative*) for the use of speech-acts in particular relation to the act of promising. Searle used the term constitutive of those rules which call into being and define units of the social or linguistic world which have no independent existence. If this conception is enlarged to include all rules of definition by constitution, then the earlier identification of constitutive rules with paradigmatic relations becomes more accurate. The term regulative referred to those rules which provide for the correct use of acts. Thus a constitutive rule might have the form *X counts as Y*, whereas a regulative rule would be represented as *If X do Y*.

Since the concept of a speech-act arose from the idea of speech as social action, it should require little argument to see that the counterpart of the speech-act in the social world at large, where ends are achieved by verbal and non-verbal means acting in concert, is the social act. There is an equivalence between the speech-act and the social-act which arises in one obvious, and another less obvious way. The obvious equivalence is exemplified by the speech-act of agreeing as performed by the words 'Yes' or 'I agree' and the social-act of agreeing as performed by nodding the head. Similarly the act of bidding farewell is in many respects unaltered by the substitution of 'Goodbye' for a wave of the hand.

The second kind of equivalence stems from the interdependence of syntagmatic and paradigmatic relations. If the reply

> It's three o'clock.

to the demand

> Tell me the time.

is placed in the response class *obeys* or *complies* by virtue of its relation with the demand, then the act of sitting down in response to the instruction

> Sit down.

must stand in a certain paradigmatic relation to the utterance

> It's three o'clock.

In fact they must be members of the same equivalence class (at least as they are used in this context). Thus non-verbal activities will be subject to description as rejoinders, refusals, protests, etc., even though their physical action characteristics when seen out of context, give no clue to the nature of their verbal counterparts.

For the remainder of this analysis it will be assumed unless stated otherwise, that the elements of structure are speech or social acts, defined by constitutive rules, and deployed in well-formed strings governed by regulative rules.

Deep Structure

One of the most fascinating facets of generative linguistic research has been the exploration of grammatical 'deep structures'. A number of people in other disciplines have adopted the concept and applied it literally or analogically when describing the profound structure of underlying reality of events as realised in the observed patterns of observation and measurement. One must remember when considering such interpretations, the great diversity of meanings which have been read into the original concept of deep structure, and the varying degrees to which different authors modify and extend the concept to suit their own need.

Meetham (1969: 652) gives a general definition of linguistic deep structure in the following terms:

> The deep structure of an item (say a sentence) is a representation of it which shows its semantic relations more directly than its surface structure does, and which takes the form of a structural description. . . .

Deep structures of a kind could function in two ways. They could be part of the mental apparatus which the actor used when forming and interpreting novel strings of behaviour, or they could be confined to the system of artificial rules which are used to represent the properties of the DCS. In the next few pages a number of uses for a concept like deep structure will be described, without giving further emphasis to the idea discussed previously that generative models of a language or DCS, and the generative process used by the speaker or actor *in vivo* are not necessarily identical.

The idea that organised patterns of behaviour have behind them some unseen cognitive structure is by no means new. Bartlett (1932: 201) wrote of cognitive 'schemata' in terms which could apply to the general properties of a behavioural structure:

> 'Schema' refers to an active organisation of past reactions, or of past experiences, which must always be supposed to be operating in any well-adapted organic response. That is, whenever there is any order or regularity of behaviour, a particular response is possible only because it is related to other similar responses which have been serially organised, yet which operate, not simply as individual members coming one after another, but as a unitary mass. Determination by schemata is the most fundamental of all the ways in which we can be influenced by reactions and experiences which occurred some time in the past. All incoming impulses of a certain kind, or mode, go together to build up an active, organised setting: visual, auditory, various kinds of cutaneous impulses and the like, at a relatively low level; all the experiences connected by a common interest: in sport, in literature, history, art, science, philosophy, and so on, on a higher level.

Similarly Tolman (1948: 192):

> (The brain) is far more like a map control room than it is like an old-fashioned telephone exchange. The stimuli, which are allowed in, are not connected by just simple one-to-one switches to the outgoing responses. Rather, the incoming impulses are usually worked over and elaborated in the central control room into a tentative cognitive like map of the environment. And it is this tentative map, indicating routes and paths and environmental relationships, which finally determines what responses, if any, the animal will finally release.

The common implication of such remarks is, of course, that the orderly stream of behavioural events which the outside observer notices is not the product of a simple process, in which each item is derived in some simple way from one or more of its antecedents. Instead the succession of events arises from a complex cognitive structure in the actor, and in the case of communicative ability gives rise to another in the observer, thus effecting the communication between the two. We might assume that this structure plays a (different) role in the generation and interpretation of behaviour, but the difference between generative and interpretive representations is not always emphasised. (This is not to be confused with the different roles of a linguistic deep structure in generative and interpretive semantics.) In the case of a single message being transmitted from emitter to receiver, the generative and interpretive roles of the underlying representation could be quite distinct. In the interplay of a social interaction, however, the distinction is not so clear. Each actor presumably has his own recollections of the course of events, together with his own goals, beliefs, attitudes, interpretations and so on. Clearly this is rather like Bartlett's schema or Tolman's cognitive map, and we shall assume for the present that it may be placed in the overall picture of a quasi-linguistic behavioural structure as the 'deep structure' of that particular behaviour sequence, although it might also be likened to the semantic representation to which each deep structure would stand in one-to-one correspondence in a classical Chomskian scheme. In so far as each item of behaviour, then, is derived from the deep structure of the actor, and then contributes to the deep structure of actor and observers, the generative and interpretive roles of deep structure are inextricably linked. When one of the observers becomes the actor, his conception of what is going on in the interaction, which was previously an interpretive deep structure, becomes part of the generative procedure by which he selects his next item of output. The deep structure as it exists for any actor at any moment is essentially synchronic, although embodying a sequence of events. But as new information is received the picture changes, both by addition and reinterpretation, so the actor's behaviour over a period of time is guided not so much by *a* deep structure as by a diachronically linked series of deep structures or social representations.

The specifically linguistic use of the notion of a deep structure and the term itself were introduced by Chomsky (1965). This is how he located the idea of deep structure in the theory of syntax.

> The phonological component of a grammar determines the phonetic form of a sentence generated by the syntactic rules. That is, it relates a structure generated by the syntactic component to a phonetically represented signal. The semantic component determines the semantic interpretation of a sentence. That is, it relates a structure generated by the syntactic component to a certain semantic representation. Both the phonological and semantic components are therefore purely interpretive. Each utilises information provided by the syntactic component concerning formatives, their inherent properties, and their interrelations for a given sentence. Consequently, the syntactic component of a grammar must specify, for each sentence, a *deep structure* that determines its semantic interpretation and a *surface structure* that determines its phonetic interpretation. The first of these is interpreted by the semantic component; the second by the phonological component.
>
> It might be supposed that surface structure and deep structure will always be identical. In fact, one might briefly characterise the syntactic theories that have arisen in modern structural (taxonomic) linguistics as based on the assumption that deep and surface structures are actually the same. . . . The central idea of transformational grammar is that they are, in general, distinct and that surface structure is determined by repeated application of certain formal operations called 'grammatical transformations' to objects of a more elementary sort. If this is true (as I assume, henceforth) then the syntactic component must generate deep and surface structures, for each sentence, and must interrelate them. . . . For the moment it is sufficient to observe that although the Immediate Constituent analysis (labelled bracketing) of an actual string of formatives may be adequate as an account of surface structure, it is certainly not adequate as an account of deep structure.

Chomsky (1965: 16)

Two things should be noted. First, that Chomsky's remarks apply to the formal description of the (English) language, they are not to be taken as a description of the machinery of the speaker—hearer. Secondly, the crucial point about linguistic deep structure is that it is *different* from the surface structure, not that it is found to 'exist'. Perhaps the deep structure is best viewed as a conceptual convenience like a 'line of force' or a 'free north pole' in magnetic theory. These are *inventions* which are retained because of their usefulness, rather than because of their demonstrable reality. As with so many scientific propositions, it is more reasonable to say the language works as if it had a deep structure of a certain kind, than to say it has that kind of deep structure.

In producing a generative grammar the utility of a deep structure is twofold. Firstly, it allows the differences of kind between syntactic and semantic representations to be separated from the many-to-one and one-to-many mappings that exist between surface structure and semantic representation. Instead of being confounded in one stage, these two types of relation are handled in two separate stages with deep structure providing the 'staging post' between them. Secondly, the addition of the transformational component that mediates between deep and surface structures elevates the computational power of the grammar from the equivalent of a push-down stack to the equivalent of a Turing-machine.

The definition of deep structure as the input to the semantic component would allow us to talk of the deep structure of any code. The interesting feature of natural languages is that this definition leads us to the conclusion that deep and surface structures are different, since there are so many cases where the same semantic representation has several surface forms, or (perhaps more interestingly) the same surface form has several semantic representations. For example:

> 'The dog chased the cat'.

and

> 'The cat was chased by the dog'.

would for most purposes be regarded as alternative formulations of the same meaning. (Active and passive forms have been shown to have different occasions of use, depending on the desired emphasis for example, so the selection is not entirely arbitrary — Osgood, 1971 — but both propositions have the same truth conditions, which is the essential criterion of synonymy here.) The active or passive forms of the sentence are handled by Chomsky's (1965) grammar as optional transformations forming two distinct surface structures from a single deep structure.

Conversely

> 'The shooting of the hunters was awful'.

has two meanings which cannot be distinguished by the labelled bracketing which represents surface structure. It is said to be ambiguous in deep structure. Similarly the sentences

> 'John is easy to please'.

and

'John is eager to please'.

which look so similar in their surface structure are seen to be quite distinct semantically when one asks who is pleased and who is pleasing? It is sometimes said that the issue of deep structural ambiguity is a minor matter (as indeed it is to the pragmatist) as so many other cues would serve to disambiguate the utterance in practice. That, however, is only to misunderstand the point. The argument is not intended to show how the world's misunderstandings arise from the lurking dangers of deep-structural ambiguity, but that the English language is constituted in such a way that the arrangement of elements in a string which specify the sounds (or marks) which could convey that message, and the abstract formulations which could be said to represent its meaning(s), are not necessarily similar or in one-to-one correspondence. Therefore one cannot study meaningful communication in such a system by observing performance alone. A more serious criticism is that meaning is not to be inferred from individual sentence structures taken in isolation, as most grammars would seem to suggest.

It is of no interest here to debate the relative merits of the different kinds of deep structure proposed by Chomsky (1965), Fillmore (1968) and many others. The deep structure of social interaction will certainly turn out to be sufficiently different from that of English sentences, to make a detailed comparison pointless.

A number of social scientists have drawn explicitly on the notion of deep structure in describing their view of social reality (Harré and Secord, 1972; Cicourel, 1973), but not in relation to the kind of material considered here.

Notions rather like deep structure abound in other branches of science. A good example is the geneticists' distinction between genotype and phenotype. As with deep and surface structure, a particular point of the distinction is that the two need not stand in one-to-one correspondence. Flowers whose colours are derived from a dominant red gene (R) and a recessive white gene (w), by simple Mendelian inheritance, look just as red whether their genotype is RR or Rw.

By now the concept of deep structure may seem so ubiquitous as to be an inevitable and uninteresting property of any communication system, but this is not so. Remember, for example, the four ways in which a code might be constituted, as described in Chapter 1, only one of which has a deep structure. It seems that a social interaction is meaningful in the way that such a 'deep-structure' code is meaningful. In either case the substitution, transposition or regrouping of events will affect the meaning assigned to a string by the native actor, but alone the surface structure is not the whole story. Ambiguity remains, extra information has to be read between the lines. The speaker has to be credited with mental attributes which are never explicitly represented in the string. As part of the process of attribution, we read logical consequences into the actor's statements. If he says he believes John to be more intelligent than Mary, and Mary more intelligent than Sam, we assume that he holds John's intellect in higher regard than Sam's. If he says he killed his dog he must believe his dog is dead. The inferences are not all logical deductions. Some belong more to the realm of psycho-logic than logic. If the actor chooses one of two courses of action bearing equal cost, we assume its outcomes are more desirable for him. If he supports a political party and believes they will reduce taxes, we might assume he supports them because he would like his taxes reduced. The inferences are not always unambiguous, however. A small boy, caught with a bag full of apples and accused of stealing from the Colonel's orchard, might protest his innocence. In which case he is innocent, truthful and informative or guilty, lying and seeking to deceive? The surface structure of events is ambiguous and does not tell us which is the case while the base rules embodying the spectator's beliefs about the kinds of mental attributes which make up internally consistent states of mind, say that only those two 'deep structures' are possible. To infer that the boy was guilty, truthful and seeking to deceive would be an illogical inference — an ill-formed deep structure. Such is the requirement for consistency in our schemata representing the circumstances, actions, thoughts, feelings and motives of others, that in courts of law, for example, attempts to deceive may be thwarted and false representations disclosed merely by the detection of inconsistency. However, to specify formally just what it is for such an account to be consistent would be quite another matter.

Of course the actual base rules and deep structure involved in any situation would be far more complicated than these simple examples, but it is pointless to speculate further on their exact nature at the present.

The fact that such attributions are made does not necessarily imply that human beings are constituted in such a way that their behaviour is shaped by a process of efficient causality involving desires, emotions and beliefs in precisely the same roles they play in our everyday accounts and representations, any more than Chomsky's grammar implies that there are masses of brain tissue which excite in response to deep structure phrase markings. The system of beliefs held about human behaviour can be very important in understanding the course of events even if it is incorrect, just as the folk medicine of a native tribe may be a poor description of pathology but still, in a sense, explanatory of the rituals which attend the sick-room. The concern here is with formal rather than efficient causality: the structural resemblance between the observed courses of events and their social-representational counterparts.

One further analogy may clarify the concept of a social deep structure still further. Social interaction has earlier been likened to a game of chess. The analogy is used to draw attention to the importance of shared rules and conventions, symbolic behaviour, turn taking and so on; but in many respects the only chess game which really resembles an interaction is that played by enthusiasts by way of letters or telephone calls. Each 'move' of the game is transmitted back and forth as a message, and we as outside observers are able to intercept the messages and show that they follow an orderly sequence. But that sequence, represented let us say by a transitional probability matrix, does poor justice to the game of chess. In order to understand what is happening, we must reconstruct from the sequence of messages, the board on which the game is played, and the private conception of the state of play which is held by each player. It is the state of play resulting from recent moves, rather than the recent moves themselves, which shape the future, and give the transmitted messages the appearance of an orderly sequence. Only by working from a conception of the board and the rules which transform its present state to future moves is any real prediction or comprehension of the course of events possible. The particular sequence of messages (surface structure) and the states of play on the two boards (deep structures) are both peculiar to *that particular game*, whereas the base rules constraining the states of play which could exist, and the transformation rules (and tactics) by which a state of play becomes a plan of action, are properties of *the game of chess*, and are common to all occasions. Now it may be argued that any sequence of moves from the known starting position uniquely specifies the resulting board positions, so the notion of a separate deep structure is dispensable in this case, but there are games whose very essence is to discover the opponent's deep structure from the surface structure of play, as in the schoolboy game of 'battleships'. Here the deployment of warships on an imaginary sea is unknown to the enemy and must be discovered by the firing of test shots, whose effect is reported. The (base) rules of the game specify the possible fleets which may be set up at the outset. Thus each player constructs a map (deep structure) which is unknown to the other. Then by reference to certain rules (transformation rules) and tactical considerations (performance variables) he engages in a sequence of overt moves (surface structure) designed to locate and destroy the enemy fleet.

The fact that each actor in an interaction has his own private and often idiosyncratic conception of the history of events and its meaning, should introduce enough ambiguity to justify the introduction of some kind of cognitive schemata, social representations or deep structures into the analysis of behavioural sequences.

There are no standard ready-made methods for discovering the deep structures and transformation rules of a language, but a hypothetico-deductive procedure is appropriate. Although no routine procedure exists (or is conceivable) which would produce the transformational rules and the principles of deep structure for a novel language given only a corpus of surface structures to go on, it is not difficult to see in principle how conjectures about these things could be tested by deducing from them the observable consequences they might have for the content of the material people can recall from past interactions, and its relation with their original form.

All of this, however, is to take us some way from the immediate task in hand. The time has come to attempt a reasonably comprehensive account of the structure and the structuring principles of some speech-act sequences.

4

BREAKING THE CODE

TERMS like 'the grammar of behaviour' and 'surface structure' seem to imply a theory-driven method of analysis, as opposed to an inductive or data-driven one. In many other respects, however, the analysis of behaviour sequences, using quantitative methods to distinguish and classify events, and to determine their sequential arrangement, has much of the character of a syntactic (or at least structural) analysis rather than a parametric one.

In this chapter, an attempt will be made to provide a fairly comprehensive, although necessarily superficial, picture of the structure of discourse by combining concepts and methods from the ethological study of *behaviour sequences* and the linguistic analysis of *surface structures*. In doing this, the first problem is that a meandering and sometimes apparently seamless flow of behaviour has to be divided into separate units or chunks for a discrete sequence analysis to be possible. This is the stage of 'unitisation', 'segmentation' or 'parsing' as it is variously called.

Unitisation

> The search for the units of behaviour, their organisation and their empirical validation, thus constitutes *the* central problem of behavioural analysis.
>
> Condon and Ogston (1967: 221)

The growing interest in the 'stream of behaviour' in recent years has prompted a number of authors to consider the problems of dividing that stream into units suitable for further analysis. The suitability of the units is the key issue, since a behaviour stream may be partitioned easily enough, giving reproducible segments of many different sorts and sizes, without necessarily capturing the 'natural' units of behaviour whose recurrence in different circumstances and combinations is the essence of a structured system. Barker (1963) warned of the dangers of employing artificial behaviour 'tesserae' in place of the natural behaviour units.

> Behaviour units are natural units in the sense that they occur without investigation by the investigator; they are self generated parts of the stream of behaviour. Behaviour tesserae, on the other hand, are alien parts of the behaviour stream in the sense that they are formed when an investigator, ignoring or dismantling the existing stream of

133

behaviour, imposes or chooses parts of it according to his own preconceptions and intentions.

Barker (1963: 2)

In a way this may be overstating the case. It makes the natural unit of behaviour sound like an object in the physical world, which one would find without any effort of subjective interpretation, while the tesserae alone depend on cognitive activity. The distinction is not really that clear. All attempts to partition the behaviour stream involve a large measure of subjective judgement and theoretical prejudice. At best one can only make careful and critical use of the necessarily judgemental data.

It is useful to consider just what is implied by the use, in other contexts, of the term unit. What is it to say of a thing that it is composed of certain units? One defining criterion has to do with planes of cleavage or weak points. A structure is expected to break under stress in such a way as to preserve the units but to yield at the joins between them. Such a criterion would support the view that bricks are units in the construction of a wall, or that atoms are the units of molecular structure. In what sense, then, can one break a behaviour stream to see where the gaps appear? Interruptions or extraneous stimuli have been used for this purpose, and are found to be perceived differently when presented at a boundary point in the behaviour stream. This principle has been particularly popular in studies of the psychological reality of linguistic structures. Fodor and Bever (1965) found that clicks played to subjects in the vicinity of a sentence phrase-boundary were recalled as being closer to the boundary. There is a tendency to perceive and process extraneous material as if it occupied spaces between natural behavioural or perceptual units. Argyle (unpublished) found interruptions by a second speaker were viewed as most appropriate when falling at the end of a sentence, less so at the end of a clause, and least appropriate in mid-clause. Another way of stressing the behaviour stream to see where it breaks is by making it a recall item in a memory task. Johnson's (1965) study of the psychological reality of phrase structure may be viewed in this light. His subjects were asked to recall sentences, and the transitional error probabilities in recall (the probabilities of recalling a word wrongly, given that the previous word was correct) were found to correspond to the phrase boundaries of the grammarian's descriptive tree structure. This experiment corresponds to the idea of unitisation by fragmentation. Yngve (1973) distracted subjects in mid-sentence by turning on a cue light which they had to cancel. Typically they carried on speaking by going back to the beginning of the clause or phrase, completing it and then finding they had forgotten what was to have come next. This suggests that the clause unit had been placed in a different store from the remainder of the sentence prior to the interruption, so the experiment provides a means of identifying the units in which verbal material is transferred from one store to another.

The other criterion which comes to mind, in considering the application of the term unit in other contexts, is that the various structures which are observed should use the same units in different combinations. Returning to the example of bricks as units of the wall, it is clear that the many styles of brickwork which are found, use (or could use) essentially the same bricks in different configurations. A comparison of two different styles would show that the internal relations of each brick were invariant, and quite unaffected by the 'context' in which they occurred. Morphological relations between each brick and its neighbours would account for the variance in building techniques. To employ this criterion, one would need to split the behaviour stream into very fine units, and then assess their contiguous occurrence in larger-scale fragments. This might be possible by the use of a cluster analysis technique, in which the raw data was a matrix of temporal intervals between items rather than dissimilarities. Or again, the log-survivor curve, which is usually used to identify single activities which occur in bouts, at random or in overspaced series, might be used to look at the distribution of time intervals between items of different sorts. The relativistic nature of such analyses becomes apparent in that criteria of sequential order are now being fed back into the detection of unit boundaries, hence the conclusion reached here, that the analysis must proceed by repeated revisions of each stage in the light of the others, rather than by a linear process in which each is completed before the next may begin.

To summarise them, one might justify the conclusion that a sequence of events $/a/b/c/d/$ consisted of two units X ($/a/b/$) and Y ($/c/d/$) on two grounds. The sequence when disrupted might be found to break at the b/c interface, more readily than the a/b or the c/d; and $/a/b/$ or $/c/d/$ might be found together in a variety of contexts, while $/b/c/$, $/a/d/$, $/a/c/$ and $/b/d/$ were not.

With the exception of the investigations of phrase structure in sentences, these principles have not been used much in unitising studies. Instead, subjects have been asked directly to identify activity boundaries in particular sequences of action; or experimenters have laid down their own explicit procedures. In either case it is assumed that a unit is self-evident to someone, and that the things which appear to the observer as units, really are units in the technical sense.

The investigators who have developed their own unitising procedures include Auld and White (1956), Scheflen (1964) and Condon and Ogston (1967). Auld and White were studying interviews, and found reliable unitising to be the first major problem. They used verbal criteria such as dependent and independent clauses; elliptical sentences; anacoluthon (false starts); aposiopeses (incomplete utterances); affirmations; denials with explanation; and 5-second periods of silence. Units defined in such terms have the advantage of being identifiable on audio-recording, or even in transcripts (with the possible exception of the silences). They claim that the method is independent of intonation, pauses, punctuation and capitalisation, and it was found to yield a 97% reliability between two judges. Scheflen reported larger units of social interaction which were hierarchically organised and punctuated by postural shifts of different magnitudes. *Points* each consist of several sentences, and are marked by different head positions; *positions* involve a series of points lasting some 5 minutes or so, and terminated by a gross postural shift involving at least half the body; *presentations* last for an entire interaction of minutes or hours, and are delimited by changes in bodily location.

In Condon and Ogston's study, slow-motion films of interaction were scrutinised. The activity of participants was found to be highly structured, appearing on the films and in transcript as a series of 'waves within waves' (perhaps a reference to the mathematics of Joseph Fourier). Each interactor was found to display 'self-synchrony' as his body 'dances in time with speech'. There was also a synchrony between actors, and between the visible and bioelectric activities of each individual.

The studies of Scheflen, and Condon and Ogston point to an interaction structure which is hierarchically organised. At any one level of description one event succeeds the next, while each is composed of smaller units, and contributes to larger ones. That in itself is hardly surprising. It is difficult to think of anything which is not hierarchically organised in that sense, and the interdependent processes of constitution and regulation in hierarchical structures have already been discussed. The emphasis on hierarchy does, however, point to a danger which may otherwise be missed. In talking of *the* units, and *the* sequence of events in social interaction, it would be quite misleading to assume that such regularities only exist at one level of description, or that different observers are necessarily reporting on the same level of the hierarchy.

The hierarchical structure of social behaviour, and its attendant complications, appear again in those studies of unitisation which have used the judgement of subjects as the index of discontinuity. Several other aspects of judgement may be affected by the level of description to which a subject attends, and conversely, other aspects of judgement may also *change* the level of description at which the subject operates. Newtson (1973) investigated both these effects in a study of attribution and unitisation. In the first experiment subjects viewed a video-taped social interaction, and marked its unit boundaries by activating an event recorder. The subjects were assigned to one of two conditions in which they were told to observe the fine or coarse segmentation of the behaviour stream. The subsequent attributions made by the two groups were then compared, and found to show the following differences. Subjects who had been marking fine unit boundaries

1. were more confident of their impressions,
2. made more dispositional attributions,
3. had more differentiated impressions.

In a second experiment, the reverse process was studied making the level of the subjects' analysis the dependent variable. Subjects viewed a video-tape of a man building a 'molecular' model, again marking unit boundaries by activating an event recorder. The control subjects saw the uninterrupted construction procedure, whereas the tape played to the experimental group included an unexpected event (the actor removed one shoe, and rolled up his trouser leg). After this rather bizarre occurrence subjects were found to record more behavioural units per minute. In other words, they had been 'switched' to a finer-grained analytical mode.

Dickman (1963) also investigated subjects' judgements of behavioural units, and again the hierarchical pattern emerged. Filmed sequences of activity were shown to subjects, and then represented as a sequence of cards each corresponding to a very small segment of the behaviour. The subjects then sorted the cards into groups of consecutive cards, so that each group corresponded to a behavioural unit in the judgement of that subject. Different subjects elected to attend to very different levels of description. The results were presented as a 'broken histogram'. Each vertical bar on the page represented one subject's interpretation of the behaviour stream. The time axis was marked on the ordinate. The bars had gaps at the points which subjects identified as transitions from one behavioural unit to the next. The overall pattern appears to be hierarchically organised in that the event boundaries recognised by subjects using coarse units are also used by the fine unitisers, in addition to their own fine distinctions. So a few boundaries are recognised by all subjects from the coarsest to the finest unitisers, a few more by all but the very coarsest unitisers, and so on. This need not have been the case, and one can imagine the results for a non-hierarchical system where the gross boundaries do not coincide with any of the fine boundaries.

Those disciplines which have shown greatest interest in behaviour sequences — linguistics and animal ethology — have paid relatively little attention to the problems of unitisation, and reasonably so. They deal with classes of behaviour like morphemes in one case and fixed action patterns in the other, whose boundaries are not particularly ambiguous. The problem becomes much more severe when the analysis turns to human NVC which is both continuous and creative. Then elaborate unitisation studies become necessary. In the analysis of discourse, however, with speech-acts as the chosen units, there should not be too much difficulty. For the time being, then, we can turn to the much harder problems of categorisation and sequence analysis on the assumption that a boundary between speech-acts is a thing which the trained observer or the native actor can recognise reasonably easily, reliably and accurately.

Before leaving the topic of unitisation altogether, it is worth recalling that there is a different approach, for which no units would be required. Some kinds of behaviour might be regarded as continuous. NVC, for example, might be more appropriately represented by a continuously changing relation between space, time and body-loci, than as a series of state-to-state transitions. This could be represented by equations, or trajectories as discussed in later chapters.

Categorisation

Existing Classifications

There are many studies in the literature which use or recommend event taxonomies, and they differ in a number of respects:

1. Some reports describe particular classifications, whereas others describe the methods by which novel schemes may be produced for novel situations.
2. Human behaviour may be classified (often using linguistically based methods) or animal behaviour may be classified (usually using ethological techniques).
3. 'Syntagmatic' and 'paradigmatic' structures may be related or not.
4. Acts or activities may be classified.
5. The taxonomy may apply to social behaviour in general, or only to its verbal aspects.
6. Verbal classifications may treat the constative (propositional), illocutionary, functional, stylistic, or prosodic features of the utterances.
7. Distinctions may be represented as dimensions, features or categories.
8. The classification may be a general one, or restricted to particular activities and situations.

These features are interrelated in various ways. Some like (1) and (2) are independent: all four combinations of methods or findings with animal or human behaviour are sensible. Others are in nested relations, such as (5) and (6): the distinction between constative/illocutionary/functional/stylistic/prosodic analyses is only relevant if one is studying speech. Some distinctions like (1) methods/findings are unrelated to the usefulness of the study for the purpose in hand (which is not to say the distinction is redundant). Others, like (4) acts/activities, are clearly polarised, with only one possibility suiting the present need.

At this stage it is valuable to consider both the kinds of study which deal with speech-event taxonomies, and those which deal with taxonomic methods more generally, although in the latter case the ostensible subject matter of the classifications often seems quite irrelevant.

Taxonomies of both human and animal behaviour are potentially useful, but in different ways. A study of human behaviour may be used to provide a classification of speech-acts or social acts directly, or it may be used to inspire discovery procedures leading to a novel taxonomy. Clearly, the animal studies are only likely to fulfil the latter role.

The relation between syntagmatic and paradigmatic structures is probably the most important single aspect of the classification schemes, and the point at which most taxonomies fail. The discussion of syntagmatic and paradigmatic structures by Saussure (1916), of regulative and constitutive rules by Searle (1965, 1969), and of alternation and sequencing rules by Ervin-Tripp (1969) all describe these two vital and necessarily related aspects of linguistic or action structure. Barker's (1963) plea for the use of natural units rather than artificial tesserae is also answered in some measure by a taxonomy in which syntagmatic and paradigmatic structures are related. The failure to follow this doctrine is so nearly universal, that the various classification schemes will be discussed here in the light of their other distinguishing features, since most are at fault in this respect. Only one classification (van Hooff, 1973) seems to escape this criticism.

In so far as the behaviour stream consists of a number of discrete behavioural events or acts, which occur in larger groups or episodes, it should be possible to devise a taxonomy for either the acts which make up an episode, or the functions which the episodes serve. The latter might be called activities. So, for example, the individual acts of stating, questioning, refuting, denying and explaining, might all be part of the episode or activity of arguing. The study by Bjerg (1968) suggests an intriguing breakdown of the behaviour stream into a series of *agons*, which are classified as *explicit*, *implicational* and *meta-agons*; and further sub-divided to form such categories as the agons of power, esteem, love, distributive justice, responsibility, aid-advice, pity-consolation, and so on. These would appear to be types of activity rather than types of act, which limits their usefulness in this study. One does not 'do' power, love or esteem, in quite the instantaneous way that one might insult, reproach or question. Similarly a paper by Ferrara (1973), which suggested four classes of social behaviour: *positive, negative, raises problem, solves problem*, could be said to deal in activities rather than acts. The point of this study was to demonstrate a recording method rather than a classification scheme, so the weakness of the taxonomy might be excused. The constraints of Ferrara's circular chart showing who did what to whom and when, would, however, militate against a more elaborate classification.

Both speech and social acts are relevant to a discussion of event taxonomies. While the present concern is mainly with speech-acts, the ultimate goal is to include verbal and non-verbal social behaviours. The distinction has a particular importance at present in that some of the levels of description which have been documented for verbal behaviour have no obvious non-verbal counterparts, for example the distinction made in the next section between constative, illocutionary, functional, stylistic and prosodic classifications.

A number of utterance typologies, particularly those which have originated in developmental linguistics, have concentrated on the propositional or constative aspects of the utterances, while neglecting the performative aspects. Inspired by the case grammars (like that of Fillmore, 1968), many authors divide the child's utterances into those dealing with changes of state as opposed to static relations, those referring to agents, objects, instruments or locations and so on, but have little to say of the performative repertoire of the child.

Classifications which take account of illocutionary forces appear to be the most promising at present. None of these can be discarded for the time being.

Functional classifications of language have been relatively commonplace over the years, presenting a bewildering diversity of categories, united by such common themes as the distinction between the transmission of information, the regulation of social encounters, and the expression of self as a spontaneous activity. Miller and McNeil (1968) describe a number of functional schemata which authors have used in the past, employing terms like expression, persuasion, description, identify, objectify, standardise and so on. Some but not all of these functional descriptions could be identified with particular speech-acts. It seems to be the case with a number of functional schemes that the categories are not mutually exclusive, but they do cover all utterance types between them. The same could be said of Robinson's (1972) fourteen functional categories, namely: avoidance of worse activity, conforming to norms, aesthetics, encounter regulation, performatives, regulation of self, regulation of others, expression of affect, marking of emitter, marking of role relationships, reference to the non-linguistic world, instruction, enquiry and meta-language. The study of spontaneous talk carried out by Soskin and John (1963) employed the six-category scheme of expressive utterances, excogitative utterances (an interesting class which most authors omit), signones (which report the speaker's present state), metrones (which express values and obligations), regnones (which regulate the other's behaviour by request, instruction or permission), and structones (which convey information). Halliday (1970) discussed language use in the light of three aspects of function which all utterances serve to some degree; ideational (the expression of propositional content), interpersonal, and textual (concerning the relation of language to itself and its situation).

A number of speech or behaviour classifications have dealt with features of performance which might be regarded as stylistic variations rather than event classes. For example, Leary (1957) used a circular chart with eight segments, to represent an individual's personality as shown in his social interaction style. The eight segments were labelled managerial-autocratic, responsible-hypernormal, cooperative-overconventional, docile-dependent, self-effacing-masochistic, rebellious-distrustful, aggressive-sadistic, and competitive-narcissistic. Each segment bore a double label denoting the virtue of that style in moderation, and its fault when practised to excess. Mehrabian (1972) distinguished between utterance styles on the bases of immediacy and denotative specificity. Utterances such as

'They enjoyed themselves.'

and

'I think they enjoyed themselves.'

would be distinguished by their differences in immediacy, whereas

'I smoke because I enjoy it.'

and

'One smokes because one enjoys it.'

would differ in denotative specificity. Fielding and Fraser (1978) studied the effect of an addressee's role on the verbal style of the speaker. Addressees were chosen for whom the speakers had different liking, familiarity and respect, to produce a $2 \times 2 \times 2$ experimental design. The monologues intended for these different classes of addressees were found to differ on four dimensions: productivity, nominal/verbal style, qualification and disfluency.

Finally there is the prosodic level of description. Gunter (1966) used the possible prosodic variations in utterances as an index of their relevance to their context, arguing that such usages as recapitulation, replacement and addition each have their own characteristic prosodic contour.

Since so many considerations in the theory of structures point to categorical rather than dimensional descriptions, it is a pity that many authors regard any taxonomic study as necessarily dimensional. This may be because of the temptation of using factor analytic techniques whose scope and flexibility have no equal among the categorical methods. A particular interesting study by Benjamin (1974) is limited for the present purpose by the use of a dimensional model. This may seem like an easily surmountable criticism, since dimensions may be used to characterise a space, in which clusters represent categories. In practice, however, the information which is selected and emphasised in the construction of a dimensional model is often the wrong basis for the sort of categorisation proposed here. Benjamin's paper is nevertheless worth describing in some detail. Called 'Structural analysis of social behaviour', it explores the paradigmatic rather than the syntagmatic structure of interaction. It deals with the similarities and differences of behavioural types and styles rather than their combination into larger units of activity. Benjamin produced a three-dimensional model of interaction styles. The three dimensions were activity, affiliation and interdependence. Behavioural opposites, antidotes and complements were found to occupy similar positions in the semantic space relative to one another. Autocorrelation studies, inter-subject correlations and factor analyses all supported this structure. When used with clinical material the model was a source of insight for patients, evoking such comments as 'I'm treating my son just as my father treated me' or 'I choose boyfriends who are mean to me in the same way my mother was'.

Many different kinds of classification are used in social anthropology, principally the taxonomy, paradigm, key and tree. The relation between such schemata and the way they would handle objects Q, R, S, A, B, C, D, distinguished by features a_1, a_2, b_1, b_2, c_1, c_2 is represented in Figure 17.

Let us assume for the time being that in rejecting the dimensional model we can accept categorical rather than feature-analytic alternatives. These are in many respects similar, the main differences being that categories are mutually exclusive

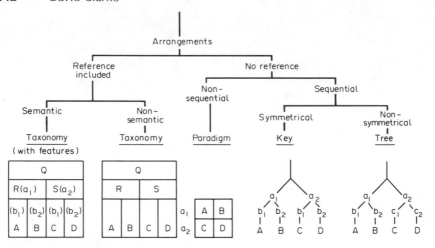

FIG. 17   The meta-structure of classifications (after Collett, 1975).

and features are not. If the search for a category scheme leads to a system which has one and only one category for each speech-act, then all well and good. If that is not possible, those same 'categories' can be treated as features and allowed to combine. In either case the outcome is much the same. A category scheme is, after all, only like a feature matrix in which each possible feature combination has been treated as a separate category.

A large number of speech-act and social-act classifications are rendered unsuitable for the task by their restriction to particular behavioural settings or types. Best known of the special classifications is that devised by Bales *et al.* for use on problem-solving groups (Bales and Gerbrands, 1948; Bales, 1953). In the more competitive situation of arguing or bargaining a slightly different repertoire of responses and tactics are observed. These are assigned to ninety-nine classes by Carter (1951); to the four dichotomies of indirect/direct, deceptive/undeceptive, offensive/defensive and inductive/non-inductive by Krause (1972); and three sets of features by Morley and Stephenson (1977). Their three feature sets are mode (such as offer, accept, reject, seek), resource (praise, information, suggestion) and referent (self, other, both, etc.). Thus each utterance might be expected to have one mode, one resource and one referent.

Again with the countless studies of therapeutic interviews using content analytic techniques (reviewed by Marsden, 1965) the particular categories, features or dimensions used are too restricted for a general theory. The classroom is another popular setting for specialised content-analytic studies (e.g. Coulthard, 1973; Flanders, 1970; Sinclair and Coulthard, 1975).

Other authors have presented classifications which were specially geared to certain segments of the behaviour stream, rather than particular behavioural settings. Ervin-Tripp (1964) and Schegloff (1968) classify the means and stages by which conversations are initiated, while Schegloff and Sacks (1973) discuss pre-closing and closing sequences. Most of Sacks' 'adjacency pairs' function as specialised sub-taxonomies in their own right, and so they are rather hard to relate to any generalised system.

Many classification schemes fail by discarding too much relevant information. There is no point in identifying each behavioural type with a point in a three-dimensional space, for example, if one cannot infer from its position all the factors relevant to the use of that behavioural item.

There are many other examples of taxonomies which could be cited, but the few given here as illustration will serve to show the main varieties and some of their shortcomings.

Exemplary taxonomies

Those classifications which survive the various criticisms mentioned above have something special to offer this kind of study, although none of them provides an ideal classification which can be adopted as it stands.

The first one to deserve special mention is the classification of performative utterances offered by Austin (1962). The concept of a performative utterance is in any case central to the model of discourse structure proposed here, but that is not to say that the particular types or examples used by Austin have any special psychological relevance. His five-fold classification into verdictives, exercitives, commissives, behabitives and expositives does not seem particularly persuasive. It was not constructed with any view to its use in a sequence analysis and therefore (quite reasonably) took no account of the 'syntagmatic structure' of discourse. Furthermore, by Austin's own admission the list is not exhaustive and possibly not even representative. The singular usefulness of Austin's work at this stage of analysis is not to provide a ready-made typology of speech acts but to remind us of the rich diversity of verbal events, and the subtlety of the distinctions which are apparent to the skilled language-user. All too often this subtlety is lost in such coding dichotomies as positive/negative or ego-centric/alter-centric. It should be a goal of the utterance taxonomist to preserve something of the subtlety and richness of Austin's scheme, if not the particular categories he used. If it should turn out that such subtlety is not altogether necessary at some later stage, the classification can be simplified much more easily than an oversimplistic scheme could be elaborated.

One scheme which goes a long way towards satisfying all the criteria is by Searle (1975). He suggested twelve features, according to which speech acts should be sorted into their respective categories. These were:

1. The point or purpose, rather like illocutionary force.
2. The 'direction of fit' between world and words. Whether the words had

to conform to the world as in a description, or the world had to fall in line with the words as in a command.

3. Expressed psychological state such as hope or intention.
4. The strength of the utterance, as in the difference between suggesting and insisting.
5. The status or role of speaker and addressee.
6. The relation of the locution to the interests of speaker and addressee, as in the difference between a threat and a promise.
7. The relation with the rest of the discourse, as in the difference between a statement and an answer.
8. Certain differences in propositional content, for example past or future events making the difference between reporting and predicting.
9. Whether the speech-act is necessarily carried out in speech, as opposed to those acts like classifying, for instance, which can be done verbally or non-verbally.
10. Whether certain external institutions are required to support the speech-act as in excommunicating, or passing sentence.
11. Whether an explicit form is available, as in "I declare that . . .", but not "I hint that . . .".
12. The style, as in the difference between announcing and confiding.

The first three criteria are the most important, and by their application Searle arrived at five main speech-act families:

1. *Representatives* have the force of stating, fit words to the world and express a *belief* (that *p*).
2. *Directives* have the force of commanding, fit the world to the words and express the *wish* that the hearer H does an action *A*.
3. *Commissives* have the force of promising, fit the world to the words, and express the *intention* that the speaker S will do an action *A*.
4. *Expressives* have the force of expressing, no direction of fit and show that the speaker is in psychological state *P*, such as hope, that speaker S or hearer H will have a stated property, such as good health.
5. *Declarations* have the force of enacting a change, they fit the world to the words *and* the words to the world since they both describe the change to be made, and in being said make it so. They express no state but have propositional concept *p*, as in 'This fête is now open'.

The next study of particular note is that by van Hooff (1973). This was an analysis of chimpanzees' behaviour, so it is interesting here for its methods rather than its findings. Van Hooff warned of the dangers of incautious segmentation:

> The great problem was what subdivision of movements and postures should be regarded as behavioural elements. Behaviour is a continuous stream of movement which can be split up in a number of more or less stereotyped recurring elements. The question is, however, how far does one split up and where does one lump? Most

students of primate behaviour have not worried too much about this and have presented catalogues in a matter-of-fact manner. Especially in experimental studies, the catalogues are relatively small so that a great deal of lumping and/or selection must have been done.

van Hooff (1973: 80)

Behavioural categories for the chimps were, naturally, based on the physical similarities between patterns of movement and posture. Associations between behavioural elements were then studied by various means. The frequencies of occurrence of different behaviours in the same time period were correlated, to establish a picture of their possible similarities. Some behaviours were found to be involved in predictable transitions as antecedents more often than sequiturs, or vice versa. This suggests a dichotomous distinction between items which initiate activity or commitment to act, and those which continue or terminate the activity. This is an idea which is also suggested by Sacks' work, and which will be considered again later. Flow diagrams are given depicting the most common behavioural transitions, in something like a finite-state grammar. The particularly striking technique used in this paper, however, is the elicitation of higher-order behavioural elements *from the pattern of transitional frequencies between the primary elements*. This is Saussure's doctrine of related syntagmatic and paradigmatic structures, presented (independently) in another discipline and in quite different terminology. The matrix of transitional frequencies between elements was transformed into a correlation matrix showing for each pair of items the extent to which their transitional frequencies with other items correlated. This correlation matrix was then subjected to multivariate analysis. A principle components analysis suggested the existence of seven behavioural dimensions or systems labelled affinitive, play, aggressive, submissive, excitement, show and comfort. A cluster analysis of the data produced a hierarchical dendrogram in which much the same behavioural classes emerged.

Finally two papers by Osgood (1968, 1970) dealt with the semantic relations between interpersonal verbs (IPVs), on the assumption that our language structures the verbal representation of social behaviour in much the way that the actor structures the behaviour itself. Some 200 or so IPVs were selected from *Roget's Thesaurus* (1959) and subjected to an intensive semantic analysis. The initial sample of 210 IPVs represented the most familiar examples of the 210 categories in the *Thesaurus* which contained verbs of interpersonal *intention* (such as *to punish*; but not *to strike with a whip*, which is a concrete behaviour). All the verbs were acceptable in the linguistic frame $PERSON_1 \ldots PERSON_2$. The verbs were then classified on the six *a priori* features of (A) associative/dissociative, (B) initiating/reacting, (C) directive/non-directive, (D) tension-increasing/tension-decreasing, (E) ego-oriented/alter-oriented, and (F) supraordinate/subordinate. The validity of verb coding on the six features was checked by asking (1) Are the clusters of words having identical feature code-strips closely synonymous in meaning? and (2) Are words with opposed coding on only one feature and identical on all others, minimally contrastive and on the appropriate feature? Test (1) was sometimes successful (e.g. forgive, pardon and excuse were all coded +A −B −C −D −E +F), and sometimes unsuccessful (punish, condemn and ridicule were all coded −A −B +C +D −E +F). Test (2) was also partially successful (e.g. impress/inform differed on ego-oriented/alter-oriented), while there were failures with such items as confuse/shame which are distinguished only on ego-oriented/alter-oriented and court/retard which differ only on the associative/dissociative feature. The contingencies between features were examined, and additional features added to improve the apparent validity of the system on criteria (1) and (2) above. Thus a list of ten features was produced (A) moral/immoral, (B) potent/impotent, (C) active/passive, (D) associative/dissociative, (E) initiating/reacting, (F) ego-oriented/alter-oriented, (G) supra-ordinate/subordinate, (H) terminal/interminal, (I) future/past, and (J) deliberate/impulsive. A theory of semantic interaction was then introduced, in which small linguistic frames were used to test for the opposition of binary features. The frame ' . . . prayed', for example, would distinguish between human and inhuman nouns, while 'he . . . successfully' might be used to detect the feature of goal-achievement. This technique was then used to draw up a 'target matrix' of interpersonal verbs by adverbs. The cells of the target matrix were then coded for anomaly (−1), permissibility (0), and appositeness (1). The target matrix was used as a basis for factor and cluster analyses of underlying dimensions and features, for comparison with the empirical data from groups of subjects who were asked to perform the same judgemental task on the target matrix, and for cross-cultural comparisons. No single, unequivocal category scheme emerged from this study, and the interpersonal verbs being classified were somewhat different from the speech-acts which are used in our analysis, so there is no need to consider in great detail the various factor and cluster solutions which were obtained, or their detailed comparison or evaluation. Suffice it to say that, as with other studies described in this section, the methods used in Osgood's work are of more immediate use here than the findings are.

By now the immense problems facing the utterance or event taxonomist should be apparent. No perfect solution exists in the literature to date, but several authors have pointed the way to a workable classification. It seems that a synthesis is required, which employs the notion of related syntagmatic and paradigmatic structures from Saussure, the context-sensitive discovery procedures of van Hooff or Osgood, and the speech-act concept and subtlety of classification suggested by Austin. A synthesis of much this kind will be attempted in the next two sections.

Experiment 12: Classification of Utterances

Introduction

The taxonomic problems raised by this kind of research have similar counterparts in linguistics, where formal methods exist for classifying the constituents of a language. One such method, the procedure of *test-frame analysis*, is described in detail in Fries (1952), where it is used to show that the conventional school-grammar distinction between nouns, verbs, adverbs and so on, is not perfectly suited to the structure of modern English. (This is yet another example of the principle of classification by commutability, as in van Hooff's procedure.)

The test-frame procedure is a simple means of deriving a paradigmatic structure of equivalence classes defined on the set of morphemes in a language, which reflects the syntagmatic structure of sentences. The test frame itself is a well-formed sentence from which a single morpheme has been deleted. Other morphemes are then inserted in its place and the new sentence judged to be well- or ill-formed. All morphemes which lead a particular test frame to be well-formed are (in that respect) equivalent. When the procedure is repeated with a number of test frames and a number of morphemes, it is found that the equivalence relations which are established between morphemes form a partition of the set, with something like eight morpheme classes in the quotient set.

So, for example, the frame

The . . . was on the table.

would be a well-formed sentence when completed with *book, lamp, jar, candle, pen, paper* and so on; but not with *blue, hard, heavy, extravagant, noisy, run, walk, sit, congratulate, prevent*; or *shamefully, graciously, ponderously* or *reluctantly*. Thus a class like NOUN is crudely characterised by instantiation, and distinguished from ADJECTIVE, VERB and ADVERB. Two aspects of this procedure should be noted. First, the test-frame technique as used here is for detecting syntactic rather than semantic equivalence (in so far as the two are really separable), so the substitutions in the test frame are only required to preserve the well-formedness of the string. The criterion of *salve veritate* which would be used in a semantic analysis does not apply. Therefore in the example above, 'The unicorn is on the table', or even 'The prospect is on the table' could be seen as acceptable. Secondly, it is true for the most part in a language like English that the constitutive rules are context free. Therefore morphemes which are equivalent in one context are equivalent in all. A perfect partition is formed on the morpheme set, with each morpheme realising one and only one part of speech. There are some exceptions but they are rare enough to pose very little problem. These are cases where the same morpheme appears in two categories depending on its context, showing equivalence relations in one context which it does not show in another. For instance, the word *smile* in the sentences

'Wipe that smile off your face.'

and

'She felt she could smile.'

acts as a noun and a verb respectively. In the first case but not the second it is equivalent to *tear*, and *expression*; and in the second case but not the first it is equivalent to *cry*, and *succeed*.

In this experiment the test-frame procedure is adapted to the needs of discourse analysis, in rather the way suggested by Harris (1952). The test frames are scaled up, so to speak, becoming well-formed dialogues in place of well-formed sentences, and the interchangeable units become speech acts in place of morphemes.

Method

The experiment was conducted in two parts: the first to produce a preliminary set of utterance classes by test-frame analysis; and the second to reduce that set by the detection of further equivalence relations, using a *single-linkage cluster analysis.*

1. *Test-frame analysis.* Twenty subjects took part in this stage of the experiment, all of whom were female students of occupational therapy, between the ages of 18 and 25.

Each subject was given a response form as shown in Figure 18 divided by faint

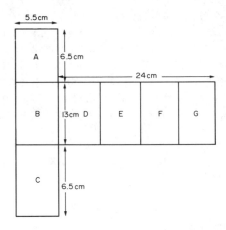

FIG. 18   Taxonomy experiment — response form.

horizontal lines into 120 spaces the size of a short handwritten utterance. Sections A and C contained 10 spaces each, and sections B, D, E, F and G 20 spaces each. The subjects were told that the experiment was designed to tap their expertise on a matter of common knowledge to them. They were assured that it was not a test of individual ability, and that there was no single correct answer against which their responses were to be evaluated. They were also assured that their individual contributions would be treated confidentially.

The subjects were asked to write their name, age, address and occupation in the space above sections D, E, F and G, and were invited to take any notes they wished on the experimental instructions in the space below D, E, F and G.

They were then asked to write 40 lines of realistic dialogue in the spaces in sections A, B and C, taking care to keep the two speakers 'in register' so that every odd-numbered space, counting from the top of the page, would contain an utterance by speaker X, and every even-numbered space an utterance by speaker Y. This hypothetical, but well-formed dialogue invented by each subject was to function as the test frame in the next part of the experiment. In producing the dialogues subjects were asked to bear in mind the diversity of roles and settings which can contribute to dyadic encounters, and to try between them to encompass a variety of normal dialogue types. They were told that each utterance or line of dialogue should consist of one 'move' and only one move. The implications of this instruction were explained to the subjects. They were told that 15—20 minutes had been set aside for this stage of the task, and were asked to use small but clearly legible writing.

When all subjects had finished that part of the task, filling parts A, B and C of the response form with dialogue, the next phase of the experiment was explained. Sections A and C of the dialogue were to remain constant as a context, while plausible substitutions were produced for all the twenty utterances in section B. Each utterance was to be given four alternatives, written on the corresponding lines of sections D, E, F and G. Subjects were told that they should choose their alternative utterances so that their insertion in the original transscript would produce another well-formed and meaningful dialogue, although its meaning need not be that of the original. Thus the criterion was one of meta-syntactic well-formedness, without the introduction of semantic anomaly, but the subjects were not asked to preserve the same meaning. Each utterance was still to consist of a single move.

The subjects' most difficult instruction was as follows. They were to construct the matrix of interchangeable utterances in such a way that any combination of columns gave a well-formed dialogue. So their task on reaching line 12, say, was not simply to restore line 11 to its original, single utterance state, and produce five versions of line 12 which were compatible with the single line 11; rather the task was to produce five versions of line 12 which would fit any of the five versions of line 11, and then five versions of line 13 which would fit any of 125 combinations of lines 11 with 12, and so on. This was difficult since the entire substitution matrix of 5 × 20 utterances was equivalent to 5^{20} (95, 367, 431, 640, 625 or 9.5×10^{13}) dialogues, each of which was required to be well formed. The task would have been inconceivable, had the subjects not had a conception of dialogue as a set of response types, each with a multiplicity of different realisations. It is one matter to produce a string of twenty event classes with five examples of each class, and a very different matter to produce 95 million million event strings, in accordance with specified constraints.

Eighteen of the twenty subjects finished the task within the allotted time of 45 minutes giving 360 sets of five interchangeable utterances from their sections B, D, E, F and G. The two subjects who were unable to finish in the available time contributed a further fourteen sets of five utterances between them, giving 374 potential utterance categories in all, each with five examples.

2. *Cluster analysis*. There was no reason to suppose that each category, formed in phase (1) was unique. The experiment could just as well have produced many more or many less categories, depending on the number of times the procedure was carried out. The same is true with a sentence test frame: morpheme classes may be produced *ad infinitum*, but there are only eight (approximately) which are unique and mutually exclusive. So the problem was to assess the redundancy of the 374 categories, and represent them as members of larger classes of utterances forming a true partition of the set of speech-acts. This was the purpose of the second stage of the experiment.

The 374 groups of five utterances were presented on file cards to twelve subjects who were asked to sort them into piles of functional equivalents as they saw them. More subjects with a knowledge of psychology were used for this task than in the earlier experiments. It was felt that some familiarity with similar abstract tasks of behavioural taxonomy might be an advantage, while the experiment was sufficiently novel that subjects seemed unlikely to be influenced by their knowledge of particular psychological findings.

Results

The outcome of the first stage of the experiment was a set of 374 groups, each of five equivalent utterances, of which examples are given below.

In the second stage of the experiment all twelve subjects completed the sorting task on the 374 five-utterance groups in 1—4 hours. The number of piles used varied considerably, with a mean of 45.5 and a range of 167 (from 7 to 174). The distribution is too skewed to be described by its standard deviation.

The data from these twelve assortments was then subjected to a single-linkage cluster analysis (Jardine and Sibson, 1971). Because of the unusual size of the data matrix, special computer programs had to be written, using the following procedure. The data from the twelve subjects were recorded as twelve lists of 374 items. Each subject's data consisted of a number of sub-lists showing the groups of items that subject had identified. The elements in each sub-list, the sub-lists in each subject list, and the subject lists in the data corpus were in random order. The data were fed to the computer in that form. A first program then read these lists, and converted them to a 374 X 374-item matrix, showing for any pair of items the number of subjects who put both in the same pile. Since the relation of 'being in the same pile as . . .' is reflexive and symmetric (and also transitive), the communalities of the matrix were all 12, and cell ij contained the same value as cell ji for all i and j.

The 374 × 374-item matrix was too cumbersome to print or interpret in full, so a second program was used to scan the matrix for high values, printing out in the following format:

$$X_1 \qquad I_1 \qquad J_1$$
$$X_2 \qquad I_2 \qquad J_2$$

where X is a specified number of subjects relating two items, and I and J are item numbers. The program was constructed so as to print each pair once only, thus avoiding the listing of:

$$X_1 \qquad m \qquad n$$

and

$$X_1 \qquad n \qquad m,$$

from the raw matrix which contained both.

From these results a dendrogram could be constructed directly, as shown in Figure 19. If the results are to be interpreted correctly, it must be emphasised

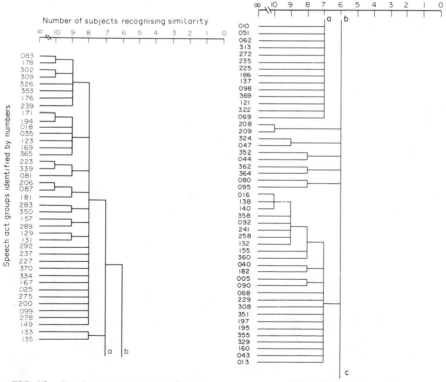

FIG. 19   Dendrogram of speech-act types.   FIG. 19   (continued)

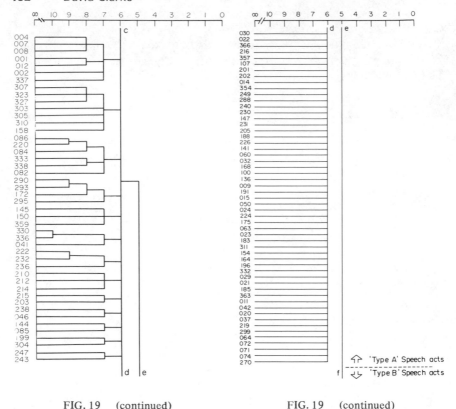

FIG. 19 (continued)   FIG. 19 (continued)

that this is a *single-linkage cluster analysis*. That is to say that an item is viewed as having a dissimilarity or distance from a pre-formed cluster equal to its distance from the *nearest member* of that cluster. This is the simplest analysis computationally, an overriding consideration with a data matrix of this size. However, it has the disadvantage that under conditions of intransitive similarity (where A is like B is like C is like D; but A and D are very dissimilar) a single linkage program represents as perfect clusters, structures which are really chains or clines (rings). In this way it shows more clusters than say a centroid linkage analysis, which unites clusters when their centroids fall within the criterion distance. Consequently, centroid analysis tends only to produce ball clusters where everything is similar to everything else, as opposed to the possible chain clusters where everything is similar to something (but *not everything*) else. However, centroid linkage analysis has the disadvantage of failing to preserve the same cluster structure under all monotonic transformations of the raw data.

Since the large matrices were held in store as a long list, there was a danger

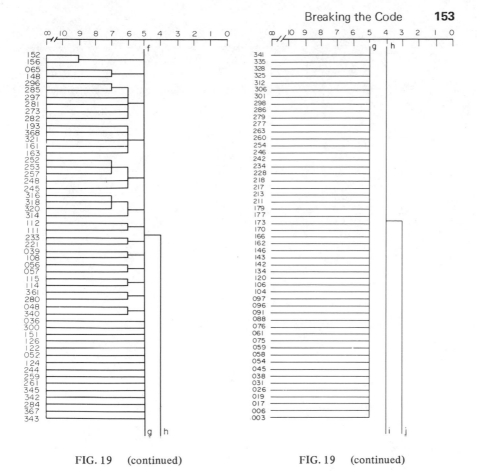

FIG. 19   (continued)   FIG. 19   (continued)

of rows and columns going out of register at some stage of the operation. Had this happened the dense clusters which the program identified would have had no intuitive validity. This did not seem to occur, and the eight small clusters formed by the agreement of ten out of twelve subjects contained the following groups:

    16   Yes doesn't he.
             Oh yes.
             I think so too.
             That's true I think.
             I agree with you there.

   138   Yes
             Indeed

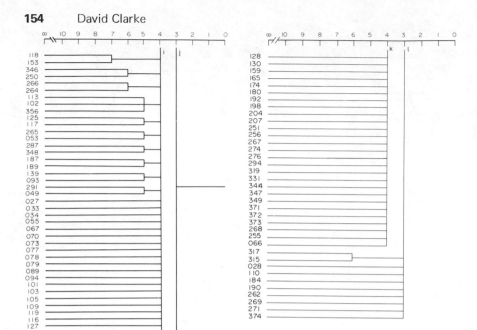

FIG. 19   (continued)   FIG. 19   (continued)

            Of course
            Affirmative
            Yes

140   I agree
            Yes
            I agree with you
            Affirmative
            So do I

and:

83   What about your daughter?
            Is your daughter married?
            Your daughter.
            Has your daughter any plans?
            Is your daughter settling down yet?

178   Does your brother know what he wants to do?
            What about your brother?
            And how's your brother getting on?
            And your brother?
            How about your brother?

All too often the five alternative utterances given by the original twenty subjects were near paraphrases of each other, but there are a number of interesting instances of dissimilar utterances being used as (legitimate) alternatives in a given context, for example the inclusion of 'Yes' with 'No' in the same group.

Discussion

The result was in some respects disappointing. The dendrogram does not show a neat hierarchy of clusters and no definitive utterance classes emerge. Consequently the plan had to be abandoned to replace each utterance in the original transcripts by the class in which it was placed by the cluster analysis, and then do a sequence analysis on equivalence classes. As the dendrogram emerged it became apparent that one cluster was present, to which more and more single items accrued as the similarity criterion was relaxed. In the case of something like half the items, they form no sub-clusters, and only join the main system when the similarity criterion drops to three, four or five out of twelve subjects in agreement.

The shortcomings of this analysis do, however, suggest a number of interesting properties of the discourse system. The paradigmatic structure or constitutive rules of the system appear to be *context dependent*, to a very large extent. It is quite clear that a number of the five-utterance groups have no clearly visible function when viewed out of context. This implies that it is not the particular utterances which need to be classified, so much as the utterances *as used in particular contexts*. This is in marked contrast to the case of sentence grammars, which are based on constitutive rules which are largely context-free. This might be counted as a major difference between the syntax of the language, and the 'meta-syntax' of discourse, and a great complication for the future of this kind of research.

This could explain the division in the dendrogram between those items which are part of the main cluster and those which are not. It could be a reflection of the difference between the 'first pair part' and 'second pair part' of Sacks' 'adjacency pairs'. The first item, like a question for example, is usually couched in a form of words which would be recognisable in isolation from any context, whereas its sequitur (such as an 'answer') is only recognisable as such when it is seen in its context. If this were so, the first member of each adjacency pair in the transcripts would be part of the main cluster structure and the second member one of the isolates. Conversely, the main cluster (which may be arbitrarily defined as the group formed by the half or thereabouts of the total number of items which aggregate at similarity level 6) would contain a high proportion of first pair parts, and the remainder of the dendrogram would contain a high proportion of second pair parts. Thus if the two types of utterance are called A and B respectively, we would expect the original transcripts to contain alternating As and Bs significantly more often than strings of As or strings of Bs. This may be tested by examination of the four-celled transitional frequency table showing the number of AA, AB, BA and BB transitions. The cell values are 10, 74, 72 and 95 respectively. $\chi^2 = 6.72$, d$f = 1$, $p < 0.01$, two-tailed (Siegel, 1956). This suggests that, contrary to the hypothesis, the tendency is for As and Bs to group together more often than they alternate. This could be due to the atypical dialogues produced by a small number of the eighteen subjects who contributed nineteen inter-utterance transitions each to the contingency table of 342 transitions. The nineteen-item contingency tables of the eighteen subjects to complete the generation task, when considered individually, show that ten subjects produced dialogues with more transitions in cells AA and BB than AB and BA, whereas eight subjects produced dialogues having more AB and BA transitions than AA and BB transitions. The pattern does not seem particularly clear. Suffice it to say that the hypothesis that types A and B occur in alternation finds no clear support in these data.

The number of utterances represented in the dendrogram is so great that a summary of the types of utterance represented by each part of the diagram is hard to produce. A sample of ten five-utterance groups of type A showed four questions, two affirmations, one request for confirmation, one agreement, one suggestion and one opinion, while ten groups of type B showed four statements, three opinions, one question, one affirmation, and one evaluation. There is perhaps some tendency for the group B to contain a higher proportion of statements (which would be hard to classify out of context as say answers, denials, proofs, and so on), while group A contains a number of the more identifiable performatives. It also seems very likely that, given the complexity of the task, the second group of twelve judging subjects failed to work at the correct level of abstraction, so that items bearing a superficial similarity were carefully classified and the more idiosyncratic ones treated as stragglers. If the various conversations from which the utterance groups were drawn passed through phases of commonplace social talk, and unique topic talk, then we should expect to find AA strings and BB strings rather than an alternation of As and Bs.

The type A and B utterances do not seem to be the peculiar contribution of two distinct subject groups. The frequency distribution of number of type A utterances used over subjects is unimodal. (The number of subjects using 1 or 2, 3 or 4, 5 or 6 type A utterances out of a possible 20, and so on, were 1, 1, 1, 1, 5, 3, 4, 2, 0, 0, respectively.)

There is little point in delving further into the possible interpretations of the dendrogram, when the one thing it is known not to represent is the all-important utterance taxonomy which could be used in the next stage of analysis. In future, attempts to produce such a taxonomy must take greater account of subjects' limited powers of abstraction, the degree to which the constitutive rules of the DCS are context dependent, and the resulting impossibility of representing type classes by instantiation, or listing, alone.

Some of these difficulties might have been overcome if the present experiment had used a cluster analysis of single utterances, each with a representation of its context, in place of the five-utterance groups. However, the problem of the subjects' limitations, and the difficulty of representing context-dependent categories, would still have remained. The next section proposes a new taxonomy which was written in the light of these problems.

A Theoretical Taxonomy

It seems clear from Experiment 12 that the units or speech-act classes which would figure in a 'grammar of conversation' are not quite like the familiar morpheme classes used in the study of syntax. The category of speech-act that an utterance belongs to is largely context dependent. A given form of words will be seen as a member of one category if it occurs in one context, and a member of another category if it occurs in another. This means that the categories cannot be derived from a simple test-frame procedure, and they cannot be represented by instantiation (or listing of constituent elements). Furthermore, it means that the two stages of analysis, categorisation and sequence analysis, can no longer be treated as independent operations. Any workable taxonomy will have to relate closely to studies of syntagms, in order to capture the relations of categories to contexts.

As a particular category scheme cannot be elicited or tested except in conjunction with a study of sequences, the new taxonomy, which is described below, was worked out *a priori* rather than by observation of the behaviour stream. The categories were then used in a formal description of sequential patterns, so that the categories and the sequencing rules could be tested together in a single experiment. Furthermore, as the categories cannot be represented by instantiation, category names were used like those which Austin used for his performative utterances such as Threat, Promise, Invitation, and so on. In a way this allows us to by-pass the details of the constitution of categories for the time being, because the names do not have to specify exactly what is to count as a *threat* or as a *promise*. If sufficiently unambiguous definitions are given for the category names, then it is up to the subjects to identify each category when it occurs, or to see how a given abstract category could be represented in a particular form of words, making reference to the context if need be. Clearly, all of this must lead to some falsifiable proposition about the categories if they are to have any use, and it does. Predictions made about sequences will fail unless the subjects use the categories consistently. When investigating sentences, one assumes subjects can recognise words, otherwise they could hardly perform consistently on a task involving sentences. Here we shall be investigating speech-act sequences in the assumption that clear regularities will only appear if subjects are consistent in their recognition of the speech-act types themselves.

When one considers the everyday vocabulary that describes speech-acts, several things are apparent. It is a very rich and subtle lexicon, which suggests that people find it useful to label their social world in this elaborate way and to make fine distinctions between its various forms. Since each speech-act name describes a form of activity, each has its counterpart in the form of a verb. *Threat* becomes *to threaten, a promise* becomes *to promise* and so on, and it is in the verbal form that an interesting distinction appears. When used in a sentence, describing some piece of conversation, these verbs take direct or indirect objects, which are sometimes previous speech-acts and sometimes not. It seems to be the case that when the verb describing a speech-act takes as an object a previous speech-act, then it is describing a quality which attaches not so much to the utterance as to the relation between utterances, and that is something that can only be identified in context. When the verb describing a speech-act takes objects which are not previous speech-acts, it seems to be describing intrinsic properties of the utterance which could be detected without reference to the context. For example, verbs like *answer, deny, disagree, comply* all take as their objects previous questions, statements or commands. (He answered the question. She disagreed with the statement. They obeyed the command.) Whereas verbs like *state, recommend, promise* do not have this property, and all are recognisable without reference to their context. The distinction is not perfect since some speech-acts seem to belong in either group. Questioning seems at first like a context-free activity: one questions a person on a particular matter, and no reference need be made to previous utterances. On the other hand, one may also question a statement, and use the term to indicate the relation of 'calling into question' another utterance or passage of talk. This distinction does not form an integral part of the utterance taxonomy, but it should be borne in mind as an indicator that there are apparently two facets to the way we describe items of discourse. Both sorts of category are used in the following taxonomy in much the same way, although it may prove useful at some later date to make a much clearer distinction between labels for items and labels for the relations between items.

The starting-point for the construction of the taxonomy itself was the idea that the essence of the social use of language is the direction of the behaviour and attention of others. Therefore the first categories to come to mind were the various modes of instruction: *Command, Request, Advise, Permit*, adding *Prohibit* (as the negative version of *Command*) and *Warn* (as the negative form of *Advise*). *Question* was viewed as similar to request, except that it invites verbal rather than non-verbal responses. The information carrying categories (those whose function is predominantly constative) then came in as a secondary consideration, because of their use as responses to the directive categories. This is in the spirit of Jakobson's (1972: 80) remark that 'efforts to interpret imperatives as transforms of declarative propositions falsely overturn the natural hierarchy of linguistic structure'. In addition to those acts which initiate and complete sequences of task-oriented activity, categories were included to allow for socio-emotional processes such as *Praise, Thank, Blame* and *Confess*. Categories were inserted where they seemed to represent alternative courses of action having different occasions of use and different consequences, and deleted when they would fit all the contexts of other categories. In this way the taxonomy was designed around the principle of paradigms in relation to syntagms, and was checked against the criterion of meta-syntactic rather than meta-semantic structure (categories were not treated as unique simply because they carried a unique 'meaning', but only if they had unique occasions of use). The taxonomy was regarded as complete when all the commonplace sequences of events which came to mind could be represented simply and accurately, and when all relevant acts from the lists by Osgood (1968), Austin (1962) and Bjerg (1968) could be represented. A number of checks were made on the internal consistency of the system, but they rely upon the sequencing rules described in the next section. In a few cases the categories did not appear to be mutually exclusive as they stood, so their definitions were modified so that one class should only include those items which could not be accommodated in the other more specific class, so for instance *Assert* is only used where *Answer* does not apply. The final list of forty-five categories was

1	# (a symbol used for the boundaries between connected episodes of talk)		
2	Command	24	Greet
3	Prohibit	25	Thank
4	Request	26	Blame
5	Question	27	Accuse
6	Advise	28	Confess
7	Warn	29	Offend
8	Permit	30	Sympathise
9	Offer	31	Challenge
10	Promise	32	Boast
11	Threaten	33	Apologise
12	Assert	34	Pardon
13	Justify	35	Bid Farewell
14	Accept	36	Pacify
15	Reject	37	Fulfil
16	Comply	38	Joke
17	Refuse	39	Laugh
18	Answer	40	Terminate
19	Agree	41	Attend
20	Deny	42	Cheer
21	Continue	43	Minimise
22	Praise	44	Complain
23	Defer	45	/ (speaker change symbol)

Later on this set of categories will be used as the basis of an experiment on sequencing rules. The rules of sequence will be processed to provide further information on the relations between the categories, as they were used in this experiment.

The Analysis of Sequences

Standard Methods

In mathematics the analysis of temporal processes is commonplace, but is usually concerned with the changing magnitude of a continuous variable with time, as in the analysis of waveforms by Fourier methods, or in the various kinds of time-series analysis. Our problem is rather different. We have to trace the order in which a system progresses from one to another of a set of discrete events or states. The methods for doing this are usually described as a series of possibilities ranging from the simple, convenient (and often implausible) models such as the Markov chain, to the complex, plausible and difficult methods, such as those provided by linguistic analysis. This range of possibilities is reviewed in Hutt and Hutt (1970). Slater (1973) describes a number of ethological techniques for the analysis of sequences. Farrell (1970) also considers the same series of sequence types, not as methods of analysis but as models of conscious devices. Several different models of sequential structure have already been described but for the sake of clarity some of their most important features and distinctions will be repeated here.

The simplest model, and one of the most widely used in ethology, is the Markov chain. This relates each event to its immediate antecedent, on the assumption that the occurrence of that event in a given interval of time, or at a given point in the sequence, depends only on the nature of the previous event. The information for such an analysis is conveniently represented as a matrix whose rows correspond to the different events as they occur as antecedents, and whose columns correspond to the events occurring as sequiturs. Any event in a real sequence is, of course, the sequitur to the one before it and the antecedent to the one which follows, so the matrix represents a continuing process and not just a number of isolated transitional frequencies. The χ^2 statistic is often used to detect significant variations in transitional frequency in such a matrix. Raush (1972) discusses the use of transition matrices as a representation of the sequential structure of human social behaviour, pointing out that even the simplest matrix can be used to show up some interesting properties of the behaviour stream as a whole. Some matrices clearly represent 'absorbing chains' of behaviour, in which certain states may be entered readily, but cannot be left. In these cases the system tends to be drawn towards such states over a period of time, and captured with no chance of escape. A 'regular chain' is one in which every state can follow every other with some probability, so that no transition is absolutely impossible. 'Cyclical chains' can arise in which a succession of states is likely to occur over and over again in the same order. It is an interesting feature of such matrices that they allow long-term predictions to be made from observations of short-term relations between events, provided the assumptions of the Markov model hold. For example, one can work out from a simple transition matrix the likelihood that the system will visit any given state in n moves after a particular starting-point, or the probability that n moves hence the system will be in a particular state. As we saw earlier, Jaffe, Feldstein and Cassotta (1967) found that a Markov model of the alternation of speakers in a dialogue gave a satisfactory account of their data.

Markov models are not acceptable for the more complex aspects of interaction as the experiments reported here have shown. They may still be used as a useful first approximation to more complicated kinds of sequential pattern, but more precise analyses will almost certainly lead to the use of non-Markovian descriptions. The idea that the brain functions as a Markov device ceased to be readily acceptable many years ago. Lashley (1951) wrote that associative chain theories of mental functioning, in which each element of a chain of central processes served to arouse the next by direct association, was untenable, and went on to suggest that the organisation of human activity should be regarded as essentially language-like.

One obvious refinement of the Markov model is to relate each event not just to one antecedent, but to several, creating different orders of linear stochastic process. Altman (1965) compared zero-, first-, second-, third- and fourth-order models of the social behaviour sequences of his Rhesus monkeys, finding the fourth to be the best. Chomsky (1957, 1959) considered such processes as models of English syntax, under the names of finite state or type-3 grammars. He concluded that they were very unsatisfactory because of the existence of 'nested' structures. Sequences of the form A( )B where the propriety of B derives from the presence of A regardless of the length or content of the string ( ), are impossible to represent in a transitional matrix of finite order. It can be argued that a matrix of finite order will still provide an adequate approximation to a system which can generate outputs of the form A( )B, but objections still exist. The amount of data required becomes prohibitive. A fourth-order transition matrix for a system having fifty states would have over 300 million cells. It would probably be an inappropriate model to describe the generative processes of such a system even if it could approximate the output, and because frequencies are usually obtained by direct observation, they could not be used in studies of competence, unless the procedure were modified to include subjects' estimations of transitional propriety in place of probability.

Isolated pieces of information about the sequential structure of the behaviour stream can be obtained without recourse to more complex models. The frequency of occurrence of pairs of items in the same time intervals can be correlated (van Hooff, 1973) and the correlations used in factor and cluster analyses. This shows up any class or dimension of activity which may be used to label sub-sets of the behavioural repertoire which occur contiguously. The distribution of time intervals between successive occurrences of the same behaviour may be recorded to see if the behaviour is randomly distributed in time, is overspaced or produced in bouts. In the log-survivor technique, for example, each possible time interval between successive occurrences of the relevant events is plotted against the log of its frequency of occurrence (Odum, 1971). This gives a straight line for randomly spaced events, one which is bowed towards the origin for events which occur in bouts, and one which bows away from the origin for overspaced events. The reason for this is simple. An event with a probability of occurrence in any time interval of p, regardless of how long ago it last occurred, will occur immediately after its last occurrence on the proportion p of occasions. Let us call the probability of its not happening q, that is $q = 1-p$. On the remaining q occasions it will occur in the second time interval on the proportion p of occasions, an overall proportion of qp. So the sequence of events will get as far as the third interval on q^2 occasions and will terminate at that point on q^2p occasions. So in general the interval between successive occurrences of the event will be found to be n on a proportion $q^{(n-1)}p$ of occasions. This is an exponential function which appears as a straight line in a semi-log plot.

Several of these approaches to sequence analysis, and the *a priori* taxonomy described above, will be combined in the next study on the sequential structure of idealised speech-act sequences.

Experiment 13: Stochastic Analysis

Introduction

In this study the problem of utterance or event classification was set aside so as to look at more elaborate kinds of sequential pattern, and to use techniques sensitive to more than just first-order transitional probabilities, without having to establish a new empirical taxonomy first. To do this, the data were collected in pre-categorised form, rather than as audio tapes or orthographic scripts, using the *a priori* category scheme described in the last section.

Method

Thirty-three subjects from the subject panel of the Oxford University Department of Experimental Psychology came into the laboratory and were given the list of utterance categories and definitions shown in Appendix D. They were also told to use the symbol # like an 'event' to mark the boundary between two topics and ## to mark the boundary between two different dialogues. Each subject then received a response sheet marked out into 100 consecutive boxes, each containing a space to write A or B to differentiate the identities of two 'speakers', and a space to write one of the utterance types. Subjects were asked to produce 100 lines of hypothetical dialogue using this notation of A's and B's for speakers, the speech-act types for their utterances, and the additional punctuating symbols for the boundaries of topics, or whole conversations.

Analysis and Results

The data were coded numerically for computer analysis. Each class of event (including the delimiters) was given a number, and the contributions of different subjects separated by a special code number, so that the overall data-base could be input to the computer in the form of a single list of 3332 numbers. One feature of the coding was that utterances of 'speakers' A and B were given the same speech-act code numbers, but with positive and negative signs respectively. This allowed the computer to keep track of speakers A and B independently, and, more importantly since these were only arbitrary names, to tell whether any pair of utterances had come from the same or different speakers, regardless of whether they were both A or both B (in the case of pro-active pairs), or A followed by B as opposed to B followed by A (in the case of reactive pairs). Multiplying any two codes gives a negative product if they are reactively related, and a positive product if they are proactively related, *regardless* of which speaker is which.

Frequency distribution

The first analysis looked at the relation between frequency and rank frequency with which items were used. We expected to find something like 'Zipf's law' which applies to word frequency in text, namely $fr = k$ (where f is the absolute frequency of use for an item, r is its rank frequency and k is a constant). Instead we found $f\sqrt{r} = k$, or, as it turns out in practice, a plot of $\log f$ against $\log r$ with a slope of $-\frac{1}{2}$ instead of the -1 predicted by 'Zipf's law'. The gradient is approximate as Figure 20 shows. The down-turn at the right of the graph can be overlooked as it is likely to be largely artifactual. Plotting f against r means that the least numerous items are found on the far right of the curve, and since these are therefore the least reliable, some departure from the rest of the pattern is to be expected. Furthermore, since f plotted against r is necessarily a descending monotonic function, all departures must appear as a down-turning 'tail', so it is not surprising that that is what shows up in the data as plotted.

The relation $f\sqrt{r} = k$ remains unexplained.

Log-survivor functions

The log-survivor plot (explained earlier) was used to examine the distribution of intervals (that is numbers of intervening events) between consecutive uses of topic boundary symbols (see Figure 21) and conversation boundary symbols (see Figure 22).

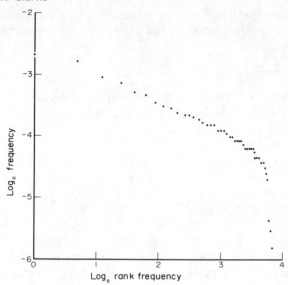

FIG. 20   'Zipf's Law' plot of frequencies of item use.

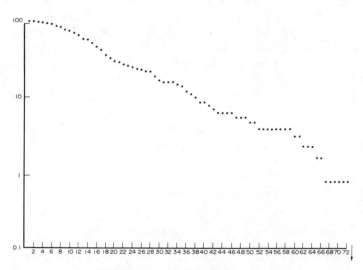

FIG. 21   Log survivor function. Distribution of run lengths between topic delimiters (excluding runs containing conversation delimiter).

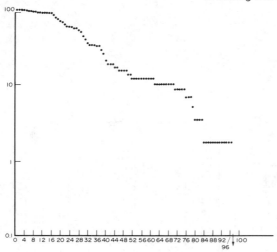

FIG. 22   Log survivor function. Distribution of run lengths
between conversation delimiters (excluding runs containing
script delimiter).

In so far as the curve for topic delimiters descends evenly, while that for conversation delimiters has an abrupt down-turn after about sixteen events these
graphs appear to indicate that, in this corpus at least, conversation length is
regulated, but topic length within individual conversations is not. This accords
with the intuition that there are many ways and reasons for saying that a conversation must end, but fewer for saying that while it may continue it is time
the topic were changed.

Cluster analysis

A separate transitional frequency matrix was drawn up for the reactive and
proactive relations in the sequences, and a computer 'concordance' produced for
all items. A cluster analysis of items was then calculated from their similarities of
use, taking all the cell values relating to any pair of items in the reactive and proactive transitional frequency matrices, and correlating them to give a measure of
similarity between that pair of items (see Figure 23). As discussed earlier this is
based on commutability, not similarity *per se* and hence 'syntactic categories'
emerge containing items with apparently different significance, but similar occasions of use such as comply and refuse, answer and defer, reject and accept. This
is as it should be, and a sign that the *post hoc* classification based on observed
sequences has worked correctly.

Transition mapping

In a further analysis a χ^2 value was calculated for each cell in the transitional

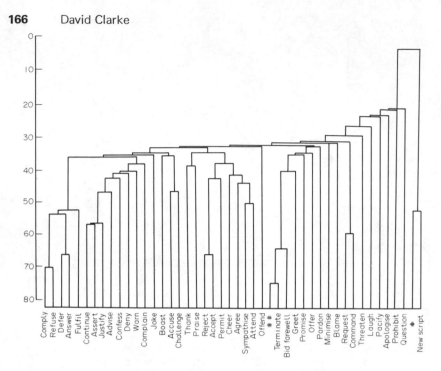

FIG. 23   Dendrogram of speech-act types.

frequency matrices with more than five entries, so that 'chains' of two commonly
related events could be detected. These two-events chains were then used with
the computer concordance of items to identify longer chains of related behaviour.
The most common chains were combined to show the conversation system as a
network, in which each node represents a type of utterance, each arrow a common transition, and each path through the network a possible conversational
format (see Figure 24).

It should be noted in this connection that any reassembly of long chains or
extended networks from small fragments has attendant dangers. In this case an
informal 'chain analysis' was carried out to discover any frequent n-item chains
in the raw data by replacing common pairs with a new symbol, adding a row and
column to the transition matrix and looking for a pair that includes that pair,
and so on (Dawkins, 1976). Even then chains of only a few items in length had
to be used to build the network in Figure 24, which cannot, therefore, be
guaranteed to represent all and only the common longer chains in the corpus.
This may even be an impractical objective *in principle* with such a diagram, since
it only shows first order relationships, and therefore distorts higher-order contingencies.

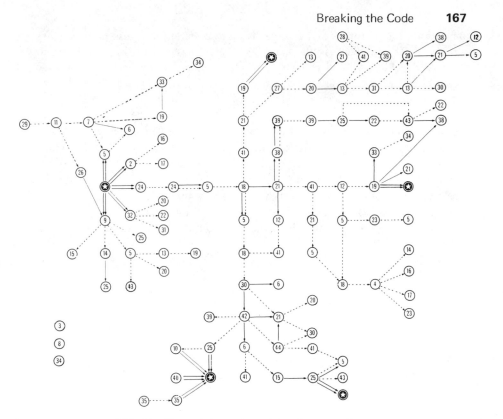

FIG. 24   Network map of transitions between utterances.

For instance, chains ABC and DBE would be mapped

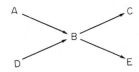

and the map read to imply the existence of ABE and DBC which are not in the 'data' of this example. Overall such transition maps, though not easily bettered, are far from ideal representations of nth order contingency, where $n > 1$.

Discussion

This study concludes the section using data-driven 'codebreaking' methods as such. Unlike the previous approach, which might be called 'secondary experimentation', the picture which emerges is more coherent, but also perhaps more superficial. The problem is this. A corpus of data has to be scanned for certain regularities which will be recorded, at the expense of others which will be ignored. The only real criterion for this, when it is done quantitatively and mechanically, is frequency of occurrence. In a commonplace phenomenon like desultory conversation the most frequently occurring regularities may seem the most banal to 'discover', and they need in no sense be more important than those discarded for being infrequent. In fields like animal ethology where similar methods are employed to better effect on the whole, common sense has less to say, and the likelihood that detailed studies will look disappointingly like a pale imitation of everyday know-how is correspondingly less.

It is now time to turn away from corpus-based methods to consider a more theoretically motivated approach to the investigation of sequential structure in discourse and action.

5

THEORIES AND MODELS
OF STRUCTURE

THE FIRST step in building a generative model of conversation structure will be
to introduce some new concepts and notations. This requires a rather different
approach from the empirical description of given sequences described in the
last chapter. Interesting though that can be, it still leaves us some way short of
a grammar of conversation, couched in the form of a system of interrelated
rules which will produce all and only the strings of sensible discourse. For that,
one would have to turn from the kinds of analysis described above, which
are ethological techniques, to the procedures of linguistic analysis as used by
generative grammarians. The latter approach differs from the former in two
striking ways. It is not corpus based. The complexity of the sequences is such
that one cannot record strings and then apply some routine procedure to unravel
their grammar although that is sometimes possible for sequences of animal
behaviour (Marshall, 1965). Instead the investigator has to postulate some kind
of underlying regularity of the generative rule system, from which predictions
may be made about the observed forms of behaviour. This is the familiar hypothetico-deductive methodology of most empirical sciences. Usually it has been
the case that linguists used the rules to predict what would and would not count
as a well-formed string, thus embarking on a kind of analysis by synthesis
(Neisser, 1967); while psycholinguists, in so far as they could interpret the rules
as descriptions of the generative mechanisms *in vivo*, used them to predict
variables such as response latency and accuracy on a variety of verbal tasks.
It is not standard practice in either discipline to collect large samples of spontaneous talk for analysis.

The second distinctive feature of 'linguistic analysis' is that it deals not only
with the observed items of behaviour known as *terminal elements* (because their
production marks the termination of their generative history) but also with
non-terminal elements. These are hypothetical units like *noun phrase,* and
sentence which feature in the rules for producing well-formed strings, but not
in the strings themselves. By using terminal and non-terminal vocabularies, such
a system can generate a hierarchical structure with any number of embedded
sub-units.

Let us now adopt the policy of attempting to synthesise rather than analyse the discourse system, and ask what kind of rules or processes one could imagine in a generative system for discourse, and how they could be represented. The representation is relatively easy using an extended version of Chomsky's rewriting rule system, in which notation it is possible to compare rules of a number of different kinds. Any generative process has to turn something into something else. It must have an initial state and a terminal state. The process serves to replace the former with the latter. Hence the archetype for all generative rules is one showing the replacement of one state of affairs with another, or one string rewritten to form a second. This was essentially Post's (1943) argument in setting up the rewriting rule as the basis of his canonical systems in which all symbol manipulating processes and disciplines could be represented in a similar format. We can write the generative rules in the form

$$A \rightarrow B$$

meaning A rewrites to, or is replaced by B. Clearly the basic generative processes must be *addition*

$$A \rightarrow A + B$$

deletion

$$A \rightarrow \emptyset$$

($\emptyset$ being the usual symbol for a null event, or empty set)

substitution

$$A \rightarrow B$$

and *transposition*

$$A + B \rightarrow B + A.$$

The addition rule as it stands is ambiguous:

$$A \rightarrow A + B$$

could mean that the rule is to be used recursively producing A, A + B, A + B + B, A + B + B + B, . . . which is the way such rules appear in Chomsky (1957); or as part of a Markov process in which A and B represent a succession of terminal elements, in which case any further rewriting must use rules beginning

$$B \rightarrow$$

or

$$A + B \rightarrow.$$

To make this quite clear it is necessary to use an additional symbol & to represent the 'growing point' of those strings which can only be rewritten at one locus. So, for example, the rule

$$A + \& \rightarrow A + B + \&$$

is quite unambiguous and cannot be used recursively. Indeed the symbol &

need not have any 'meaning' at all to work as a growing point marker provided it figures in the rules in the way shown above.

We can now represent a variety of different rules and processes in the same form for comparison. A simple Markov chain would be generated thus:

$$A + \& \to A + B + \&$$
$$B + \& \to B + C + \& \text{ and so on.}$$

More commonly the rules would provide for a variety of different rewritings so one would see

$$A + \& \to A + B + \&$$
$$\to A + C + \& \text{ and so on.}$$

Such a Markov process could be allowed to terminate at any point by the rules

$$\& \to \# \,(\# \text{ is the symbol for a string delimiter})$$
$$\# \to \emptyset$$

or it could be made to terminate only after some suitable event D by the rules

$$D + \& \to D + \#$$
$$\# \to \emptyset.$$

A higher-order linear stochastic process producing a type-3 language would use rules such as

$$A + B + \& \to A + B + C + \&.$$

The more elaborate languages all use some kind of tree structure or nesting system. These can be generated by recursive

$$A \to A + B$$

or non-recursive rules

$$A \to B + C.$$

Furthermore, the rules can be context free

$$A \to B$$

or context dependent

$$P + A + Q \to P + B + Q$$
$$R + A + S \to R + C + S.$$

Context-free rules characterise the type 2 language, and context-dependent rules characterise the type 1 language of Chomsky's classification.

Finally in the type O language, or transformational grammar, a system of base rules working by divergent substitution

$$A \to B + C$$

produces a deep structure, which is transformed to surface structure by complex rules combining the operations of addition, deletion, substitution and transposition:

$$A + B + C \rightarrow C + D + A.$$

One could also imagine a grammar containing rules of convergent substitution

$$A + B \rightarrow C.$$

Two other general classes of rule are worth considering here: rules which operate from left to right but allow for nesting

$$A + ( ) + \& \rightarrow A + ( ) + B + \&$$

and rules which work from left to right, erecting non-terminal items from terminals. These are of particular interest to the student of interaction, because they allow one to produce nested structures without their having the paradoxical quality of being derived by two people fron non-terminal antecedents which are never communicated. Such rules may easily be used in computer simulations, where the machine has only to detect the presence of a left half rule in an incomplete character string, and replace it with the corresponding right half. Furthermore, the rules may be different for each actor or persona, may have probabilities attached to their use, and use different behaviour categories for different roles, if need be.

One of the main advantages (and complications) of working with sequences is that so many disciplines have developed conceptual schemes, tools and notations for the description of sequential patterns and their origins. Cryptography and linguistics, genetics and embryology, strategic analysis and computing are all concerned with sequences of events, states and structures, and each has its own methods of analysis. The 1930s and 1940s were a particularly rich period during which time the foundations were laid for general systems theory and cybernetics, operations research and automata theory, and it is to disciplines like these that we must turn next to review very briefly some of the conceptual tools of the sequence analyst's trade.

General Systems Theory was the brainchild of a biologist, Ludwig von Bertalanfly, who was intrigued by the property of living organisms, that they seem more than a mere sum of their parts. The concept of a living *system*, later extended to other mechanical, socio-economic and abstract examples, introduced the idea of a trajectory of behaviour or of growth. That in turn requires for its exploration certain distinctions defining classes of system: open or closed, determinate or probabilistic, feed-back or open-loop, equilibrium or non-equilibrium, and so on. Each of these basic features can introduce complex configurations into the behavioural trajectory of a system, which can only be recognised and interpreted by knowing which system features can produce them.

Cybernetics, the study of self-regulating (usually negative feedback) systems, was christened by Norbert Wiener, after the Greek word for a steersman or helmsman. The property of self-navigation in the literal case of an automatic pilot, or the metaphorical case of a thermostat, depends on the detection and correction of discrepancies between intended and actual effects of behaviour. A *feedback loop* is created so that one of the inputs to the system tells it of the effects of its output, and stability is produced by *negative feedback,* in which excessive effects are used to counteract or limit their own causes. For example, as a room overheats the boiler is turned off, or as a plane drifts to starboard the rudder is turned to port.

Things are not quite that simple in reality. Simple feedback systems have a *lag.* They correct for things too late, and so they tend to *oscillate.* They may control the *position* of the target variable directly, or they may determine its *rate of change*, or *acceleration*, or some combination of these. When a car is in equilibrium its accelerator pedal position corresponds to its speed, in disequilibrium it corresponds to its acceleration or rate of change of speed.

The social skill model of social behaviour, like the motor skill model on which it was based is a cybernetic model with a feedback loop (Argyle, 1967). It predicts the automatic maintenance of equilibrium by compensatory reactions to change (the intimacy equilibrium hypothesis of Argyle and Dean, 1965). This is just one example of cybernetic explanation for sequential patterns of social behaviour.

Operations Research began in earnest during the Second World War as the application of scientific and mathematical methods to military (especially tactical) problems such as the optimisation of convoy sizes or equipment replacement schedules. Naval applications of mathematical analysis date back to at least the end of the last century with the calculation of Lanchester exchange ratios for naval battles. Aerial applications tend to be somewhat more complex because of the three-dimensional movement of aircraft, and land warfare is the hardest of all to model because of the irregularities of terrain.

Again the analysis, prediction and optimisation of sequences of events and behaviour turned out to be crucial as it has been in subsequent peaceful commercial uses of O.R. Game theory and decision analysis, both described in other sections of this book, are specific examples of O.R. methodology for the analysis of sequences and strategies. From these we get the concepts of *pay-off matrices, optimal* and *sup-optimal solutions*, *zero-sum* and *non-zero sum games*, the *minimax strategy*, the *minimisation of regret*, and the *saddle point.*

Markov Theory, or the analysis of probabilistic chain reactions, is of course crucial for the understanding of behaviour sequences. It is based on the idea that (certain) chains of events are defined by the transitional probabilities (or conditional probabilities) with which each possible event or state could follow previous events or states. The probabilities themselves are (or for this kind of analysis *should be*) constant. This is the property of *stationarity*. Some states have such a low probability of being followed by anything else that the system tends to get stuck in them. These are *absorbing states*. As the elapsed time tends to infinity, the probability that the system will have got into and stayed in one of these tends to the value 1.0. Markov mathematics provides various theorems and tools for calculating the likelihood that the system will end up in one state rather than another, the likelihood it will visit a given state in a given time from a given starting state, and so on. Useful though its concepts are, the methods of Markov analysis are seldom strictly applicable for the present purpose as their assumptions, like that of stationarity, rarely hold for interesting stretches of human social behaviour.

Automata Theory is the study of, and proof of, theorems about abstract (computer-like) machines (see especially Minsky, 1972). It arose largely from the work of the mathematician Turing, who was concerned to determine the limits of computability, or if you like the boundary between what all conceivable forms of mathematics could and could not do. In order to prove that some problems were impossible even for those branches of mathematics which were yet to be invented, he had to find a way of characterising these, and finding the limits of their calculating power in generic form. To do this he invented a hypothetical device, now called a Turing machine, which is rather like an imaginary computer, although computers as we now know them had not been invented then. All calculations can be described as a mapping from one string of symbols to another, by a series of steps or transformations. A similar formulation in terms of rewriting rules was being created at about this time by Post, and it was this which was to provide the basis and the format for Chomsky's linguistic system. Although most people are used to carrying out such transformations on sheets of two-dimensional paper (often ruled into squares in the early days of school arithmetic), Turing was able to show that all the same calculations could be carried out on a one-dimensional page, or paper tape, also ruled into squares with one character per square, provided it was infinitely long. The other component of a Turing machine is a hypothetical 'head', rather like the recording and playback head of a tape-recorder, which contains a small finite state machine. This can read whatever symbol is on the adjacent square of tape, and according to the symbol it finds, and its own previous state, move the tape a specified distance either way, write a new symbol in that square and go into a new state. The essential rules that the machine follows, or which specify in abstract what it is, are of the form 'if you are in state q_i and you find the symbol s_j move d_{ij} squares, write the symbol s_{ij} and go into state q_{ij}'. (The subscripts simply indicate that state q_i and input s_j determine the values of q_{ij}, s_{ij} and d_{ij}.) These groups of five specifications or quintuples can be abbreviated to:

$$(q_{i1}, s_{j1}, q_{ij1}, s_{ij1}, d_{ij1})$$
$$(q_{i2}, s_{j2}, q_{ij2}, s_{ij2}, d_{ij2}) \text{ and so on.}$$

When built into the finite state component of the head they specify the function of that particular Turing machine and enable it to carry out the corresponding family of computations. But there is a marvellous twist to all this. The quintuples, the specification of how the machine is to operate, indeed what machine it is to be, can be *written onto the tape,* leaving the head itself with a bare minimum of rules allowing it to read that section of tape and refer back to it for each new instruction. In other words, it can follow what is written on the tape as a program. This is now called a Universal Turing Machine.

This twist in the story has various striking consequences. Firstly it sets the scene for the invention of the programmable digital computer as a real physical machine. Secondly, it provides the mathematical tools and the format for theorems of computability. But most importantly from our point of view it gives a language — the quintuples and their finite state interpreter — in which any possible kind of determinate sequential pattern can be described and produced, no matter how complex.

This may seem like taking a sledgehammer to crack a nut. Attractive though brain/automaton comparisons are, it is often argued that the brain, though large, is not infinite, and certainly not set out like Turing's imaginary machine. Would not a simpler version be adequate? And the answer seems to be 'yes' in most cases. If a series of restrictions are added to the Turing machine then simpler versions called *linear bounded automata, push-down stack automata* and *finite state automata* are created. Together with the Turing machine itself, these correspond to Chomsky's four main classes of grammar called types 0, 1, 2 and 3 according to the number of additional restrictions on their Turing equivalent (the full transformational grammar) which is needed to produce them.

The finite state machine or type-3 grammar is of special interest for many analysts of behaviour sequences. It can be specified without a tape, as a set of rules according to which each combination of a state and an input will produce a particular next state and next output. These quadruples, which take the form

$$q_i, s_j, q_{ij}, s_{ij},$$

are best pictured as a state-space diagram in which, as the name suggests, different points in space represent different states as in Figure 25.

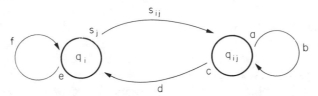

The quadruple q_i, s_j, q_{ij}, s_{ij} is represented, meaning: if in state q_i, and input is s_j, go to state q_{ij}, outputting s_{ij}. Represented with arbitrary letters, the remaining quadruples of this system are:

$$q_{ij}, a, q_{ij}, b$$
$$q_{ij}, c, q_i, d$$
$$q_i, e, q_i, f$$

FIG. 25   State-space diagram.

Although much simpler and more manageable than Turing-machine notation, this is also a powerful representation of families of sequential possibilities – behaviour grammars – which can distinguish patterns which stochastic or Markovian treatments cannot. For example, a finite state system can represent and reproduce sequential dependencies of indefinitely (although not infinitely) high order, quite economically.

Artificial intelligence. It is a natural progression from the use of hypothetical computers to model behaviour patterns, to the use of real ones, and an interesting step whether the goal is pragmatic – to produce more 'intelligent' machines by some means or other – or scientific – to set up and test models of human intelligent activity using computers as a tool.

Artificial intelligence (see, for example, Boden, 1977) has produced a number of notations and formats appropriate to the modelling of behaviour sequences, whether implemented on computers or not. In particular these have arisen from work on the computer processing of natural language. *Production systems*, for example, are sets of circumstance action pairs, usually written

$$C \Rightarrow A$$

meaning *if condition C is satisfied, then do action A.* Lists of these form a very straightforward 'program notation' for behavioural rules and grammars. The individual productions (rules) are relatively independent of one another and can be investigated separately in a way that most model elements cannot.

Behavioural rules can be complex and their conditions often require a number of logical operations like *and, or* and *not* to specify them. Winograd (1972) produced an elegant notation for representing such conditions graphically in which] means *and,* and | means *or.* So

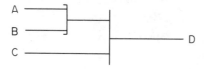

would mean *if (A and B) or C, then D.* In this way the interrelationship of sequencing rules can be represented in a kind of logical 'circuit diagram'.

Woods' (1970) system for natural language parsing provides another powerful sequence modelling notation. Called RATN's for recursive augmented transition networks, these are like the state space diagrams shown above, except that they are augmented to leave a structured trace of any path they follow successfully through the system, which then becomes the final parsing description of that sentence. They are also recursive, in the sense that a piece of the network can refer to the whole within which it is embedded. For example, one stage in testing for the well-formedness of a sentence can be to see if a sub-component of that sentence is a complete sentence in its own right. This is done by having a transition map for the 'outer' sentence, one node of which is an instruction to pause and use that whole map again as a sub-component of itself, in determining whether the sub-string at that point is also a sentence. Newell and Simon's (1972) treatment of problem-solving strategies and their computer simulation has also produced concepts and notations relevant to the analysis of action sequences, such as the problem-behaviour graph or PBG, and the distinction between depth-first and breadth-first search strategies.

Generative linguistics is a source of so many concepts and notations for behavioural sequence analysts that it has been made the subject of a chapter in its own right.

Although it has not been possible to do them justice here, conceptual schemata like these will be absolutely essential if the study of behaviour sequences is to be put on a sounder and more coherent theoretical footing.

Readers who are unfamiliar with the ideas mentioned in the last few sections will find a good introduction by reading Waddington (1977), Beishon (1971), Ashby (1956), and Alexander (1977). A most entertaining presentation of similar concepts is also to be found in Hofstadter (1979), where the ideas are partly described, partly illustrated, and partly woven into the structure of the text itself, in a kind of self-illustrating figure.

Theoretical physics may also be a useful source of ideas, in trying to pin down the elusive line of demarcation between the forms which behaviour sequences can and cannot take.

Symmetry is always an important concept in any science of structure, but it has recently been discovered that the great symmetries of the natural world are inextricably linked to its conservations. Neither could occur without the other.

The translation symmetry of natural laws necessarily implies conservation of linear momentum. Likewise, rotational symmetry goes hand in hand with conservation of angular momentum, and temporal symmetry with conservation of energy. The moral of this story is that the detection of symmetries, or variables over which the fundamental properties of the system are constant, tells us much more about its basic organising principles than might be expected.

One very peculiar symmetry seems to characterise sequences of human social action, and that is fractal symmetry or scale invariance. It has the property shared by certain structures in nature, like the edge of an ice crystal or the profile of a coastline, that its shape appears the same over a range of magnifications. A picture of the water's edge where the sea meets the land has a shape when traced from which you cannot tell whether the picture was taken from a few hundred metres or a few hundred kilometres. Similarly the description of action sequences often takes a form in which a few minutes' conversation between two individuals could not be distinguished from a decade of exchanges between two nations. Consider the following:

. . . by this time a stalemate had been reached. The demands of one side, backed up as they were by threats of an unreasonable and vindictive kind, could only be held in check by a counter-threat, that if any further action were taken then revenge would follow.

In a way the plot is quite explicit. The structure of the dilemma is made quite clear. It is not just by virtue of vagueness of description that this account, and other more detailed elaborations of it, could describe a play-ground squabble or a cold war. Rather it is that the overall units, and principles of combination, that make up concerted periods of action, conflicts, projects and plans are much the same on any scale. This idea has already been used extensively as a justification for the approach taken in this book, of studying in the micro-social world those sources of pattern and regularity that we most need to understand on the macro-social scale. But the suggestion raised by the implications of physical symmetry goes much further than that. There is an exciting, but as yet unexplored theoretical possibility, that the mere existence of invariances in behaviour organising principles despite differences of scale, will specify to a large degree what these principles must be.

The interrelation of effects over different levels of description and different scales has always been a problem in science, but recently the mathematics of renormalisation groups has been put forward as a possible tool for tackling problems such as this (Wilson, 1979; Llewellyn-Smith, personal communication).

Now that the basic vocabulary of generative rule modelling has been introduced, it is time to build some tentative models of discourse structure, starting with simple *a priori* versions in this chapter, and then going on to base more detailed models on particular conversational situations in the next chapter.

The starting-point is a simple Markovian structure whose rules can be described in the rewriting notation introduced earlier. First-order rules of the form

$$A + \& \rightarrow A + B + \&$$

are used in the next study to specify proactive relations between speech-act types, while reactive sequences, involving a speaker change (/), are controlled by second-order rules:

$$A + / + \& \rightarrow A + / + B + \&.$$

The speaker changes themselves are inserted by first-order rules in the proactive system:

$$A + \& \rightarrow A + / + \&.$$

Experiment 14: A Simple Rule Model

Introduction

The purpose of this experiment is to bring together the *a priori* category scheme and the procedures for sequence analysis discussed earlier, to evaluate both together in a single experiment on the syntax of conversation. The experiment worked by synthesising strings rather than by analysing them. Three sets of utterance strings were made up, a set of artificial sequences derived from the rule model being tested which was called *Backchat*, and a second set from a random procedure using the same categories. This procedure was called *Joker*. The strings produced by Joker were to function as a lower-limit control, so that the ordering of items produced by the grammar could be compared with a random series. The third group was made up by subjects using the same category list to represent ideal, perfectly acceptable conversations. This was the upper-limit control.

There were two hypotheses. The first was that the Control strings would be rated as significantly better than those produced by Joker. This was an important aspect of the experiment as the strings were all presented to the subjects as sequences of abstract categories in the form

A   Invite
B   Accept   Question
A   Answer.

This was unfamiliar to the subjects, and could have been the wrong way to elicit judgements about sequencing rules. To establish then, that subjects can use information in this form to assess how meaningful a general class of conversations would be, without being given any complete examples, one must first be sure that they can detect the gross distinction between the random and 'perfect' strings with ease.

The second hypothesis was that the rule governed strings produced by Backchat would be rated as significantly better than those produced by Joker. In a way this was an easy test. The least one might expect of a rule system is that it represents the world more accurately than a random string does. In practice the result is only of use if it is very significant. Once a first attempt at a grammar has been tested against a random control, it can serve as a further baseline for testing improved versions and so on. In this way a succession of more and more sophisticated grammars could be produced, each tested against its predecessor, so that as the grammars themselves became more refined, the tests to which they were subjected would also become more stringent.

The representation of the strings to the judges was a problem. Backchat, Joker and Control were all produced in the form shown above. The original plan was to give those strings to an intermediate group of subjects who would see them one item at a time and turn them into specific transcripts. They might be shown

A   Question
B   Answer

for example, and realise those as

A   Do you have change for a pound?
B   Yes, I have some silver right here.

This procedure was followed in a pilot study in which the intermediate subject group (the translators of categories to sentences) worked blindly not knowing which strings were supposed to be sensible and which were random. They were asked to rate the difficulty they had in thinking of a sensible example of each. The examples were then passed to a 'blind' group of judges. The *judges'* ratings showed no clear difference between Backchat and Joker, but there was a very clear pattern in the *translators'* ratings of *difficulty*. They had found it much harder to realise the random strings sensibly, although with effort and often at the expense of the exact category definitions they had succeeded. In so doing they had obliterated precisely those differences between Backchat and Joker which the experiment was supposed to detect. So the utterance category strings were presented to judges directly in the final version of the experiment.

It must be remembered that an experiment of this kind is made more or less convincing by the specificity of its predictions. It is no great feat to find a perfect correspondence between artificial and natural strings if the coding categories are few enough and simple enough. To take an extreme case, a system with only two categories, such as *speak* and *reply* let us say, would be simple to use in a grammar, but the predictions could be so general as to be worthless. Hypothesis 1 is a safeguard against this to some extent, since a category system which is grossly oversimplified cannot even express the distinction between extremes of sense and nonsense.

The grammar itself, Backchat, is very primitive. It is a Markov system with a few elaborations, made up according to the conversational institutions of the author. It produces dialogue consisting of forty-three speech act categories, together with the symbols # (the string delimiter) and / (for speaker change). The use of a separate symbol for / allows each speaker to use more than one speech act per turn-at-talking. The rules are all of the form

A + & → A + B + & (rules of proaction) or
A + / + & → A + / + B + & (rules of reaction).

The reactive rules are the only departure from a simple Markov model. The rules are presented here in the form of a matrix to save space. The proactive matrix represents the rule

A + & → A + B + &

as a 1 in the cell where row A and column B intersect. All the matrices presented in conjunction with this experiment follow the convention of using rows for antecedents and columns for sequiturs. In the proactive matrix column 45 shows that the speaker change / can occur after certain speech acts. In some cases the symbol 1+ occurs in the cell, showing that whenever that row is entered the speaker change will be selected with a probability of 0.5. Had this provision not been made, the strings would have consisted mainly of long monologues. If when working from the proactive matrix the generator encountered the symbol / it then transferred control to the reactive matrix to find which sequiturs were available reactively for the antecedent labelling that row. In this way rules of the form

$$A + / + \& \rightarrow A + / + B + \&$$

were used to control reactive contingencies. The matrices of proactive and reactive rules which made up Backchat are shown in Figures 26 and 27.

SEQUITUR NUMBERS

```
ANTECEDENT NUMBERS 0000000001111111111222222222233333333334444444
                   1234567890123456789012345678901234567890123456
                   ..............................................
 1  #            0111111101000000000000000100000001001000000000011+
 2  Command      0000000001101000000000000000000000000000000000001+
 3  Prohibit     0000000101101000000000000000000000000000000000001+
 4  Request      0000000010010000000000000000000000000000000000001ı
 5  Question     0000000000000000000000000000000000000000000000001
 6  Advise       0000000000010000000000000000000000000000000000001+
 7  Warn         0000000000010000000000000000000000000000000000001+
 8  Permit       0011011000000000000000000000000000000000000000001+
 9  Offer        0000000000000000000000000000000000000000000000001
10  Promise      0000000000000000010000000000000000000000000000001+
11  Threaten     0000000000101000000000000000000000000010000000001+
12  Assert       0000100000000000000100000000000000000000000000001+
13  Justify      0000000000000000000000000000000000000000000000001
14  Accept       0000000000000000010001000000000000000000000000001+
15  Reject       0000000000010000000000010000000100000000000000001
16  Comply       1000100000000000000000000000000000000000100000001+
17  Refuse       0000000000100000000000000100000010000000000000001
18  Answer       0000100000000000010000000000000000000010000000001+
19  Agree        0000000000000000010000000000000000000000000000001+
20  Deny         0000000000110000000000000000001000001000100000001
21  Continue     0000000000000000010000000000000000000000000000001+
22  Praise       0000000000000000000000000000000000000000000000001
23  Defer        0000000000100000000000000000000010001000000000001
24  Greet        1000000000000000000000000000000000000000000000001
25  Thank        1000000001000000000010000000000000000000000000001+
26  Blame        0000000000010000000000000100000000000100000000001+
27  Accuse       0000001000010000000000010000000000000000000000001+
28  Confess      0000000001000000000000000000000001001000000000001
29  Offend       0100000001000000000000010100000000000000000000001+
30  Sympathise   0000000110000000010000000000000001000001001+
31  Challenge    0000000000000000000000000000000000000000000000001
32  Boast        0000000000010000001000000000100000000000000000001+
33  Apologise    0000000110010000000000000000000000000000000000001+
34  Pardon       0000011000000000000000000000010000000001000001+
35  Bid farewell 1000000000000000000000000000000000000000000000001+
36  Pacify       0100011000001000000000000001000000000000000000001+
37  Fulfil       1000000000000000000000000000000000000000000000000
38  Joke         0000000000000000000000000000000000000001000001+
39  Laugh        0000000000000000000000000000000000000111000001+
40  Terminate    1000000000000000000000000000000000000000000000000
41  Attend       0000000000000000000000000000000000000000000000001
42  Cheer        0000100110000000000000000000000000000000000000001+
43  Minimise     0000000000000000000000000000000000000000000000001
44  Complain     0000000000000000010000000000000000000000000011+
45  /            0000000000000000000000000000000000000000000000000
```

FIG. 26   Proactive rule matrix.

SEQUITUR NUMBERS

```
ANTECEDENT NUMBERS 000000000111111111122222222223333333333444444
                   123456789012345678901234567890123456789012345
                   .............................................
 1  #              011111111000000000000000000000000001000000010
 2  Command        011010101110000110000010000000000000000000000
 3  Prohibit       011010101110000110000010000000000000000000000
 4  Request        000010001100000110000010000000000000000000000
 5  Question       000010000000000110000000000000000000000000000
 6  Advise         000010000000011000000001000000000000000000000
 7  Warn           000010000000011000000000100000000000000000000
 8  Permit         000000000000011000000001000000000000000000000
 9  Offer          000010000000011000000001000000000000000000000
10  Promise        000010100000011000000001000000000000000000000
11  Threaten       001010100010000000000001000000001000000000000
12  Assert         000010000000000111000000000000000000010000000
13  Justify        000010000000011000000000000000100000000000000
14  Accept         100000000000000000000010000000000000100000000
15  Reject         010011100000000000000010000000000000000000000
16  Comply         100000000000000000000100100000000000100000000
17  Refuse         010111100010000000000010000000000100010000010
18  Answer         000010000000000001110000000000000000110000000
19  Agree          100000000000000000010000000000000000100000000
20  Deny           000010000000100000011000010000000000000000000
21  Continue       000010000000000001110000000000000000000000000
22  Praise         000000000000000000010000000000000000000000100
23  Defer          000010000000011000000001000000000000000000000
24  Greet          100000000000000000000010000000000000000000000
25  Thank          100000000000000000000000000000000000000000100
26  Blame          000000000001000011000000000010000000000000000
27  Accuse         000010000000000010000001000000000000000000000
28  Confess        000010000000000000000011000000100000000000000
29  Offend         001010100010000000000001101000000100000000000
30  Sympathise     000000000000000000010010000000000000000000000
31  Challenge      000010000000110000000000010000000000000000000
32  Boast          000010100000000000000001100110000000000000000
33  Apologise      000000000001100000000000000001000001000000000
34  Pardon         100000000000000000010000000000000000000000000
35  Bid farewell   100000000000000000000000000000001000000000000
36  Pacify         000000000100000000000011001000000000000000000
37  Fulfil         000000000000000000000000000000000000000000000
38  Joke           000000000000000000000000000000000000011000000
39  Laugh          100000000000000000000000000000000000011100000
40  Terminate      000000000000000000000000000000000000000000000
41  Attend         000000000000000001000000000000000000000000000
42  Cheer          000000000000000000001000000000000011000000000
43  Minimise       100000000000000000000000000000000000000100000
44  Complain       000011001100000000000001000100000100000100000
45  /              000000000000000000000000000000000000000000000
```

FIG. 27   Matrix of reactive rules.

Method

Three groups of strings were produced for comparison and ratings by judges. One group was derived from the grammar (Backchat), one group contained random strings (Joker) and one group was produced by subjects, who arranged categories according to their definitions to represent typical sequences (Control). There were ten examples of each dialogue type, each ten items in length, not counting episode boundaries #. The categories and their definitions are given in Appendix D.

The ten Backchat strings were produced in the following way. Each started from an episode boundary #. The proactive matrix showed which items could follow #. One of these was selected at random (using a table of random numbers in Fisher and Yates, 1963) to become the first item in the string. There was a probability of 0.5 (again introduced by the random number tables) that a / would follow # and the first item would be drawn from the reactive table. This first item was then used to locate a row of the proactive table in which its sequiturs were recorded. One of these was selected at random to become the second item, and so on until ten separate strings of ten items in length had been produced.

The ten Joker strings were produced by selecting items at random from the forty-four possibilities (excluding /) to make up ten item strings. So as to avoid long monologues which would have resulted if / had only had a probability of 1/45 of occurring at any point, it was given a probability of 0.5 of occurrence after *every* speech act. Examples of the strings used in the experiment are shown in the transcripts in Appendix E.

An important failing of first-order rule systems can be seen in the output strings from Backchat. *Question* was specified as a legitimate sequitur to *Question* in accordance with earlier results on question–answer nesting. But for a first-order rule system such an association is recursive, so long sequences of unanswered questions can be formed. The difficulty can only be overcome with more elaborate rule schemes.

The thirty examples were typed on to file cards, each with a randomly assigned code number by which subjects could identify it on their response sheet. Each of the ten subjects rated the thirty examples for plausibility, in a different order and without knowing about the three different types.

Results

The experiment was treated as a three-factor design: 3 dialogue types or C(onditions) $\times$ 10 E(xamples) $\times$ 10 S(ubjects). C was a fixed effect, E was a random effect nested in C and therefore represented as E(C), and S was a random effect fully crossed with C and E(C). This is the design that was used in Experiment 5, and a description of its analysis may be found in Chapter 2. The data were analysed using the statistical program for analysis of variance BMD 8V (Dixon, 1973: 693–704). The results of the analysis are shown in Table 8.

F' for the main effect C (the three dialogue types) = 29.02; df = 2, 25; $p<0.001$. (The critical value of F for df = 2, 25; α = 0.001 is 9.22.)

F''_C = 25.26; df = 2, 33; $p<0.001$. (Critical value for df = 2, 30; α = 0.001 is 8.77.)

The other main effect, that of examples, gives an F ratio of $F_{E(C)}$ = 6.69; df = 27, 243; $p<0.001$. (Critical value for df = 24, 120; α = 0.001 is 2.40.)

The mean ratings for the three dialogue types are plotted in Figure 28.

TABLE 8   *Experiment 14. Analysis of variance*

Source	SS	df	MS
Mean	5729	1	5729
S	74.56	9	8.285
C	488.5	2	244.3
E(C)	235.9	27	8.737
S × C	17.73	18	0.9848
S × E(C)	317.2	243	1.306

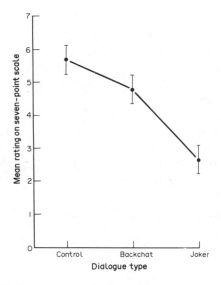

FIG. 28   Mean rating of three dialogue types on seven-point scale.

The confidence interval of 0.84 shown is the least significant difference interval for $p < 0.05$ (two-tailed) from Fisher's LSD multiple comparison test (Kirk, 1968: 87).

Two further calculations were done on the matrices of 0s and 1s making up the grammar Backchat itself. These both describe systematic properties of the grammar and make it easier to summarize its overall form.

The first calculation was a cluster analysis. The paradigmatic structure of the grammar, the way in which items may exchange for each other in particular contexts is related to the syntagmatic structure, the way in which items combine to form strings. The proactive and reactive rule matrices summarise the syntagmatic structure of Backchat. The paradigmatic structure may be represented in the following way. Any pair of items will share some of their permissible occasions of use and not others. (In the extreme cases they may share all or none of each other's occasions of use.) So the similarity between items in the way they form combinations may be measured by counting the number of occasions of use they share. An occasion of use includes both the sequiturs two items may share and the antecedents they may share. For example, if AB and AC are permissible sequences then one occasion of use is shared by B and C, also if *XZ* and *YZ* are permissible sequences then *X* and *Y* share an occasion of use. Such a similarity measure could be misleading if two quite dissimilar items were represented as similar because of all the occasions of use which apply to neither. So the matrix of 0s and 1s cannot be processed simply by counting the number of times that a 1 corresponds to a 1, and a 0 to a 0, for any two pairs of items. Instead the following expression was used. If the set of occasions of use appropriate to an item A is *a*, the set of occasions of use appropriate to B is *b*, and the set of occasions of use appropriate to A and B is *ab*, then

$$\frac{100ab}{a + b - ab}$$

is the percentage of occasions of use applying to A or B which applies to both A and B. In other words, it is the intersection of the two sets expressed as a percentage of their union. A special program was written to process the matrices of proactive and reactive rules, and print a similarity matrix for every pair of items. The results of this program were used in a single linkage cluster analysis performed by hand, and summarised in the dendrogram in Figure 29.

The other calculation was a critical path analysis. The rule matrices of Backchat were constructed in such a way that every item or state of the system could be reached from every other. This is not always the case and it would be quite possible to devise similar matrices in which discrete 'islands' of activity could each be toured internally, but none could be reached from any other. In this case, while every state can be reached from every other state, the least number of transitions required differs from one pair of states to another. A further program was written to examine the proactive and reactive rule matrices and print out for every pair of items the shortest path length between then. This is an asymmetrical matrix since the shortest distance from A to B is not necessarily the same length as the shortest path from B to A. The results of this analysis are summarised in Table 9. Category 45 has no sequiturs as such and hence no specific path lengths attached to it.

Discussion

The hypotheses were confirmed. There is significant variance accounted for by the three different dialogue types. The control dialogues were given the highest rating, followed by Backchat, with Joker last. Backchat was rated as being worse than the control set, by a difference of 0.89 between means on the

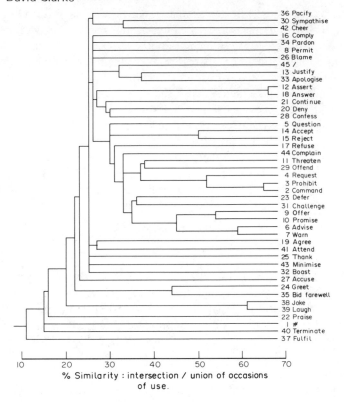

FIG. 29   Cluster analysis.

seven-point ratings scale, which is just significant at 0.05 (critical value 0.84). Joker was rated as worse than Backchat by 2.15 which is significant on the LSD test at 0.001 (critical value 1.53), and of course Joker is also worse than the Control condition ($p<0.001$).

So, as predicted, the control strings are seen as much more realistic than random ones. Subjects can make such judgements reliably even when presented with information in this abstract form, and with the particular category set which was used. The artificial strings produced by Backchat were given significantly higher ratings than those produced by Joker, while appearing to be worse than the control strings by a margin which is only just significant.

The variance due to the differences between examples was also significant ($p<0.001$), but the examples effect reached this level of significance by a much smaller margin than the effect of the three dialogue types.

The cluster analysis demonstrates several interesting features of Backchat. No two items are identical in their occasions of use. This is the criterion which was chosen at the outset for deciding when two categories should be regarded

TABLE 9   *Minimum path analysis*

SEQUITUR NUMBERS

```
ANTECEDENT NUMBERS  0 0 0 0 0 0 0 0 0 1 1 1 1 1 1 1 1 1 1 2 2 2 2 2 2 2 2 2 2 3 3 3 3 3 3 3 3 3 3 4 4 4 4 4 4
                    1 2 3 4 5 6 7 8 9 0 1 2 3 4 5 6 7 8 9 0 1 2 3 4 5 6 7 8 9 0 1 2 3 4 5 6 7 8 9 0 1 2 3 4 5
                    . . . . . . . . . . . . . . . . . . . . . . . . . . . . . . . . . . . . . . . . . . . . .
 1  #               2 1 1 1 1 1 1 1 1 1 2 2 4 2 2 2 2 2 2 3 3 2 3 2 1 2 2 2 3 3 2 2 1 3 3 1 2 3 3 3 3 3 2 3 1 1
 2  Command         2 1 1 2 1 2 1 2 1 1 1 1 4 1 2 2 1 1 2 3 3 2 2 1 3 2 2 4 5 3 3 4 3 2 2 3 2 2 4 4 2 3 3 3 2 1
 3  Prohibit        2 1 1 2 1 2 1 1 1 1 1 4 1 2 2 1 1 2 3 3 2 2 2 3 2 2 4 5 3 3 4 3 2 2 3 2 2 4 4 2 3 3 3 2 1
 4  Request         2 2 3 2 1 2 2 3 1 1 2 4 1 2 2 1 1 2 3 3 2 2 1 3 2 2 4 5 3 3 4 3 2 2 3 2 2 4 4 2 2 3 3 2 1
 5  Question        3 2 3 2 1 2 2 4 3 3 2 3 2 3 3 3 1 1 2 2 2 3 3 4 3 2 4 5 5 5 5 4 2 3 4 3 3 4 4 2 2 3 4 2 1
 6  Advise          2 2 3 3 1 2 2 3 3 2 3 4 1 1 1 3 2 2 3 3 2 2 3 3 1 2 4 5 3 3 4 3 2 2 3 4 4 5 5 2 3 4 2 3 1
 7  Warn            2 2 3 3 1 2 2 3 3 2 3 4 1 1 1 3 2 3 3 3 2 2 3 3 1 2 4 5 3 3 4 3 2 2 3 4 4 5 5 2 3 4 2 3 1
 8  Permit          2 2 1 1 2 1 2 2 2 2 4 2 1 1 2 2 3 3 2 2 2 1 2 4 5 3 4 4 3 2 3 3 3 3 5 5 2 4 4 2 3 1
 9  Offer           2 2 3 3 1 2 2 3 2 3 4 2 1 1 3 2 2 3 3 2 2 3 3 1 2 4 5 3 4 4 3 2 3 3 4 4 5 5 2 3 4 2 3 1
10  Promise         2 2 3 3 1 2 1 3 3 2 3 3 2 1 1 3 2 2 2 2 1 2 3 3 1 2 4 5 3 4 4 3 2 3 3 4 4 5 5 2 3 4 2 3 1
11  Threaten        2 2 1 3 1 2 1 2 2 2 1 3 1 2 2 2 2 2 2 2 3 3 3 3 2 1 3 4 2 2 4 3 2 2 3 1 1 4 4 2 3 3 3 3 1
12  Assert          2 3 3 3 1 3 3 3 3 3 2 2 3 3 4 2 2 1 1 1 2 4 3 3 2 4 5 3 4 4 3 3 2 3 4 4 4 5 5 2 1 4 3 3 1
13  Justify         2 2 3 3 1 2 2 3 3 2 3 3 4 2 1 1 3 2 2 3 3 2 2 2 4 5 3 2 4 3 2 1 3 3 4 4 4 2 3 3 3 3 1
14  Accept          1 2 2 2 2 2 2 2 2 2 3 3 3 3 3 3 3 2 2 1 1 3 2 1 3 3 4 4 3 3 2 3 4 2 3 4 4 4 1 4 3 2 2 1
15  Reject          2 1 2 3 1 1 1 3 2 2 2 3 1 2 2 2 2 2 2 2 5 2 2 3 1 1 3 4 2 3 4 3 1 2 3 3 3 5 5 2 3 4 2 3 1
16  Comply          1 2 2 2 1 2 2 2 2 4 3 3 3 3 2 2 3 3 3 1 3 2 1 3 3 4 4 3 3 2 3 4 2 3 4 4 4 1 3 3 2 2 1
17  Refuse          2 1 2 1 1 1 1 3 2 2 1 3 1 2 2 2 2 2 2 2 2 3 2 3 2 1 3 4 2 2 4 3 1 2 3 2 2 3 3 1 3 2 3 1 1
18  Answer          2 3 3 3 1 3 3 3 3 3 2 2 3 3 4 2 2 1 1 1 2 4 3 3 2 4 5 3 4 4 3 2 3 3 4 4 5 5 1 1 4 3 3 1
19  Agree           1 2 2 2 2 2 2 2 2 3 3 3 3 3 3 3 3 3 2 2 1 1 3 2 2 3 3 4 4 3 3 2 3 4 2 3 4 4 4 1 4 3 2 2 1
20  Deny            2 3 3 3 1 3 3 3 2 2 3 1 1 2 2 4 2 2 2 1 1 1 2 4 3 3 2 4 5 3 4 2 1 2 3 3 4 5 5 1 2 4 4 1
21  Continue        2 3 3 3 1 3 3 3 3 3 2 2 3 3 4 2 2 1 1 1 2 4 3 3 2 4 5 3 4 4 3 2 3 3 4 4 5 5 2 3 4 3 3 1
22  Praise          2 3 3 3 3 3 3 3 3 2 4 5 4 3 3 4 4 4 4 3 2 4 3 1 4 4 5 5 4 4 3 4 5 3 4 5 5 5 2 5 4 1 3 1
23  Defer           2 2 3 3 1 2 2 3 2 2 3 4 1 1 1 3 2 2 3 3 2 2 3 3 2 2 4 5 3 3 4 3 1 2 3 4 1 5 5 2 3 4 3 3 1
24  Greet           1 2 2 2 2 2 2 2 2 3 3 5 3 3 3 3 3 3 4 4 3 4 3 1 3 3 3 4 4 3 2 4 3 2 4 2 3 4 4 4 4 4 3 2 1
25  Thank           1 2 2 2 2 2 2 2 2 1 3 4 3 2 2 3 3 3 3 3 3 2 1 3 2 2 3 3 4 4 3 3 2 3 4 2 3 4 4 4 2 4 3 1 2 1
26  Blame           2 2 2 3 2 3 2 3 2 2 2 2 1 2 2 3 3 3 1 1 2 2 3 3 3 2 2 3 1 3 4 3 1 2 3 2 3 5 5 1 3 4 3 3 1
27  Accuse          3 3 3 3 1 3 1 4 3 2 3 2 1 2 2 4 2 2 2 1 2 3 4 4 2 1 3 1 2 3 5 4 2 2 4 2 4 5 5 2 3 4 3 3 1
28  Confess         2 2 3 3 1 2 2 3 2 1 3 3 1 2 3 2 2 2 2 2 2 2 3 3 1 1 3 4 2 2 4 3 1 1 3 1 4 4 4 2 3 3 3 2 1
29  Offend          3 1 1 3 1 2 1 2 2 2 1 3 2 2 2 2 2 2 2 2 3 3 2 4 2 1 1 2 1 2 5 4 2 3 4 1 2 4 4 2 3 3 3 3 1
30  Sympathise      2 2 3 3 2 2 2 3 1 1 3 4 2 2 2 3 3 3 1 3 2 1 3 3 1 2 3 4 2 2 4 3 3 3 3 1 4 2 2 2 4 1 2 3 1
31  Challenge       2 2 3 3 1 2 2 3 3 4 2 1 1 3 2 2 3 3 2 2 3 3 2 2 4 1 2 3 3 4 2 1 2 3 3 4 4 5 5 2 3 4 3 3 1
32  Boast           3 3 3 3 1 3 1 4 3 3 3 3 1 2 2 4 2 2 2 2 1 3 4 4 2 1 1 2 2 3 1 1 2 2 4 5 5 2 3 4 3 3 1
33  Apologise       2 2 3 3 2 2 2 3 1 1 3 4 1 1 1 3 3 3 3 3 2 2 3 3 2 2 4 5 3 2 4 3 2 1 3 3 4 4 4 1 4 3 3 3 1
34  Pardon          1 2 2 2 2 1 1 2 2 2 3 5 2 2 2 3 3 3 2 4 3 2 3 2 1 3 3 4 3 4 3 2 3 3 2 2 4 3 3 1 4 2 2 2 1
35  Bid farewell    1 2 2 2 2 2 2 2 3 5 3 3 3 3 3 3 3 4 4 3 4 3 2 3 3 3 4 4 3 3 2 4 3 1 3 4 4 4 4 4 4 3 2 1
36  Pacify          2 1 2 3 2 1 1 3 2 1 2 3 1 2 2 2 2 2 2 3 2 1 1 2 3 1 1 4 3 2 2 3 3 3 3 2 4 2 2 3 1
37  Fulfil          1 2 2 2 2 2 2 2 2 3 3 5 3 3 3 3 3 3 4 4 3 4 3 2 3 3 3 4 4 3 3 2 4 4 2 3 4 4 4 4 4 3 4 2 2
38  Joke            2 3 3 3 3 3 3 3 3 4 4 6 4 4 4 4 4 5 5 4 5 4 3 4 4 4 5 5 4 4 3 5 5 3 4 5 1 1 2 5 4 5 3 1
39  Laugh           1 2 2 2 2 2 2 2 2 3 3 5 3 3 3 3 3 3 4 4 3 4 3 2 3 3 3 4 4 3 3 2 4 4 2 3 4 1 1 1 4 3 4 2 1
40  Terminate       1 2 2 2 2 2 2 2 2 3 5 3 3 3 3 3 3 4 4 3 4 3 2 3 3 3 4 4 3 3 2 4 4 2 2 3 4 4 4 4 3 4 2 2
41  Attend          3 4 4 4 2 4 4 4 4 4 3 3 4 4 5 3 3 2 2 1 3 5 4 4 3 5 3 4 5 5 4 3 4 4 5 5 3 3 3 4 5 4 4 1
42  Cheer           2 3 3 3 2 1 2 3 1 1 4 4 2 2 2 4 3 3 3 3 2 2 4 3 1 3 4 5 4 4 4 3 3 3 3 4 5 1 1 2 4 4 2 3 1
43  Minimise        1 2 2 2 2 2 2 2 2 3 3 3 3 3 3 3 3 4 4 3 4 3 2 3 3 3 4 4 3 3 2 4 4 2 3 4 4 4 1 4 3 4 2 1
44  Complain        3 2 3 3 1 1 2 4 1 1 3 3 2 2 2 3 2 2 2 2 1 2 3 4 2 1 3 4 2 1 5 4 3 2 4 1 4 2 2 2 3 1 3 1 1
45  /
```

as different. The nodes of the dendrogram nearly all fall in the similarity range 20–60%, so the categories used are fairly evenly spaced in the domain of syntagmatic similarity. It has already been stressed that this grammar (like any syntax) assigns items to the same category on the basis of similar combinatorial properties and in spite of semantic differences. So not surprisingly semantic opposites with similar occasions of use are clustered together such as Prohibit and Command, Advise and Warn, Accept and Reject. The directive acts Prohibit, Command and

Request fall into one group, together with the sanctions Threaten and Offend, while less directive acts such as Advise and Warn cluster with rewards like Offer and Promise.

The minimum-path analysis is of special interest as it illustrates a possible application for this kind of research, which could develop from the study of rules of sequence. An activity map could be derived by placing all the different acts making up a particular situation in a multidimensional space, so that the distances between pairs represent their minimum path length. In this way the presence of groups of related acts which make up coherent episodes may be detected. There is some technical difficulty involved in that the path distances between states are not necessarily symmetrical, whereas multi-dimensional scaling techniques deal with symmetrical relations. Nevertheless, it is clear in principle how such an investigation would proceed, given a more elaborate grammar. Perhaps most importantly, minimum-path information brings into the system the first strategic considerations, which would enable one to predict which of several courses of action in the present is most likely to lead to certain outcomes in the future, or which would lead to the desired outcome most directly. If this kind of predictive information could be derived in future from studies of the sequential structure of bargaining and conflict, it would prove to be a powerful tool with practical and theoretical implications.

Study 15: A Simple Computer Model

A computer simulation of the same model was also written, which places the forty-three speech-act names in sensible sequences, by looking up in the computer's memory all the sensible sequiturs to the last event, and then making a random choice between them. The simulation also decides when speaker change is appropriate and prints out one of two speakers' names (A or B) accordingly. The simulation marks the boundary between separate phases of talk (such as topics) by printing the symbol #. As an example of what the program produces, its first few lines of output are reproduced below:

```
        #
A:   COMPLAIN
A:   CONTINUE
B:   DENY
B:   TERMINATE
        #
A:   COMPLAIN
B:   QUESTION
A:   REFUSE
A:   APOLOGISE
B:   ACCEPT
```

This is a very simple simulation, but as an exercise in the combined use of algebraic and text-handling programming languages (FORTRAN and SNOBOL) it was very useful, and it illustrates in very simple form the equivalence and intertranslatability of rule and computer models for instrumentalist conceptions of 'rule'.

The original production of strings was done in FORTRAN outputting the sequences in integer coded form, and then these integer strings were read and translated by a subsequent SNOBOL program into the format shown above.

The greatest shortcoming of this model in both its manual and computer versions is that it is only a first-order Markov system. Each item is only related to its immediate antecedent (not counting speaker-changes). A more sophisticated grammar would include more information, not just by going to higher orders of stochastic series, but by drawing on the repertoire of rule types outlined earlier in this chapter. In this way a grammar could be constructed which could account economically for relations between widely separated items. Almost certainly the grammar would be required to derive its information from the output string of terminal items to date, so that any participant could use his own rule system, without direct access to non-terminal features of the other's behavioural stream. Such a grammar would include non-terminal items but they would be thrown up in 'cascades' from the terminals, to be rewritten by hierarchical rules to further non-terminal and terminal items. There would have to be a separate (and possibly different) grammar for each interactor. At present the rules simulate the interaction as a whole, and could not possibly serve as a model for the psychology of a single participant. When the rules are reformulated in such a way that one rule set corresponds to the mentality of each actor, modifications can be introduced to simulate interpersonal and intercultural differences, conflicts of interest and belief, and the interaction of personal and situational determinants of the behavioural output. When each actor has his own rule system, the notion of deep structure or individual representations of social structure can be brought into play.

The simple categories may have to give way to a more elaborate feature system which preserves some of the sub-structure of each speech act. The problem here is that in order to simulate dialogue you need to have an output language which is rich enough to do justice to interesting forms of interaction, but at the same time sufficiently simply formatted for the computer to interpret and write it. This problem does not arise for the computational linguist whose 'terminal vocabulary' (the set of morphemes to be used in sentence building) is finite. In dialogue simulation there is no such finite set, and so a finite or recursively definable vocabulary has to be established to represent the indefinitely large set of possible output units. The 'Backchat' model only used speaker name and speech-act type in its notation, so a single item of output might be represented as

A: QUESTION

This is very crude, and potentially ambiguous since the next line might be:

B: ASSERTION

without us knowing whether the question has been answered, or:

B: ANSWER

without us knowing whether the answer was a statement of fact, an opinion or an expression of feeling. Furthermore, a simple construction such as:

A: QUESTION
A: QUESTION
B: ANSWER

does not make it clear which question was answered. The surface structure of the dialogue is inadequately represented.

Going to the other extreme, our everyday use for reported speech is too open-ended to serve as a vehicle for simulation. As a compromise, a notation was developed which works like functional or operator-argument notation in mathematics, or the frame system of the early 'case grammars'. A main verb defines each utterance type, and a string of parameters *which is peculiar to that type* defines its relation with the people and the other events. So, for instance:

THREAT (A, B, x, y, z)

would mean *A threatens B with x unless condition y is met within (time) limit z.* The choice of parameters to go with each act-type is interesting in itself, and an aspect of speech-acts which has not been examined. The fact that in questioning someone you need an *issue* to question them *about*, while in threatening you need a *penalty* to threaten them *with*, relates to work on the relations between the logical structure of speech-acts and the syntactic structure of the locutions in which they are realised. This notation, while computationally manageable, also allows one to disambiguate surface connections, as in:

QUESTION (A, B, a)
QUESTION (A, B, b)
ASSERTION (B, A, a)

and to set up simple rules of inference such as:

IF: COMMAND (A, B, x)
AND: PERFORM (B, x)
THEN: COMPLY $(B, COMMAND (A, B, x))$.

This last example also illustrates the recursive use of the notation.

In the next study a restricted version of this scheme was used in a simulation of question and answer patterns.

Study 16: Push-down Tree Structures

Introduction

As we have already seen, conversational sequences and especially question—answer sequences can contain segments of discourse 'nested' or 'embedded' within one another, and this raises special problems when representing sequential patterns in rule or computer models. It has also been suggested that the problems (and remedies) are not unlike those raised in Chomsky's early work on sentence structure and its reproduction from formal grammars (see esp. Chomsky, 1957). The nesting may be simple as in

$$Q_1 \ Q_2 \ A_2 \ A_1$$

where Q_n and A_n are an associated question—answer pair, or more complex, as in

$$Q_1 \ Q_2 \ Q_3 \ A_3 \ A_2 \ A_1$$

or

$$Q_1 \ Q_2 \ A_2 \ Q_3 \ A_3 \ A_1$$

but not

$$Q_1 \ Q_2 \ A_1 \ A_2$$

(assuming Q_1 and Q_2 come from different speakers). As usual it is hard to specify the pattern by listing the combinations which could occur, but the rule that must be followed is like that for nesting of brackets in mathematical expressions.

Reading $(_n$ for Q_n
and $)_n$ for A_n

the well-formed examples above become

$$(_1 \ (_2 \ )_2 \ )_1$$
$$(_1 \ (_2 \ (_3 \ )_3 \ )_2 \ )_1$$
$$(_1 \ (_2 \ )_2 \ (_3 \ )_3 \ )_1$$

and the ill-formed example

$$(_1 \ (_2 \ )_1 \ )_2$$

This principle was embodied in a programme which used the frame notation described above, where Q_n and A_n would be represented

     1. A: QUESTION/n.
     2. B: ANSWER/n.

The Model

The crux of the model was the data-structure in which the present state of the conversation was stored. The possibility of several unanswered questions 'piling up' in some circumstances, suggests that a tree structure should be used with its terminal branches as conversational 'loose ends', but priority rules determining the order of answering embedded questions require the properties of a push-down stack. The program was finally made to behave satisfactorily by combining the two into a kind of branching stack devised by Peter Hancock, which was called a 'push-down tree'.

In its ordinary unbranching form a push-down stack is a kind of store, memory or queue with the property that the last items to be entered are the first to be retrieved, like the spring-loaded stacks of trays in a self-service cafeteria from which the name comes. A tree in its simple form is a divergent branching data structure in which each item may be linked to, or lead to the accessing of several more, and each of these to several more still, and so on. The two principles were combined as a push-down tree model of question and answer queues in the following way. A question—answer sequence has to begin with either one or else with several questions by the first speaker, and then a speaker change. This would lead to a single commitment to answer or continue being stored by the model in the former case, or in the latter case by a number of possible points of continuation with equal priority, which could be represented as the end points of a fan of lines, like a hand with fingers spread apart. Each of these 'finger ends' can then give rise to direct answers, in which case it ceases to be an extant option or obligation for response, and is deleted, or else some further question or questions could fan out from its end, and so on. The interesting thing is that all of the permutations of question, counter-question and answer that make logical sense according to the principle of nested brackets, and no ill-formed ones, can be generated if the following principles are followed:

1. The outstanding commitments are mapped as a push-down tree.
2. Items are only responded to when they form the end of a branch.
3. Terminal (branch ending) questions may be followed in the sequence by an answer, and deleted from the tree, *or*
4. They may be followed by one or several counter questions by the next speaker, in which case they become (temporarily) buried in the tree and inoperative.

This may or may not indicate something about the kind of data structure used in memory to indicate where a conversation has 'got to', but it seems to generate the appropriate array of sequential combinations. The principles are rather like an extended version of the grammar for mirror-image languages, also based on the notion of nested bracketing regularities (Chomsky, 1956); or a simple phrase-structure grammar of the type

$$S \rightarrow S_a \ S_b \qquad\qquad (1)$$
$$\rightarrow Q_n \ A_n \qquad\qquad (2)$$
$$\rightarrow Q_n \ S \ A_n . \qquad\qquad (3)$$

This can reproduce the example

$$Q_1 \ Q_2 \ A_2 \ Q_3 \ A_3 \ A_1$$

from the starting-point or axiom S, in the following way:

S	
Q_1 S A_1	by rule 3,
Q_1 S_a S_b A_1	by rule 1,
Q_1 Q_2 A_2 S_b A_1	by rule 2,
Q_1 Q_2 A_2 Q_3 A_3 A_1	by rule 2.

See also Miller (1967) for a similar treatment of mirror-image languages and grammars.

The current state of the data structure was printed out at intervals during the program run (but could be suppressed). The program could also be modified to run as a string parser and analyser as well as a generator. It made all binary choices with a probability of 0.5, which gives a very deeply nested sequence. This switching parameter could be adjusted with resulting changes in the output.

In some ways the modification of the category scheme to produce one of the frame-bound features would be like the transition to a predicate calculus from a propositional calculus. A further modification would be to allow for the generation of group as well as dyadic interactions.

To summarise the generative process that might be used in such a model, let us consider the way in which an incomplete dyadic interaction would be continued. Each individual would have his own rule set, and a cognitive representation of the state of play, showing the beliefs, attitudes and intentions attributed to the actors, and a surface structure showing the history of events. Note that unlike a sentence grammar, this kind of rule system cannot completely derive its deep structure, and then transform it to the surface. The cyclical nature of the process demands that an event which arises in the deep structure of one actor be realised in the surface structure of behaviour, and thus pass into the interpretive deep structure of the other actor, where it interacts with the rules to select a new item of behaviour which passes to the surface and so on.

The counterparts of deep and surface structures are not static in social interaction, but they grow and change with each new event. The actor's mental map of the social world influences the production of behaviour, and in this sense surface structure is produced from deep structure; but as both parties act, their world view changes to incorporate the actions and their consequences, and in this sense deep structure is derived from surface structure, and of course from other sources of information concerning situations, roles and so on.

```
$$$$$$$$$$$$$$$$$$$$$$$$$$$$$$$$$$$$$$$$$$$$$$$$$$$$$$$$$$$$$$$$$$$$$
  DUMP OF SESSION SO FAR
$
$ CURR..SPEAKER = B
$
$ DUMP OF CURR.SET
$ TERMINAL - : 1/          BRANCH : 11  3    2    1  /  COUNT  =  4
$$  CARDINAL OF SET =  1
$...................................................
$ DUMP OF OPP.SET
$$TERMINAL  :  10         BRANCH :  3   2   1   /  COUNT  =  3
$$  CARDINAL OF SET =  1
$...................................................
$$$$$$$$$$$$$$$$$$$$$$$$$$$$$$$$$$$$$$$$$$$$$$$$$$$$$$$$$$$$$$$$$$$$$

19    A: QUESTION /10

20    A: QUESTION /10
$$$$$$$$$$$$$$$$$$$$$$$$$$$$$$$$$$$$$$$$$$$$$$$$$$$$$$$$$$$$$$$$$$$$$
$ DUMP OF SESSION SO FAR
$
$
$ CURR.SPEAKER = A
$
$ DUMP OF CURR.SET
$$  SET EMPTY
$ DUMP OF OPP.SET
$$TERMINAL  :  17         BRANCH : 11  3   2   1  /  COUNT  =  4
$$TERMINAL  :  20         BRANCH : 10  3   2   1  /  COUNT  =  4
$$TERMINAL  :  19         BRANCH : 10  3   2   1  /  COUNT  =  4
$$  CARDINAL OF SET =  3
$...................................................
$$$$$$$$$$$$$$$$$$$$$$$$$$$$$$$$$$$$$$$$$$$$$$$$$$$$$$$$$$$$$$$$$$$$$

21    B: QUESTION /20
$$$$$$$$$$$$$$$$$$$$$$$$$$$$$$$$$$$$$$$$$$$$$$$$$$$$$$$$$$$$$$$$$$$$$
$ DUMP OF SESSION SO FAR
$
$
$ CURR.SPEAKER = B
$
$ DUMP OF CURR.SET
$$TERMINAL  :  17         BRANCH :
$$TERMINAL  :  19         BRANCH :
$$  CARDINAL OF SET =  2
$...................................................
$ DUMP OF OPP.SET
$$TERMINAL  :  21         BRANCH :
$$  CARDINAL OF SET =  1
$...................................................
$$$$$$$$$$$$$$$$$$$$$$$$$$$$$$$$$$$$$$$

22    A: QUESTION /21

23    A: QUESTION /21

24    A: QUESTION /21
$$$$$$$$$$$$$$$$$$$$$$$$$$$$$$$$$$$$$$$$$$$
$ DUMP OF SESSION SO FAR
$
$ CURR.SPEAKER = A
$
$ DUMP OF CURR.SET
$$  SET EMPTY
$ DUMP OF OPP.SET
$$TERMINAL  :  17         BRANCH : 11  3    2    1  /  COUNT  =  4
$$TERMINAL  :  24         BRANCH : 21  20  10  3   2   1  /  COUNT  =  6
$$TERMINAL  :  23         BRANCH : 21  20  10  3   2   1  /  COUNT  =  6
$$TERMINAL  :  22         BRANCH : 21  20  10  3   2   1  /  COUNT  =  6
$$TERMINAL  :  19         BRANCH : 10  3   2   1  /  COUNT  =  4
$$  CARDINAL OF SET =  5
$...................................................
$$$$$$$$$$$$$$$$$$$$$$$$$$$$$$$$$$$$$$$$$$$$$$$$$$$$$$$$$$$$$$$$$$$$$

25    B: ANSWER    /24

26    B: QUESTION /19
$$$$$$$$$$$$$$$$$$$$$$$$$$$$$$$$$$$$$$$$$$$$$$$$$$$$$$$$$$$$$$$$$$$$$
$ DUMP OF SESSION SO FAR
$
$
$ CURR.SPEAKER = B
$
$ DUMP OF CURR.SET
$$TERMINAL  :  22         BRANCH .   21  20  10  3   2   1  /  COUNT  =  6
$$TERMINAL  :  17         BRANCH :   11  3    2    1  /  COUNT  =  4
$$TERMINAL  :  23         BRANCH :   21  20  10  3   2   1  /  COUNT (=  6
$$  CARDINAL OF SET =  3
```

Line number

Speaker name

Speech act type

Line number questioned

Memory 'dump', showing the present state of the 'push-down tree'

FIG. 30   Question and answer simulation.

It must be stressed yet again, that the system described here, although described in realist terms, is not necessarily a valid model of the actor's real mental processes. If it serves to simulate observed patterns of behaviour, and the judgements to which they lead, it will be a *plausible candidate* for that status, but no more. If it does not simulate the behaviour (that is it does not achieve observational adequacy) then it is certainly *not* a representation of the actor's mental processes.

The rule models described in this chapter were rather simplistic and governed by *a priori* notions of structure alone. They were formal and mathematical in a rather narrow sense, and they contained none of the extra-linguistic influences of role or motivation that would be found in real talk, let alone the differences in background knowledge and in the interests of the speakers that could lead to conflict or misunderstanding.

In the next chapter the conception of a generative rule model will be broadened considerably to include a variety of social and circumstantial influences on behaviour, in an attempt to reproduce the overall properties of three specific, complex and practically problematic social situations. But first it will be necessary to introduce a more anthropomorphic conception of what is to be modelled, and how it may be represented in a less mechanistic way. It is time to consider what might be called 'the human aspect'.

6

THE HUMAN ASPECT

LET us suppose that the purpose of this line of research is to produce something rather like a map of the social world, a systematic representation of what things there are, what possibilities exist for action, how they are interconnected, and which ones lead on to which others. Like a map, its usefulness would be as an aid to navigation in a strange and confusing place. By knowing what our choices were, and what they would lead to, the chances would be much increased of our ending up where we wanted to be, whether as individuals or organisations. The map we use in the social world most of the time comes from common sense, but often it lets us down and it could do with some extension and improvement. So, to pursue the analogy, what properties would a better map have? *Accuracy* is probably too obvious an answer. The facts which the map represents could be made more and more precisely true. But that may not be the main failing of the common-sense map at all. We usually assume it is, and our scientific efforts are geared more to the production of greater accuracy than to any other objective, but there are other aspects of a good map, too, and if those are the ones which common sense most lacks, perhaps we should change our approach so as to remedy what is worst in our present picture, and not what is already satisfactory. *Scope* or *generality* may be what is most lacking, but again I suspect not. Our common-sense map of social reality does not seem particularly as though it tells us about some aspects of everyday experience and not about others, as if there were a big white area on one side of the map marked 'not yet charted', although this is perhaps representative of the way many people see deviance, or mental disorder.

Consistency is also important. A map would be no help if it were constructed in such a way that contradicting inferences could be drawn from it about positions and distances. Likewise *completeness*. It might be embarrassing if all the level-crossings or T-junctions were missed out. Finally there is *coherence*, which is perhaps the most important and elusive property of all. This seems to be where common sense lets us down badly, and where most remedy is required. It is as if the common-sense map of the social world did not come in the form of a single organised diagram at all, but a mountain of disparate entries on separate scraps of paper giving the location and description of each geographical feature, but in no particular order or scheme. It might well be accurate, general, consistent and complete but still lack coherence and hence usefulness as a map. This, I think, is much of the problem with the everyday picture of the social world, and our scientific approaches to social psychology only repeat the same mistake. Ordinary social intuition probably does better on accuracy than any of the other criteria listed above, with its performance falling off rapidly through the list of generality, consistency and completeness, to a nearly total lack of coherence. And yet in using our scientific tools to improve the map, we repeat the same priorities with all the attention going to accuracy and virtually none to methods of consolidation. The same failing is not found in the advanced sciences where consolidation is a major priority. The integration of the four fundamental forces in nature, for example, has long been a major goal for theoretical physicists.

The approaches which follow are not aimed so much at improving accuracy or extending the scope of our picture of the everyday world, as at unifying it into a coherent model. (Of course the five criteria of the map analogy should not be treated as totally independent. Inconsistency must jeopardise accuracy, generality and completeness are the same property but differently distributed, and so on. Nonetheless the general point holds.) What we need more than anything is to organise the insight we already have about human conduct into a more systematic and usable form. The methods used here, unusual though they are, are chosen for the emphasis they give to integration and coherence, and the relatively low priority accorded to new 'facts' as isolated additions to the catalogue of available information.

To speak of maps and of coherence is to deal with the structure of a system rather than with causes or laws of a more familiar kind. That may be no bad thing. In turning to the natural sciences for inspiration, we assume that the causal sciences must set the paradigm, and overlook the structural sciences like chemistry, anatomy and crystallography. The *structure* of social action and the social world may be as important as its causes, and very often the course of an argument or the plot of a novel has as much to do with architectonic principles as with the precipitation of one event by another. In Aristotle's terms the formal causation of action and experience may reflect more about its real nature than the efficient causes.

It is usual to assume that when dealing with arrangements of matter in space, a structural account is in order, and when dealing with patterns of events over time, a causal account is called for, but this tendency is not binding. There are quite rightly exceptions to it, such as the structurally oriented study of language adopted by generative syntacticians. Although the latter structures are diachronic (arranged through time) as opposed to more familiar synchronic patterns, they are structures nonetheless and lend themselves to structural explanation. For this, it is usual to turn to the notion of templates (Harré, 1977). Whereas effects come from causes by the mediation of causal laws, realised in material entities and processes, structures come from templates (which are other structures) by way of translation mechanisms and procedures. Phenotypes come from genotypes by way of m-RNA intermediates, sentences from grammars by transformational and other rules (in the formal model at least, if not in actual sentence production). Synchronic structures come from synchronic templates, and so too must diachronic structures. It would be a metaphysical nonsense and an unhelpful explanatory concept to think of diachronic structures coming from diachronic templates. Although the synchronic templates in real systems do often change with time, that does not make their structure diachronic.

This emphasis on structural investigation does not contradict causal explanations — it simply reverses the priority, just as the physicist may choose to see particles as primary and their interaction as secondary; or else may stand the picture on its head by treating fields as primary, and their discontinuities (masquerading as particles) as derivative. The difficult relationship between individual and social psychology is also open to such reversals with the social matrix given original status, and personas (people) treated as its granulations, instead of the more obvious idea that people are what really *exist*, and society is entirely consequent upon their interaction with one another, in ways determined by their properties as individuals (Harré, personal communication).

To take the structure of social action as the phenomenon and its templates as the issue is not to embark on a psychology of 'faculties' whose parts would have names like memory, cognition, or emotion. Rather it is to look for general structuring rules or principles behind the evident occurrence of particular behavioural (or experiential) configurations.

There is an important difference, however, between the diachronic structures of the social world and the synchronic structures of the physical one. Physical explanations are reductive, and they look to the nature of the parts to explain the whole. Molecules have a form dictated by the properties of their constituent atoms and thence by their sub-atomic particles, and so on (perhaps!). It is as if the natural world is driven from the bottom up, and so by looking to finer and finer levels of structure, the origins of the pattern we first noticed, the evident order, can be retraced. With social organisation, the *opposite* seems true. It is the whole that dictates the selection and arrangement of the parts. Now reductive explanation does *not* work. To dissect the patterns of human action into finer and finer parts is not to retrace their genesis and discover fundamental building blocks, it is to move further and further from the sources of pattern towards a dead-end filled with nothing but trivia. This is why so many 'scientific' procedures seem to lead nowhere when applied to human action. The task of the social or behavioural scientist is not to take things to pieces to see what they are made of, it is to put them together to see what they are part of. This might be called upward explanation or contextualising, as opposed to downward explanation or reducing. The patterns we should be looking for in social action are not caused by the bits and pieces, the blueprint of this organism is not in its cell. It is the opposite. The grand designs are more fundamental (as well as more important) than the fine details, and they imprint themselves on the sub-components whose arrangements they determine.

For other reasons, more familiar in the natural sciences, it is synthesis, not analysis that is required. If the phenomena we observe in the world are called P, and the explanations we want for them are x, then we want to find an x such that

$$x \supset P$$

not, as is the fate of most inductive and data-driven procedures, such that

$$P \supset x.$$

What is at issue is the fundamental principles of (human) nature from which observed occurrences can be deduced, not the set of possible inferences for which our observation and experience are axiomatic. Here, the *analysis* of behavioural sequences and structures in its usual sense is inappropriate. It seeks to start with sequences as they are to be found, and then to process them to form 'conclusions' or 'findings'. Real scientific enquiry, as Chomsky (1965) pointed out for linguistics, would do quite the opposite. Later in this chapter some approaches will be illustrated in which the aim is to reproduce behaviour patterns from explicit principles, not to 'analyse' behavioural structure as such. Postulated processes serve for the reconstruction of hypothetical products.

In attempting such generative models, coherence is once again a key consideration. The aim of the investigation is intensive rather than extensive understanding, in which all the different parts and relations of a given structure may be accounted for; whereas more traditional research designs would seek to determine the general properties of a single structural element in the context of a large number of the structures in which it was found. This emphasis is quite common in other structural subjects and is the basis for radical new developments in idiographic and case-study methodology (de Waele and Harré, 1979).

The extensive, nomothetic strategy is often assumed to produce stronger and more generally valid findings than intensive idiography, but as de Waele has argued, this can be misleading. Two classes of generalisation must be distinguished. *Aggregate propositions* are produced by processing information about a set of entities or observations, but the problem is that they may not be distributive. That is they may not apply to the individual members of the set, just because they are true of the set as a whole. If there are 2.8 times as many children as mothers in a town, it does not mean there are 2.8 children in every family. The ratio applies to the aggregate number of children and families, not to individual cases. Other fallacies of aggregation, which may tend to creep into research designs, may be subtler and harder to detect. *General propositions* about a set, on the other hand, apply to all the members of the set, and these can be guaranteed by an *intensive* design where the relation between variables is established in each case and then aggregated (generalised), as opposed to aggregating each variable in turn, and examining the relation between aggregates. A town where every person owns a house is not the same as a town where all the people own all the homes. In the case-by-case intensive method, relations are established for each instance in turn, and if they are common to all instances then there is no danger of false generalisation.

The growing need for idiographic research methods has been accompanied by an increasing awareness of the limitations of experimental methods. The commonest criticism of the traditional experimental approach to social psychology has been that it produces unrealistic artificial situations with little external validity (that is little relation to real life). Even more seriously the experiments have often been treated as a discovery procedure and an end in themselves, instead of the last stage in an elaborate sequence of theoretical conjecture and logical or mathematical reasoning. All too often no real theory is proposed at all, and studies concerned themselves only with observable phenomena, unlike the real sciences which are about unseen forces, processes and structures as *evidenced* by observable phenomena. Experiments, in other words, were often taken out of the context of the scientific method proper, and misused.

Of course not all sciences use experimental methods, so in any case this approach cannot be the universal hallmark of scientific investigation. There must be criteria according to which problems are suitable or unsuitable for experimental treatment. For example, the things we take to be causes in the system must be manipulable as independent variables in the study. But if we are looking for determinants of human destiny it would be an absurd contradiction to suppose that the same factors can be the forces to which we respond in shaping our lives, and at the same time easily (and ethically) manipulable for the sake of seeing what happens. Just as in cosmology there may well be causes and effects, but not ones we can tamper with unless we want to confine our attention to the minor variations, the fine tuning of the social world. A system to be experimented on as a 'black box' must have relatively little memory and a simple transfer function, if this is ever to be inferred from input—output observations. If each input produces an immediate corresponding output, then the association between the two can be described; but if any experience in the lifetime of an organism can affect any other, how ever much later, and in combination with countless other factors, the task of tracing cause and effect becomes nigh on impossible. Although so many fruitful analogies have been suggested between computers and brains, no one has been rash enough to believe that the experimental approach we use with humans would tell us anything useful if applied to the input—output transactions of an unfamiliar computer, programmed in a strange language.

Experimentally tractable systems need to be 'open', to allow transaction with the experimenter's observations and manipulations, whereas many complex processes of feedback and self-regulation, including those which are found in interpersonal relationships, are disrupted by scientific intrusion, and turned into something else by the very process of measurement. There are many other problems, too, with the experimental study of human nature: the importance of meaning; the seemingly non-mechanical nature of the social actor; the complexity and changeability of the processes at work; the elaborate interaction of variables; the effects of culture; and the unsuitability of complex systems in general for atomistic studies, where each part is studied in turn, hoping their properties will add up to an understanding of the whole.

The real issue is not with input—output regularities or behaviour patterns anyway, but with the psychological processes that produce them. The distinction between product and process is crucial. The social world as we know it is the product (and in our studies the evidence), but what is at issue scientifically is the process (psychological or otherwise) that produces it.

It is likely that action-regulating processes differ from one individual to another, and respond differently from one circumstance to another, but this raises no special problem, as the advocates of the P X S (or Person-by-Situation) interaction seem to think (Magnusson, 1981). Any mechanism, from a car to a calculator, responds differently to different circumstances. That is what its transfer function or input—output characteristic describes. It summarises the behavioural properties of that mechanism, and it may differ from one individual to the next. Behaviour is a person-dependent function of circumstance, just as skidding is a car-dependent function of cornering speed, but in each case the useful approach is to partial out how each individual works, treating behaviour as an individual-specific function of experience, as distinct from those functions that specify the distribution of individual differences in a population.

Much of the controversy about the best way to do social psychology has centred on an alternative programme put forward by Harré and others and variously called 'the New Paradigm', 'ethogenics', or 'ethogeny', meaning the genesis of meaning. Only a very cursory summary of the main ideas will be possible here. For further details see Harré (1977, 1980). As the name ethogenics suggests, the central idea is that what we mean in everyday life (and should mean for scientific purposes) by *explaining* a piece of social behaviour, is working out its meaning not its precipitating circumstances or *causes* as such. Harré is very critical of the 'Old Paradigm' as he calls it for producing non-explanatory accounts of social behaviour — mere 'critical descriptions' which use scientific tools to say what social behaviour is like, but not how it got that way. This is like the point above, that *processes* are at issue, not *products* in themselves. Furthermore, Harré says that even when experimental social psychology does seek process explanations it often resorts to narrow, inappropriate and out-of-date conceptions of process. In the advanced sciences, according to Harré, the idea that every observed phenomenon is an effect, and that we should find the corresponding cause or causes, has ceased to occupy the centre of the stage. Far more crucial these days is the idea that material objects and systems have a constitution which confers on them a nature — a set of powers, capacities and tendencies which manifest themselves as the behaviour of the system. Which of the powers is expressed at any one time depends on circumstance, the *enabling conditions* which allow one behavioural mode to express itself rather than another. These are not causes in the old sense. They act on the system and its properties, not directly on the 'effect', and the effect itself is produced by the system, in virtue of its nature, not by the cause *per se*. So, for instance, when an object is released and falls we should not say that gravity has caused its descent. (Gravity was there all along, before it began to fall.) Rather that a property it has, namely potential energy (due to its mass and position in a gravitational field), gives it an enduring tendency to fall, expressed when the enabling condition is supplied, namely a clear path to the ground. Likewise we should not speak of action as caused by stimuli or changing circumstances. Rather it is an expression of the constitution of the organism, explicable by reference to that constitution, and merely switched from one mode to another by the influence of external circumstance.

The powers, tendencies and capabilities of the social actor — what he can do — are determined largely by what he *knows how to do*. A knowledge of the social world, its conventions and regularities is at the heart of the system. A data base, or *cognitive resource*, is what controls our social being (in some respects as linguists would claim that competence controls a linguistic performance) and the task of the social analyst is to discover what the individual's *cognitive resource*, his social competence, consists of. *That* is the explanation of social behaviour, and so the layman's everyday theory of sociality becomes a prime candidate for scientific status. In a sense everyday theory has to describe how behaviour is produced, because it is from that theory that behavioural obligations are read off. It is true not just by description but also by prescription. What it holds to be so, it makes so.

This is entirely compatible with a functionalist version of psychology, as we shall see later, in which the sources of action, thought and feeling are described as abstract processes realised in the brain much as computer software is realised in hardware. Those processes are what psychology and ethogenics are all about, not the behaviour which they produce. Perhaps in the person as in the computer, the powers of the system and the operating characteristics of its software are for most practical purposes co-extensive. However, one should be wary of taking the computer analogy too far. Weizenbaum (1976), and Dreyfus (1972) have offered extensive accounts of the respects in which the mind is not computer-like. They say the information-processing-system view of people is a dangerous oversimplification, both intellectually and practically.

So much for the nature of the explanation to be sought. The methodology, as in all science, is largely dependent on analogy (Harré, 1976). The transition from observing the behaviour of a system, to understanding the processes which produce it, is not simple or direct. It depends on likening the system to another with better-known machinery. This *source* of analogy can then be used to set up an *icon*, a speculative model in which the real system is imagined to have the mechanics and properties of the analogical one. Comparison of the behaviour of the real system and the hypothetical behaviour deduced from the icon shows up errors in the theory and gives specific grounds for modification. In this way the real generative process, and the descriptions of it offered by the icon, may be expected to converge in due course.

The cognitive resource, or the actor's theory of sociality, is itself expressed in two ways, and discovered from the consolidation of these two types of evidence. Firstly, action or performance P_1 bears the hallmark of the belief system that produced it, but so too does the stream of *accounts* or talk in support of action, performance P_2, which accompanies it. Whether offered in justification, explanation, or mere commentary people use talk to make sense to others of the things they do and say, and that talk, the set of their *accounts*, is privileged information about the sense their actions make to them, and hence the source of those actions. These accounts set the format and the basic content of what we should regard as explanatory material.

Study 17: Retrograde Modelling

Introduction

The models of the previous chapter were formal, and in a way arbitrary. They arose from the need to test certain classes of formal device as possible generators or 'behaviour grammars' for patterns in discourse, in the first case matrices of first-order conditional dependency, and in the second case 'push-down tree' data-structures running a 'case grammatical' or frame-like event notation. They were evaluated according to a rather vague and general notion of the resemblance (or lack of it) between their output and the characteristics of discourse. They were *not* related to any particular corpus or type of discourse. Their processes were *not* derived from a consideration of the nature of talk in any particular situation, and their object was not to reconstruct a particular set or type of conversational instances either as individual examples or general descriptions.

In this study and the two that follow it, the reverse is the case. These were all based on a particular corpus of conversational material (real or hypothetical, reported or recorded), and they set out to analyse and state the regularities of the corpus in such a way that the same sequences, and other instances of their type, could be reproduced, or 'generated' from an explicit model.

As we have seen before the real problem always arises with sets of sequences and their reproduction, rather than with individual sequences, and yet it is usually a set of sequences which it is important to capture, since the situation under consideration typically produces a variety of sequences, rather than a single recurring chain. The studies in the following group of three attempt in their different ways to characterise sets of sequences having a particular thing in common, namely their past history. Clearly a technique for characterising the set of possible futures or continuations which are possible given a certain state-of-affairs, or history, has a special significance both for our understanding of how patterns of events develop with time, and for practical considerations of forecasting events, and for solving problems by predicting the effects of alternative policies; although other sets of sequences with different things in common are also amenable to this kind of analysis.

Aims

The aims of this study were to produce a combinatorial model of a particular type of (problematic) social interaction, that is to decompose and characterise the individual elements or events from a set of examples, and the underlying constraints or 'shaping factors' that regulate their occurrence, in such a way that a model representing those and only those facts would reproduce all the example sequences, other 'well-formed' examples of that type, and no 'ill-formed' examples.

Producing the Corpus

A naturally occurring corpus of examples is unsuitable for this purpose, because it would not contain the sets of sequences which were equivalent in the sense of being alternative versions or continuations of the same discussion. A role-playing procedure, however, can re-create the same situation over and over again and collect alternative versions of the ensuing interaction. In this study the role-playing was passive, in the next two it was active.

The corpus of material for this study was collected with examples of two other similar situations in a study by Argyle et al. (1981), of situational differences in social behaviour sequences. A group of ten subjects from the Oxford University Psychology Department subject panel came into the laboratory, where they were given brief written descriptions of the situation analysed here (and the two others for the comparative study). They were asked to produce a detailed written description of how the whole situation might go, including a more detailed version of the opening circumstances they had been given. They were told to include dialogue and explanations for events, and to invent further characteristics of the people and situation if they wished, provided they were consistent with the framework given. The subjects were asked to take 20—30 minutes over this part of the task, and were given an idea of the detail and style required, in the form of a short extract from a novel and our own version of the situational summary on which it might have been based.

The situation which subjects were asked to describe in detail for this study was that of a customer trying to return an item of clothing to the shop where it was bought. Subjects were told that the customer had found the clothes did not fit, and had brought them back for alteration, or to have them exchanged for clothes of a different size. The shop assistant refused to change the garment, as it had been worn, and wanted £3.00 for an alteration, which the customer thought unreasonable.

The ten written accounts of how this situation would develop (the scripts) were then the material for the subsequent analysis.

Constructing the Model

The main aim of this model was to attempt for sequences of discrete events the kind of analysis and reconstruction which system dynamics (e.g. Forrester, 1972) achieves for continuous time-series data. In systems dynamics, the behaviour of a system, such as a city, an industrial sector, or in the most famous case the world system of economic and ecological inter-actions, is described as a set of continuous scalar variables that fluctuate with time. The purpose of the model is to capture the interrelationship of the variables in such a way that their past profiles can be reconstructed and their future course projected, and the likely effects of present, or alternative policies studied. The network of interrelationships between variables is first plotted as an 'influence matrix', and then particular relationships recast as (differential) equations showing how each variable fluctuates as a function of the others. This is specified on the basis of *a priori* assumptions about the nature of the variables and their interactions, and tested according to the ability of the hypothetical model to reconstruct the time course of the relevant variables over their recorded history. Iterative solution of the equations for successive values of t gives rise to a reconstruction of the system's behaviour up to the present, and a projection of its behaviour into the future (in so far as the assumptions of the model are, and remain, valid).

In one way the problem posed by analysis and modelling of discrete event sequential data is much the same, but in other ways rather different. The spirit of Forrester's hypothetico-deductive approach seems very appropriate. With behaviour sequences, as with other modelling problems, the point is not to induce some general description from what has been observed to occur, but rather to postulate some system of underlying factors, principles and constraints from which observed patterns can be reconstructed, and novel patterns projected.

The mechanics of the model, on the other hand, must be different. Since the behaviour to be reconstructed is a succession of discrete events, the representation of variables and their interrelationship must be different. Variables become event types or categories, and the regularity to be reproduced is their tendency to occur (or to seem plausible when conceived as occurring) in some orders rather than others. Their interrelationship is more problematic in this case however, since, unlike the continuous variables of a system dynamics model, they are not continuously present, so the invariant property by which the model is defined, regardless of time, cannot be the synchronic network of intervariable influences on which a system dynamics model is based. There is, nonetheless, a clue to be found in the format of the continuous variable models. Typically they take the form of a set of equations, one for each variable, showing how it varies as a function of others, for instance:

$$a_t = f_1(a_{t-1}, b_{t-1}, c_{t-1} \ldots),$$
$$b_t = f_2(a_{t-1}, b_{t-1}, c_{t-1} \ldots)$$

and so on. This is only to take the very simplest case where values at t only depend on earlier values, and therefore the equations can be solved separately. In practice

$$c_t = f_3(a_t, b_t, c_{t-1}, d_t \ldots)$$

would be more likely, and more problematic to solve, but the principle remains the same.

Suppose then that the variables in the present model, the occurrence of events of discrete types, were to be set out similarly so that event type e_j was specified by a rule

$$e_j \leftarrow x$$

meaning it could occur at any time provided the preceding string of event types satisfied condition x, some formula of occurrences and non-occurrences of previous events, such as

$$(b \ v \ c) \wedge \bar{d}$$

meaning b OR c have occurred AND NOT d, and so on for all j.

In other words, the only regularities that can occur in such a model are produced by a necessary condition that the string-so-far must satisfy for the (possible) occurrence of each event. This is called a retrograde model, as it deals with the relation of each event to its *past history*. In some circumstances several events may be appropriate, in which case the model would select between them at random, and in no circumstance (if the model is correctly constructed) would *no* event be appropriate, so that that run of the model ground to a halt.

This is a framework that was adopted here, and the following procedure was drawn up (after Forrester, see Rivett, 1978) for the construction of the model:

1. Reduce given scripts to sequences of coded event categories, developing a category list as required for overt events and states. Tabulate for each event type its number, category and the strings in which it occurs.

2. Similarly list and tabulate all covert events and states which like the non-terminal vocabulary of a grammar would be necessary to describe production states and conditions, but not part of the output as reported. For instance, it

may be convenient in the model to have a covert variable called PRESENCE, switched on by the overt-event ARRIVAL and switched off by the event DEPARTURE, and which figures in the conditions for reported story events without being one itself.

Transfer all categories and their description and code number to file cards.

3. Redescribe the ten original sequences as strings of overt (and covert) event types, revising typology where necessary.

4. Tabulate for each event type, which others influence it (that is form part of its rule or necessary condition) and which others it influences.

5. State for all overt and covert events the prior circumstances necessary for its occurrence, with logical connectives such as *if, and, or, then,* and so on.

6. Tabulate and plot diagrammatically the conditions of occurrence of each event/state and then reverse tabulate so as to show future implications of each event.

7. Transcribe the rules of the model (step 5) on to the appropriate event cards (step 2) in standard notation (contained in the key to the model).

8. Run the model, working along behaviour sequences one event at a time, determining at each stage which candidates for 'next event', have their condition satisfied, and if there is more than one, selecting between them at random.

9. Check that all the originally given strings can be generated from the rules, and no nonsensical ones. Revise the model until this criterion is met. Generate novel strings.

10. Experiment with the model to determine emergent properties such as stability, recycling, oscillation, etc., and their source.

11. Experiment with behavioural strategies for different participants to see which produce the desired effects.

12. Use this information to interact with the real system (if there is one).

13. Evaluate and document model strengths and weaknesses.

The full and ideal procedure given above may be modified and short-cut in specific instances, and in this case stages 1, 2b, 3, 5, 7, 8, 9 and 13 were the only ones to be carried out in detail, together with informal or partial versions of stages 2a and 4, as a useful guideline.

The Model

The final version of the model after several unsatisfactory runs and revisions is given below:

(1) Event codes

1. Incident begins.
2. Incident ends.
3. Customer buys clothing.

4. Customer takes clothing home.
5. Customer tries on clothing at home.
6. Customer finds clothing does not fit.
7. Customer returns clothing to shop.
8. Customer asks that clothing be changed/altered at shop's expense/money refunded.
9. Shop refuses customer's request.
10. Shop gives justification for refusal, for example points out that clothing has been worn.
11. Shop offers alteration at £3.
12. Customer refuses shop offer.
13. Customer objects to shop offer/policy as unreasonable.
14. Customer feels angry.
15. Customer becomes tense/anxious/distressed/impatient.
16. Assistant consults manager.
17. Customer feels anger at discrepancy between shop and advertising policy.
18. Customer encouraged by thought of being in the right.
19. .Shop refuses to improve offer.
20. Customer declares clothing unworn (in a sense).
21. Customer suggests worn look of clothing arose in the shop before sale.
22. Shop suggests worn look of clothing should have been sorted out at time of sale.
23. Customer asks for manager/senior.
24. Assistant declines to summon manager/senior.
25. Assistant summons manager/senior.
26. Shop makes a point of trying to look helpful.
27. Shop asks if clothing is satisfactory apart from size.
28. Customer says clothing is satisfactory apart from size.
29. Customer points out that clothing is wrong size.
30. Shop points out it is governed by standing policy.
31. Customer argues that shop policy does not apply in this case.
32. Manager feels/shows impatience.
33. Shop improves offer.
34. Customer accepts shop's offer.
35. Customer says handling of complaint/outcome is not satisfactory.
36. Customer withdraws custom (i.e. goes elsewhere).
37. Customer and shop arrange to implement final decision.
38. Manager/senior arrives.
39. Manager/senior leaves.
40. Assistant explains problem to manager/senior.
41. Manager/senior tells assistant to deal with problem.
42. Manager/senior feels/expresses dissatisfaction with assistant's handling of something.

43. Shop examines clothing.
44. Shop asks customer what trouble is (with clothing).
45. Customer says when clothing was bought (recently).
46. Shop says no comparable substitutes in stock.
47. Shop says it has been left too long (return of clothing).
48. Customer asks for better/another offer.
49. Customer threatens legal action/press/consumer group/withdrawal of custom.
50. Customer leaves.
51. Shop/manager apologises for inconvenience.
52. Customer regrets purchase.
53. Customer very relieved.
54. Shop says customer should have tried on clothing in shop.
55. Customer says was in too much of a hurry to try clothing on.
56. Customer says could not bring back clothing sooner (excuse).
57. Customer knows she is in wrong.
58. Customer dismisses assistant.
59. Customer goes looking for manager.
60. Customer agrees to see manager.
61. Assistant becomes upset/unhappy.
62. Customer receives altered clothing.
63. Customer is satisfied/happy.
64. Shop asks if clothing worn.
65. Customer feels depressed/unhappy.
66. Customer says she should have been allowed to try clothing on.
67. Shop points out trying on not possible — because late.
68. Customer explains problem to manager.
69. Shop encourages customer to seek legal advice.
70. Shop assistant enters.
71. Shop agrees to customer's request.
72. Shop assistant leaves.
73. Shop relieved, satisfied.
74. Shop assistant becomes annoyed/angry.
75. Customer says she is long-standing customer.
76. Customer says assistant said clothing was right size.
77. Assistant denies having said clothing was right size.
78. Shop gives reason for improvement in offer (i.e. customer has been long-standing customer).
79. Customer asks for higher authority yet.

(2) Key to rule notation

33   event '33' (has occurred).
←   may occur if.

Ø   no events.

&   end of string so far.

and both events/strings required for condition to be satisfied

or   either event required for condition to be satisfied.

$\overline{33}$ event '33' has *not* occurred.

([} indicate scope of logical operators, e.g.

)] } 19 and (32 or 17) vs. (19 and 32) or 17.

else alternative formula for that event.

t   then. At any time later in the string, not just 'next'.

n   next. ≡ tøt.

,   separates symbols in formula, otherwise meaningless.

(3) Rule set

1. 1 ← Øn&
2. 2 ← 34
    else 35
    else 36
    else 37
    else 39
    else 50
    else 59
    else 71
3. 3 ← 1n&
4. 4 ← 3n&
5. 5 ← [4 or (4 n 63)] n&
6. 6 ← 5n&
7. 7 ← (6n&) or [6n (14 or 52 or 65) n&]
8. 8 ← (7 or 29) t [$\overline{34}$ and 71] and [$\overline{27}$ or (27t28)] and [$\overline{44}$ or (44 t(29 or 68)] and [64 or (64t20)] and [$\overline{66}$ or (66t67)] and [$\overline{76}$ or (76t77)] and $\overline{8}$n&
9. 9 ← 8t ($\overline{34}$ and $\overline{71}$) and [$\overline{27}$ or (27t28)] and [$\overline{44}$ or (44t (29 or 68))] and [$\overline{64}$ or (64t20)] and [$\overline{66}$ or (66t67)] and [$\overline{76}$ or (76t77)] and $\overline{9}$n&
10. 10 ← (8 or 9 or 11 or 13 or 19) t ($\overline{34}$ and $\overline{71}$) and [$\overline{27}$ or (27t28)] and [$\overline{44}$ or 44t(29 or 68)] and [$\overline{54}$ or (54t55)] and [$\overline{64}$ or (64t20)] and [$\overline{66}$ or (66t67)] and [$\overline{76}$ or (76t77)] and $\overline{10}$n&
11. 11 ← (7 or 8 or 29) t ($\overline{34}$ and $\overline{71}$) and [$\overline{27}$ or (27t28)] and [$\overline{44}$ or 44t (29 or 68)] and [$\overline{54}$ or (54t55)] and [$\overline{64}$ or (64t20)] and [$\overline{66}$ or (66t67)] and [$\overline{76}$ or (76t77)] and $\overline{11}$n&
12. 12 ← (11 or 33) t ($\overline{34}$ and $\overline{71}$) and [$\overline{27}$ or (27t28)] and [$\overline{44}$ or (44t (29 or 68))] and [$\overline{54}$ or (54t55)] and [$\overline{64}$ or (64t20)] and [$\overline{66}$ or (66t67)] and [$\overline{76}$ and (76t77)] and $\overline{12}$n&
13. 13 ← (9 or 10 or 11 or 19 or 22 or 30 or 33 or 47 or 67) t ($\overline{34}$ and $\overline{71}$)

and [$\overline{27}$ or (27t28)] and [$\overline{44}$ or (44t(29 or 68))] and [$\overline{54}$ or (54t55)] and [$\overline{64}$ or (64t20)] and [$\overline{66}$ or (66t67)] and [$\overline{76}$ or (76t77)] and $\overline{13}$n&

14. 14 ← (6 or 9 or 10 or 11 or 19 or 22 or 24 or 30 or 32 or 46 or 47 or 54 or 67 or 72 or 74 or 77) t ($\overline{14}$ and $\overline{33}$ and $\overline{34}$ and $\overline{37}$ and $\overline{51}$ and $\overline{53}$ and $\overline{57}$ and $\overline{62}$ and $\overline{63}$ and $\overline{69}$ and $\overline{71}$)

15. 15 ← (7 or 8 or 9 or 10 or 12 or 13 or 14 or 16 or 19 or 20 or 22 or 23 or 24 or 25 or 30 or 32 or 35 or 38 or 43 or 46 or 47 or 48 or 54 or 57 or 59 or 60 or 61 or 64 or 67 or 68 or 70 or 74 or 75 or 77) n&

16. 16 ← [$\overline{25}$ and (8 or 12 or 13 or 14 or 15 or 20 or 21 or 23 or 24 or 29 or 31 or 35 or 45 or 48 or 49 or 58 or 59 or 60 or 61 or 65 or 66 or 72 or 74 or 76 or 79) n&]

17. 17 ← (9 or 10 or 19 or 30 or 47 or 54) t ($\overline{34}$ or $\overline{71}$) and [$\overline{27}$ or (27t28)] and [$\overline{44}$ or (44t(29 or 68))] and [$\overline{64}$ or (64t20)] and [$\overline{76}$ or (76t77)] and $\overline{17}$n&

18. 18 ← (12 or 16 or 17 or 25 or 33 or 40 or 42 or 60 or 69) n&

19. 19 ← 11 t ($\overline{33}$ and $\overline{62}$ and $\overline{71}$) and (12 or 13 or 14 or 15 or 30 or 32 or 41 or 48 or 49 or 55 or 56 or 74) and [$\overline{27}$ or (27t28)] and [$\overline{44}$ or (44t (29 or 68))] and [$\overline{54}$ or (54t55)] and [$\overline{64}$ or (64t20)] and [$\overline{66}$ or (66t67)] and [$\overline{76}$ or (76t77)] and $\overline{19}$n&

20. 20 ← 7 t ($\overline{34}$ and $\overline{71}$) and [$\overline{27}$ or (27t28)] and [$\overline{76}$ or (76t77)] and $\overline{20}$n&

21. 21 ← (10 or 20)n&

22. 22 ← 21n&

23. 23 ← $\overline{38}$ and [(9 or 10 or 12 or 13 or 19 or 22 or 24 or 30 or 35 or 46 or 48 or 54 or 67 or 77) n&]
     else ← $\overline{38}$ and [(9 or 10 or 12 or 13 or 19 or 22 or 24 or 30 or 35 or 46 or 48 or 54 or 67 or 77) n (14 or 15)n&]

24. 24 ← 23n&

25. 25 ← $\overline{38}$ and [(8 or 12 or 13 or 14 or 15 or 20 or 21 or 23 or 24 or 29 or 31 or 35 or 45 or 48 or 49 or 58 or 59 or 60 or 61 or 65 or 66 or 72 or 74 or 76 or 77) n&]

26. 26 ← 38n&

27. 27 ← $\overline{34}$ and $\overline{71}$ and [(8 or 20 or 26 or 29 or 43 or 46 or 68) n&]

28. 28 ← 27n&

29. 29 ← (7 or 8 or 20 or 28 or 38 or 40 or 43 or 44 or 45 or 75 or 76) n&

30. 30 ← (8 or 9 or 10 or 11 or 12 or 13 or 19 or 20 or 24 or 31 or 32 or 35 or 45 or 51 or 66 or 68 or 75) n&
     else ← [(8 or 9 or 10 or 11 or 12 or 13 or 19 or 20 or 24 or 32 or 35 or 68 or 75)n (14 or 15)] n&

31. 31 ← (10 or 13 or 20 or 30) n&
     else ← (10 or 13 or 20 or 30)n(14 or 15) n&

32. 32 ← 38 and $\overline{39}$ and [(11 or 12 or 13 or 31 or 35 or 48 or 49) n&]

33. 33 ← 11 and [(12 or 13 or 16 or 20 or 21 or 30 or 35 or 40 or 48 or 49 or 61 or 66 or 68 or 75 or 78) n&]

else ← 11 and [(12 or 13 or 16 or 20 or 30 or 35 or 48 or 61 or 68 or 75) n 15 n&]

else ← 11 and [(16 or 40 or 68 or 38) t (51 or 32) n&]

34. 34 ← (11 or 33) and [(11 or 19 or 22 or 30 or 33 or 46 or 47 or 51 or 53 or 57 or 61 or 63 or 74) n&]

35. 35 ← 9 t $\overline{63}$ and [$\overline{27}$ or (27t28)] and [$\overline{54}$ or (54t55)] and [$\overline{64}$ or (64t20)] and [$\overline{66}$ or (66t67)] and [$\overline{76}$ or (76t77)] and $\overline{35}$ n&

36. 36 ← (13 or 19 or 24 or 35 or 49 or 50) n&

37. 37 ← (34 or 71) and [(34 or 36 or 39 or 51 or 71 or 73) n&]

38. 38 ← $\overline{38}$ and (14 or 16 or 25)

39. 39 ← 38 and [(34 or 36 or 37 or 41 or 50 or 63 or 71 or 73) n&]

40. 40 ← 38 t $\overline{40}$

41. 41 ← 38 and [(40 or 68) n&]

42. 42 ← 38 and (25 or 40 or 41) n&

43. 43 ← (7 or 8) and $\overline{34}$ or $\overline{71}$ and [($\overline{9}$ and $\overline{16}$ and $\overline{19}$ and $\overline{25}$ and $\overline{33}$ and $\overline{39}$ and $\overline{53}$ and $\overline{58}$ and $\overline{60}$ and $\overline{63}$ and $\overline{78}$ and $\overline{43}$) n&]

44. 44 ← (7 or 8 or 38 or 43) n&

else ← (7 or 8 or 38 or 43) t (15 or 52) n&

45. 45 ← (7 or 8 or 10 or 13 or 20 or 21 or 43 or 44 or 46 or 48 or 64) n&

else ← (7 or 8 or 10 or 13 or 20 or 43 or 44 or 46 or 48 or 64) n (14 or 15 or 65) n&

46. 46 ← (8 or 9 or 11 or 12 or 16 or 19 or 28 or 29 or 40 or 43 or 47 or 48 or 51 or 68) n&

47. 47 ← (9 or 10 or 20 or 40 or 43 or 45 or 68) n&

48. 48 ← 11 t $\overline{34}$ and [(9 or 11 or 12 or 13 or 14 or 15 or 17 or 18 or 29 or 31 or 35 or 38 or 40 or 49 or 68 or 75) n&]

49. 49 ← $\overline{34}$ and $\overline{71}$ and [(9 or 10 or 12 or 13 or 19 or 24 or 30 or 31 or 35 or 46) n&]

else $\overline{34}$ and $\overline{71}$ and [(9 or 10 or 12 or 13 or 19 or 24 or 30 or 35 or 46) n (14 or 15 or 17) n&]

50. 50 ← (9 or 10 or 12 or 13 or 19 or 24 or 30 or 34 or 35 or 36 or 37 or 49 or 62 or 69 or 71 or 72 or 74) t ($\overline{27}$ and $\overline{44}$ and $\overline{50}$ and $\overline{54}$ and $\overline{64}$ and $\overline{66}$ and $\overline{76}$) n&

51. 51 ← (16 or 26 or 33 or 34 or 38 or 40 or 49 or 62 or 68) n&

52. 52 ← $\overline{63}$ and $\overline{71}$ and [(6 or 9 or 15 or 19 or 25 or 65) n&]

53. 53 ← 15 t [(33 or 34 or 37 or 50 or 71 or 78) n&]

54. 54 ← $\overline{34}$ and $\overline{66}$ and $\overline{67}$ and $\overline{71}$ and [(7 or 8 or 9 or 19 or 29 or 30 or 40 or 68) n&]

55. 55 ← $\overline{66}$ and $\overline{67}$ and 54n&

else $\overline{66}$ and $\overline{67}$ and [(54 n(14 or 15 or 57) n&]

56. 56 ← 47 n&

57. 57 ← (13 or 20 or 31) and [$\overline{18}$ and $\overline{23}$ and $\overline{27}$ and $\overline{44}$ and $\overline{57}$ and $\overline{64}$ and $\overline{66}$ and $\overline{76}$] n&

58. 58 ← $\overline{72}$ and [(9 or 10 or 12 or 13 or 19 or 23 or 24) n&]
    else ← $\overline{72}$ and [(9 or 10 or 12 or 13 or 19 or 23 or 24) n (14 or 15) n&]
59. 59 ← $\overline{38}$ and (24 or 58 or 72) n&
    else ← $\overline{38}$ and [(24 or 58 or 72) n (13 or 14 or 15 or 17)] n&
60. 60 ← 25 n&
    else ← 38 n&
61. 61 ← (12 or 13 or 15 or 31 or 35 or 36 or 49 or 58 or 75 or 76) t [($\overline{61}$ or $\overline{73}$) n &] and $\overline{34}$ and $\overline{71}$
62. 62 ← (34 or 37 or 71) t $\overline{12}$ and $\overline{62}$ n&
63. 63 ← (4 or 10 or 33 or 62 or 71) and $\overline{63}$ n&
64. 64 ← $\overline{20}$ and $\overline{21}$ and $\overline{34}$ and $\overline{40}$ and $\overline{68}$ and $\overline{71}$ and [(7 or 8 or 29 or 38 or 43 or 45) n&]
65. 65 ← (6 or 9 or 19 or 24 or 34 or 52 or 61) t ($\overline{14}$ or $\overline{33}$ or $\overline{34}$ or $\overline{37}$ or $\overline{51}$ or $\overline{53}$ or $\overline{57}$ or $\overline{62}$ or $\overline{63}$ or $\overline{69}$ or $\overline{71}$) and $\overline{65}$ n&
66. 66 ← $\overline{54}$ and $\overline{55}$ and $\overline{34}$ and $\overline{71}$ and [(9 or 10 or 12 or 13 or 14 or 15 or 29 or 31 or 77) n&]
67. 67 ← 66 n&
68. 68 ← 38 and [(13 or 15 or 26 or 35 or 38 or 40 or 44 or 51) n&]
69. 69 ← 49 t [($\overline{27}$ or (27t28)] and [$\overline{44}$ or (44t(29 or 68))] and [$\overline{66}$ or (66t 67)] and [$\overline{76}$ or (76t77)] and 69 n&
70. 70 ← 72 t $\overline{70}$
71. 71 ← 8 and (8 or 12 or 16 or 31 or 49 or 51 or 56 or 75 n&)
    else [38t (40 or 43 or 68) n&]
72. 72 ← (13 or 23 or 31 or 35 or 48 or 49 or 58 or 60 or 61 or 74) n&
73. 73 ← (34 or 50) t ($\overline{73}$ n&)
74. 74 ← (12 or 13 or 15 or 31 or 35 or 49 or 58) t [($\overline{34}$ or $\overline{71}$ or $\overline{73}$ or $\overline{74}$) n&]
75. 75 ← (9 or 12 or 13 or 14 or 15 or 19 or 30 or 31 or 35 or 36 or 48 or 49 or 68) n&
76. 76 ← $\overline{34}$ and $\overline{71}$ and [(8 or 9 or 12 or 13 or 14 or 15 or 19 or 29 or 31 or 45 or 49 or 54 or 57) n&]
77. 77 ← 76 and [(43 or 61 or 74 or 76) n&]
78. 78 ← 75 t ($\overline{78}$ n&)
79. 79 ← 38 t ($\overline{34}$ and $\overline{71}$) t ($\overline{79}$ n&)

Running the Model

Three instances of output from the model are given below, from three different stages in its development. The last run was produced by the final version of the model given above.

(1) First run

1. Incident begins.

3. Customer buys clothing.
4. Customer takes clothing home.
5. Customer tries on clothing.
6. Customer finds clothing does not fit.
14. Customer feels angry.
7. Customer returns clothing to shop.
29. Customer points out clothing is wrong size.
16. Assistant consults manager.
15. Customer becomes tense/nervous/anxious/distressed/impatient.
8. Customer asks that clothing be changed/altered at shop's expense.
27. Shop asks if garment is satisfactory apart from size.
28. Customer says garment is satisfactory apart from size.
9. Shop refuses customer's request.
52. Customer regrets purchase.
11. Shop offers alteration at £3.
46. Shop says no comparable substitutes in stock.
45. Customer says when goods were bought (i.e. recently).
12. Customer refuses shop offer.
74. Shop assistant becomes annoyed.
25. (Shop) assistant summons manager/senior.
38. Manager/senior arrives.
68. Customer explains problem to manager/senior.
48. Customer asks for better offer.
19. Shop refuses to improve offer.
14. Customer feels angry.
49. Customer threatens legal action/Press/consumer group/withdrawal of custom.
33. Shop improves offer.
63. Customer is satisfied/happy.
34. Customer accepts shop's offer.
37. Customer and shop arrange to implement final decision.
50. Customer leaves.
2. Incident ends.

(2) Second run

1. Incident begins.
2. Customer buys clothing.
4. Customer takes clothing home.
5. Customer tries on clothing at home.
6. Customer finds clothing does not fit.
7. Customer returns clothing to shop.
8. Customer asks that clothing be changed/altered at shop's expense/money refunded.

44. Shop asks customer what trouble is.
14. Customer feels angry.
75. Customer says she is long-standing customer.
29. Customer points out that garment is wrong size.
64. Shop asks if garment worn.
43. Shop examines goods.
15. Customer becomes tense.
 9. Shop refuses customer's request.
10. Shop gives justification for refusal – points out that clothes have been worn.
45. Customer says when goods were bought (recently).
47. Shop says it has been left too long (i.e. return of clothing).
20. Customer declares goods unworn (in a sense).
30. Shop points out it is governed by standing policy.
13. Customer objects to shop's offer/policy as unreasonable.
11. Shop offers alteration at £3.
56. Customer says handling of complaint/outcome is not satisfactory.
12. Customer refuses shop offer.
46. Shop says no comparable substitutes in stock.
34. Customer accepts shop's offer.
73. Shop relieved, satisfied.
57. Customer and shop arrange to implement final decision.
35. Customer says handling of complaint/outcome is not satisfactory.
30. Shop points out it is governed by standing policy.
50. Customer leaves.
 2. Incident ends.

(3) Third run

 1. Incident begins.
 3. Customer buys clothing.
 4. Customer takes clothing home.
 5. Customer tries on clothing at home.
 6. Customer finds clothing does not fit.
52. Customer regrets purchase.
 7. Customer returns clothing to shop.
20. Customer declares goods unworn (in a sense).
 8. Customer asks that clothing be changed/altered at shop's expense/money refunded.
54. Shops says customer should have tried on clothing in shop.
15. Customer becomes tense/anxious/distressed/impatient.
43. Shop examines goods.
44. Shop asks customer what trouble is with clothing.
29. Customer points out clothing is wrong size.

76. Customer says assistant said goods were right size.
61. Assistant becomes upset/unhappy.
77. Assistant denies having said goods were right size.
25. Assistant summons manager/senior.
38. Manager/senior arrives.
68. Customer explains problem to manager/senior.
71. Shop agrees to customer's request.
63. Customer is satisfied/happy.
39. Manager/senior leaves.
37. Customer and shop arrange to implement final decision.
50. Customer leaves.
 2. Incident ends.

Evaluation and Discussion

By and large the model achieved its targets. To a reasonable approximation the outputs it could produce seem to correspond to the set of sensible versions of the dispute being studied. It demonstrated (or at least employed) a rather interesting property of behaviour sequences, that they can best be described *backwards* showing where each event has come from, rather than forwards showing what every possible combination of circumstances could lead to. Subsequently a complete set of retrospective, and initially piecemeal descriptions of sequential fragments can be 'turned round' by the formal mechanism of the model, so that taken all together they can be used to make projections of possible futures.

It might be said that little has been learned about real behavioural processes by this exercise, since the rules are entirely arbitrary, apart from their capacity to reconstruct given and similar sequences. However, it is interesting to note what *kinds* of rules are required to do that. It will be seen that the rules in this model are of two types, one that could be called pseudo-Markovian rules and the other interlocking bracketing rules. Pseudo-Markovian rules say which events can follow which others, such as

$$a \leftarrow b\,t\,\&$$

meaning *a* can occur if the string-so-far finishes with *b*. Interlocking bracketing rules say that certain events can occur provided necessary events have occurred to create a suitable state of affairs for their occurrence, which itself may be of indefinite duration, and further provided that none of a different set of events which would nullify that state of affairs has subsequently occurred. An instance would be the rule

$$a \leftarrow (b \vee c \vee d) \wedge \bar{e} \wedge \bar{f} \wedge \bar{g}.$$

The rules only specify necessary conditions, not sufficient conditions, so one can write a rule to allow an event, but not write a rule which will necessarily make it happen. This creates a problem in that pseudo-Markov rules may allow a to follow b, but cannot ensure that it will, since an interlocking bracketing rule may allow for something else to happen instead. Now, since b is no longer last event the $b \rightarrow a$ sequence will never be completed. One possible solution would be to give pseudo-Markovian rules priority over interlocking bracketing rules.

On the whole the pseudo-Markovian rules control reactive behaviour like answering a question, or objecting to something unreasonable; interlocking bracketing rules control proactions like the introduction of new suggestions or strategies.

The other main characteristic to emerge from the model is the preponderance of 'trivial' rules in the sense that the plausible output of such a model depends in large measure on the explicit representation in the rules of obvious constraints, such as the implausibility of two consecutive arrivals by the same person in the same place without an intervening departure, or the inappropriateness of saying something to someone in a place where they have not yet arrived. If these kinds of rule are omitted the model does silly things, and if they are included they take up most of its bulk, in order to set the scene for a few more interesting and hypothetical regularities to be tested. Remedies for this are tried out in the subsequent models.

In general the rules are formatted rather like the 'productions' or circumstance $\Longrightarrow$ action pairs of a 'productive system', except that they are back to front, specifying a circumstance for each action, rather than an action for each circumstance. However, the architecture of this rule system is non-hierarchical, so phases or modes of behaviour cannot be invoked by calling special modules or subroutines of the rule system, which would almost certainly be an advantage with a more sophisticated model. The decision of whether to structure the model hierarchically depends on the theory of behavioural organisation that each model is used to test.

Sometimes an event may require two seemingly unrelated descriptions, one relating it to the past and one to the future. For example, the same remark may be an answer in relation to the preceding question and an insult with respect to the subsequent protest. This model cannot deal with such double categorisation.

There is no theory of categories in the model, and no explicit rationale for the vocabulary of events in the situation being as it is, nor are any relations between categories expressed other than serial order.

One of the main problems arises with the coding of implicit events. If, for example, one of the given instances includes a consultation between shop assistant and manager, that must imply that the shop assistant has explained the problem to the manager, although that may not be stated (and hence not coded) explicitly. In another version explanations of the problem to the manager may be mentioned explicitly and a category created for it. Now, is the first instance to be recoded, so as to include an implicit event only explicitly mentioned in the second instance, in which case each coding must be continually reappraised in the light of other examples? Or is an additional kind of rule to be added to say one event type, wherever it occurs, also implies the occurrence of others (which may not always be true)? And if not, how are future events which are activated by an event when it is explicit, also to be activated by it when it is implicit? There is no easy solution to this. The present model used explication by recoding as far as possible, although that is a clumsy and ultimately rather limited solution.

There were numerous other more specific difficulties with the formulation of rules, such as the tendency for parenthetical references to thought and feeling to arrest otherwise connected chains of overt behaviour; the tendency for some event pairs to be reversible such as stating a choice and giving the reason; and the problem of drawing the line between probable contingencies stated in a few rules, and obscure possibilities stated in very many.

Overall the model seems to be an interesting but far from ideal way of stating and testing generative behavioural rules. Its main drawbacks are the lack of real explanatory psychological context; the time and care that is required to produce a relatively crude reproduction of a relatively simple behavioural situation; and the high proportion of uninteresting rules that are needed to make the model behave sensibly.

In the next study a different format altogether will be adopted, in order to try to remedy these disadvantages.

Study 18: Hierarchical Modelling

Introduction

In the previous study there was a tendency not to see the wood for the trees. The description of the behavioural structures and regularities involved was all on the same level, and it was a level of rather fine detail at that. As was noted at the time, this has several disadvantages. The model becomes slow and tedious to produce and interpret. It is rigid and very literal, so obvious regularities of behaviour have to be included as explicit rules which take up much of the model. All sense is lost that the behavioural pattern is not just present on one single level of description, when in fact the different phases and stages of the sequence form a kind of macro-structure, with other finer aspects of the pattern forming the sub-structures of the larger pieces.

Moreover, there was a kind of arbitrariness about the level of description used, in that the whole episode could well have been a single event in a longer-term story, or conversely each of the individual events could have been the whole substance of a micro-analysis of its own substructure. If, as seems likely, much the same kind of rules and regularities would have been found on any of these different levels of description, the implication is that the structure in question is a hierarchical or 'top-to-bottom' one, and not at all like a 'left-to-right' chain reaction as portrayed in the model.

Perhaps the essential feature of such a situation is not the way one event follows another in succession after all, but the way in which the whole encounter needs to consist of certain major phases (which could occur in various orders, but probably not all), and the way each of those phases consists of some necessary and some optional sub-components, and so on.

This is merely to introduce a familiar idea in a more specific form. It has been suggested earlier that rule models of conversation sequences may fulfil much the same function that a generative grammar does for linguists, but not particularly that the same kind of rules or grammars would be involved. From the outcome of the last study, however, and the remarks above, it seems that something very like a phrase-structure grammar may be appropriate, with or without the transformational component that would turn it into a full-blown transformational generative grammar of action (Păun, 1976; Frentz, 1976).

This seems likely to offer not only a more faithful reproduction of the real behavioural structure, but also a more practical research strategy, in that a global and self-contained description would be produced first, and then broken down in successive stages to finer and finer levels of detail. The process could be stopped at any point giving a complete, although perhaps rather general picture of the sequence, whereas the previous model was built by a procedure which was detailed from the outset, but was in a much more serious sense incomplete until the very end. If such procedures were to be used to represent and interact with real problems and dilemmas as they occurred, one requirement would be that they could work in 'real time', keeping pace with the course of events. For a single meeting or argument, of course, that would never be possible, but for a series of meetings with breaks in between it might be, provided the method of analysis could itself work on a flexible time scale, sacrificing detail for speed where necessary.

This study, then, was an attempt to produce a model of a more literally 'grammatical' kind from a new corpus of active role-played disputes.

Producing the Corpus

The corpus of material on which this model is based, was again produced by role playing, for the reasons given with the previous study. Twelve volunteers from the subject panel (eleven women and one man, aged 18–42) came to the laboratory in six pairs. Each pair took part in the same five role-played exercises. One was a practice, and the subsequent four were tape-recorded, becoming respectively the material for this study, the next one, and two others which will not be reported here. The six versions of the same problem produced by the six subject pairs were the corpus for this study. Their role-play task was defined by a pair of different though factually consistent written briefings or preambles, given to the two subjects on each trial. The two preambles used to generate the corpus for this model are given below.

(1) Brief for Mr/Ms Harrison

You have just moved into a house of your own for the first time. It has been very hard to scrape enough money together to buy it, but you have finally managed to get a rather run-down property. At present the mortgage repayments are taking all the money you can spare, so it will be some time before you can have work done, even on the house itself, let alone the garden, which looks like a jungle with rambling thornbushes and delapidated fencing. As soon as you have any spare money the first priority will be to buy a decent bed in place of the make-shift camp-bed that is breaking your back every night.

Your neighbours on one side seem very pleasant, but the Johnsons on the other side are reputed to be a rather bossy and self-opinioned family. Local gossip has it that they tend to be quite unreasonable and unpleasant to newcomers as a point of principle, but if you can stand up for yourself and not be bullied they come to respect you in time and mellow considerably.

You have decided that if they try to get nasty you can always play your trump card, and complain about the incessant barking of their dog. If the worst comes to the worst you would even threaten legal action, as you were told that in cases like this the courts can make the owner silence his dog, if need be, by sending it to the vet for an operation.

Although having nothing personal against the neighbour (or the dog) you are determined to stand your ground if they try anything. You have just had a rather terse phone call from Mr/Mrs Johnson to say he/she is coming round to see you. . . .

(2) Brief for Mr/Mrs Johnson

You are a devoted animal lover living in a small suburban house. You find your neighbours are often unsympathetic to your love of animals, and you sometimes suspect you are rather unpopular in the district, for taking a strong line on so many local issues, especially where animal welfare is concerned. However unpopular you may be with local people, you still have your one real joy in life, your old and devoted sheepdog Bess.

Your main worry at present is that your new neighbour Mr/Ms Harrison has shown no signs of repairing the dividing fence between your two gardens, and there is every chance that Bess will stray through the broken fence and out of the ungated back entry onto the main road. You have to let Bess into your own garden while all the family are away at work, as she could not possibly be shut in the house or car all day long, but now you are afraid to let her out. Poor Bess has been so miserable that she has howled and yelped pathetically for her old freedom which is now so mysteriously denied.

The fence in question has posts on the Harrisons' side, and so, in your understanding of the law, the responsibility is theirs. You will take legal action if you have to, to make them do their duty. After all you are as hard up these days as anyone, and have neither the means or the inclination to pay other people's bills for them.

You feel that as a possible legal action is involved, you must take a firm line from the outset, as any leniency or tolerance for delay would weaken your case in court. You have phoned to make an appointment, and are on your way round now to do some straight talking. . . .

Clearly the objectives of the two people, and the interpretation they put on events, are quite contradictory, and the two preambles were written with a view to producing a stalemate for the role-players to extricate themselves from.

The form of the dilemma was prompted originally by the idea that a common and problematic stalemate is produced by the following kind of exchange:

> A: Do X
> or else I shall carry out threat Y against you.
> B: I shall not do X
> and if you do Y to me I shall do Z to you.

That is the 'threat and counter-threat' dilemma.

> A: DEMAND
> : THREAT
> B: REFUSAL
> : COUNTER-THREAT.

In this case it would take the form

> JOHNSON: Mend your fence
> or I shall take legal action.
> HARRISON: I cannot afford a repair
> and if you sue me I shall sue you over the noise your
> dog makes.

A further twist or circularity to the dilemma, of course, is that it is open to Johnson to reply that the noise from the dog would stop if only it could be left to exercise in a securely fenced garden. And so the plot thickens. In practice, however, the role-players were much more inclined to see the problem as a co-operative problem-solving enterprise in which everyone's preferences must be considered, rather than an antagonistic encounter in which each side tried to force their choice of solution on the other.

The six recorded discussions, which were between 4' 8" and 9' 49" in length, were then transcribed orthographically and used in written form as the basis and the test of the model.

Constructing the Model

A taxonomic tree was produced by consideration of the task the subjects had been given, the preambles and an informal inspection of the first transcript. The tree consisted of the main phases and stages the encounter might be expected to have *a priori*, such as courtesy and greeting at the outset; presentation of the problem (since it soon became evident to the participants that they did not have the same version of 'the facts'); attempts at joint problem-solving; and so on. These main stages as set out in idealised 'logical' sequence, were then elaborated into their various sub-components and numbered hierarchically, that is with 3.1.2. standing for phase 3, sub-component 1, sub-sub-component 2, and so on.

This tree of episode parts, and parts of parts, was further elaborated as required when new categories of events were found in the six transcripts. The version shown in Figure 31 is the final one, after all modifications were complete.

The six transcripts were then coded so that the terminal or branch-ending categories from the tree were mapped to them in the appropriate sequences, as an abbreviated representation of their form. The task for the model was now to reproduce these sequences of codes (and perhaps others of a similar type). Unfortunately, it turned out that the order of occurrence of events in the transcripts was a scrambled (or to put it more optimistically 'transformed') version of the ideal sequence suggested by the taxonomic tree.

Figure 32 shows the first of the six transcripts as the sequence of event codes that occurred (the *surface structure*), the idealised sequence in number code order of the same sub-set of possible events, the specific trace through the taxonomic tree that would produce the latter, and its relation with surface order.

Corresponding diagrams were prepared for the other five transcripts, which showed a similar mismatch between ideal and observed sequences. It was as if subjects had started upon one phase of the interaction (as we conceived of it), jumped ahead or back to another one before it was complete, then resumed the first, and so on. So what we took originally to be successive stages of the encounter were actually produced more in parallel than in series. At this point it was decided to separate out two parts of the model or grammar. The first, very like phrase structure rules or a base structure component (Chomsky, 1965) would, by a series of rewrites, define which sub-trees of the overall taxonomic tree had appeared in observed sequences, as if in their idealised order. It is tempting to liken this to a deep structure as a convenient label, although at this point the linguistic metaphor is particularly weak.

In the next section the rules of the taxonomic tree and the generating rules for observed 'deep structures' are given.

The harder task was to summarise the relation between the deep and surface orderings in which the events occurred, the equivalent of the transformational component. This seemed to follow a statistical rather than a determinate regularity, which is summarised in a table and graph in the next section.

For all the possible events from the taxonomic scheme, considered in their ideal or 'deep structure' order, the greatest, least and mean displacements backwards and forwards in sequence are shown. This may look deceptively regular since the earliest events can only be delayed, and the last brought forward. The overall downward slant of the three curves is a product of logical necessity rather than contingent fact.

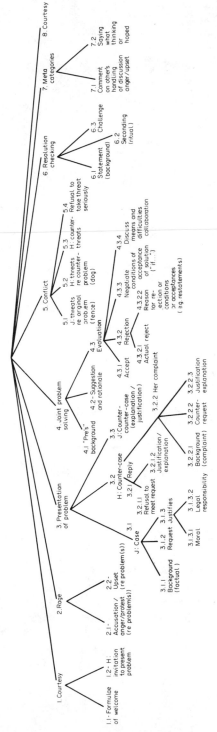

FIG. 31 *A priori* tree-diagram for dispute between neighbours.

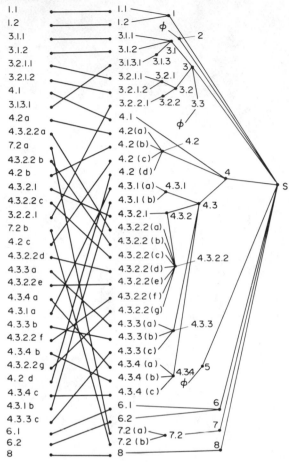

FIG. 32   Transformed surface structure.

The Model

Taxonomic Tree Grammar

S → 1, courtesy + 2, rage + 3, presentation of problem + 4, joint problem-solving + 5, conflict + 6, resolution + 7, meta-categories + 8, courtesy.

1 → 1.1, formulae of welcome + 1.2, H: invitation to present problem.

2 → 2.1, accusation/anger/protest re problem + 2.2 upset re problems.

3 → 3.1, J: case + 3.2, H: counter-case + 3.3, J: counter-counter-case.

4 → 4.1, background + 4.2, suggestion and rationale + 4.3, evaluation.

5 → 5.1, J: threats (re fence) + 5.2, H: threats (re dog) + 5.3, H: counter-threats + 5.4, refusal to take threat seriously.

$6 \rightarrow 6.1$, statement + 6.2, seconding + 6.3, challenge.

$7 \rightarrow 7.1$, comment on others' handling of discussion + 7.2, statement of what thinking/hoping.

$8 \rightarrow \emptyset$.

$3.1 \rightarrow 3.1.1$, background + 3.1.2, request + 3.1.3, justification.

$3.2 \rightarrow 3.2.1$, reply + 3.2.2, her complaint (H).

$4.3 \rightarrow 4.3.1$, accept + 4.3.2, rejection + 4.3.3, negotiation of conditions of acceptance + 4.3.4, discussion of means.

$3.1.3 \rightarrow 3.1.3.1$, moral + 3.1.3.2, legal responsibility.

$3.2.1 \rightarrow 3.2.1.1$, refusal to meet request + 3.2.1.2, justification/explanation.

$3.2.2 \rightarrow 3.2.2.1$, background + 3.2.2.2, counter-request + 3.2.2.3, justification/explanation.

$4.3.2 \rightarrow 4.3.2.1$, rejection + 4.3.2.2, reason for rejection or conditions of accep-tance.

Observed sequences: Grammar

S	$\rightarrow 1 + 3 + 4 + 6 + 7 + 8$	
	$\rightarrow 1 + 2 + 3 + 4 + 5 + 6 + 7 + 8$	
	$\rightarrow 1 + 3 + 4 + 5 + 6 + 7 + 8$	(2)
	$\rightarrow 1 + 2 + 3 + 4 + 5 + 8$	
	$\rightarrow 1 + 2 + 3 + 4 + 5 + 6 + 7$	
1	$\rightarrow 1.1 + 1.2$	(3)
	$\rightarrow 1.1$	(3)
2	$\rightarrow 2.1 + 2.2$	
	$\rightarrow 2.1$	
	$\rightarrow 2.2$	(2)
3	$\rightarrow 3.1 + 3.2$	
	$\rightarrow 3.1 + 3.2 + 3.3$	(5)
4	$\rightarrow 4.1 + 4.2 + 4.3$	(3)
	$\rightarrow 4.2 + 4.3$	(3)
5	$\rightarrow 5.1 + 5.2 + 5.4$	
	$\rightarrow 5.1 + 5.3$	
	$\rightarrow 5.1 + 5.2$	(2)
	$\rightarrow 5.1$	
6	$\rightarrow 6.1 + 6.2$	(4)
	$\rightarrow 6.1$	
7	$\rightarrow 7.2$	(2)
	$\rightarrow 7.1$	(2)
	$\rightarrow 7.1 + 7.2$	
8	$\rightarrow 8$	
3.1	$\rightarrow 3.1.1 + 3.1.2 + 3.1.3$	(6)

3.2   → 3.2.1 + 3.2.2   (6)

4.3   → 4.3.1 + 4.3.2 + 4.3.3 + 4.3.4   (3)

      → 4.3.2 + 4.3.3 + 4.3.4

      → 4.3.1 + 4.3.2 + 4.3.3   (2)

3.1.3 → 3.1.3.1

      → 3.1.3.1 + 3.1.3.2   (5)

3.2.1 → 3.2.1.1 + 3.2.1.2   (4)

      → 3.2.1.2   (2)

3.2.2 → 3.2.2.1   (2)

      → 3.2.2.1 + 3.2.2.2

      → 3.2.2.1 + 3.2.2.3   (2)

      → 3.2.2.1 + 3.2.2.2 + 3.2.2.3

4.3.2 → 4.3.2.1 + 4.3.2.2   (4)

      → 4.3.2.2   (2)

TABLE 10   *Transformations: Summary of displacement scores*

Item	Minimum displacement	Maximum displacement	Mean displacement
1.1	0	0	0
1.2	0	0	0
2.1	5	39	18.0
2.2	17	52	31.5
3.1.1	−3	0	−1.33
3.1.2	−3	20	2.2
3.1.3.1	−5	43	15.0
3.1.3.2	−8	25	7.91
3.2.1.1	−8	27	6.17
3.2.1.2	−16	22	2.16
3.2.2.1	−11	14	−1.67
3.2.2.2	−4	29	15.7
3.2.2.3	−9	17	6.9
3.3	−12	16	−0.24
4.1	−10	16	1.33
4.2	−34	17	−4.30
4.3.1	4	20	9.89
4.3.2.1	−31	4	−17.0
4.3.2.2	−43	13	−8.0
4.3.3	−46	6	−10.0
4.3.4	−26	4	−3.25
5.1	−27	8	−10.1
5.2	−22	−3	−13.2
5.3	−11	−11	−11.0
5.4	−17	−17	−17.0
6.1	1	7	2.67
6.2	0	3	1.40
7.1	−49	0	−18.8
7.2	−23	0	−13.1
8	−13	0	−2.29

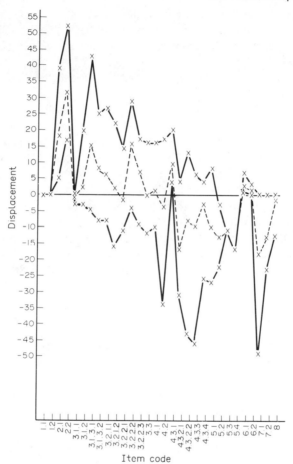

FIG. 33 Minimum, maximum and mean displacement
values.

Discussion and Alternative Procedure

The main drawback with this model, as we have seen, is the mismatch between the ideal order of events generated by the model, in which each major function within the episode is dealt with and finished with separately before the next one begins, and the actual order of events as observed, where the logically distinct phases of the encounter all seem to be scrambled together. Given the difficulty of describing the transformational relation between these ideal and observed sequences precisely, the effective force of the model is that of a generator of consistent sub-vocabularies from the overall event-lexicon, rather than a generator of 'sentences' or sequences *per se*.

The second drawback is that, as in the previous model, issues of psychological interest, having to do with rivalry, loyalty, trust, defensiveness and so on, tend to become submerged in the technicalities of model writing. The answer, as the next study will show, seems to lie in a reappraisal of the notion of 'model' and its relation with a realist theory of underlying processes shaping and controlling behaviour.

Before moving on to the last of this group of three models, it is worth just mentioning an alternative modelling procedure. It was not used here, as it makes a theoretical assumption which is implausible for this kind of material, but which might be applicable elsewhere. The assumption is that a 'jigsaw theory' of structure is appropriate, or a theory of endogenous templates as it might be called (see Harré, 1977). The modelling procedure is for those kinds of permutable structures where the nature or valency of the pieces is the determinant of their possible combinations, like the pieces of a jigsaw fitting together, or atoms combining to form molecules. In the case of conversation, however, it is much more plausible to think of exogenous structuring, of outside factors like beliefs and expectations of speakers, governing the concatenation of remarks, not their intrinsic structural properties.

For sequences or structures where intrinsic regulation of wholes by parts is more in order, the procedure would be:

1. Redescribe the observed sequences, coding or emphasising those features to be accounted for by the model.
2. List similarities and differences amongst the examples in the corpus.
3. Describe the variety of initial states and outcomes and the apparent links between them.
4. Partial out major phases and sub-systems of interaction.
5. Decompose data into individual events, states, circumstances and other elements.
6. Make inventory and standard vocabulary for elements detected in 5.
7. Characterise parts, emphasising features such as predictability, difficulty, social desirability, mutual availability, and so on, which would influence their use, and determine their 'valency'.
8. Identify links between events and 'regulating factors' including necessary and/or sufficient conditions, facilitators, inhibitors, modifiers, enablers, and so forth.
9. Restate these in time variant terms which are not peculiar to particular (unstated) contextual circumstances.
10. Generalise as far as possible to a form that would be true of other events and episodes.
11. If possible axiomatise the system, distinguishing between derived and underived regularities, and the rules of their derivation.
12. Restate elements and relations in standard notation permitting regenera-

tion of possible sequences, such as a recursive augmented transition network (Woods, 1970), state space diagram (Minsky, 1972) or production system (Anderson, 1976).

13. Run the model, estimating exogenous variables, choosing free variables, and generating endogenous variables and their 'history' over time.
14. Evaluate and compare with real sequences, and other criteria of adequacy.
15. Use for prediction of and interaction with real systems.

This procedure is given in outline only, since in its details it would almost certainly need to be accommodated to the peculiarities of each case. Even then there is a danger of focusing too much on *a priori* research recipes, at the expense of particular issues and particular evidence.

In the next study an attempt will be made to construct a theory-testing model, as opposed to a mere data-reproducing one of the kind which can in other respects seem arbitrary, and theoretically implausible.

Study 19: Goal-net Modelling

Introduction

What should a behavioural model be a model *of*? The tempting answer is *behaviour*. But taken too literally that can lead to the kind of problems illustrated in the last two studies. All that is likely to be achieved is a formula or procedure for reproducing behavioural patterns which says nothing of real processes, and is not built out of natural types of sub-components. Such a model may have very useful applications as an experimental system in its own right, showing how behaviour may be affected by new, and as yet untried, circumstances, but as a discovery (or evaluation) procedure for process theories it has little to offer. For that purpose the model should be a representation of the underlying system of processes and entities that govern the behaviour, built in such a way that it reproduces the behaviour, but *not* a representation of the behaviour *per se*.

Ideally the end point would look something like Figure 34, although in

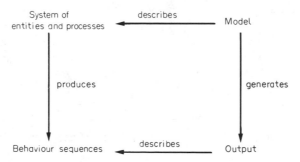

FIG. 34   Role of models – first version.

practice it is a lot to expect a single formulation to function both as an intelligible description of psychological processes *and* a procedure for producing descriptions of all and only the patterns of behaviour these processes would produce. It may be more realistic to divide these requirements as shown in Figure 35, so that the former demand is satisfied by a *theory*, probably stated in a natural language, while the latter is satisfied by a *model of the theory* realised in some form like an algorithm or grammar. The relationship between model and theory is, of course, more complex than that. The model also exemplifies the theory, while the theory describes and entails the model.

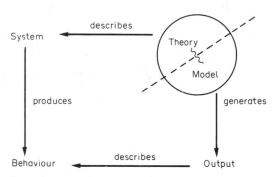

FIG. 35   Role of models — second version.

The real problem arises in producing a theory to describe the system, and in particular, in choosing the right type of 'substrate' for that theory. Six of the main possibilities will be discussed below:

Entity theories. Most explanatory theories in natural science (and often in common-sense psychology too) work by postulating entities, things, or material objects, such as fundamental particles which endure over time, and have as their distinguishing characteristics attributes like mass, charge, or 'colour'. These attributes determine the transactions between fundamental entities, and those transactions regulate or constitute the gross behaviour which we might hope to explain. In a rather similar way common-sense psychology refers to conscience, belief, attitude, personality, and so on, as things which, like the actors in a play, have their own characteristics determining their interrelations and hence the overall 'plot', in this case of the behaviour sequence. However, when looked at more closely these things are not like entities at all. *The belief that p*, for instance, is not all that much like an element in a mental structure that can combine and interact with others according to its properties, in the way that an atom may join and influence one molecule and then another. There is no conservation of identity (or equivalent energy-mass total). In fact the belief behaves more like a transient state of affairs, an event (albeit covert) in the sequence to be explained, than like a part of the 'machinery' that produces it. To explain overt behaviour by reference to mental states is to derive a diachronic structure from a diachronic template (Harré, 1977) which is clearly unsatisfactory. It is perhaps more helpful to see mental state terms as parts of the sequence of events, rather than explanations for it, and hence to regard common-sensical 'explanations' of behaviour as interpolations of missing data from the complete record of the phenomenon, while the question of why these elaborate descriptions must follow certain patterns in order to be plausible and 'well-formed' belongs to a different and more scientific realm of explanation.

Jigsaw theories. Given the structural emphasis of this field of research it is tempting to treat elements of behaviour sequences, not so much as being arranged by some process external to them, as being capable of spontaneous recombination according to their own 'valencies' — a theory of endogenous structure (like so many in nature) where parts combine to form wholes, simply by virtue of their intrinsic combinatorial propensities. As a notational device (or model) this has its attractions, but as a realist theory its metaphysics are wildly implausible. Taken to extremes it would go something like this. The social world consists of various types of events, each with inbuilt constraints determining which other events it will combine with to form the 'diachronic molecules' that we are aware of as our experience, our lives, careers, interactions, relationships and so on. Note there is no place in this theory for persons or their properties as such (although it may be a distinguishing feature of an event that it is the behaviour of one person rather than another). The events merely form themselves into chains.

Events and laws or rules. Another possibility would be to have a theoretical substrate consisting of a set of entities, and a separate 'rule book' for exogenous constraints and regulatory factors producing regular sequences. These two ingredients of theory are very like the constitutive and regulative rules discussed by Searle (1965). Again the first problem to arise is the difficulty of seeing this as a realist theory. How can events waiting to happen, and the regularities with which they could happen, be real parts of an (ultimately) material process? By making the system consist of events and laws (rather than, for instance, people with different behavioural patterns) an extreme form of functionalism is being proposed, in which elements of the explanatory system are taken to be no more than (or to be characterised by no more than) their behavioural tendencies and capacities. In some disciplines, particularly electronics, this has proved extremely successful. To call components in a circuit a switch, resistor, amplifier, inductance and so on is to describe what they do and the role they play in the whole *as if* it were a description of what they are and how they are constituted. The application of this conceptual transformation to psychology will be discussed later.

Common-sense mentalism. Looking at the preambles for these role-playing studies it is possible to imagine a good deal of the interaction that would take place without employing any special theory. Common-sense analysis and reasoning suggests that the actors would feel and want certain things, realise some possibilities and not others, import certain implicit goals about continued good relations, ans so on. Perhaps the explicit model need be no more than an explication of the implicit common-sense model. Certainly common-sense reasoning can suggest useful concepts and processes for an explicit theory to test, but this should be taken more in the spirit of an analogy between neighbouring descriptions than the overlay of an implicit body of knowledge with its explicit counterpart. Cases such as this are really of interest only in so far as they require us to propose processes and regularities that are outside (but if possible consistent with) common-sense psychology.

Means-end hierarchies (Harré, personal communication). These are rather like 'scripts, plans and goals' (Schank and Abelson, 1977). The situation from which each dialogue comes, and by which it is shaped, could be seen as a hierarchy or network of inter-connected goals, and the means for the two participants to achieve them. During the course of their discussion, they are using these goal-maps as a reference, rather like the board in a two-person board game, except that it is incompletely known to each of them at the outset, and as the discussion proceeds they have to build up a shared conception of the board, as well as trying to navigate through its various paths and branches to a mutually acceptable outcome.

This is specially attractive as it makes the model a representation of social competence, both in the sense of ability and in the sense akin to linguistic 'competence'. The system becomes a set of interconnected 'ways of doing things', which could in principle include procedures for acquiring and deleting other procedures, modifying procedures, calling one as a sub-routine from another, and so on. This is the view that will be explored further in this study.

Situations. One last possibility worth introducing at this point is the concept of the social situation as an explanatory notion. It seems to have two quite different meanings, each raising its own problems. As used in the psychological literature, a situation is a kind of set-piece occasion, like an interview or dinner party, defined by its own cluster of artefacts, rules of behaviour, cast of characters, and so on (Argyle *et al.*, 1981). Again the problem of realist interpretation arises. A situation seems to be a rather ephemeral thing which does not so much exist as occur, and hence seems more a candidate to be explained than to explain anything else (such as the structure of particular sets of behaviour sequences).

In everyday usage a situation is a state of affairs or state-of-play in a game or a protracted enterprise. It would be a nonsense to begin a history, for instance, by saying that by the turn of the century the situation was a summit meeting. A far more likely predicate to 'the situation' would be a description of the current disposition of world powers, military and economic forces, and motives. Similarly a chess 'situation' posed as a puzzle in a newspaper is an instant from a game, not a cluster of features defining a type of occasion of play. On this view of situations, they become more realistic, but are reduced to points or stages within the sequence rather than explanatory frameworks within which it occurs, and they relate to the sequence as a whole more as a cursor sweeping along a slide rule, than as a theory of logarithms according to which the scale as a whole is laid out.

Before outlining the present study *per se*, another special objective should be mentioned. The last two studies, like this one, set out to decompose collections of behaviour sequences and then reproduce them (and other similar tokens of the same type) from explicitly stated rules and principles. This was, however, largely *post hoc*: the analysis was based on the sequences themselves, and was therefore explanation after the event. Instead, it would be theoretically more interesting and practically more useful to be able to derive the model that will predict the sequences, from the prior circumstances which influenced the sequences, without consulting the sequences themselves. In this study a model will be constructed from the *preambles* that defined the role-play exercise, and only tested against the sequences themselves as they were recorded.

Producing the Corpus

The corpus for this study was produced in the same way as that for the previous study, on the same occasion, using the same subjects. The preambles are given below:

Brief for Jo(e)

You live in a small two-bedroomed flat, which you found some time ago and now share with Pat, a friend from work. The flat is rented, in your name, from a landlord who had no objection to your sharing with a friend, provided you will take *personal* responsibility for the way the place is kept, and for the regular payment of rent. Pat is always very punctual in contributing his/her share of the money, which is fortunate as you seem to be permanently broke and could not afford to pay all the rent yourself, even for a short while.

At first the arrangement worked very well, but lately Pat has become increasingly untidy and unreliable. Things came to a head a few days ago when the landlord called to find that Pat had gone off to work after you, leaving the place unlocked and in a filthy state. The first you knew of this was an angry phone call from the landlord to say that unless things improved dramatically you would both have to leave. Pat's slovenly ways had irked you for some time, but you had tried not to complain in case he/she left and you had to manage financially or find a new partner — an unwelcome prospect as your other friends all have their own homes and you would have to take in a stranger. It seems the best solution would be to get Pat to mend his/her ways and to stay on in the flat. You really do not want him/her to leave.

Now you feel you must clear up these problems as soon as possible. They have been preying on your mind and causing you to sleep badly. On some occasions you have even taken to drowning your troubles in whisky — a real danger sign as you do not usually drink much.

Pat has just come home from work and you feel it is time for a talk. . . .

Brief for Pat

> You live in a small two-bedroomed flat with Jo(e), a friend from work. The arrangement began when you first moved to the district to take your present job, and Jo(e), who was already living there, said he/she could do with someone to share the flat and the burden of paying the rent. The landlord, who deals directly with Jo(e) for the most part, seems quite happy about this state of affairs, and so were you at first.
>
> Lately though, you have been feeling that a place of your own would be better where you could spread yourself and your things without having to listen to Jo(e)'s incessant nagging about tidiness. Although the flat is not his/hers, Jo(e) seems only too ready to play the heavy-handed parent, and to try to scold you into fitting his/her lifestyle.
>
> Now you feel you are stuck. You would really like to leave, but Jo(e) is financially and perhaps emotionally dependent on your being there. The last straw is that Jo(e) has started drinking rather heavily, which makes him/her even more authoritarian. As the drinking problem gets worse you wish more and more that you could leave, but at the same time you feel more guilty about the prospect of doing so.
>
> The whole problem could not have come at a worse time, as you are already under heavy pressure at work, and although you do not usually worry about work when you are at home, you have been finding yourself so pre-occupied with deadlines and targets just lately, that even your basic routine has had to be neglected. Twice you have gone to work without your lunch, and last week you forgot your money on one occasion, and omitted to lock the flat on another. You really cannot cope with any more pressure just now. It would solve everything in a way if you had an excuse to just walk out.
>
> The time has come to sort the matter out with Jo(e). You have just returned from work to find Jo(e) waiting for you in one of his/her moods. . . .

Constructing the Model

A separate map of goals and means for each participant was drawn up by consideration of the preambles. In doing so it became apparent that various kinds of relations needed to be represented, including a goal implying a sub-goal; goals or sub-goals being incompatible, in that doing A precludes B (or the converse, or both); sub-goals in AND or OR relations with each other in the accomplishment of goals; and so on. The notation that was used for this was modified from Winograd's (1972) notation for syntactic relations in his natural language understanding program.

The two individual goal structures are given in Figures 36 and 37.

The separate goal maps were then compiled into a common structure, *as if all the facts were known to both participants*, although in fact this overall perspective had to be created during discussion, rather than being available at the outset. One such composite is shown in Figure 38, with *interpersonal* goal differences unknown to either party at the beginning dotted in.

Some slight embellishment of the diagram was necessary in the light of the observed sequences, but it seems that the underlying principle holds good. The version in Figure 38 is basically the original produced from the preambles, with only a minimum of embellishment required to account for the extract shown below from the beginning of the first dialogue.

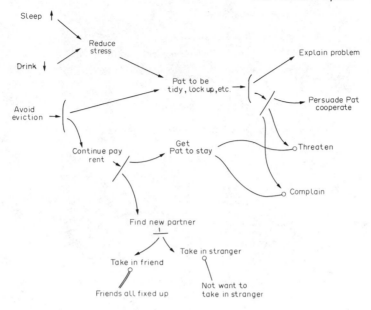

FIG. 36   Goal map for Jo(e).

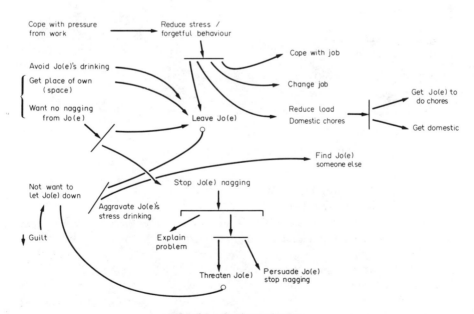

FIG. 37   Goal map for Pat.

Key to figures 36, 37 and 38

A → B   B is a means to A.

A —• B   Doing A would prevent you from doing B.

A → | → B / → C   B *or* C are means to A.

A → [→ B / → C   B *and* C are needed for A.

A ⟹ B   A (a fact not a goal) is counter to B.

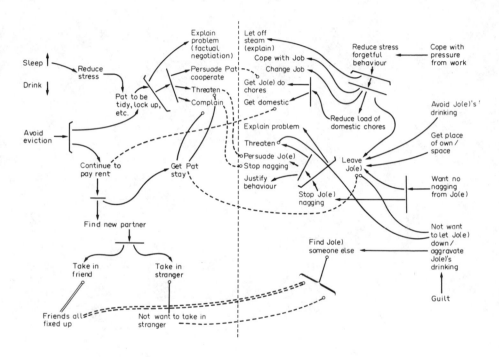

FIG. 38   Composite goal map for Jo(e) and Pat.

A: Hello Jo(e), I'm back.

B: Hi, how was your day?

A: Oh, as bad as usual. Got a lot of stuff to get on with, I never seem to have any spare evenings these days.

B: Mmm.

Pat, you know the landlord rang me up last week.

A: Mmm.

B: Seems he came by on Tuesday — er — wasn't expecting him and — er — when he came in the flat was unlocked.

A: Oh really?

B: Mmm. He was very cross about it. He said it was in an absolute tip too. I mean that was the day you had a half day — you had the morning off didn't you?

A: Of yes, yes um — I must have rushed off I think and forgotten to lock the door.

B: Mmm. The landlord seems to be a bit of a fuddy-duddy and he likes things all neat and clean and everything. Wants to . . . people to walk in.

A: Well there couldn't have been much mess, only the breakfast things probably.

B: Mmm, well he said one of the bedrooms was really untidy with everything about too, lying on the floor.

A: Well it's not his business to go in people's bedrooms surely.

B: Mmm.

A: I mean it can't make much different to the flat and how things are run whether the bedroom's untidy or not. I mean I'm sorry I left the door — the door open that was just an oversight and a mistake and well perhaps he's got a complaint there but it's none of his business whether my bedroom happens to be slightly untidy.

B: He was really cross with me. Nasty, he was threatening to bring in cleaners every week and make us pay for them and things like that and I don't want that.

A: Well I'm sorry about that I mean I don't know what he's on about, it's only sort of an unmade bed and clothes and papers all over the place it's nothing that needs cleaners.

The Rules

Of course the goal maps do not constitute a generative model in themselves. They are like a data base without a program. The rules for their consultation and elaboration need to be added. Assuming each person has a version of the map with what he knows so far marked on it and the remainder of the other person's representations 'pencilled in' (that is, the potential parts of his picture to be discovered in the course of discussion are in a state of virtual representation). These rules would be something like

1. Start turn.
2. Mark in new goals or connections discovered during last turn.
3. If this new material blocks a previously declared goal of yours, acknowledge and (optionally) end turn.
4. Otherwise declare sub-goals of yours which block other person's recently revealed suggestions or plans.

5. Suggest a new path element from the map as known to you which is not yet blocked and part of a 'solution' (that is, such that all necessary *AND* and *OR* relationships are satisfied).
6. End turn.

These maps and rules seem in principle capable of reproducing all the role plays, with some further additions and elaborations, but it will not help to try to go into all of the necessary details here.

Discussion

It seems that this kind of scheme provides a reasonable compromise between descriptions of plausible psychological processes, and reproduction of behavioural patterns in detail. In principle these two objectives should go hand-in-hand, and increasing success with one should bring increasing dividends for the other, but in practice, as has been seen, a trade-off seems to be more common, in which descriptions of process and reproduction of product are each pursued at the expense of the other.

One particular construction in such goal maps is of special interest (below) which will behave as a race. If A is declared first it will inhibit B and hence prevent *its* inhibition of A ever being apparent, and vice versa.

Finally to return to a point of general methodology: it has been a constant theme of this book that behaviour sequences in general and conversation sequences in particular are a rather special topic, and pose special problems for analysis.

In the early studies analysis was taken very literally and the methodology was largely inductive. As the emphasis moved from analysis to modelling, the inductive element became less obvious, but was always present, in the sense that the data collected and examined at the outset dictated, if not the form and content of the theory, then at least the set of predictions it was to make. The hunt was on, in other words, for a theory to reproduce or account for certain given data. This is like adding an additional constraint to the simple four-stage view of 'the scientific method' to make it read: (1) observation, (2) theory, (3) deduction of testable hypotheses, (4) test empirically, in such a way that the predictions deduced at stage 3 are required to be *the same as* the observations mentioned at stage 1.

That very requirement becomes the essence of the test (stage 4). The process is a closed loop running not merely from observation to observation, but looping back on itself to the very *same observations* that the procedure began with.

Throughout this book has been a steady progression away from inductive methods for studying sequences, and towards hypothetico-deductive ones. There is still one more step in the progression to be advocated but not implemented here, and that is to open the loop, so that the predictions that test a theory need no longer be equivalent to the observations that suggested it.

The point would not then be merely to find theories to account for new data, but to find *new theories*, which predict something or other (and it does not matter too much what, as long as it does not turn out to be empirically false). This may seem like a hair-splitting distinction but it now seems crucial and often misunderstood in some quarters at least. The reason is that new processes — real scientific discoveries — and processes that account for new phenomena are quite independent categories of things, and any given process can be in one or other or neither or both, so searching for the processes behind new phenomena, in order to find *new processes* is a bad strategy. A new phenomenon is both an unnecessary and an insufficient starting-point for the discovery of a new process. New processes are discovered (by and large) by the conceptual manipulation and extension of old processes *in the imagination of the scientist.*

Seen in that light the future task will not be to do with the collection and analysis (or modelling) of behaviour sequences in the first instance, but with the questions 'What more could there be than psychological processes as we know them?' and 'What observable consequences or products would these new possibilities entail?' If it should turn out that new theories of process which are interesting and plausible in their own right suggest an examination of behaviour sequences as a crucial test, then so be it. But to begin with particular sequences and hope they will lead to an interesting new process or theory is all too often to start at the end and look for a beginning.

Further methodological implications of these studies will be discussed in the concluding chapter, but in the meantime there is the question of practical applications to consider. The *raison d'être* from which this sequence of studies began was to look for better practical problem-solving tools, based on an understanding of sequential mechanisms, and that is what must be considered next.

7

APPLICATIONS

CLEARLY, the analysis of sequences of remarks or behaviours or various other events, lends itself to many applications in the field of practical problem-solving. Usually what we mean by a problem (at least when referring to the kind of problems about which something helpful might be done in principle) is a series of events which is showing signs of culminating in something undesirable, unless we take the right course of action. Practical problem-solving has to do with identifying that right course of action (and executing it). The right course of action is the one which produces the best combination of good outcomes with high probabilities, which means we need to know the outcomes of the various policies we might adopt, and that in turn means we need to know how the sequence of events in question (or if you prefer the 'system' underlying and producing it) would react to various contingencies we might supply. And *that* means understanding the mechanics of the system whereby different contingencies interact to produce different chains of events over time. In short, we need to be able to analyse and model the system producing the sequences of events in question, in order to interact with it optimally.

This idea is nothing new. In the making of economic forecasting models (Newbold, 1973), global systems dynamics models (Forrester, 1972), in various branches of operations research (Makower and Williamson, 1967; Battersby, 1975; Lighthill, 1978) and in engineering design, this is essentially how scientific approaches are used in resolving design and policy dilemmas.

In principle the same idea translates into the sphere of problems involving discrete items of human behaviour: actions, decisions, messages, and so on. In practice, however, some new tools are required, since the problems mentioned above all obey physical or quasi-physical laws, in which mass and energy are conserved, for example (relativistic effects notwithstanding!), and so networks may be envisaged in which the rate at which material, value, energy, or some other 'substance' flow into any junction sum to the total rate at which they leave through various outflows. This means that differential equations describing rates of change of level or flow with time tend to balance around any single node, and the overall system conforms to comparatively straightforward mathematical representations, often in the form of families of simultaneous differential equations.

With behaviour sequences, the treatment is not so straightforward, and there is considerable scope for the development of improved representations, although methods of gaming and simulation (Wilson, 1968) and the tools of General Systems Theory (Bossel *et al.,* 1976) have been applied quite successfully to complex social and political processes. This is why advances in the apparently 'ivory tower' field of conversation analysis may have implications for other fields, at least in the role of a 'tool-building' discipline like statistics or computing.

What seems to be needed is a body of scientific knowledge and technique that is as relevant to the solution of 'human' problems in interpersonal, intergroup and international relations, as ideas originating in natural science, mathematics and engineering are for the solution of quantitative problems in the traditional fields of military and commercial operations research (Lord Todd, 1980). Perhaps a better knowledge of psychological fundamentals and their methods of representation will serve here, just as physical notions of quantity, rate of change, conversation and probability have done in providing theories of queuing patterns, networks, and price fluctuations, for example.

One potentially fruitful connection which deserves more attention in the future is the use of individual psychological concepts to explain the behaviour of large groups and organisations such as nations or corporations. It is already standard practice to use common-sense psychology as an explanatory model for large collectives, and so it would not be all that surprising if techniques from scientific micro-psychology were to be applicable too. Furthermore, it is interesting to speculate that the apparent appropriateness of psychological metaphors for governments, or large companies, may be due not so much to the fact that such bodies have in a sense 'memory', 'intention', 'concern' and so on like individuals as to the fact that the individual mind is less of a singular entity than we like to think, and has far more internal 'politics' going on than we usually recognise. Maybe the analogy works because the mind is like an organisation, not because an organisation is like a mind.

One constraint on the application of scientific techniques to practical problems is that specific given instances usually have to be analysed, not general cases or laboratory surrogates. It is for this reason that many pure research methods do not lend themselves well to such applications, since they require the construction of experimental situations, not the analysis of naturally occurring ones. Methods based on sequence analysis or behaviour grammar writing, however, are not generally limited in this way, and may be applied as well to historical records or newsfilm, as to idealised laboratory data.

Soluble problems, as has been said before, involve the future, and the sciences of the future whether strategic analysis, policy optimisation or technological forecasting involve the extrapolation of known factors, and the means of choosing the best alternatives. In doing this, the study of progressions of events is always crucial, but the methods that have been developed so far for dealing with successions of categorically distinct events and states are crude compared with those for analysing and modelling time-varying continuous functions. The need to select between options requires the detection of optima, but again combinatorial optimisation, or the selection of a best sequence or permutation from a set of alternative permutations is not as straightforward or well developed a business as the selection of optimal values for a set of continuous variables, such as the coordinates of àn ideal point on a control surface or space.

Discrete-state models do exist, as we have seen in automata theory, game-theory and decision theory, but in no case do they come very close to a representation of behaviour-generating processes, and the latter two fields really only serve to integrate probability and pay-off information given a knowledge of available strategies and their consequences; they do not provide the kind of *calculus of strategy*, which is the applied aim of sequence analysis methodology.

In classical decision theory (Kaufmann and Thomas, 1977), the only part of the decision process to be formalised and provided with optimal techniques, is the selection of a best path through a decision tree *once the tree itself has been provided, together with the pay-off for all outcomes, and the probability of occurrence of all branches.* But as many decision analysts now recognise, that is the least of the problem. Of far greater concern is the way in which we detect and construe the decision situation in the first place, in order to arrive at a decision tree. If we knew more about that, then it might be possible to improve and perhaps even to automate the processes which monitor patterns of events over time, deciding when decisions are called for, what alternatives are to be chosen between, and what historical precedents are to be considered. Although this is still a remote possibility, again it seems that the development and application of techniques like the writing of behaviour grammars (or even 'history-grammars'), offers one of the best prospects.

Not all important and problematic systems are interactive, of course. Some patterns and trends of events will go on the same way whatever we do, at least as individual and group agents if not as a species. In these cases the question is not which of the possible interactions between our policies and the system would produce the best outcome, but what course of events is the system most likely to produce regardless of our influence. The issue in this case is one of forecasting rather than decision or control. This too has its importance, even though it is not quite as good to know that the future has certain things in store whether we like it or not, as it is to be able to determine what the future is to be. The information is still very useful. In the words of the old saying: 'We cannot control the wind, but we can at least trim our sails', or at any rate we could if we had enough prior warning of where the gusts might come from and when. Weather forecasting and economic forecasting have both had their pay-off, and even when the forecast events cannot be altered, other decisions can help us enjoy or avoid them as the case may be. The usefulness of forecasting methods is catching on in other areas too, from the prediction of new developments in technology (Wills *et al.*, 1972) to the forecasting of social and political changes (Forrester, 1972); but there are still many areas where in spite of its obvious usefulness, forecasting is not yet feasible. This is largely because of the gap between the nature and assumptions of our methods, and the nature of the events we would like to forecast.

The most basic approach to forecasting is extrapolative, assuming that trends or cycles can be identified in the past behaviour of a system which will continue into the future. Yet again it seems the familiar obstacle arises. When the pattern to be identified and extrapolated is either made up of the interplay of scalar variables, or else stochastic transitions between events and states, then the methods exist. Otherwise they do not, and it is quite distinctly 'otherwise' that many of our most important and problematic social mechanisms operate. One only has to consider how present forecasting methods might be applied to the plot of a play, the text of an argument, or the content of tomorrow's news-papers, to see that linguistic kinds of regularity, which as I have argued here are typical of many other human activities besides just language, expose and perhaps offer the solution to, quite new orders of pattern, and to the problems of forecasting which they raise.

More sophisticated forecasting methods work not by extrapolating the observed behaviour of the system, but by deducing what new behaviour would emerge if the processes operating in the past were to interact with the circum-stances to be expected in the future. This might be called *process* as opposed to *product*-based forecasting, and as we have seen one of the best examples of this is the technique of system dynamics. Here the basic processes are often straight-forward and quite obvious, and our intuitive grasp of them serves us well as a point of departure. What is lacking is a method for deducing the behavioural *consequences* of these processes which are at work. Such is the nature of the processes most often involved (namely multiloop feedback processes) that our intuitions are quite unable to translate a good grasp of the process itself into a prediction of how it will behave, and that is where special techniques are needed.

This argument seems equally appropriate for many social or behavioural problems and it is to be hoped that the system dynamics approach (which needless to say was designed for *continuous* systems) will soon be matched by a discrete-state counterpart based upon, and suitable for, the analysis of human action.

Such an approach could provide us with discrete but non-Markovian time-series forecasting and control methods of enormous utility. In realising this aim the emphasis will have to be on the development of tools, rather than on the accumulation of 'findings' *per se*. That is the spirit of the other 'tool-building' disciplines like statistics, O.R. and computing, and in a way it is the spirit of this book. While some of the studies described here will, I hope, be taken to establish new 'facts' of language and social interaction, that is still the *least* significant aspect of what I have tried to do. The particular questions asked, and the answers found, were often no more than instances of *types* of problem, and testing-grounds for approaches which will produce their real pay-off when developed further and applied to much graver problems than I have attempted to analyse here.

One of the main difficulties of managing a complex discrete-state system can be illustrated by the analogy with a road map that was used in Chapter 6. Let us suppose that all the possible courses of events to be considered are set out as the possible routes on a map. Decision points where the sequence of events may be turned one way or another correspond to the road junctions. The object of the exercise is to navigate through this maze of possibilities, so as to arrive at the place (the state of affairs) you want, without passing through any unduly undesirable points on the way. That is to say, the means cannot be sacrificed to the ends. Given an incomplete and usually incoherent knowledge of the 'map' in question, the navigator (or problem-solver) is in danger of failing to recognise crucial junctions for what they are. It is true that many of the choices will be immaterial, in that they are easily revocable, and lead to alternate segments of a route from any of which the desired journey can be completed, since they rejoin further along. Other junctions, however, lead into unconnected sub-maps, to which one is then entirely committed, or in systems jargon one is then 'locked in'. Unfortunately these key decision points do not look any different from inconsequential decisions, unless the overall structure of the map is known, and in dangerous situations, they may occur much earlier than people expect, so that ill-attended choices will have determined the outcome before the decision-maker or problem-solver has started to consider the alternatives seriously enough.

A sequence analysis which shows where the decision points are in relation to the whole map, and where they lead to, can be a life-saver. One dramatic example of this can be seen in the analysis of human behaviour in burning buildings, done by the Fire Research Unit at the University of Surrey, and based in part on the methods of the present author (Canter *et al.*, 1978). This showed, amongst other things that very early actions after the raising of a fire alarm, in hotels and hospitals especially, seemed at the time to have little bearing on the actors' chances of survival, but they were in fact the major determinants of the outcome. On the other hand, later and apparently more consequential choices could do little to alter a fate which had already been unwittingly sealed.

Here the sequence analysis, mapping and decomposition of behavioural accounts showed clear indications of the way that changes in design of buildings, fire regulations and training in emergency procedures could reduce mortality and morbidity.

Getting out of a burning building is a conflict or a 'game' against nature and strategic choices may be relatively static and simple. But in interpersonal or intergroup conflict, where both sides have strategies and choices to make, the need for systematic representation and selection of alternatives is rather greater.

In Figure 39 the first few rounds of a simple verbal conflict are shown. This map was taken from an exploratory study, in which a number of argument 'scenarios' were used to reproduce a particular dilemma over and over again. Each pair of subjects was given an incomplete script which led them into a certain kind of dilemma or impasse. The script then ended abruptly, and the subjects had to role-play the remainder of the interaction. By repeated use of this procedure with different pairs of subjects, we were able to examine a number of possible 'futures' for each 'past' or scenario, and to follow the con-

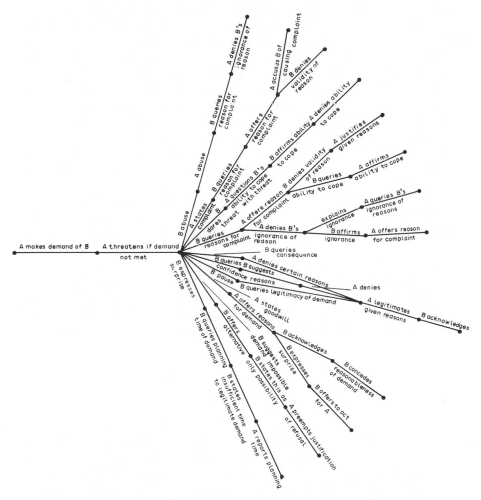

FIG. 39   First four nodes of a conflict situation taken from a role-playing enactment of two scenarios.

sequences of early selections between tactical alternatives. Nine different scenarios were used in building up the tree diagram. Note that nearly all the nodes are 'divergent' as one would expect in a pure tree, while the one 'convergent' node of the type more typical of a network renders quite immaterial B's previous choice between 'queries consequence' followed by 'queries confidence' on the one hand and 'pause' on the other.

In a more realistic case the map may be even more network-like, so there would be fewer crucial or purely divergent choice points.

These examples reinforce the point that a suitable representation of the transitional or sequential structure of a system's interactive behaviour could be a valuable decision-making tool. But the point must be made yet again, that unless the system is first order these simple 'road-maps' are *mis*-representations of the facts. What a better representation would turn out to be is the main question behind this whole area of research. In the case of Figure 39, for example, it is all very well to point to the consequences of 'convergent' and 'divergent' nodes occurring in a map, but in practice they are not as easy to identify or represent as this example would suggest. How is one to know, for instance, when a convergent node is drawn on the assumption that the immediately following sequence is common to several prior sequences, that later divergent nodes are not controlled or 'switched' by the differences in the prior pathway? There is no simple solution to this since any amount of time could pass between the controlled and the controlling events. In other words, for all we know, the system could be of indefinitely high order, and the behavioural nodes in the map far from equivalent to system 'states' in the technical sense that would give them uniform implications for the future regardless of their prior history (Minsky, 1972).

In the next study a real problem, that of disruptive behaviour in school classrooms, will be considered, using a more elaborately derived transition map than that discussed above. This brings us closer to the point where sequence analysis methods can produce findings with real practical implications, although in this case the difficulty remains of making valid inferences about long behavioural chains from first-order transition diagrams.

Study 20: Classroom Disruption

Introduction

Disruptive behaviour in school classrooms has been a practical problem for teachers, and a research problem for educationalists for some time now. Usually the classroom itself has been regarded as a 'black box' into which causal factors enter from the structure of society, the organisation of the school, the constitution of the children and the nature of their families (Parry, Jones and Gay, 1980). These factors are then usually taken to blend (in some uninteresting or untraceable way) into a result emerging from the black box of classroom life, namely an incidence of disruption which may be very great or very small, depending on the causal factors.

This seems to overlook the truism that classroom behaviour, disruptive or otherwise, is a matter of what teachers and pupils *do*, and should be studied as such, *in situ.* Furthermore, the supposedly 'causal' factors such as macro-social structures in the school catchment area are unlikely to be changed just to provide a remedy for this problem. Nor can a bilateral solution be introduced whereby teachers and pupils undertake to dispense with the problem in some way, since (we assume) the pupils who were motivated to refrain from disruption would do so anyway, and the others would not. In neither case would such a 'solution' produce a disinclination to disruption where it did not exist before.

The remedy seems, on the face of it, to lie in understanding and changing the way in which teachers' methods of handling disruptive classrooms affects the incidence and outcome of those disruptive episodes. In short, the teachers seem to need help in finding better management strategies for disruptive pupils, which means looking at the processes of teacher—pupil interaction as a behavioural structure over an extended period of time. It is rather surprising that this approach has been so rare, and in some quarters is viewed as being so unappealing, since it is common practice in the study of the *pedagogical* behaviour of teachers and pupils (see especially Flanders, 1970).

The present study is only exploratory, and is presented in the spirit of a 'worked example' of some of the ways in which sequence analysis of conversation and related behaviours may illuminate problems such as classroom disruption. Much more extensive data collection and analysis would be needed before firm conclusions could be drawn. The results of pilot work presented here are to be taken as illustrating the form, but *not* the content of a serious sequence-analytic treatment of classroom disruption.

Method

The study was carried out in conjunction with Dr. William Parry-Jones and Mrs. Brenda Gay of the Oxford Education Research Group, who ran the first part of the study, contacting schools, observing lessons, devising coding schemes for teacher and pupil acts, and coding the data into integer sequences from which the sequence analysis *per se* could be carried out.

Twenty lessons were observed in two secondary schools, and disruptive incidents recorded as a 'blow-by-blow account' in the form of notes, narrative and reported speech.

Results

The events in eight of the lessons were 'parsed' and classified by Gay and

Parry-Jones according to the coding scheme in Appendix F. This was repeated independently as a reliability check and found to be approximately 95% reliable. Each lesson was represented as a number of disruptive incidents between which there was uninterrupted teaching or organising (code 27). Each disruptive incident was described by a string of integer-coded categories, for example (27) 21, 1, 10, 22, (27). Analysis began with a Markovian treatment (e.g. Rausch, 1972). A transitional probability matrix was then constructed showing the number of transitions from every category to every following category, as observed across all eight lessons. The expected frequency for each cell in this matrix was calculated using the expression:

$$\text{expected cell value} = \frac{\text{row total} \times \text{column total}}{\text{grand total}}$$

The observed and expected frequencies were used to calculate χ^2 for each cell, or:

$$\frac{(\text{observed} - \text{expected})^2}{\text{expected}}.$$

This was not a true χ^2 statistic in several respects but the threshold value of 3.84, above which a real χ^2 would be significant at $P<0.05$, $df = 1$, served as a cut-off value to identify the transitions where observed and expected frequencies were sufficiently different to merit further analysis. Sixty-one transitions satisfied this criterion as being the transitions from one category to another which are more (or in one case less) frequent than might be expected by chance. The negative transition was between category 22 and category 1 indicating that teachers in this study give explicit commands to pupils regarding their disruptive behaviour *less* often than chance would suggest, once it had been stopped (which of course is as one would expect).

The transitions which satisfy this criterion are plotted in Figure 40. The diagram is divided into columns showing teacher acts (heading T) and pupil acts (heading P).

In order to simplify and summarise the information contained in Figure 40 the diagram was scanned for the presence of 'recycling groups'. A recycling group is a set of categories between which transitions can be made indefinitely, but once a transition is made out of the set re-entry is unlikely during that sequence, or in the ideal case of equivalence classes in an ergodic system re-entry would be impossible. Three groups emerged which correspond to different discourse modes between teacher and pupils called 'Hard commands', 'Soft strategies' and 'Discursive'. The transitions between them and the remaining categories are shown in Figure 41 and the groups are shown in detail in Figure 42.

A further summary was produced by dividing the teacher act categories into two sets, 'authoritarian' and 'non-authoritarian', and the pupil act categories

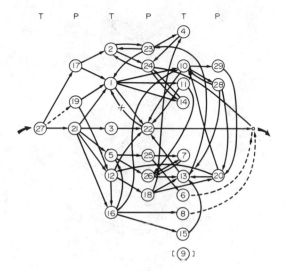

FIG. 40 Transition map for all teacher and pupil acts,
where observed frequency (O) and 'chance' frequency (E)
were different according to the criterion $\dfrac{(O-E)^2}{E} > 3.83$.

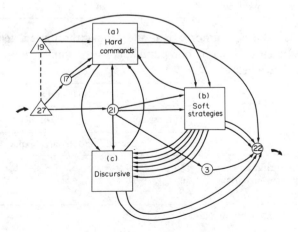

FIG. 41   Main recycling groups and their interrelations.

250   David Clarke

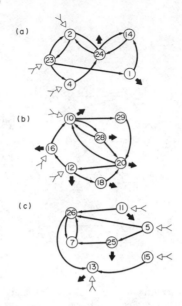

FIG. 42   Internal structure of recycling groups.

into two sets, 'desirable' and 'undesirable'. These sets are shown in the table below.

Acts	Category code
'Authoritarian' teacher acts	1, 2, 3, 4, 7, 9, 11, 14, 15
'Non-authoritarian' teacher acts	5, 6, 8, 10, 12, 13, 16
Desirable pupil acts	18, 19, 20, 21, 23, 26, 28, 29
Undesirable pupil acts	22, 24, 25

The transitions from all 'authoritarian' and 'non-authoritarian' teacher acts to 'desirable' and then to 'undesirable' pupil acts were summed and a χ^2 test was carried out as shown below:

		PUPIL ACTS				
		Undesirable		Desirable		Total observed
		observed	expected	observed	expected	
TEACHER	Authoritarian	14	17.9	52	48.1	66
ACTS	Non-authoritarian	36	18.1	45	48.9	81
	Total	50	—	97	—	147

$\chi^2 = 2.32$, d$f = 1$ (10% trend, one tailed).

Although this test did not prove significant there was a trend ($p < 0.1$) showing the more 'authoritarian' teachers' acts tend to be followed by 'desirable' pupil acts and 'non-authoritarian' teacher acts tend to be followed by 'undesirable' pupil acts.

It must be re-emphasised that with these few preliminary data this can only be offered in the spirit of a 'worked example' showing how certain methods may be applied to the problem of classroom disruption when better data are available. It would be most inadvisable to treat the outcome of the study as a proven 'result', as the above statistical test indicates that the most tempting conclusion to draw has a rather higher probability of being wrong given the data used than one would have of tossing a coin four times and getting four heads in a row. This is an unacceptably high probability of error, if firm conclusions are to be drawn.

Discussion

The analysis described above is intended to illustrate possibilities for the treatment of these kinds of data, rather than to show reliable and valid conclusions. More observational data would be needed before the relative frequencies of transitions could be compared meaningfully and thus the likelihood of any given category following a certain antecedent category could be calculated.

The rather crude division of teacher acts into two groups would need to be revised for subsequent studies: at least three groups for different kinds of teacher strategy are likely to be useful, as suggested by the 'recycling groups' that emerged. Again more data are needed to confirm these groups. It seems useful to retain a division of pupil acts into 'desirable' and 'undesirable' outcomes and initiating acts, but degrees of 'undesirability' might be distinguished. With more observational data, hypotheses regarding the outcomes of certain teacher strategies could be tested. Such analyses would involve not only simple transitions from one category to another, but whole sequences of events which had been set into motion in certain circumstances. Also critical choice points could be identified where a sequence can be turned in one of two directions leading, perhaps inexorably, to the restoration of peace or the escalation of conflict. A knowledge of such points could prove important for theory, training and the practice of classroom-management skills.

Study 21: Vector Space Analysis of Life Histories

Introduction

Finally let us turn to a different approach, and a different sense of 'application' of methodology: that is an application not to a practical problem, but to a different area of pure research.

First the new technique. This was suggested and largely programmed by John Collins, a physicist who was at the time working in Oxford as a research assistant. It is based on methods used widely in Physics and General Systems Theory and employs the idea of *vector spaces* describing force fields (Dorny, 1975). The main difficulty with any sequence analysis, as we have seen a number of times already, is that of producing a single general description of a set of related but different sequences of events, which is broad enough to be common to the set, and yet specific enough to be peculiar to it. In other words, it has to characterise *all* and *only* the sequences of the type it purports to describe. It is often preferable for behavioural purposes that the sequences should be described as a succession of event types in discontinuous or event time, and that the general description should be some kind of combinatorial formula or rule. However, the other possibility exists, that we think of real time as a continuous variable, with the passage of which another group of continuous variables fluctuates in magnitude, in which case we have a much more familiar, and in some respects much more tractable description of time-serial data. At this point the usual treatment is to consider each descriptive variable as a time-dependent function

$$a = F_1 (t),$$
$$b = F_2 (t)$$

and to consider the nature of F_1, F_2, etc., by means of autocorrelation, cross-correlation or regression of the various time-series involved, with or without the introduction of lags.

The present technique is different. If there are n different descriptive dimensions in addition to time, then the n different values that describe any particular 'state-of-affairs' at a point in time may be treated as the coordinators of that state in a 'vector space' having n dimensions corresponding to the n measuring scales on which that state of affairs was originally described. Now, with the passage of time one state gives rise to another, and one point in the space succeeds another as the place which represents the present state of affairs. In this way a trajectory is drawn out as time passes, rather as if a moving object in an n-dimensional space were describing a series of arcs and curves under the influence of a number of unseen force fields. Any number of different trajectories may be produced by the same force fields given different initial conditions. And conversely, provided they have an appropriate shared regularity, any number of trajectories may be described by one static timeless map showing the fields it would take to produce them. That, in essence, is the principle of this technique.

The subject-matter for the present study was not the time course of a conversation, but the pattern of people's lives, as represented by the brief autobiographical accounts they gave us as part of the procedure described below.

Method

Fourteen subjects contributed to the study in a single laboratory session.

There were seven females and seven males aged 19 to 50, obtained through the subject panel of the Oxford University Psychology Department. First of all the subjects were asked to make an outline autobiography on rough paper, listing the key events in their lives in chronological order. When they were satisfied with it, this was transferred to a response form with a vertical column of boxes in which the life events could be written. Since these served as mnemonics for the subjects but not as data *per se*, subjects were told that important life events that they would rather not identify should nevertheless be included in the list, but labelled only with a private code or symbol such as an asterisk or an exclamation mark, which they alone would understand later on.

Then the subjects were asked to put in another column their age at the time of each event, so that there would be a real time measure to use in subsequent calculations of rates of change of perceived life states.

Then finally for this stage of the task, they were asked to enter in further boxes beside each life event, a rating for their life at the time of the event (as opposed to a rating for the event itself) using the following scales:

Happiness
Confidence
Control (their locus of control from internal to external)
Success
Busyness
Maturity
Self-esteem

The idea behind each scale and the general technique of scaling were explained to the subjects in some detail, and they were given time for discussion and questions, but the range of values to be used was not specified. This was partly so that subjects could use numbers in a way that was natural to them, assuming that some people would prefer to think in percentages from 0 to 100, while others might be more at home with a bipolar scale including negative and positive values from -7 to $+7$ for instance. These possibilities were discussed with the subjects. The second and more important reason for idiosyncratic scaling was that we did not want to impose artificial limits on each scale in the form of inescapable ceilings or floors. Some subjects might want to indicate that maturity had increased steadily with time, without 'running out' of the scale on which to convey this. Similarly, someone who set out to use values 0 to 10 might suddenly encounter an event which should be called 12, without wanting to rescale the entire list.

In order that we could rescale subjects' values later on to form a common scale, they were also given a second task, in which they scaled standard events in the terms of the scales they had used for their own lives. For each of the seven scales, they were asked to give a value to a high and a low event (specified by the experimenter) and to the neutral point as they saw it. For example:

BUSYNESS   1. Working around the clock to
                  establish a career
               2. Convalescing at home after
                  a long illness
               3. Neutral point

New target events had to be provided for this calibration task, since the events
the subjects had scaled from their own lives were not comparable. Even then it
seemed that asking how they would react to these target events in terms of their
own scales was not necessarily a comparable question for all subjects so we also
asked them to scale how they thought the *average person* would react to the
target events provided.

A third part of the task was then included to check the assumption that more
standardisation was to be expected in ratings of the average person's reactions
to target events than in people's ratings of their own likely reactions. For this,
the same target events were re-used, but now with standard seven-point scales,
which were common to all subjects, who rated each event according to their
own reaction, and what they saw as the average person's reaction.

That then concluded the data collection.

Analysis and Results

Calibration

It was indeed the case that variance in ratings of the average person's reaction
to target events was lower than variance in the subjects' ratings of their own
likely reaction to the same events, so the decision was justified to base calibration
on subjects' ratings of target events for average persons, rather than their own
idiosyncratic scales.

> Average variance for ratings of 14 target events as subjects would react:
>   1.35
> Average variance for ratings of 14 target events as 'the average person'
>   would react: 0.90

Ratings from task 2, of the target events as they would affect an 'average
person', in terms of subjects' own idiosyncratic scales, were then used to calculate
a separate calibration equation for each scale and each subject, showing how
that scale may be transformed into common units for comparison between
subjects. For example for subject 1, scale 1, it was

$$y = 0.250x - 1.250.$$

In other words, each raw datum offered by that subject on that scale needs to
be multiplied by 0.25 and have 1.25 subtracted from it, to turn it into a standard
form, comparable with other subjects.

Re-scaling

All data from task 1 (except, of course, for age) were rescaled in this way, so that they now read as a time ordered list of coordinates, showing for each subject, at each age, the point in the 7-D space that their life trajectory was passing through, with the coordinates in comparable units. So, in effect, we could picture (in coordinate geometric terms) a single seven-dimensional space with the fourteen life-trajectories of the fourteen subjects described within it.

Smoothing

Next the trajectories had to be smoothed to form a set of even curves, instead of a succession of straight line-segments joining the measured points. A smoothing algorithm was used which constructs a continuous curve without sharp corners in it, but nonetheless passing through all the original data points representing the life events.

It is worth noting that time is not a *dimension* of the space, but varies along each trajectory, once again like a route on a map. Consequently the trajectories are not necessarily monotonic in any plane, and may loop back on themselves to visit the same point or state more than once, at different times. These two passes through the same point, however, may not have the same implications for the future, as the curve will have been running in different directions and with different velocities and hence different momentum vectors at the time.

Time interpolation

Coordinates were then worked out for points on each curve between reported life events, at regular time intervals, typically every 6 months.

Vector field estimation

In the mechanical analogy that this analysis employs, every trajectory will continue in the same direction at the same rate unless acted upon by a force field. Conversely the direction and magnitude of the vector field that acts at any point can be calculated from the departure of the trajectory from a straight line of uniform velocity, over the next time interval, as shown in Figure 43.

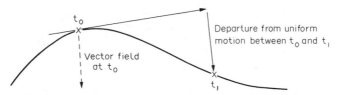

FIG. 43   Derivation of vector field from deviations in
trajectory.

Momentum

Vector fields at different times and for different objects are only comparable if the equivalent of inertial mass for the particles is a constant. Since any displacement will be produced in proportion to field strength and in inverse proportion to the inertial mass of the 'particle' (or conversely since its tendency to move ahead undeflected will be proportional to its momentum which is the produce of its mass and its velocity), the mass of the particles needs to be known in order to map apparent displacement figures to a standard measure of vector field strength.

'Mass' in this case means the propensity to be unaffected by outside forces, and as it happens one of the seven originally scaled dimensions, namely locus of control, has just this implication.

Consequently the locus of control dimension was 'removed' from the space, which then became six-dimensional, and was used as a unipolar measure of mass. The lowest possible value was rescaled to zero.

Now the vector field associated with all the points along all the trajectories could be computed in equivalent terms.

Interpolation

The next job was to find out what was going on in the spaces between the trajectories. This was a matter of taking a weighted average of values from nearby points whose value was known because a trajectory went through them. How, though, should the averages be weighted? How does the correlation between fields at different points vary with distance? An answer to the latter question was calculated by taking auto-correlations along each trajectory to provide a weighting function for use in the spaces *between* the trajectories. Towards the edges of the space the life-curves tend to 'rebound', so in this region the auto-correlations tend to be negative. This is like saying that towards the edges of the space there is a strong repellent field, or that the edges of the space 'curl up'. This is likely to be a reflection to some degree of a real tendency for motion towards extreme values to be reversed, but further exaggerated by the constraints of the scaling procedure.

Minkowsky coefficient

For an abstract 'space' such as this 'life-space', the geometry of the space itself is uncertain. For ordinary common or garden three-dimensional space, we take it for granted that the distance d between two points with coordinates $(x_1 \ y_1 \ z_1)$ and $(x_2 \ y_2 \ z_2)$ is given by

$$d^2 = (x_1 - x_2)^2 + (y_1 - y_2)^2 + (z_1 - z_2)^2$$

or more generally

$$d = \sqrt[n]{\delta x^n + \delta y^n + \delta z^n \ldots}$$

where $n = 2$. This is the rule of which Pythagoras' theorem is the two dimensional special case, n is called the Minkowsky coefficient for the space, and may take other values besides 2.0. In a 'city-block' metric it is 1, since the shortest distance between two points is the sum of vertical and horizontal distances in the city grid between them, diagonal journeys being impossible. (The phrase 'as the crow flies' of course serves to remind us that the crow has a Minkowsky co-efficient of 2 wherever it goes!)

For this analysis the Minkowsky coefficient was assumed to take its 'normal' value of 2, although alternative values may be useful to remedy geometrical anomalies. The fields themselves can be described by local variations in the Minkowsky coefficient as in the relativists' dictum 'space tells particles how to move, particles tell space how to bend'.

Integration

The scalar field strength at any point may be obtained by integration over vector field values. The relation between the two may be thought of in the following way. Let us suppose the fields are a system of hills and valleys over which a ball is rolling. Valleys or 'attractor basins' represent points towards which it is drawn, hills represent 'resistance points' or points of repulsion. Vector fields are descriptions of the direction and steepness of slope (that is rate of change of height) and scalar fields are like the absolute 'heights above sea level' that describe the terrain most simply.

Table 11 shows part of a 'slice' through the space in scalar field terms.

It is rather hard to visualise since it is more complex than a slice through a three-dimension space in which two coordinates vary and one is fixed. This is a slice through a six-dimensional space, representing the effect of conjoint variation of two variables while four remain fixed. In this instance variables 1 and 2 are being swept to form the plane, while numbers 3, 4, 5 and 6 are held constant at the mid-range value of 0.0. One feature of this slice seems to be a group of four out of the five positive points down near the $-1.0, -1.0$ corner, typically interspersed with small values, although the value of -0.5989 at $-1.0, -0.6$ is an exception. There is another low peak at $-0.6, + 0.8$, again surrounded by small negative values.

Discussion

In principle a representation such as this, when considered for the whole space, can make certain predictions, in the sense that the trajectory of a new 'life' or particle can be projected given its initial direction and velocity of motion, and its mass.

TABLE 11   *Slice through scalar field*

Variable coordinates defining positions in slice		Fixed coordinates: parameters of the slice being scanned				Scalar field strength
A	B	C	D	E	F	
−1.0	−1.0	+0.0	+0.0	+0.0	+0.0	+0.0863
−1.0	−0.8	+0.0	+0.0	+0.0	+0.0	−0.1301
−1.0	−0.6	+0.0	+0.0	+0.0	+0.0	−0.5989
−1.0	−0.4	+0.0	+0.0	+0.0	+0.0	+0.1898
−1.0	−0.2	+0.0	+0.0	+0.0	+0.0	−0.0904
−1.0	+0.0	+0.0	+0.0	+0.0	+0.0	−0.1841
−1.0	+0.2	+0.0	+0.0	+0.0	+0.0	−0.1897
−1.0	+0.4	+0.0	+0.0	+0.0	+0.0	−0.1727
−1.0	+0.6	+0.0	+0.0	+0.0	+0.0	−0.1300
−1.0	+0.8	+0.0	+0.0	+0.0	+0.0	−0.0723
−0.8	−1.0	+0.0	+0.0	+0.0	+0.0	+0.2730
−0.8	−0.8	+0.0	+0.0	+0.0	+0.0	−0.0749
−0.8	−0.6	+0.0	+0.0	+0.0	+0.0	−0.2686
−0.8	−0.4	+0.0	+0.0	+0.0	+0.0	−0.1154
−0.8	−0.2	+0.0	+0.0	+0.0	+0.0	−0.0792
−0.8	+0.0	+0.0	+0.0	+0.0	+0.0	−0.1586
−0.8	+0.2	+0.0	+0.0	+0.0	+0.0	−0.2026
−0.8	+0.4	+0.0	+0.0	+0.0	+0.0	−0.1545
−0.8	+0.6	+0.0	+0.0	+0.0	+0.0	−0.0925
−0.8	+0.8	+0.0	+0.0	+0.0	+0.0	−0.0278
−0.6	−1.0	+0.0	+0.0	+0.0	+0.0	+0.1432
−0.6	−0.8	+0.0	+0.0	+0.0	+0.0	−0.0872
−0.6	−0.6	+0.0	+0.0	+0.0	+0.0	−0.2440
−0.6	−0.4	+0.0	+0.0	+0.0	+0.0	−0.3018
−0.6	−0.2	+0.0	+0.0	+0.0	+0.0	−0.3117
−0.6	+0.0	+0.0	+0.0	+0.0	+0.0	−0.2952
−0.6	+0.2	+0.0	+0.0	+0.0	+0.0	−0.1992
−0.6	+0.4	+0.0	+0.0	+0.0	+0.0	−0.1131
−0.6	+0.6	+0.0	+0.0	+0.0	+0.0	−0.0333
−0.6	+0.8	+0.0	+0.0	+0.0	+0.0	+0.0247
−0.4	−1.0	+0.0	+0.0	+0.0	+0.0	−0.0900
−0.4	−0.8	+0.0	+0.0	+0.0	+0.0	−0.3859

The analysis raises certain problems when used with this kind of material. Firstly, the true initial conditions of life trajectories are not known. Initial motion in the space may be due to fields in the vicinity of the starting-point or to intrinsic motion — as if the particle had been 'lobbed into play' so to speak.

The mass of data generated by the technique is considerable. At any point the above calculations may require 10^8 numbers to be stored in order to calculate a given type of field description. This calls for special data packing and unpacking routines on all but the largest computers.

This was only an informal study, from which no specific findings may be expected. It was an experiment in the everyday sense, something which was tried out to see whether and how it worked, but there was no formal quantitative assessment of the success of the method or the accuracy of the output. That would require a number of additional calculations. As it stands the usefulness of the study lies not so much in the particular calculations and their outcome, as in the spatial analogue for representing and summarising sequences which it introduces into our conceptual and descriptive repertoire. It is a worked example of a different conception of event sequences and their origins.

Finally the analysis treats the life system as closed, and dependent only on its own history and on factors predictable from its present state, for the determination of its future course. Random cross-impacts like ill health or unemployment which are not systematic correlates of prior state, but affect the future dramatically, can only be treated as 'noise'. For that reason the method is probably more suitable for sequences like conversations and arguments, which are arguably closed in the requisite sense. Nevertheless this method, which is not yet common in psychology, has considerable potential for future applications, as do any powerful techniques which may emerge or can be developed to capture the possible range and variations in sequences of events, using known circumstances as the fixed parameters of a generative forecasting model.

8

CONCLUSIONS

THE PLAN for a structural analysis of conversations and other action sequences has been started, and will probably turn out to be at least as long and complex a business as the analysis of grammar. Its completion is way beyond the scope of a single book, or even a single career, but the story so far has a number of implications for future research which should be considered.

Better rules describing the legitimate futures which may arise from a given past may be proposed and tested by computer modelling, so as to be used in forecasting and the optimisation of plans and policies. Computer models could be used not only for the discovery of surface rules, but could also be extended to provide a critical path analysis of negotiations and conflicts. The various alternative moves available in each state of play could be weighted for probability and cost. In this way a program could predict the future course of critical interactions, and so serve in training and advising those who have to confer and bargain under difficult circumstances.

The training of mental patients in social skills (Trower *et al.*, 1978) is already based upon a similar model of interaction structures to some degree, and a more specific description of surface structure would be particularly useful in that field. Working from the social-skill model of behaviour (Argyle, 1967) the social skill therapists/trainers find rules of interpretation and performance relatively easy to conceptualise and express. The greatest difficulty is with the organisation of behaviour, and the relations between perception, motivation and performance. This is the *translation* process of the social skill model, which this project originally set out to study.

A grammar of social behaviour would provide a formal system for predicting the likely responses of an individual, in a variety of different situations. It could also be modified to give a summary statement of the differences between individuals, not just in terms of their response repertoire, but also in terms of their peculiar way of reacting to situations of different kinds. That could lead to a new kind of personality theory describing person and situation interactions, rather than just discovering their existence and asserting their importance.

The grammar of a behavioural system would be at least a plausible candidate as a model of the generative process used by the actor *in vivo* to regulate his behaviour. Further experiments could be carried out to see whether the structural properties suggested by the grammar, and the formal operations performed on them really did correspond to the actors' generative process.

It is to be hoped that a greater understanding of these aspects of interaction management would facilitate all sorts of practical improvements in the resolution of conflict, the treatment of mental disorder, and the promotion of communication and understanding between people.

Evaluation of Methods

One of the main emphases of this project has been the development and evaluation of new methodology. There are a number of ways of looking at conversation sequences, which can be found in several different disciplines: from speech-act theory in philosophy, through linguistic pragmatics, to the ethnomethodological 'conversation analysis' technique used by micro-sociologists. All these methods proved useful, at least as a source of ideas, but it seemed that individually, and perhaps also collectively, they fell a good way short of producing the kind of comprehensive, coherent account of discourse structure that was wanted. So we set about collecting and developing methods to try to overcome some of these shortcomings, both for the sake of research on conversation sequences *per se*, and with a view to the wider applications of sequence analysis and modelling methods, in the study of any pattern of actions and events over time. (These might include the progression of phases and stages in long-term interpersonal relationships — which is now a major part of a new research programme which has developed out of the work described here — or the systematic and projective analysis of policies and strategies for dealing with various kinds of conflict, or other problems, rather as economic forecasting models and engineering design models are now used to represent complex patterns of interacting factors and to predict their responses to possible changes in their structure or their environment.)

So, one outcome from the project, in addition to the substantive findings on discourse structure reported above, has been a synthesis, and to some extent an extension of the methods available for analysing sequences of events. In outline the main approaches that were explored, and the issues they raised, were as follows.

'Secondary Experimentation'

The obvious experiments to do on social interaction would involve manipulating the contributions of one person and observing the effects on the other(s). However, this would only be to break up the very interdependence between acts that was under study. Instead one can use indirect, or 'secondary', experiments in which conversations are allowed to proceed naturally, and then recordings or transcripts of them used as experimental material in subsequent studies, in which subjects carry out tasks such as classifying extracts, reordering parts and replacing deletions, thereby showing to what extent and in what way the original talk conformed to shared expectations of structure. The main limitation of this approach is that separate studies have to be used for separate facets of conversation structure, so the end product tends to look rather piecemeal.

Inductive Sequence Analysis

This method is the mainstay of most research on behaviour sequences and involves a four-stage analysis of recorded material. In the first stage the recording of a period of interaction is divided into discrete units of activity and speech, while the second stage involves the classification of these units into recurring types. Stage 3 is the analysis of the particular sequences in which these types have been found to occur, and stage 4 is to chart the relation of the form of the sequences to their meaning or implications for the actors.

This plan was followed and elaborated in various ways. The main problem arises with stage 2, the classification of behaviour. This has to be based on the *significance* of the behaviours rather than their physical form, and needs to be elaborate enough to capture the subtlety of an interaction. Furthermore, the classification has to correspond with the natural divisions between behavioural alternatives. All behaviours which occur in similar circumstances have to be placed in the same class, while any two behaviours whose conditions of occurrence are different have to go into different classes. Otherwise stage 3, the sequence analysis, would have to embody differences between members of a class and similarities between the members of different classes, which would clearly defeat the object of the classification. The problem is like that of deciding which parts of speech are necessary in writing the grammar of a language. An arbitrary classification of words using, for instance, one-letter words as one class, two-letter words as another, and so on, does not make for an elegant grammar because this is not the property which determines when a word is grammatically appropriate. On the other hand, a classification into nouns, verbs, adjectives and so on, makes the job of grammar-writing much easier because all the words in such a class can be used in a similar way in sentence construction.

One way of making up the right behaviour categories is to take a sensible sequence of behaviour, and ask which other actions would have been equally appropriate in place of each one which occurred. (This is the basis of 'test-frame analysis' or the 'test of commutation' in linguistics.) It poses a special problem when used with social behaviour, as it requires behaviours to be described in terms which can be transferred from one context to another. Unfortunately the meaning of an item of social behaviour differs from one context to another, so the behaviour stream has to be described as a succession of meanings or functions before the technique can be applied. This raises the issue of what a behavioural 'meaning' is, how it is best described, and how it can be identified from recorded material.

The main limitations of the second approach turned out to be that it requires a large corpus of data, which rules out the 'anatomical' analysis of particular debates, for example, and that the only criterion for extracting certain fragments of structure as 'significant' is their frequency of occurrence. Since conversational patterns are relatively familiar anyway, a tabulation of the most frequently observed constructions tends to be uninteresting.

A priori Modelling

Another part of the research described here was based on the idea of a 'behaviour grammar' for conversations: a set of generative rules reproducing the orderly succession of utterance types in conversation, just as a more literal grammar reproduces the strings of morphemes which are well-formed sentences in a given language. This approach, as used by linguists, is theory-driven rather than data-driven and is not based on the detailed analysis of a corpus of examples. Instead, it begins with a set of structural assumptions about the organisation of sequences, represented in such a way as to define a procedure for the enumeration of all and only those strings which are consistent with its principles. The correspondence or non-correspondence of these with the type of sequences which were chosen to be modelled is then the main test of the adequacy of the grammar, and the main source of revisions and improvements. The studies we carried out along these lines raised two main issues. Firstly, there was the class of grammar to be employed: Chomsky's classification of finite state, context-free, context-sensitive and transformational grammars for languages (corresponding to finite-state, push-down stack, linear bounded and Turing automata) did not appear to include an appropriate class to model the peculiarities of conversational structure. Secondly, a formal generative model must have an interface language in which to describe its output, which is at once simple and mechanical so the rules of the model can regulate it exactly, and rich and powerful enough to describe the phenomenon in detail. These objectives are hard to reconcile but a workable compromise was found.

Analysis and Modelling of Case Studies

What is wanted from a sequence analysis is not a set of propositions or summary measures that are deducible from observed sequences, but some representation of system structure *from which* the set of observed sequences can be deduced or predicted. Realising this, the next step was to turn to an approach in which particular case studies, or situations for which there were a number of example sequences, became the focus. The aspects of the situation which seemed important in determining the resulting sequences were then extracted informally and embodied in a specific rule model (for which discrete-state system dynamics, goal networks, and transformational grammars were used as exemplary formats). This then allowed predictions to be made about which sequences such a process would produce, to be tested against *observed* sequences, and in principle provided a practically useful model on which further experiments could be done to anticipate the effect of changes in background circumstances or the actors' behavioural strategies.

Of the four approaches, this last one seems most fruitful for further work but they all have drawbacks. On the whole it could be said that the first two methods (which are largely data-driven) can be relied upon to produce an end product, although what they produce can often be obvious and uninteresting. The last two methods being more theory-driven have on the whole the opposite characteristic. They do not always work, but when they do the result is often unexpected and valuable.

Theoretical Issues

During the project a number of more general issues relating to the nature and origins of sequential regularity had to be considered. Briefly, the main conclusions were as follows.

The Syntax of Action

In certain ways social behaviour is like language and understanding it is like writing a grammar. As with syntax a crucial task is to produce a canonical generative representation of a set of sequences of discrete events arranged in time according to their type classes; there is a semantic classification of the events interacting with their 'syntactic' arrangements; the end-product is as much an explication of tacit lay knowledge as an empirical study of an unfamiliar domain; structural models are set up and tested hypothetico-deductively; and some of the arguments for attributing a deep structure to sentences turn out to apply as well to social behaviour sequences.

Hierarchical Structure

Human action (like most other things) is hierarchically structured with large units being made up of combinations of smaller units, and so on. More remarkably it seems that the larger structures dictate the properties of their subcomponents, unlike the phenomena of the natural sciences where the reverse is true. Whereas it makes sense to analyse natural phenomena reductively, since patterns and structures may be traced back to their origins by reducing them to their parts, behavioural structures, on the other hand, become less explicable as they are more finely partitioned, and the task is principally one of synthesis rather than analysis. Social objects need to be put together to find what they are part of in order to understand them, not taken to pieces to see what they are made of, although that may often be the key to their systematic *description*.

Models of action structure must reconcile the 'top–down' hierarchical nature of individual planned performance, with the necessarily 'left-to-right' or real-time chain reaction quality of interpersonal exchanges. Most of the tractable formalisms can do one or the other, but not both in combination. When a decomposition or 'parsing' of particular sequences is necessary for descriptive purposes, it proceeds best from 'top-to-bottom' (that is from large-scale units towards finer and finer sub-classifications) rather than the reverse, although many quantitative taxonomic techniques that are used for this purpose work 'bottom-to-top', or by the aggregation of small clusters into larger ones.

Synthesis and Coherence

Many studies of sequences have produced piecemeal results in which components of complex behavioural systems are separated out and described in isolation. Often that is only to reproduce the least mysterious and problematic aspects of behaviour. The real difficulty lies in capturing the interplay of parts in elaborate behavioural complexes, in some kind of synthetic statement which is rigorous, complete, consistent, and coherent. Atomistic studies do not even attempt this and fail; they pursue the opposite goal and so take us further and further in the wrong direction.

Choice of Paradigm

One way of describing the relation between old paradigm and new paradigm social psychology as they have been called, is to say that while both try to reconcile scientific knowledge and human affairs, the 'old paradigm' starts with the scientific methods and tries to apply it to human action, while the 'new paradigm' starts with the conception of action we use in everyday life and tries to make it more scientific, by removing gaps and inconsistencies. Both paradigms can be used to examine behaviour sequences, but on the whole the latter seems the more fruitful.

It may turn out to be a mistake to spend too much time on the development and evaluation of paradigms, since real science is driven by issues and theories, not by methods. The important thing is to pick a problem and solve it, then another, and another, not to pursue ways of doing research *per se*. The methods can often be completely *ad hoc*, and in a way are better if they are, as they are then likely to be tailored to suit the problem in hand, rather than the reverse. If a general paradigm does emerge, or a body of technique which is applicable to a whole range of problems, then that is better recognised in retrospect than in prospect. Above all the mistake should be avoided of embarking on endless methodological preparations, for the day when the techniques are sufficiently perfected and the *real* research can begin in earnest: that day never comes.

However, a few broad guidelines can provide a useful orientation, even if there are no recipes for good research, and never could be. For me, the key belief on which the scientific methods rests, and which crops up repeatedly in the writing of scientists and philosophers of science, is the idea that there are many layers and orders of reality, existing and interacting on different levels of scale and abstraction. Some are readily apparent and make up the world of ordinary experience, sometimes called surface phenomena. Others are hidden in some way, and it is these that science seeks to discover. Many images and metaphors are used to describe this state of affairs, but whether it be seen as drawing aside a great veil, tunnelling beneath the landscape of experience, or peeling off successive layers of an onion, everyone is agreed that it is what lies behind or beyond the surface phenomena that is important. These hidden processes and structures may be responsible for the appearances of the surface, or they may themselves be the effects of more obvious causes. Hidden causes of apparent effects are of special interest of course, partly because of the sense they give us of explaining the given facts (the literal meaning of 'data'), and partly because we want prediction and causes tend to entail effects logically, or processes entail their products, in a way which is not reversible. This also seems to be one of the chief reasons why inductive methods are usually treated as the poor relation of hypothetico-deductive ones. There is no reason to suppose that a process can be inferred from its products because they do not determine it, whereas knowing (or postulating) the process it *is* possible to infer the products and thus test the conjecture that was made. In short, hypothetico-deductive methods offer a way of getting beneath the surface phenomena, whereas inductive ones can only produce observations and generalisations about them, which is not the object of the exercise.

This seems to be the great failing of much social psychology and the reason why it is perennially criticised for 'discovering' the obvious. All too often this discipline in particular fails to make any distinction between surface phenomena and underlying processes, and hence tends to study things which, if the distinction were to have been made, would surely count as surface material and therefore not worthy of study in themselves (although they may provide evidence for the evaluation of theories about what is really at issue, namely the processes and structures that underlie them). This could hardly be otherwise since social psychology is ostensibly about the stuff of everyday life and common-sense experience. It no more stands to be discovered how people behave in day-to-day life than it would be true to say that the great imponderables of natural science include the colour of grass or the source of rain. What *is* in question is the constitution of the 'machinery' *by virtue of which* everyday action and experience has the properties it has.

Figure 44 shows how the whole scheme might look when applied to behaviour sequences.

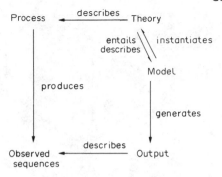

FIG. 44   Anatomy of a sequence model.

The observed sequences are the surface phenomena, and the process that produces them is the object of enquiry. This is not directly accessible in itself, but theories which purport to describe it may be conjectured at, and then modelled in such a way as to generate outputs which describe a set of hypothetical behaviour sequences. The adequacy of the theory and the model based upon it then depend on the extent to which the sets of hypothetical and real sequences are co-extensive.

The next step is crucial, and often is taken the wrong way. All too often a new and related surface phenomenon is chosen for the next 'cycle' of the procedure, so that a chain of studies builds up, having as their linking element the coherence of the surface phenomena they investigate, but providing no particular coherence or direction for the explanatory ideas they invoke. By contrast in the advanced sciences the next question is more often 'What further processes could there be which are similar to or related to these?', rather than 'What other similar phenomena could we find explanations for?'. Figures 45 and 46 show these two alternatives schematically.

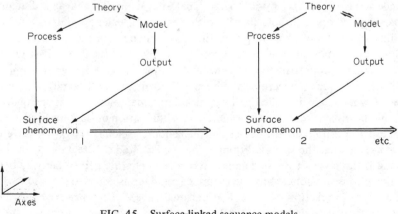

FIG. 45   Surface-linked sequence models.

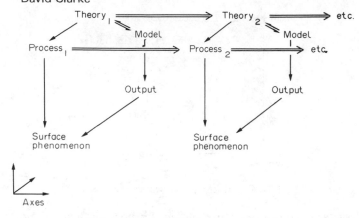

FIG. 46   Theory-linked sequence models.

As these diagrams show, the key difference is the position of the linking 'backbone' in the structure. In the first instance it is a connection between the phenomena investigated, while in the second it is the interrelation of the theories proposed and the processes discovered. Sciences structured in the former way inevitably read like a catalogue of rather arbitrary, unrelated experiments, while the latter structure gives the sense, which is so marked in the natural sciences, of a systematic account of natural processes being built up which can (when the need arises) be told without reference to experimental evidence, and yet make good sense. In social psychology, however, if the experiments are removed from the account, nothing remains. The history of experimentation is all there ever was.

What, then, lies below the surface phenomena of behaviour sequences? In answering this question there is a problem which seems to be peculiar to the social and behavioural sciences. When the physical sciences break through the surface levels of reality, by and large what they come to next is a domain of stable explanatory concepts like charge, mass, spin, valency and so on. These are rather well-behaved concepts in that they do not contradict one another, definitions do not change with context, and the entities themselves seem to have invariant properties no matter what the time or place of observation may be. Further enquiry concerning the deeper fundamentals ultimately runs into a layer of what might be called philosophical imponderables, such as the quantisation and possible reversibility of time, and the unification of the four fundamental forces. The position in the social and behavioural sciences is rather different. Here it seems that the very first thing to be encountered on breaking through the surface is the layer of imponderables. Explanation hardly gets under way before running into issues concerning the nature of mind, consciousness, freedom of the will and the interaction of social and personal causes. The answer cannot be to retreat into a mere description of the surface, and yet those who break through this layer are all too apt to drown in the quicksand that lies just below. Perhaps the only strategy is to recognise it as conceptual quicksand, and accept that permanent structures and tunnels cannot be built as they can in the explanatory rock below the landscape of physical science, but that nonetheless there are patches viscous enough, and suspended logs inert enough, that one can navigate from one to another, using each as a platform from which to reach or exert leverage on the next, but only at the expense of displacing the starting-point in the other direction. All movement is relative and all constructions temporary, but by choosing the pieces carefully, enough stability may be created to operate practically in this fluid domain, and repeatedly to build a new conceptual raft to stand on, at least before the old one has sunk beneath one's feet.

Returning to the point that the postulation of new processes is primary, and the discovery of new phenomena secondary, there is a further reason for this besides the point made above that it leads to a knowledge structure with more than mere surface coherence. Let us suppose that there is a set of known phenomena abutted by a set of further phenomena, not yet discovered, and likewise sets of known and unknown processes, as shown in Figure 47. In some cases it

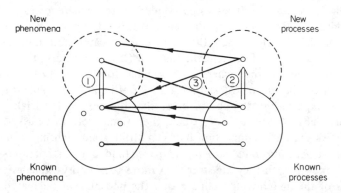

FIG. 47   Sets of known and unknown phenomena and
processes.

may also be known which processes produce which products as shown by the linking arrows. If the set of known phenomena is extended (arrow 1) and then explanations sought, the chances are that familiar processes will provide adequate explanation (arrow 3) and no real discovery will have been made. The only way to ensure that novel processes are discovered is to follow arrow 2 in search of new possibilities in the process domain by imagination or conjecture, after which it does not matter too much whether the phenomena they 'predict' are novel or familiar.

All this talk of imagination might seem distinctly unscientific but it is in precisely these terms that many great scientists have talked about the theoretical side of their work. If we are to emulate the successes of the natural sciences, one of the lessons we must learn is that scientific ideas are not motivated by new collections of data, nor by set experimental procedures and paradigms, but by the creativity that can imagine stranger and stranger processes at work in the world, combined with the skill to be right in those imaginings, and the discipline to evaluate them sceptically. Far from seeking to 'inspire fresh empirical research' as is so often said (Berkowitz, 1979), the role of theory in science is not just to provide the means to a greater end. The substance and the purpose of science is in itself to develop and evaluate better, deeper and more general theories. The collection and analysis of data has no part to play except in so far as it provides one of the means to that end.

The form the theories should take can differ widely with the phenomena, the purpose and the discipline in question, but the stock formula that theories should describe cause-and-effect connections, or point to a cause for each observed effect in the world, is one of the least satisfactory possibilities (Harré and Secord, 1972). For one thing, a long list of ordered pairs describing causes and their respective effects gives a relatively shallow and incoherent picture of what is going on. Moreover, since it does not tell us how the cause—effect connection is embodied in the world, it leaves us wondering from where it was so magically summoned by the appearance of the cause. It is one thing to believe that effects are summoned into existence by the occurrence of causes, but quite another to believe that the cause—effect tendency is too. On the contrary, that must have been there all along — but where, and in what form? If I say that a match is alight because it has been struck, then I am offering an intelligible if somewhat incomplete explanation. If I go on to say that the next match I take from the box *would* light, *if it were to be* struck, then I am likely to be asked how the match knows that. The connection between striking and lighting (if indeed it is true) must be *built into the nature of the match* (and in the case of safety matches into the box on which they are struck). A more satisfactory explanation for the behaviour of the match would tell me that the phosphor of the match head has a number of high-energy chemical bonds, which are only just stable, and which, given a small input of energy, will break down releasing the bond energy as heat and light (and, incidentally, keeping the process going). This also explains why the head will burst into flames if warmed gently in another more subdued flame and so on.

The same principles apply to behavioural theories. It may be true that some stimuli bring about some responses, that circumstances largely determine actions, but how and in what form is that tendency built into human nature? Answers to that question should take pride of place in psychological theories, whether they be expressed at physiological, genetic, mathematical or other levels of description and abstraction.

This inevitably leads us to consider the nature of 'mind' and the ways in which its properties determine its behaviour. We need a way of considering what it *is*, in order to frame explanations of what it *does*, and since we are considering its constitution we will need to concentrate on structures and existent processes, rather than just occurrent processes. On this view the 'process' of social interaction, for example, will not do so as an object of study, as it is only part of what happens, and not part of what exists. It is too ephemeral and too variable to count as part of a constitutive description of any process (in the sense of a mechanism), which could by its existence explain the occurrence of anything else.

From the standpoint of the outside observer the surface phenomenon that needs to be explained is the regular dependence of action upon circumstance, but to the actor himself there is also a mediating chain of 'mental events' such as thoughts, feelings, perceptions, memories and decisions which also seems to be part of the surface phenomenon which is directly observable, albeit by introspection. Taken together, the outside world and the world of conscious mentation constitute all we know by direct experience, and the two domains seem to interact so as to produce a continuous cyclical chain reaction, with changing circumstances (1), producing beliefs (2), feelings (3), wishes (4), decisions (5), plans (6) and actions (7) in (*very roughly*) that order, as in Figure 48.

As this cyclical interaction of conscious mental activity and the outside world is all we get to know about as lay actors, we treat it as a closed, coherent explanatory domain, and any events in the cycle are taken to be explained by providing the other events from the same cycle. Thus actions may be explained by

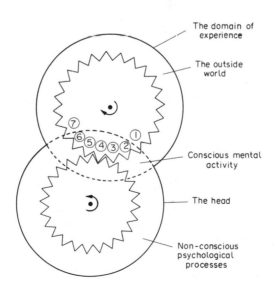

FIG. 48   Cog-wheel analogy for action, conscious experience and psychological processes.

plans, plans by decisions or goals, decisions by beliefs, beliefs by circumstances and so on. This is essentially the system of common-sense psychology and attribution. What it cannot deal with at all, of course, are questions like 'What is it in the constitution of the system that allows it to entertain and act on beliefs?' or '*How* are events in the world translated into our perceptions of them?'. This is to raise questions about quite different levels of process, which do not figure at all in common-sense psychology, but are central to scientific psychology.

There seem to be two quite distinct schools of thought about what else the mind might consist of apart from the strain of consciousness linking circumstance to actions. In one version, the domain described by psycho-analysts, there are reported to be states of mind rather like those which we experience, with names like wishes, beliefs and intentions, except that we are unaware of them. They are unconscious, or they exist in 'the unconscious', from which compartment of the mind they are apt to play tricks on us which we cannot understand or control. In the scheme of Figure 48, these are hard to represent accurately, but they could be thought of as similar in status to the states marked 2, 3, 4, 5 and 6, although not conscious as that segment of the diagram would otherwise suggest. Taken together, the events of the outside world, conscious mental events (and arguably unconscious mental events, too) make up the upper 'cog-wheel' of the mechanism whose rotation and whose parts we can experience, and which for everyday purposes we take to be the mind/world system and its processes. What I want to suggest is that this does not rotate spontaneously but is, as it were, driven around by something else, of which we are not aware, represented by the lower cog wheel in Figure 48. It is this which scientific psychology (by and large) sets out to characterise. It is not the same thing as the 'mind' in everyday parlance, but is rather the set of hidden structures and processes which organise and animate that part of the 'mind' we are aware of.

In order to pursue this any further it is necessary to change to a different and more familiar analogy, namely that with the workings of a computer. On this analogy the brain may be taken to correspond to the 'hardware' of the computer. The psychological processes of interest here become the 'software', and the behaviour of the person in response to changing circumstances would correspond to the input—output transactions of the whole system. What then of the 'conscious mind' in the sense described above? That is perhaps best likened to the 'trace' which a sophisticated computer makes as its programs run, a record laid down in memory and available to be output, showing certain key states that the program has been through, such as the value of its variables at particular times. This is an internal monitoring function of the machine, which may serve similar functions to consciousness, although it does not involve any self-awareness on the part of the computer, as far as we know. Note that this trace is not the same as the hardware, software, or behaviour of the system, although if the real software were inaccessible it might well appear as the mediating chain of events between input and output, much as we take conscious mental activity to be.

The trace and behaviour can be treated as parts of a single historical record, corresponding to the upper cog-wheel of Figure 48, while the 'software' becomes the lower cog. In either metaphor the following things are implied:

1. The mind/world system appears to cycle spontaneously, but in fact does not.
2. The process level provides a driving and organising influence.
3. The states of (1) and the processes of (2) are interleaved like the teeth of the two meshing cogs, in that states mediate between processes and processes mediate between states.
4. The real point of all this is that the mind/world system, the upper cog in Figure 48, or the combined record of inputs, traces and outputs in the computer analogy is *not* what we should be after. It is after all only the surface phenomenon, the ephemeral but regular occurrences which we want to explain. It is not the explanation of anything else and should not be the prime object of attention of our science. That should be the software, the *lower* cog in the diagram, which exists rather than just occurs, and which stands to be discovered as the synchronic template of diachronic patterns in behaviour and experience.

This attention to the psychological equivalent of software, often called functionalism, has some interesting precedents. In electronics, for example, the components of a circuit have always gone under names like switch, resistor and impedance, or on a higher level of description amplifier, detector, AND-gate, and so on. These labels usually apply to parts of the circuit that can be identified as physical entities, but very little is said by the label about their physical form. A switch can be almost anything that can interrupt or pass a current, a resistor can be anything from a coil of wire to a special-purpose ceramic cylinder. In spite of first appearances, the labels and the explanations of circuit design and performance based upon them, do not tell us what the parts are, they tell us what they do. The overall circuit has been divided up according to the function of its parts. There is an intriguing twist to this, if the circuit were not accessible, if it were a 'black box' mechanism, so that we could not enumerate its parts, and hence could not give names to their functions as such, we could still apply the same labels to the primitive operations which would in principle go to make up the overall properties of the circuit. We should be applying the same terminology to the parts of its function, instead of to the functions of its parts, but nonetheless we should have a way of characterising what it consisted of, albeit abstractly, and this would provide a way of framing and testing hypotheses about how it did what it did, and what further properties it might be expected to have. Note that these operations or functions are in a sense permanent constituents of the system, while the events and states they produce are not. It is also the case that a function in this sense is very close to a function in the mathematical sense, and so a series of mathematical functions can often be written to describe individual operations in such a way that when taken together they amount to a mathematical model of the whole system.

In this sense the description of computer software and much modern cognitive psychology is functionalist. It sets out to describe the sequences and networks of primitive operations by which observable complex performance characteristics could be accomplished (Fodor, 1981).

Of course it is likely that in the brain as in the computer, the software does not just govern output depending on input, it also incorporates input into itself in the form of new programs, or modifications to existing ones. In the computer, programming and data processing are quite distinct modes of operation, whereas in the brain, I suspect, learning and acting on what was previously learned (or inborn) are often intertwined facets of the same process.

This starts to raise problems for the simple functionalist view I have outlined here. Unlike a simple electronic circuit, the software is partly built out of the information it processes, much as the digestive tract rebuilds and extends itself using the stuff it digests. Consequently the relationship between the psychological and social domains is not just a one-way traffic. Far from being the static entity which produces society, the human psyche is, in part at least, a network of stored programs that have come *from* society and which act back upon it in a kind of socio-psychological feedback loop. That means it may be a forlorn hope to try to set out a timeless constitutive description of what the psyche is like, since it is in the very nature of its function to change itself and the environment in which it operates. Each person's life history, the top-level 'trace' as far as the individual is concerned, is a record which is not only produced by, but which also *produces* the psychological machinery we would like to describe. In that way the machinery may be as ephemeral as the behaviour it produces, and no worthier an object of description. No wonder individuals seem so different from each other, and from themselves at different stages in life.

Now, if the psyche does not hold still for us to describe it, what are we to do other than to revert to a kind of biography which says that a given person at a given time was like *such and such*? There seem to be two main possibilities. One is to study a kind of developmental meta-psychology, the rules and principles according to which the individual changes with time and with experience. (But where are they realised? Partly in the genes perhaps.) The other solution is to treat certain acquired characteristics such as skills as a kind of 'syndrome', which is not invariant across time or individuals, but which does recur and can be detected and described in *those particular cases* where it is currently to be found. In much the same way, one can say (for a given era at least) what kinds of computer programs exist, and how each type works, but not in a more general way what set of programs is to be found on a certain type of machine, which would vary from example to example and time to time. Taken a step further this leads us to see psychology as a 'science of the possible', with as much concern to say what kinds of psychological process there *could be*, as to say what kinds there are.

Perhaps the solution is this. The mind, as a complex control system, has a (largely) hierarchical structure. Changes in the lower level of control may happen quite fast, and when they occur they must be governed by higher levels of control which change more slowly. The fundaments of such a control hierarchy, from which the properties of the whole organisation arise, are to be found at the top (unlike the more familiar constitutive hierarchies of the natural world, whose fundaments are at the bottom, making for the greater success of reductionist explanation in the natural sciences). These upper levels of the control hierarchy, which are the most important explanatory structures to find out about, are also, happily, the most stable through the life-course of an individual. If we were to give greater scientific attention to these, they might well provide us with a less ephemeral object of study, and a glimpse of the heart of the mind in action, instead of the more common middle- and lower-level control routines, which respectively seem to the layman to be obvious and unimportant.

We all have access to a certain part of our own psychology. The inaccessible parts that *it* controls are no problem. The real questions will concern those parts of the system which control the accessible mind. They will be understood, as much as anything, by the study of the sequences and patterns of behaviour over time which are their product and their hallmark.

Appendix A   GLOSSARY

THE DEFINITIONS given below are not intended to provide a comprehensive explanation of the concepts, but merely to make the text more comprehensible to anyone who is unfamiliar with these terms.

Act   Meaningful behavioural event such as threat, promise, greeting, etc.

Actor   Person whose behaviour is to be explained.

Atomism   Mode of scientific analysis in which phenomena are treated independently of one another.

Base Rule   A rewriting rule in generative grammar generating the deep structure.

Centroid Linkage   Relation used in cluster analysis, meaning that the similarity between clusters is taken to be the distance between their centroids in similarity space. Centroid is like a 'centre of gravity' for the cluster.

Cluster   Group of items found to be similar during some taxonomic study or cluster analysis.

Competence   Topic of investigation involving the actor's knowledge of a system of language or behaviour, and the rules which embody or are equivalent to that knowledge.

Constative   Aspect of an utterance to do with the transmission of propositional meaning, and evaluated according to its truth or falsity.

Constitutive Rule   A rule describing the assignment of objects to classes, e.g. X counts as Y.

Critical Path Analysis   Technique for deciding which of a number of alternatives involves least cost or delay, or is 'critical' in determining overall cost or delay.

Deep Structure   The syntactic representation of a sentence most closely related to its meaning or semantic representation.

Descriptive Adequacy   Criterion for evaluating a grammar, to comply with which the grammar must generate all and only the sentences of the language, and assign the correct structural description to each.

Descriptive Competence   That part of the actor's knowledge which enables him to predict events, and assign probabilities to particular transitions between events.

Diachronic   Changing with time, and structured in the time dimension.

Ellipsis   Process of abbreviation by which incomplete messages may be transmitted intelligibly.

Emic   Mode of analysis based on the actor's judgements.

Episode   Segment of the behaviour stream containing several interrelated acts, which are not related (in the same way) to events outside the episode boundaries. The counterpart of the sentence in social behaviour.

Equivalence Class   Set of items related by some relation which is transitive, reflexive and symmetric.

Etic   Mode of analysis based on observation and measurement of behaviour.

Explanatory Adequacy   Criterion for evaluating a grammar, to comply with which the grammar must generate all and only the sentences of the language, assign the correct structural description to each, and comply with the theory of linguistic universals.

Felicity   The quality of 'happiness' or effectiveness by which a performative utterance has the desired effect.

Finite-state System   A system which can only exist in one of a finite number of states.

It may be shown that English cannot be generated by a finite-state device having one state for each morpheme; but a device which has states corresponding to nonterminal items could possibly generate English.

Generative Semantics Semantic theories in which a logical or semantic deep structure is used in the generation of syntactic forms.

Holism Mode of analysis in which phenomena are regarded as inextricably interrelated, or a group of phenomena are investigated as a whole.

Illocution A kind of performative utterance which achieves its function *in* being said.

Interpretive Semantics Semantic theories in which a semantic representation is derived from syntactic forms by interpretation of a deep structure.

Langue The language as a system (an abstraction).

Markov Chain A sequence of events in which each is governed by the preceding one. Strictly this applies to the probability of transition between events, but the term is used here of any series deriving each element from its immediate antecedent.

Moral Competence The actor's knowledge of the constraints on social behaviour, having to do with polite and respectable conduct.

Morpheme Unit of linguistic analysis, roughly equivalent to a word, or one of its meaningful sub-components.

Multiple Articulation Property of language whereby small units combine to form larger units which are meaningful in a way which is not a simple sum of their parts, and moreover this emergence of a new order of meaning occurs on more than one level of description.

Nested Conditions Feature of experimental design, in which different levels of one treatment are peculiar to one level of another.

Nested Sequences One sequence of events inserted in another, which is broken off and then resumed.

Non-terminal Elements Part of a generative grammar which do not appear as items of output, e.g. S and NP.

Observational Adequacy Criterion for evaluating a grammar, to comply with which the grammar must generate all and only the sentences of the language.

Paradigmatic Relations Formerly called associative relations. Relations between words (or events) based on their similarity, and particularly their intersubstitutability in various contexts.

Parametric Analysis Mode of scientific description in which qualities are represented by continuous variables, and interrelated by equations.

Parole Language as realised in particular acts of speech or writing.

Parsing The syntactic analysis of a sentence, especially in terms of its constituent structure.

Performance The use an actor makes of his knowledge of language or social behaviour. Actual behaviour, often taken to include the means of production of the behaviour.

Performative Utterance An utterance 'doing social work' such as promising or consoling. More properly there is a performative quality associated with every utterance. Equivalent to *speech acts*, often sub-divided into *illocutionary* and *perlocutionary* aspects.

Perlocution An utterance achieving its function *by* being said but not necessarily *in* being said, e.g. *persuade* as opposed to *urge*.

Phrase Structure Syntactic structure of a sentence as a hierarchy of constituents.

Positivism Philosophy of science placing great emphasis on direct observation and measurement. Associated in its extreme form with radical behaviourism, when applied to psychology. Propositions are only held to have meaning in so far as they imply criteria or procedures for objective verification, like 'Grass is green' as opposed to 'Murder is wicked'.

Proaction The continuity of an individual's own behaviour from event to event.

Prosodic Pertaining to the melodic sound of a sentence. The fluctuations in pitch of the first formant.

Quotient Set Set of equivalence classes making up a universe of discourse.

Reaction Relation between an actor's behaviour, and the behaviour of other actors.

Recursion Property of a generative device or rule system whereby it may revisit the same states or sequences of operations, as sub-components of their own execution. e.g. to do X you do A, then X, then B.

Regulative Rule   Rule determining the correct use of a class of objects or behaviours.
Relativism   Quality of a system describing the interdependence of the values and processes which define it.
Rule (a) Belief held by an actor about what should or should not be done in given circumstances.
 (b) Analytical device, similar in status to an equation, describing a set of behavioural patterns in the form of a procedure for producing their descriptions, but not necessarily implying (a).
Semantics   The study of meanings, and particularly the relation of meaning to form in language.
Semiotic Competence   The aspect of the actor's knowledge of a communicative system relating to the correct and meaningful use of symbols.
Single Linkage   Feature of a cluster analysis meaning that the similarity between clusters is derived from the distance between their nearest members.
Speech Act   As *performative utterance.*
Statistical Approximation   A reconstruction of a regular sequence of events, from the transitional probabilities between them.
Stochastic Sequence   A sequence governed by the transitional probabilities between events. Used here of any structure governed by transitions between overt events (whether probabilistic or not). *Linear stochastic sequence* used of any sequence of events which could be represented by transitions between *adjacent* events or strings.
Structure   An object or sequence of events made up of systematically arranged parts, characterised by the set of constituents and the relations that hold between them.
Surface Structure   A description of the output form of a sentence or event string showing the class to which each event belongs, and the relations between them, usually as a phrase structure.
Synchronic Structure   Not structured in the time dimension. Unchanging, or described without reference to its changing properties, as it exists at a particular time.
Syntagmatic Relations   Relations between the elements of a structure specially those between the morphemes of a sentence.
Syntax   The internal relations of a string.
System   A set of interrelated objects or processes, usually with a high degree of mutual interdependence.
Terminal Element   The product of a generative syntax which is output as a linguistic token, capable of being spoken or written.
Test Frame   A well-formed string with an item deleted, to test the equivalence of other items in context.
Transformation Rule   Rule relating deep and surface structures.
Transitional Probability Matrix   Matrix showing the probability that the second of two items or strings will follow, given that the first has occurred.
Translation   Process whereby the actor infers an appropriate response from the nature of incoming stimuli, and his or her own goals and beliefs.
Well-formedness   Term used in logic and linguistics to show that a succession of propositions or symbols has been correctly derived and is permissible within that system.

Appendix B EXAMPLE DIALOGUE

Experiment 1

Example dialogue

1A: Oh, yes, I've remembered now.

2B: What?

3A: What are you doing on Saturday night?

4B: Going to dinner, which is at seven o'clock and then doing a . . . singing in concert.

5A: (Oh, well . . .) Ah, and what time do you finish that, because there's a party which you're invited to!

6B: Ah, another party. I'm invited to Bill's party as well. Bill Taylor.

7A: (Mmm) Oh he didn't invite me.

8B: Oh, oh discrimination.

9A: He only said Saturday night?

10B: Saturday night, I was going to go to that straight after the concert.

11A: Oh well there's . . .

12B: Another one as well, God!

13A: Yes, oh perhaps that's why I haven't been invited, where I'm already going to a party.

14B: Mmm, I'll believe . . .

15A: Mary and Sue and Jane have got a party and I think it'll be quite a nice party, wine.

16B: (Bill probably said. . ./oh/ah/I've got/ah) Yes, where's it . . . where's it at?

17A: It's near the station.

18B: Oh Golly, Cherry Lane or something?

19A: I don't know, Pete . . . I can't remember. Pete doesn't know at the moment. He is going to find out this afternoon, where it is.

20B: Yeah, well the thing is, since we're not starting 'til eight thirty, we'll probably not finish 'til ten thirty, the concert, then we'll go to . . .

Experiment 2

Example dialogue

1A: I wonder why people associate Hull with dreary northern backwaters?

2B: Especially when Hull is so full of fascinating places of interest to all interested in how people in ports live.

3A: How much of interest in Hull do you find in port area alone?

4B: I think old and disused docks tell much of past glories, speaking in historical vein, but is much outside dock areas.

5A: Essentially I would agree that most of character of Hull lies within dock area, but so few visitors to Hull actually visit dockside.

6B: Regrettably, very few visitors ever come to Hull, let alone to see river pursuits or to trace old town walls or see churches.

7A: Excepting of course lorry drivers and commercial travellers, and even people of this nature rarely stay long enough to appreciate old town and history of place.

8B: Very few people ever hear of Beverley, and Beverley Minster must be great point of interest, not only in Yorkshire.

9A: Beverley is only one of East Yorkshire's lesser known attractions, and yet I find Beverley Minster every bit as interesting as York Minster.

10B: I think trying to make people aware of Hull's attractions is fighting a losing battle.

11A: Only solution is to introduce people here to Hull itself.

12B: I do not agree − I let people rot in their own ignorance.

13A: You must admit Hull is virtually out of reach, so to speak, and everywhere has attractions if people look for attractions.

14B: I do not like missionaries.

15A: What have missionaries to do with subject?

16B: Missionaries convert people from ignorance to bliss, of course.

17A: Somebody has to convert people.

18B: I wish you would go out to African backwoods.

19A: If only I could spend some time in African backwoods.

20B: I can see you swinging from creeper to creeper.

Appendix C   EXAMPLE DIALOGUE

Experiment 5

Zero-order dialogue

A: Virtually nothing.

B: Fine with me.

A: I joined her when she was new. We loaded steel rails in Middlesbrough. Ten years ago, that is.

B: What makes you think he is still a Party member?

A: Who said that?

B: What is Digby's game?

A: Don't you wish you were coming Gussie?

B: Will one be enough?

A: Oh, it was me. It was me made sure you would come.

B: But I don't want to go to bed.

First-order dialogue

A: Is that the way you feel?

B: Why don't you call round sometime?

A: I had a long talk with Archie the other day and he seems to think that you have undergone some sort of revolution in your political ideals. I told him I didn't think this was the case, but I'm not sure. What is your stand now?

B: Yes you can most certainly borrow it. I don't play it anymore. Though when Christopher becomes a little more proficient he will want to buy his own, and no doubt a better instrument than this.

A: I would like to say yes, but it's impossible to do so.

B: How's your new 'Hi-Fi'?

A: I'd better start thinking hard then.

B: I wonder if the manager has seen those files yet.

A: Come and see my etchings.

B: That's O.K. with me.

Second-order dialogue

A: Do you always catch this train?

B: Every week.

A: Yes the meetings only used to be every fortnight but people got so keen and interested that we decided to have more activities.

B: Have weekly meetings produced more activity, or is it just that the committee enjoyed debating the possibilities of what could be and still don't get round to doing it?

A: I'm sure those who enjoy talking about doing things don't enjoy doing things.

B: To some extent that's true, but I wouldn't use it as a blanket statement.

A: Of course, but there are many exceptions.

B: Yes but that's the general rule that applies.

A: Yes I suppose you have to be careful about generalising, but in this case it's O.K.

B: But how can you be sure in this case, surely it's no different from anything else?

Third-order dialogue

A: I'm feeling much better than I was.

B: It takes a long time doesn't it.

A: Yes, time is a factor obviously but I don't think I would have got very much better had it not been for the medicaments the doctor prescribed for me.

B: Do you know whether there is likely to be a recurrence, and if so does it mean you should have, for instance, an annual course of treatment, or will this one see you for several years or for ever?

A: I hope there'll be no recurrence.

B: Well I'm glad, and I hope things go as you anticipate them to.

A: I hope so too, we're all keeping our fingers crossed.

B: I'm sure there's no need for that. These things usually do go right.

A: Well you can never rely on the weather I suppose.

B: No, not in England, but where I come from.

Fourth-order dialogue

A: I've been meaning to get in touch with you.

B: Yes, I haven't heard from you for weeks.

A: Well you know how it is, pressure of work. I've been very busy tying up ends of my thesis, but now that I'm back in the social round we must arrange something.

B: Well you seem to have chosen your moment to reappear because I'm having a party this weekend so you may as well come to that if you're free.
A: Tell me where it is.
B: It's at my place. Starts at ten and goes on all night.
A: If it's alright with you I'll be there about midnight.
B: Yes that's fine, but please bring a bottle.
A: Champagne or beer?
B: It's up to you.

Fifth-order dialogue

A: I've never seen you here before.
B: No, it's the first time I've been here.
A: What new tack have you discovered in your research that brings you to this neck of the woods? I thought more of your books were in the other library.
B: Well actually I'm not here to work at all. I just came in to see a friend and this is the only place I know I can definitely find her at a given time of day.
A: So this is the new social Mecca.
B: Well not really. Just yet another distraction.
A: Distraction from what?
B: Distraction from my work at the office.
A: Do I take it that you don't enjoy your work.
B: No, it's not that, I really do enjoy it — that's why I don't want to be distracted from it.

Sixth-order dialogue

A: Can I come in?
B: Please do.
A: I've been trying to call you on the phone a few times but you always seemed to be out or engaged so I thought I'd pop round instead and see how you were.
B: Yes perhaps you ought to know a little bit more about our timetables. We are out three times a week which is why you couldn't get us. And we've been ringing my mother and cousin a lot lately since my mother is going away and we are going to look after the house, and my cousin is going to have a baby.
A: Well in that case there's no point in me ringing you.
B: Not really, sometimes I'm in. Anyway it's nice of you to come round.
A: Well I'm pleased to be here for both business and pleasure.
B: Well come upstairs, have some tea and then we can get down to business.

A: That's very kind of you to spare the time.

B: Well I may make some form of profit out of it, so I can afford to spare it.

Text-order dialogue

A: I heard you were in town.

B: I arrived by plane yesterday.

A: By plane — does this go down on the firm's expenses or have you suddenly won the pools?

B: Neither actually, in fact it's all a bit of a con. In fact I'd never flown before. I was talking to my friend who was coming down to the airfield at Abingdon and I managed to 'hitch' a ride with him, so to speak.

A: You lucky devil.

B: Well it's nice to get out of Oxford for a while. Where does life happen here?

A: I wish I could tell you.

B: I hope my trip hasn't been wasted then.

A: No I don't suppose so — you probably had a better time than I had here.

B: Oh I knew life on these camps was a bit low, but is it really that grim?

Real dialogue

A: I'm at 'College A'.

B: You are? Ah! You're not in 'B Hall' are you?

A: No, I'm in, um, the new building. (The first one.)

B: Oh you're not in 'C Hall'? No you're in . . .

A: No, the other one.

B: 'cause I know one girl . . . two girls in 'C Hall': Mary Evans and um Clare Jones and my cousin's in . . . just come this year. She's in 'B'. She's reading law, or should I say jurisprudence.

A: (Yes/Oh/Mmm) Whichever one you prefer. I'm a third-year physicist (final year).

B: I don't know anything about physics at all.

A: Well neither do I.

B: I never even did them at school.

[Letters substituted for proper names.]

Appendix D   DICTIONARY OF SPEECH–ACT CATEGORIES

#	'string delimiter'. This symbol marks the beginning and ending of conversations, and the boundaries between topics, or related passages of talk. In effect it means that no particular relations should be expected between utterances preceding the # sign and those which follow it. It also implies that speech-acts coming before # should be suitable ways of closing a topic or conversation, and speech acts following # should be suitable ways of starting a new passage of talk or new conversations.
Accept	choose, take some course of action made available by the other speaker, but which one is not obliged to take.
Accuse	imply guilt on the part of the other.
Advise	suggest, recommend, propose, urge. To advocate that the other take some course of action which would be to his or her own advantage.
Agree	side with, concede, recognise, acknowledge, confirm, acquiesce, concur.
Answer	supply requisite information.
Apologise	show penitence, compunction, remorse.
Assert	state, assess, reckon, report, suggest (it to be the case that . . .), inform, mention, tell, postulate, confide, describe. *This category should only be used when more specific ones like answer or deny do not apply.*
Attend	'back-channel communication' showing attention, understanding, and a willingness to go on listening, e.g. 'I see', 'Uh-huh', 'Mmm', etc.
Bid farewell	take leave, say 'goodbye', part.
Blame	reproach, recriminate, criticise, grumble, punish, shame, expose, degrade, deprecate, scold, ridicule.
Boast	claim, describe one's own virtues.

Challenge	taunt, dare, tempt, provoke.
Cheer	encourage, reassure, boost morale.
Command	direct, instruct, require to, compel, force, oblige, order. Used particularly when the speaker requires the listener to engage in activities for *the speaker's* benefit.
Complain	moan, report on misfortunes which are *not due to the listener's activities* (cp. *Blame*).
Comply	execute, perform, enact, obey. Carry out some obligation to respond, *arising from the other person's speech or behaviour* (cp. *Fulfil*).
Confess	admit to, accept the responsibility for (some misdemeanour).
Continue	elaborate, interpret, infer, illustrate, conclude, prove, demonstrate, analyse, deduce. Supply the logical or chronological continuation of some narrative, argument or theme.
Defer	postpone. Arrange or offer to carry out some response obligation at a later time.
Deny	refute, dispute, argue, repudiate, contradict, correct, revise.
Fulfil	carry out obligation (arising from the speech or behaviour of the *present speaker himself*), honour commitments.
Greet	welcome.
Joke	tease, make humorous remarks or wordplay.
Justify	warrant, explain (behaviour or speech), account for, legitimise.
Laugh	express amusement.
Minimise	make light of one's own achievements or sacrifices (e.g. 'It was nothing' or 'Think nothing of it').
Offend	humiliate, curse, attack, insult, abuse, embarrass, annoy, harass.
Offer	invite, make some course of action available to the other *at some cost to oneself* (cp. *Permit*).
Pacify	soothe, comfort, appease.
Pardon	forgive, excuse, let off.
Permit	allow, condone.
Praise	congratulate, applaud, commend, approve, exalt.
Prohibit	forbid, prevent, quash.

Promise	commit (oneself to . . .), undertake, vow that, contract, guarantee.
Question	enquire, ask about, express doubt about.
Refuse	(to carry out some response obligation arising from the speech or behaviour of *the other person*.)
Reject	decline. Turn down some course of action made possible by the other, but which did not constitute an obligation.
Request	ask to, plead, entreat, beg. Used when the speaker asks for some course of action on the part of the listener, which is for the speaker's benefit.
Sympathise	condole, reflect, commiserate.
Terminate	bring a topic or passage of talk explicitly to a close (e.g. 'That settles that, then').
Thank	express gratitude, reward.
Threaten	announce that the speaker may do harm to the hearer, in some way.
Warn	urge restraint, caution, advocate that the hearer refrain from some course of action for his own (*the hearer's*) benefit.

Appendix E EXPERIMENTAL SPEECH-ACT SEQUENCES

Experiment 14

Random string produced by Joker

```
    #
A   Thank
B   Offer
A   Question   Refuse
B   Permit
A   Warn   Warn   Attend   Greet
B   Comply
```

String produced by Backchat

```
    #
A   Offer
B   Reject   Apologise
A   Accept
B   Terminate
    #
A   Warn
B   Accept   Thank   Promise
A   Accept
```

Control string

```
    #
A   Assert   Complain
B   Accept   Justify   Offer
A   Agree
    #
    Assert   Question
B   Answer   Justify
```

Appendix F KEY TO CLASSROOM STUDY

(1–16 Teacher acts)

1. Teacher explicit command, prohibition, instruction, request to individual pupil(s) (sometimes implied, e.g. in rhetorical question).
2. Teacher explicit command, prohibition, instruction, request to whole class (sometimes implied, e.g. in rhetorical question).
3. Teacher implicit command, prohibition, instruction, request to individual pupil(s) (e.g. by naming alone or staring).
4. Teacher implicit command, prohibition, instruction, request to whole class (e.g. by using pupil's collective name, or non-verbal signals).
   (N.B. 1–4 excluded items included under 14.)
5. Teacher requests explanation from pupil regarding behaviour (i.e. disruptive).
6. Teacher accepts pupil's explanation for behaviour.
7. Teacher refuses to accept pupil's explanation for behaviour.
8. Teacher grants permission for behaviour.
9. Teacher refuses permission for behaviour.
10. Teacher gives explanation to amplify command by, for example (a) appeal to norms or rules, (b) explanation of consequences of behaviour.
11. Teacher threatens to impose sanctions.
12. Teacher makes no response.
13. Teacher encourages, reassures, placates pupil, e.g. notes awareness of pupil's difficulty.
14. Teacher alters pupil's position, excludes him or keeps him behind.
15. Teacher confiscates distracting article.
16. Teacher goes to pupil.

(17–27 Pupil acts)

17. Individual pupil(s) make initial act that leads to disruption as perceived by the teacher whether or not this was intended to be provocative.
18. The same pupil repeats the same disruptive act after an interval (i.e. referring to 17).

19. The same pupil makes a different disruptive act (not included in 28 or 29).
20. Another pupil, several pupils or the whole class contribute to the particular disruptive act (not included in 28 or 29).
21. Another pupil(s) makes a new disruptive act (not included in 28 or 29).
22. Pupil(s) stops disruptive act immediately.
23. Pupil(s) does not stop disruptive act.
24. Pupil(s) stops disruptive act but with a delay of less than x seconds (x is the reasonable length of time for compliance).
25. Pupil gives what is perceived by the teacher as a reasonable explanation for his behaviour.
26. Pupil gives unreasonable or facetious explanation or no explanation for his behaviour.
27. Interval between provocative acts or end of lesson.
28. Pupil refuses to accept teacher explanation.
29. Pupil abusive.

BIBLIOGRAPHY

ALEXANDER, I. (1977) *The Human Machine: A view of intelligent mechanisms.* St. Saphoria, Switzerland: Georgi.

ALLWOOD, J. (1976) *Linguistic Communication as Action and Cooperation.* Gothenburg Monographs in Linguistics 2. Gothenburg: University Department of Linguistics.

ALTMAN, S. A. (1965) Sociobiology of Rhesus monkeys. II: Stochastics of social communication. *Journal of Theoretical Biology*, 8, 490–522.

AMIDON, E. J. and HOUGH, J. B. (eds.) (1967) *Interaction Analysis: Theory, research and application.* Reading, Massachusetts: Addison-Wesley.

ANDERSON, J. R. (1976) *Language, Memory and Thought.* Hillsdale: Erlbaum.

ANNETT, J. (1969) *Feedback and Human Behaviour.* Harmondsworth: Penguin.

ARGYLE, M. (1967) *The Psychology of Interpersonal Behaviour.* Harmondsworth: Penguin.

ARGYLE, M. (1969) *Social Interaction.* London: Methuen.

ARGYLE, M. (1972) Non-verbal communication in human social interaction. In R. A. HINDE (ed.) *Non-verbal Communication.* London: Cambridge University Press.

ARGYLE, M. (1977) Predictive and generative rule models of P × S interaction. In D. MAGNUSSON and N. ENDLER (eds.) *Personality at the Crossroads: Current issues in interactional psychology.* Hillsdale, New Jersey: Erlbaum.

ARGYLE, M. and DEAN, J. (1965) Eye contact, distance and affiliation. *Sociometry*, 28, 289–304.

ARGYLE, M., FURNHAM, A. and GRAHAM, J. A. (1981) *Social Situations.* Cambridge University Press.

ARGYLE, M. and LITTLE, B. R. (1972) Do personality traits apply to social behaviour? *Journal for the Theory of Social Behaviour*, 2, 1–35.

ARGYLE, M. and McCALLIN, M. (1981) The rules about interrupting. In M. ARGYLE, A. FURNHAM and J. A. GRAHAM *Social Situations.* Cambridge: Cambridge University Press.

ASHBY, W. R. (1956) *An Introduction to Cybernetics.* London: Chapman & Hall.

ATKINSON, J. M. and DREW, P. (1979) *Order in Court: The organisation of verbal interaction in judicial settings.* London: Macmillan.

AULD, F. (Jr.) and WHITE, A. M. (1956) Rules for dividing interviews into sentences. *Journal of Psychology*, 42, 273–281.

AUSTIN, J. L. (1962) *How to do Things with Words.* Oxford: Clarendon Press.

BAKEMAN, R. and DABBS, J. B., Jr. (1976) Social interaction observed: some approaches to the analysis of behaviour streams. *Personality and Social Psychology Bulletin*, 2, 335–345.

BALES, R. F. (1953) The equilibrium problem in small groups. In T. PARSONS, R. F. BALES and E. A. SHILS. *Working Papers in the Theory of Action.* Glencoe, Illinois: Free Press.

BALES, R. F. (1955) How people interact in conferences. *Scientific American*, March, 3–7.

BALES, R. F. and GERBRANDS, H. (1948) The interaction recorder: An apparatus and checklist for sequential content analysis of social interaction. *Human Relations*, 1, 456–463.

BARKER, R. G. (1963) The stream of behaviour as an empirical problem. In R. G. BARKER (ed.) *The Stream of Behaviour.* New York: Appleton–Century–Crofts.

292   David Clarke

BARTLETT, F. C. (1932) *Remembering: A study in experimental and social psychology*. London: Cambridge University Press.
BASSO, K. H. (1972) 'To give up on words': Silence in Western Apache Culture. *In* P. P. GIGLIOLI (ed.) *Language and Social Context*. Harmondsworth: Penguin.
BATTERSBY, A. (1966/1975) *Mathematics in Management*. Harmondsworth: Penguin.
BEISHON, J. (1971) *Systems*. Bletchley: Open University Press.
BELLACK, A. A., KLIEBARD, H. M., HYMAN, R. T. and SMITH, F. L., Jr. (1966) *The Language of the Classroom*. New York: Teachers College Press.
BENJAMIN, L. S. (1974) Structural analysis of social behaviour. *Psychological Review*, 81, 392–425.
BERKOWITZ, L. (1979) *A Survey of Social Psychology*, 2nd edn. New York: Holt, Rinehart & Winston.
BERNSTEIN, B. B. (1962) Social class, linguistic codes, and grammatical elements. *Language and Speech*, 5, 221–240.
BJERG, K. (1968) Interplay analysis. *Acta Psychologica*, 28, 201–245.
BODEN, M. (1977) *Artificial Intelligence and Natural Man*. Hassocks: Harvester.
BOSSEL, H., KLACZO, S. and MÜLLER, N. (eds.) (1976) *Systems Theory in the Social Sciences*. Basel: Birkhäuser.
BRENNER, M. (1978) Interviewing: the social phenomenology of a research instrument. M. BRENNER, P. MARSH and M. BRENNER (eds.) *The Social Contexts of Method*. London: Croom Helm.
BRENNER, S.-O. (1975) Formal structure of messages and discourse related to personality. *Göteborg Psychological Reports*, 5(18).
BRENNER, S.-O. and HJELMQUIST, E. (1974a) Verbal interactions in dyads. I: Intensive process analysis of interactions. *Göteborg Psychological Reports*, 4(24).
BRENNER, S.-O. and HJELMQUIST, E. (1974b) Verbal interactions in dyads. II: Process analysis of interactions. *Göteborg Psychological Reports*, 4(25).
BRENNER, S.-O. and HJELMQUIST, E. (1974c) Verbal interactions in dyads. III: Effects of the interactions. *Göteborg Psychological Reports*, 4(26).
BRENNER, S.-O. and HJELMQUIST, E. (1975) Personality and the structure of speech processes. *Göteborg Psychological Reports*, 5(12).
BRONOWSKI, J. (1973) *The Ascent of Man*. London: British Broadcasting Corporation.
BROWN, P. and LEVINSON, S. (1978) Universals in language: politeness phenomena. In E. N. GOODY (ed.) *Questions and Politeness: Strategies in social interaction (Cambridge papers in Social Anthropology, 8)*. Cambridge: Cambridge University Press.
BROWN, R. and FORD, M. (1961) Address in American English. *Journal of Abnormal and Social Psychology*, 62, 375–385.
BROWN, R. and GILMAN, A. (1960) The pronouns of power and solidarity. In T. A. SEBEOK (ed.) *Style in Language*. Cambridge, Mass.: Massachusetts Institute of Technology Press.
BRUNER, J. S. (1976) The ontogenesis of speech acts. In P. COLLETT (ed.) *Social Rules and Social Behaviour*. Oxford: Blackwell.
BRUNING, J. L. and KINTZ, B. L. (1968) *Computational Handbook of Statistics*. Glenview, Illinois: Scott, Foresman & Co.
BURKE, J. P. and SCHIAVETTI, N. (1976) Effects of cumulative context and guessing methods on estimates of transition probability in speech. *Language and Speech*, 18, 299–311.
CANTER, D., BREAUX, J. and SIME, J. (1978) *Human Behaviour in Fires*. Building Research Establishment, Fire Research Station, University of Surrey.
CARTER, L. (1951) A note on a new technique of interaction recording. *Journal of Abnormal and Social Psychology*, 46, 258–260.
CHOMSKY, N. (1957) *Syntactic Structures*. The Hague: Mouton.
CHOMSKY, N. (1959) On certain formal properties of grammar. *Information and Control*, 1, 91–112.
CHOMSKY, N. (1963) Formal properties of grammars. In R. D. LUCE, R. R. BUSH and E. GALANTER (eds.) *Handbook of Mathematical Psychology II*. London: Wiley.

CHOMSKY, N. (1965) *Aspects of the Theory of Syntax.* The Hague: Mouton.
CHOMSKY, N. (1971) Deep structure, surface structure, and semantic interpretation. In D. D. STEINBERG and L. A. JAKOBOVITS (eds.) *Semantics.* Cambridge: Cambridge University Press.
CICOUREL, A. V. (1973) *Cognitive Sociology*, Harmondsworth: Penguin.
CICOUREL, A. V. (1978) Discourse, autonomous grammars and contextualised processing of information. Proceedings of conference on Gesprächsanalyse, IKB Bonn, October, 1976.
CLARKE, D. D. (1975a) The structural analysis of verbal interaction. Unpublished D. Phil. thesis, Oxford University.
CLARKE, D. D. (1975b) The use and recognition of sequential structure in dialogue. *British Journal of Social and Clinical Psychology*, 14, 333–339.
CLARKE, D. D. (1981) Orders of approximation to English dialogue. *Language and Communication*, I, 207–236.
CLARKE, D. D. and ARGYLE, J. M. (1982) Conversation sequences. In C. FRASER and K. SHERER (eds.) *Social Psychology of Language.* Cambridge: Cambridge University Press.
COLLETT, P. (1975) The repertory grid and anthropology: The Psychological Structure of a Spirit Cosmology. Oxford, unpublished.
CONDON, W. S. and OGSTON, W. D. (1967) A segmentation of behaviour. *Journal of Psychiatric Research*, 5, 221–235.
COULTHARD, R. M. (1973) The analysis of classroom language. *Social Science Research Council Newsletter*, 19th June, 5–8.
COULTHARD, R. M. (1977) *Introduction to Discourse Analysis.* London: Longmans.
CRIBBIN, J. and MARSTRAND, P. (1978) There is enough for us all if only . . . *The Times*, 26th September, p. 16.
DAWKINS, R. (1976) Hierarchical organisation: a candidate principle for ethology. In P. P. G. BATESON and R. A. HINDE (eds.) *Growing Points in Ethology.* London: Cambridge University Press.
DE WAELE, J.-P. and HARRÉ, R. (1979) Autobiography as a psychological method. In G. P. GINSBURG (ed.) *Emerging Strategies in Social Psychological Research.* London: Wiley.
DICKMAN, H. R. (1963) The perception of behavioural units. In R. G. BARKER (ed.) *The Stream of Behaviour.* New York: Appleton–Century–Crofts.
DIXON, W. J. (ed.) (1973) *BMD: Biomedical Computer Programs.* Berkeley: University of California Press.
DORNY, C. N. (1975) *A Vector Space Approach to Models and Optimisation.* New York: Wiley.
DREYFUS, H. L. (1972) *What Computers Can't Do: A critique of artificial reason.* New York: Harper & Row.
DUNCAN, S., Jr. (1972) Some signals and rules for taking speaking turns in conversations. *Journal of Personality and Social Psychology*, 23, 283–292.
DUNCAN, S., Jr. (1973) Towards a grammar of dyadic conversation. *Semiotica*, 9, 29–46.
DUNCAN, S., Jr. and FISKE, D. W. (1977) *Face-to-face Interaction: Research, methods and theory.* Hillsdale, N. J.: Erlbaum.
DUNKIN, M. J. and BIDDLE, B. J. (1974) *The Study of Teaching.* New York: Holt, Rinehart & Winston.
EKMAN, P. and FRIESEN, W. V. (1969) The repertoire of nonverbal behaviour: categories, origins, usage and coding. *Semiotica*, I, 49–98.
ERVIN-TRIPP, S. M. (1964) Analysis of the interaction of language, topic and listener. *American Anthropologist*, 66, 86–94.
ERVIN-TRIPP, S. M. (1969) Sociolinguistics. In L. BERKOWITZ (ed.) *Advances in Experimental Social Psychology*, New York: Academic Press.
FARB, P. (1974) *Word Play: What happens when people talk.* London: Cape.
FARRELL, B. A. (1970) On the design of a conscious device. *Mind*, 79, 321–346.
FELDSTEIN, S. (1972) Temporal patterns of dialogue. Basic research and reconsiderations. In A. W. SIEGMAN and B. POPE (eds.) *Studies in Dyadic Communication.* New York: Pergamon.

FERRARA, J. W. (1973) A verbal interaction recording technique for studying individuals in small groups. *Journal of Personality and Social Psychology*, 90, 207–212.

FIELDING, G. and FRASER, C. (1978) Language and social relationships. In I. MARKOVA (ed.) *The Social Context of Language*. Chichester: Wiley.

FILLMORE, C. J. (1968) The case for case. In E. BACH and R. T. HARMS (eds.) *Universals in Language*. New York: Holt, Rinehart & Winston.

FISHER, R. A. (1970) *Statistical Methods for Research Workers*. New York: Hafner Press.

FISHER, R. A. and YATES, F. (1963) *Statistical Tables for Biological, Agricultural and Medical Research*. London: Oliver & Boyd.

FLANDERS, N. A. (1970) *Analysing Teaching Behavior*. Reading, Mass.: Addison-Wesley.

FOA, U. G. and FOA, E. B. (1972) Resource exchange. Towards a structural theory of interpersonal communication. In A. W. SIEGMAN and B. POPE (eds.) *Studies in Dyadic Communication*. New York: Pergamon.

FODOR, J. A. (1981) The mind–body problem. *Scientific American*, 244, 124–132.

FODOR, J. A. and BEVER, T. (1965) The psychological reality of linguistic segments. *Journal of Verbal Learning and Verbal Behaviour*, 4, 414–420.

FORRESTER, J. W. (1972) Understanding the counter-intuitive behaviour of social systems. In J. BEISHON and G. PETERS (eds.) *Systems Behaviour*. London: Open University Press.

FRAKE, C. O. (1964) How to ask for a drink in Subanun. *American Anthropologist*, 66, 127–132.

FREEDLE, R. O. (ed.) (1977) *Discourse Production and Comprehension (Discourse Processes: Advances in research and theory*, Vol. 1). Norwood, N.J.: Ablex.

FRENTZ, T. S. (1976) A generative approach to episodic structure. Univ. South Cal., Western Speech Communication Convention. San Francisco, Cal., November: manuscript.

FRIES, C. C. (1952) *The Structure of English*. New York: Harcourt, Brace & Co.

GANDY, R. (1973) Structure in mathematics. In D. ROBEY (ed.) *Structuralism*. Oxford: Clarendon.

GARFINKEL, H. (1967) *Studies in Ethnomethodology*. Englewood Cliffs: Prentice-Hall.

GOFFMAN, E. (1972) *Relations in Public*. Harmondsworth: Penguin.

GOFFMAN, E. (1981) *Forms of Talk*. Oxford: Blackwell.

GOTTMAN, J. M. (1979) *Marital Interaction*. New York: Academic Press.

GREENE, J. (1972) *Psycholinguistics*. Harmondsworth: Penguin.

GRICE, H. P. (1957) Meaning. *Phil. Rev.* 66, 377–388.

GRICE, H. P. (1968) Utterer's meaning, sentence meaning and word meaning. *Foundations of Language*, 4, 225–242.

GUNTER, R. (1966) On the placement of accent in dialogue: A feature of context grammar. *Journal of Linguistics*, 2, 159–179.

HALLIDAY, M. A. K. (1970) Language structure and language function. In J. LYONS (ed.) *New Horizons in Linguistics*. Harmondsworth: Penguin.

HAMPSHIRE, S. (1965) *Thought and Action*. Chatto & Windus.

HARRÉ, R. (1976) The constructive role of models. In L. COLLINS (ed.) *The Use of Models in the Social Sciences*. London: Tavistock.

HARRÉ, R. (1977) The ethogenic approach: theory and practice. In L. BERKOWITZ (ed.) *Recent Advances in Experimental Social Psychology*, 10, 283–314. New York: Academic Press.

HARRÉ, R. (1980) *Social Being*. Oxford: Blackwell.

HARRÉ, R. and SECORD, P. F. (1972) *The Explanation of Social Behaviour*. Oxford: Blackwell.

HARRIS, Z. S. (1952) Discourse analysis. *Language*, 28, 1–30.

HARRIS, Z. S. (1963) *Discourse Analysis Reprints*. The Hague: Mouton.

HELLER, K. (1972) Interview structure and interview style in initial interviews. In A. W. SIEGMAN and B. POPE (eds.) *Studies in Dyadic Communication*. New York: Pergamon.

HERTEL, R. K. (1972) Application of stochastic process analyses to the study of psychotherapeutic process. *Psychological Bulletin*, 77, 421–430.

HJELMQUIST, E. (1975) Functions of messages and discourse related to personality in dyadic communication. *Göteborg Psychological Reports*, 5(19).

HOFSTADTER, D. R. (1979) *Gödel, Escher, Bach: An eternal golden braid*. Hassocks: Harvester Press.

HUESMAN, L. R. and LEVINGER, G. (1976) Incremental exchange theory: a formal model for progression in dyadic social interaction. In L. BERKOWITZ (ed.) *Advances in Experimental Social Psychology*, 9, New York: Academic Press.

HUTT, S. J. and HUTT, C. (1970) *Direct Observation and Measurement of Behaviour*. Springfield, Illinois: Thomas.

HYMES, D. (1967) Models of the interaction of language and social setting. *Journal of Social Issues*, 23, (2), 8–28.

JAFFE, J., FELDSTEIN, S. and CASSOTTA, L. (1967) Markovian models of dialogic time patterns. *Nature*, 216, 93–94.

JAKOBSON, R. (1972) Verbal communication. *Scientific American*, September, 72–82.

JARDINE, N. and SIBSON, R. (1971) *Mathematical Taxonomy*. London: Wiley.

JEFFERSON, G. (1972) Side sequences. In D. SUDNOW (ed.) *Studies in Social Interaction*. New York: Free Press.

JOHNSON, N. F. (1965) The psychological reality of phrase structure rules. *Journal of Verbal Learning and Verbal Behaviour*, 4, 469–475.

JONES, E. E. and GERARD, H. B. (1967) *Foundations of Social Psychology*. New York: Wiley.

JOOS, M. (1950) Description of language design. *Journal of the Acoustical Society of America*, 22, 701–708.

KATZ, J. J. and FODOR, J. A. (1963) The structure of a semantic theory. *Language*, 39, 170–210.

KAUFMAN, G. M. and THOMAS, H. (1977) *Modern Decision Analysis*. Harmondsworth: Penguin.

KEMENY, J. G. and SNELL, J. L. (1960) *Finite Markov Chains*. Princeton: Van Nostrand.

KENDALL, M. G. (1948) *Rank Correlation Methods*. London: Griffin.

KENDON, A. (1967) Some functions of gaze direction in social interaction. *Acta Psychologica*, 26, 22–63.

KIRK, R. E. (1968) *Experimental Design: Procedures for the behavioural sciences*. Belmont: Brooks Cole.

KOHLER, G. and ALCOCK, N. (1976) An empirical table of structural violence. *Journal of Peace Research*, 4, 343–355.

KORSCH, B. M. and NEGRETE, V. F. (1972) Doctor–patient communication. *Scientific American*, August, 66–74.

KRAUSE, M. S. (1972) Strategies in argument. *Journal of Psychology*, 81, 269–279.

LABOV, W. (1970) The study of language in its social context. *Studium Generale*, 23, 30–87.

LABOV, W. (1972) Rules for ritual insults. In D. SUDNOW (ed.) *Studies in Social Interaction*. New York: Free Press.

LABOV, W. and FANSHEL, D. (1977) *Therapeutic Discourse: Psychotherapy as Conversation*. New York: Academic Press.

LAFFAL, J. (1965) *Pathological and Normal Language*. New York: Atherton.

LAKOFF, G. (1968) Instrumental adverbs and the concept of deep structure. *Foundations of Language*, 4, 4–29.

LASHLEY, K. S. D. (1951) The problem of serial order in behaviour. In L. A. JEFRESS (ed.) *Cerebral Mechanisms in Behaviour*. New York: Wiley.

LAWTON, D. (1968) *Social Class, Language and Education*. London: Routledge & Kegan Paul.

LEARY, T. (1957) *Interpersonal Diagnosis of Personality*. New York: Ronald Press.

LEAVITT, H. J. and MUELLER, R. A. H. (1951) Some effect of feedback on communication. *Human Relations*, 4, 401–410.

LEVI-STRAUSS, C. (1968) *Structural Anthropology*. Harmondsworth: Penguin.

LIBERMAN, A. M., HARRIS, K. C., HOFFMAN, H. S. and GRIFFITH, B. C. (1957) The discrimination of speech sounds within and across phoneme boundaries. *Journal of Experimental Psychology*, 54, 358–368.

LIGHTHILL, J. (ed.) (1978) *Newer Uses of Mathematics*. Harmondsworth: Penguin.

LYONS, J. (1970) *Chomsky*. London: Fontana.

MACKAY, D. M. (1972) Formal analysis of communicative processes. In R. A. HINDE (ed.) *Non-verbal Communication*. London: Cambridge University Press.

MAGNUSSON, D. (ed.) (1981) *Towards a Psychology of Situations: An interactional perspective*. New York: Erlbaum.

MAKOWER, M. S. and WILLIAMSON, E. (1967) *Operational Research*. London: English Universities Press.

MARSDEN, G. (1965) Content analysis studies of therapeutic interviews. *Psych. Bull.*, 63, 298–321.

MARSHALL, J. C. (1965) The syntax of reproductive behaviour in the male pigeon. Oxford: Medical Research Council psycholinguistics unit report, unpublished.

MARTIN, E. (1970) Towards an analysis of subjective phrase structure. *Psychological Bulletin*, 74, 153–166.

MCCAWLEY, J. D. (1968) The role of semantics in a grammar. In E. BACH and R. T. HARMS (eds.) *Universals in Language*. London: Holt, Rinehart & Winston.

MEETHAM, A. R. (1969) *Encyclopaedia of Linguistics, Information and Control*. Oxford: Pergamon.

MEHRABIAN, A. (1972) *Non-verbal Communication*. Chicago: Aldine-Atherton.

MELTZER, L., MORRIS, W. N. and HAYES, D. P. (1971) Interruption outcomes and vocal amplitude: explorations in social psychophysics. *Journal of Personality and Social Psychology*, 18, 392–402.

MENDELEEV, D. I. (1879) *La Loi périodique des éléments chimiques*. Paris: Renau, Maulde et Cock.

MILL, J. S. (1851) *A System of Logic, Ratiocinative and Inductive*, 3rd edn. London: Parker, p. 335.

MILLER, G. A. (1951) *Language and Communication*. New York: McGraw-Hill.

MILLER, G. A. (1967) *The Psychology of Communication*. New York: Basic Books.

MILLER, G. A. and CHOMSKY, N. (1963) Finitary models of language users. In R. D. LUCE, R. R. BUSH and E. GALANTER (eds.) *Handbook of Mathematical Psychology II*. New York: Wiley.

MILLER, G. A., GALANTER, E. and PRIBRAM, K. L. (1960) *Plans and the Structure of Behaviour*. New York: Holt, Rinehart & Winston.

MILLER, G. A. and MCNEIL, D. (1968) Psycholinguistics. In G. LINDZEY and E. ARONSON (eds.) *The Handbook of Social Psychology III*. Reading, Mass.: Addison-Wesley.

MILLER, G. A. and SELFRIDGE, J. A. (1950) Verbal content and the recall of meaningful material. *American Journal of Psychology*, 63, 176–185.

MINSKY, M. (1972) *Computation: Finite and infinite machines*. London: Prentice-Hall.

MISCHEL, W. (1973) Toward a cognitive social learning reconceptualisation of personality. *Psychological Review*, 80, 252–283.

MORLEY, I. and STEPHENSON, G. (1977) *The Social Psychology of Bargaining*. London: Allen & Unwin.

MORRIS, W. N. (1971) Manipulated amplitudes and interruption outcomes. *Journal of Personality and Social Psychology*, 20, 319–331.

MURRAY, H. A. (1951) Towards a classification of interactions. In T. PARSONS and E. A. SHILS (eds.) *Towards a General Theory of Action*. Cambridge, Mass.: Harvard University Press.

NEISSER, U. (1967) *Cognitive Psychology*. New York: Appleton–Century–Crofts.

NELSON, K. (1973) Structure and strategy in learning to talk. *Monographs of the Society for Research in Child Development*, 149, (1–2), Feb–April.

NEWBOLD, P. (1973) *Forecasting Methods*. London: H.M.S.O.

NEWELL, A. and SIMON, H. A. (1972) *Human Problem Solving*. Englewood Cliffs, N.J.: Prentice Hall.

NEWTSON, D. (1973) Attribution and the unit of perception of ongoing behaviour. *Journal of Personality and Social Psychology*, 28, 28–38.

ODUM, E. P. (1971) *Fundamentals of Ecology*. Philadelphia: Saunders.

OSGOOD, C. E. (1968) Interpersonal Verbs and Interpersonal Behaviour. Report from the Group Effectiveness Research Laboratory, University of Illinois, unpublished.

OSGOOD, C. E. (1970) Speculation on the structure of interpersonal intuition. *Behavioural Science*, 15, 237–254.

OSGOOD, C. E. (1971) Where do sentences come from? In D. D. STEINBERG and L. A. JAKOBOWITZ (eds.) *Semantics: An interdisciplinary reader in philosophy, linguistics and psychology*. London: Cambridge University Press.

PARRY-JONES, W. L. and GAY, B. M. (1980) The anatomy of disruption: a preliminary consideration of interaction sequences within disruptive incidents. *Oxford Review of Education*, 6, 213–220.

PĂUN, G. (1976) A generative model of conversation. *Semiotica*, 17, 21–33.

PEARCE, W. BARNETT (1976a) The coordinated management of meaning: A rules-based theory of interpersonal communication. Manuscript.

PEARCE, W. BARNETT (1976b) Coordination and enactment of conversational episodes: a perspective on interpersonal communication. Speech Communication Association, San Francisco, December.

PEASE, K. and ARNOLD, P. (1973) Approximation to dialogue. *American Journal of Psychology*, 86, 769–776.

PIAGET, J. (1971) *Structuralism*. London: Routledge & Kegan Paul.

PIKE, K. L. (1967) *Language in Relation to a Unified Theory of the Structure of Human Behaviour*. The Hague: Mouton.

PÖRN, I. (1977) *Action Theory and Social Science: Some formal models*. Boston: Reidel.

POST, E. L. (1943) Formal reductions of the general combinatorial decision problem. *American Journal of Mathematics*, 65, 197–268.

RAUSH, H. L. (1965) Interaction sequences. *Journal of Personality and Social Psychology*, 2, 487–499.

RAUSH, H. L. (1972) Process and change: A Markov model for interaction. *Family Process*, 11, 275–298.

RIVETT, B. H. P. (1978) Planning. In J. LIGHTHILL (ed.) *Newer Uses of Mathematics*. Harmondsworth: Penguin.

ROBINSON, W. P. (1972) *Language and Social Behaviour*. Harmondsworth: Penguin.

ROGET, S. R. (1959) *Thesaurus*. Harmondsworth: Penguin.

ROMMETVEIT, R. (1968) *Words, Meanings and Messages*. London: Academic Press.

ROMMETVEIT, R. (1972) Language games, syntactic structures and hermeneutics. In J. ISRAEL and H. TAJFEL (eds.) *The Context of Social Psychology*. London: Academic Press.

ROMMETVEIT, R., COOK, M., HAVELKA, N., HENRY, P., HERKNER, W., PECHEUX, M. and PEETERS, G. (1971) Processing utterances in context. In E. A. CARSWELL and R. ROMMETVEIT (eds.) *Social Contexts of Messages*. London: Academic Press.

SACKS, H. (1967) Class notes.

SACKS, H., SCHEGLOFF, E. A. and JEFFERSON, G. (1974) A simplest systematics for the organisation of turn-taking for conversation. *Language*, 50, 696–735.

SAUSSURE, F. de (1916) *Cours de linguistique générale*. Lausanne: Bally et Sechehaye. (1974) *Course in General Linguistics*. Glasgow: Fontana.

SCHANK, R. C. and ABELSON, R. P. (1977) *Scripts, Plans, Goals and Understanding*. Hillsdale, N.J.: Erlbaum.

SCHEFLEN, A. E. (1964) The significance of posture in communication systems. *Psychiatry*, 27, 316–331.

SCHEGLOFF, E. A. (1968) Sequencing in conversational openings. *American Anthropologist*, 70, 1075–1095.

SCHEGLOFF, E. A. and SACKS, H. (1973) Opening up closings. *Semiotica*, 8, 289–327.

SCHLESINGER, I. M. (1974) Towards a structural analysis of discussion. *Semiotica*, 11, 109–122.

SEARLE, J. (1965) What is a speech act? In M. BLACK (ed.) *Philosophy in America*. London: Allen & Unwin and Cornell University Press.

SEARLE, J. (1969) *Speech Acts*. London: Cambridge University Press.

SEARLE, J. (1975) A taxonomy of illocutionary acts. In K. GUNDERSON (ed.) *Language, Mind and Knowledge*. Minnesota Studies in the Philosophy of Science, 7, University of Minnesota Press.

SEGAL, E. M. and STACY, E. W., Jr. (1975) Rule governed behaviour as a psychological process. *American Psychologist*, **30**, 541–552.

SHANNON, C. E. (1948) A mathematical theory of communication. *Bell System Tech. J.* 27, 379–423.

SHANNON, J. and GUERNEY, B., Jr. (1973) Interpersonal effects of interpersonal behaviour. *Journal of Personality and Social Psychology*, **26**, 142–150.

SHAPIRO, D. A. (1976) Conversational structure and accurate empathy: an exploratory study. *British Journal of Social and Clinical Psychology*, 15, 213–215.

SIEGEL, S. (1956) *Nonparametric Statistics for the Behavioural Sciences*. New York: McGraw-Hill.

SIMMONS, R. and SLOCUM, J. (1972) Generating English discourse from semantic networks. *Communications of A.C.M.* 15, 891–905.

SIMON, A. and BOYER, E. G. (eds.) (1974) *Mirrors for Behaviour*. 3rd ed. *Classroom Interaction Newsletter*. Wyncote, Pennsylvania: Communication Materials Center.

SIMON, H. A. (1952) A formal theory of interaction in social groups. *American Sociological Review*, 17, 202–211.

SINCLAIR, J. and COULTHARD, R. M. (1975) *Towards an Analysis of Discourse: The English used by teachers and pupils*. London: Oxford University Press.

SLATER, P. J. B. (1973) Describing sequences of behaviour. In P. P. G. BATESON and P. H. KLOPFER (eds.) *Perspectives in Ethology*. New York: Plenum.

SOSKIN, W. F. and JOHN, V. P. (1963) The study of spontaneous talk. In R. G. BARKER (ed.) *The Stream of Behaviour*. New York: Appleton–Century–Crofts.

THORNDYKE, P. W. (1977) Cognitive structures in comprehension and memory of narrative discourse. *Cognitive Psychology*, 9, 77–110.

TODD, Lord (1980) The role of scientists in the 1980's. *New Scientist*, 3rd January, p. 2.

TOLMAN, E. C. (1948) Cognitive maps in rats and men. *Psychological Review*, 55, 189–208.

TROWER, P., BRYANT, B. and ARGYLE, M. (1978) *Social Skills and Mental Health*. London: Methuen.

TURING, A. M. (1950) Computing machinery and intelligence. *Mind*, 59, 433–460.

VAN HOOFF, J. A. R. A. M. (1973) A structural analysis of the social behaviour of a semi-captive group of chimpanzees. In M. VON CRANACH and I. VINE (eds.) *Social Communication and Movement*. London: Academic Press.

WADDINGTON, C. H. (1977) *Tools for thought*. St. Albans: Paladin.

WASON, P. C. and JOHNSON-LAIRD, P. N. (1972) *Psychology of Reasoning: Structure and content*. London: Batsford.

WEBB, J. T. (1972) Interview synchrony. An investigation of two speech rate measures in an automated standardised interview. In A. W. SIEGMAN and B. POPE (eds.) *Studies in Dyadic Communication*. New York: Pergamon.

WEIZENBAUM, J. (1966) ELIZA – A Computer programme for the study of natural language communication between man and machine. *Communications of the A.C.M.* 9, 36–45.

WEIZENBAUM, J. (1967) Contextual understanding by computers. *Communications of the A.C.M.* 10, 474–480.

WEIZENBAUM, J. (1976) *Computer Power and Human Reason*. San Francisco: Freeman.

WESTMAN, R. S. (1978) Environmental languages and the functional bases of animal behaviour. In B. HAZLETT (ed.) *Quantitative Methods in Animal Behaviour*. New York: Academic Press.

WILLS, G., WILSON, R., MANNING, N. and HILDEBRANDT, R. (1972) *Technological Forecasting*. Harmondsworth: Penguin.

WILSON, A. (1968) *The Bomb and the Computer*. London: Barrie & Rockliff, The Cresset Press.

WILSON, K. G. (1979) Problems in physics with many scales of length. *Scientific American*, August, 241, 140–157.

WINER, B. J. (1962) *Statistical Principles in Experimental Design*. New York: McGraw-Hill.

WINOGRAD, T. (1972) Understanding natural language. *Cognitive Psychology*, 3, 1–191.

WITTGENSTEIN, L. (1953) *Philosophical Investigations*. Oxford: Blackwell.

WOODS, W. A. (1970) Transition Network grammars for natural language analysis. *Communications of the A.C.M.* **13**, 591–606.

WOOTTON, A. (1975) *Dilemmas of Discourse: Controversies about the sociological interpretation of language*. London: Allen & Unwin.

YNGVE, V. H. (1973) I forget what I was going to say. Paper to the ninth regional meeting of the Chicago Linguistic Society.

AUTHOR INDEX

Abelson, R. P.   38, 232
Alcock, N.   1
Alexander, I.   177
Allwood, J.   33
Altman, S. A.   39, 67, 161
Amidon, E. J.   26
Anderson, J. R.   229
Annett, J.   84
Argyle, M.   5, 6, 9, 41, 43, 110, 134,
   173, 260
   Argyle et al., 204, 232
Aristotle   15, 197
Arnold, P.   72f
Ashby, W. R.   177
Atkinson, J. M.   29
Auld, F. Jr.   135
Austin, J. L.   3, 54, 124, 143, 146, 159

Bakeman, R.   36
Bales, R. F.   8, 33ff, 54ff, 84, 122, 142
Barker, R. G.   85, 121, 133f, 139
Bartlett, F. C.   127
Basso, K. H.   29
Battersby, A.   240
Beishon, J.   6, 177
Bellack, A. A.   26
Benjamin, L. S.   141
Berkowitz, L.   270
Bernstein, B. B.   6
Bever, T.   134
Biddle, B. J.   36
Bjerg, K.   36, 139, 159
Boden, M.   38, 175
Bossell, H. et al.   241
Boyer, E. G.   36
Brenner, M.   29
Brenner, S. O.   43
Bronowski, J.   15
Brown, P.   29
Brown, R.   6
Bruner, J. S.   121
Bruning, J. L.   59
Burke, J. P.   36

Canter, D. et al.   244
Carter, L.   142
Cassotta, L.   41, 161
Chomsky, N.   5, 6, 16, 18, 85, 107, 110,
   112f, 128ff, 161, 170f, 174, 191f,
   199, 222
Cicourel, A. V.   24, 33, 121, 130
Clarke, D. D.   43, 49, 70, 78
Collett, P.   142
Condon, W. S.   133, 135f
Coulthard, R. M.   20, 25, 33, 43, 142
Cribbin, J.   1

Dabbs, D. B. Jr.   36
Dawkins, R.   166
Dean, J.   173
De Waele, J. P.   199
Dickman, H. R.   137
Dixon, W. J.   69, 88, 94, 183
Dorny, C. N.   252
Drew, P.   29
Dreyfus, H. L.   202
Duncan, S. Jr.   40
Dunkin, M. J.   36

Ekman, P.   6
Ervin-Tripp, S. M.   33, 85, 138, 143

Fanshel, D.   33
Farb, P.   20
Farrell, B. A.   85, 160
Feldstein, S.   41, 161
Ferrara, J. W.   36, 139
Fielding, G.   141
Fillmore, C. J.   6, 109, 130, 139
Fisher, R. A.   70, 89
Fiske, D. W.   40
Flanders, N. A.   26, 142, 247
Foa, E. B.   42
Foa, U. G.   42
Fodor, J. A.   6, 17, 134, 274

Ford, M.   6
Forrester, J. W.   205, 240, 243
Frake, C. O.   29, 121
Fraser, C.   141
Freedle, R. O.   20
Frentz, T. S.   33, 219
Fries, C. C.   51, 147
Friesen, W. V.   6

Galanter, E.   8, 9, 85
Gandy, R.   121
Garfinkel, H.   17
Gay, B. M.   246
Gerard, H. B.   66, 84
Gerbrands, H.   142
Gilman, A.   6
Goffman, E.   23, 24, 25, 36, 66
Gottman, J. M.   37
Greene, J.   6
Grice, H. P.   33
Guerney, B. Jr.   84
Gunter, R.   31, 116, 141

Halliday, M. A. K.   140
Hampshire, S.   2
Harré, R.   3, 5, 16, 36, 61, 112, 116,
     121, 130, 197f, 199, 201f, 228, 231,
     232, 270
Harris, Z. S.   30, 31, 149
Heller, K.   42
Hertel, R. K.   36
Hjelmquist, E.   43
Hofstadter, D. R.   177
Hough, J. B.   26
Huesman, L. R.   39
Hutt, C.   85
Hutt, S. J.   85, 160
Hyman, R. T.   26
Hymes, D.   31

Jaffe, J.   41, 161
   Jaffe et al.   84
Jakobson, R.   158
Jardine, N.   150
Jefferson, G.   22, 23, 36
John, V. P.   26, 140
Johnson, N. F.   50, 95, 134
Johnson-Laird, P. N.   38
Jones, E. E.   66, 84
Joos, M.   119

Katz, J. J.   6, 17
Kaufmann, G. M.   242

Kemeny, J. G.   7
Kendall, M. G.   57f
Kendon, A.   40
Kintz, B. L.   59
Kirk, R. E.   70, 89, 184
Kliebard, H. M.   26
Kohler, G.   1
Korsch, B. M.   34
Krause, M. S.   142

Labov, W.   6, 27, 28, 29, 31, 33, 66f
Laffal, J.   11, 66
Lakoff, G.   109
Lashley, K. S. D.   84f, 161
Lawton, D.   6
Leary, T.   140
Leavitt, H. J.   84
Levinger, G.   39
Levinson, S.   29
Levi-Strauss, C.   121
Liberman, A. M. et al.   115
Lighthill, J.   240
Little, B. R.   5
Lyons, J.   107

McCawley, J. D.   109
Mackay, D. M.   85
McNeil, D.   6, 110, 140
Magnusson, D.   201
Makower, M. S.   240
Marsden, G.   142
Marshall, J. C.   85, 169
Marstrand, P.   1
Martin, E.   85, 96
McCallin, M.   41
Meetham, A. R.   126
Mehrabian, A.   6, 140
Meltzer, L. et al.   40f
Mendeleev, D. I.   13, 112
Mill, J.   vi
Miller, G. A.   6, 8, 9, 11f, 67f, 72, 85, 107,
     110, 140
Minsky, M.   65, 174, 229, 246
Mischel, W.   5
Morley, I.   142
Morris, W. N.   40
Mueller, R. A. H.   84
Murray, H. A.   8

Negrete, V. F.   34
Neisser, U.   169
Nelson, K.   33
Newbold, P.   240
Newell, A.   177

Newtson, D.   136

Odum, E. P.   162
Ogston, W. D.   133, 135f
Osgood, C. E.   52, 129, 145f, 159

Parry-Jones, W. L.   246
Paun, G.   219
Pearce, W. Barnett   33, 42
Pease, K.   72f
Piaget, J.   121
Pike, K. L.   109
Pörn, I.   121
Post, E. L.   170
Pribram, K. L.   8, 9, 85

Rausch, H. L.   36, 160, 248
Rivett, B. H. P.   206
Robinson, W. P.   140
Roget, S. R.   145
Rommetveit, R.   30, 33
     Rommetveit et al.   42

Sacks, H.   21, 23, 25, 41, 66, 82, 122, 143, 145
Saussure, F.   7, 109, 111f, 116, 138, 145
Schank, R. C.   38, 232
Scheflen, A. E.   135f
Schegloff, E. A.   21, 23, 25, 66, 143
Schiavetti, N.   36
Schlesinger, I. M.   93
Searle, J.   3, 31, 112, 125, 138, 143, 231
Secord, P. F.   5, 16, 36, 61, 112, 121, 130, 270
Segal, E. M.   112
Selfridge, J. A.   11f, 67, 72
Shannon, C. E.   39
Shannon, J.   84
Shapiro, D. A.   54
Sibson, R.   150

Siegel, S.   47, 58, 60, 156
Simon, A.   36
Simon, H. A.   39, 177
Simmons, R.   38
Sinclair, J.   25, 142
Slater, P. J. B.   160
Slocum, J.   38
Smith, F. L. Jr.   26
Snell, J. L.   7
Soskin, W. F.   26, 140
Stacy, E. W.   112
Stephenson, G.   142

Thomas, H.   242
Thorndyke, P. W.   121
Todd, L.   241
Tolman, E. C.   127
Trower, P. et al.   260
Turing, A. M.   39, 68, 174f

Van Hoof, J. A. R. A. M.   66, 139, 144f, 146f, 161

Waddington, C. H.   177
Wason, P. C.   38
Webb, J. T.   42
Weizenbaum, J.   37, 202
Westman, R. S.   85, 121
White, A. M.   135
Williamson, E.   240
Wills, G. et al.   243
Wilson, K. G.   178, 241
Winer, B. J.   88
Winograd, T.   37, 39, 109, 176, 234
Wittgenstein, L.   33
Woods, W. A.   39, 176, 229
Wootton, A.   23

Yngve, V. H.   134

SUBJECT INDEX

Accounts
    as explanatory material 203
    decomposition of behavioural 244f
    negotiation of 36
    technique of negotiation of 120
Act 7, 12
    act/action structure 16, 112
    and activity 139
    and coding systems in classroom 26, 246ff
    and episodes 188
    and interaction in groups 34, 35
    social 3, 125, 138
        type and choice of parameters 190
Action 7, 203, 265
    act/action structure 16, 112
    analysis of human 243
    analysis of sequences of 177
    and circumstances 271
    hierarchical level of 28
    human 1ff, 198, 264
    science of 2f, 10, 20
    segments of 3
    sequences of human social 177
    social 3, 106, 116, 198
    speech as 124
    structure of 9f, 264
    structure of social 198
    syntax of 3
    system of social 20
    theory of 2f, 15
    transformational generative grammar of 219
    and utterance unit 28
Activity
    and act 139
    map of 188
Actor 4, 5, 6, 7, 8, 9, 10, 12, 14, 15, 17, 18, 36, 46, 61, 63
    communicative competence of 109
    generative process of the 261
    mental map of 193
    mental processes of 195
    native 95

    real 99, 260
    real social 16
    social 201f
    theory of sociability of the 203
Adequacy
    descriptively adequate 110
    explanatorily adequate 110
    observational 16, 110
    of the theory 267
Agons 36, 139
Algorithm 7, 255
Analogue 3
Analogy 10, 11, 12, 13, 14, 44
    computer 202, 272ff
    and icon 202−203
    linguistic 50, 106, 117
    of map 196ff, 244ff
    mechanical 255f
    and methodology 202−203
    of mind and organisations 241
    symmetrical double 106
Analysis
    categorisational 157
    of conversation 13, 16, 21, 23, 30f, 33, 241, 260
    of discourse (*see* Discourse, analysis of)
    dynamic 27
    ecological 26
    functional 27
    holistic 119
    of human action 243
    of interaction 112
    of interaction processes 20
    linguistic 20, 96, 118, 169
    parametric 119
    of script 38
    semantic 145, 147
    of sequences (*see* Sequence, analysis of)
    vs. synthesis 199, 265
Anatomy 197
Anthropology 141
Anticipation
    and conversation 83
    curve 76

and discourse generation   83
  medium-term   97
  short-term   97
  and utterance selection   83
Approximations
  to dialogue   68
  order of approximation   104
  statistical   67
  'text' orders of   72
  zero and higher order   67–74
Arrangements
  of morphemes   11
  of speech acts   11
Articulation
  double   107
  linguistic multiple   107
  tertiary   107
Artificial Intelligence   176ff
  and behaviour sequences   176
Astronomy   4
Automata
  finite state   175, 263
  linear bounded   175
  push-down stack   175, 263
  theory of (*see* Theory)
  Turing   263

Behaviour
  Artificial Intelligence and sequences
    of   176
  categories of   172, 262
  classes of   137
  context and items of   18
  and elements   13
  grammar (*see* Grammar)
  methodology and conversation sequences
    238f
  model of sequences analysis of   241
  organisation of   260
  patterns of   4, 201
  proactive   217
  reactive   217
  semantics of   16, 115
  sequences of (*see* Sequences)
  sequences and analysis of   133, 139
  stream of (*see* Stream)
  theory of   269
  trajectory of   172
  units of   133ff, 139, 264
Behavioural
  accounts and decomposition   244f
  chains   246
  configurations   15
  episodes   1
  meaning   116
  model   229f

patterns and reproduction   238
  process   216
  rules   176, 218
  science   3f, 121, 258
  structure   123, 218f, 264
  system   5
  taxonomy   112
  theory of b. organisation   217
Brain   5, 127, 175, 200, 202, 274

Calculus
  predicate   193
  propositional   193
  of strategy   242
Category(ies)
  of Bales   34, 36, 54–60, 64
  of behaviour   172, 262
  of events   30, 36
  'chameleon categories'   23
  functional   140
  list of *a priori*   159, 178 (*see* Speech-act,
    category of)
  'syntactic'   165
Cause   197
  and effects   266ff
  efficient   15, 131, 197
  and enabling conditions   202
  final   15
  formal   15, 110, 131, 197
  material   15
  personal   268
  social   269
  and social behaviour   201f
Chain(s)
  'absorbing'   160
  analysis of   166
  behavioural   246
  'cyclic'   160
  of events   231, 240, 272
  'left-to-right'   219
  of 'mental events'   271f
  of overt behaviour   218
  'regular'   160
  single recurring   203
  theories of associative   161
Chemistry   4
  structural   112
  and structural models   119, 197
Class(es)
  Austin's five performative   125
  of behaviour   137
  combinations of   119
  of elements   11, 13, 17
  equivalence (*see* Equivalence, class of)
  of information   98
  of utterances (*see* Utterances, class of)

Cluster analysis   148, 150ff
  ball clusters   152
  chain clusters   152
Code(s)
  deep structure c.   18
  elliptical   22
  of events   207ff, 217f
  encoding and decoding process   6
  hierarchical coding system   26
  sequence c.   18
  surface semantic   18
  unit c.   18
  and verbal communication   29
Cognitive resource   202f
Combination
  sequential   192
Combinatorial
  explosion   120
  formula   252
  optimisation   242
  property   14
Commonsense
  analysis   232
  knowledge   2, 196ff
  mentalism   231f
  model   232
  psychology   2, 230, 241, 272
Commutability
  classification by   147
  criterion of   17
Competence
  communicative   15, 31, 44, 60, 61, 109,
    110
  descriptive   49, 60, 63, 87, 118
  and langue   109, 110−111
  linguistic   24, 31, 232
  moral   19
  vs. performance   64, 106, 110−111,
    120−121, 123
  semiotic   19, 51, 87, 118
  social   110, 202, 232
Component
  phonological   128
  semantic   109, 128, 129
  syntactic   109
  transformational   129, 222
Computer
  and brain   200, 202
  language   11, 86
    ALGOL   7
    FORTRAN   7, 189
    PASCAL   15
    SNOBOL   189
  modelling   261
  and natural language   37
  program   7, 11, 44, 118
    BMD 8V   69, 183
    DOCTOR   37

ELIZA   37
  and rule   189
Concordance, computer   165f
Configurations
  behavioural   15
  of elements   18
  and system   10
Content
  propositional   38, 96
  of the rules   33
  rule and propositional   32
Context
  context-free activity   158
  context-sensitive discovery   146
  dependence of   38
  explanatory psychological   218
  historical   43, 65
  items of behaviour and   18
  of a sentence   32
  verbal   42, 49, 51, 54
Contingency(ies)
  asymmetrical   66
  higher-order   166
  mutual   66
  non-   66
  probable   218
  pseudo-   66
  reactive   56, 60, 72, 181
Conversation
  and adjacency pair   (see Pair)
  analysis of   13, 16, 21, 23, 30f, 33, 241,
    260
  assumptions about   45
  and control of the social world   26
  dyadic   10, 44
  and experiments   42f
  factors in the history of   98
  grammar of   117, 157, 169
  in married couples   26−27
  measurements of   40
  model of   83
  multi-party   83
  observational studies of   30
  patterns of   45, 98
  as performance   60
  realism of   71
  and reconstruction of sequences   45−51
  rules of   42
  science of   20
  and sequence analysis   247
  sequences of   14, 59, 63, 67, 219
  sequences of c. in classroom   25−26,
    247ff
  and sequential structure   50
  and simulation   39
  structure of   3, 9f, 12ff, 18, 23, 33, 35,
    44, 51f, 56, 61, 104, 106, 169
  syntax of   51, 179

theory of   3, 15
topic of   97
Corpus
   of conversational material   203ff
   of discourse   (*see* Discourse)
Cosmology   200
Criterion(a)
   of accuracy   196ff
   of coherence   196ff
   of commutability   17
   of completeness   196ff
   of consistency   196ff
   of meta-syntactic well-formedness   149
   of scope or generality   196ff
   of similarity   155
Cryptography   172
Crystallography   197
Cybernetics   172

Decision
   analysis of   173
   process of   247
   situation of   242
   theory of   242
   tree of   242
Dependency
   conditional   203
   of context   38, 155ff
   of discourse   38
Description
   canonical   116
   categorical   141
   constitutive level of   90–96
   dimensional   141
   empirical   169
   interaction sequences and mathematical
     39
   performative level of   90–96
   personal vs. situational   100
   propositional level of   90–96
   of psychological process   203
   of real generative process   203
   social objects and systematic   265
   of structure   44
Device
   formal   203
   function indicating   32
   generative   123
   hypothetical   175
   notational   231
   and simulation   39
Diachronic
   behavioural structure   13
   patterns in language   108, 109
   patterns in social interaction   108
   structure   (*see* Structure, diachronic)
   templates   198

Dialogue
   approximations to   68
   generation of   83, 96
   as hierarchy of goals   232
   performative structure of   54
   realism of   91
   social vs. task aspects of   101
   surface structure of   190
   structure of   66, 83, 90
   temporal patterns in   106
Discourse
   analysis of   29f, 33, 71, 106, 109, 112,
     117, 120f, 137
   corpus of   95, 105, 203
   discourse system (DCS)   19, 30, 45,
     64, 109ff, 114, 117f, 120, 123, 127,
     133, 155f
   and generative grammatical models   33
   generative system of   170
   meta-syntax of   155
   natural   95
   patterns of   39
   properties of DCS   16–18
   social   33
   stages of   31
   structure of   3, 27, 37ff, 54, 90, 105,
     107, 113, 142
   surface structure of   111
Distinguishers   17

Econometrics   119
Element(s)
   and behaviour   13
   and chemistry   13
   and classes   11, 13, 17
   and discourse   17, 30
   non-terminal   169
   and system   10
   terminal   169
Embryology   172
Engineering   4, 240f
Environment
   equivalent   31
   natural   1
   physical   84
   social   84
Episodes
   and acts   188
   behavioural   1
   composition of molecules and social
     14
Equations, differential   39, 240
Equivalence
   classes   30, 31, 34, 111, 122, 126, 147,
     155, 248
   equivalent units   31
   functional   31, 65

relations 147
  between speech-act and social act 125
  of utterances 110
Ethogenics (ethogeny) 201ff
Ethology
  and behaviour sequences 106, 137
Ethnomethodology
  ethnomethodologists 24, 121
  ethnomethodological studies 23
Explanation(s)
  causal 198
  common-sensical 231
  downward or reducing 198
  nature of 202
  physical 198
  of process 201
  reductive 198
  and social behaviour 201f
  structural 197
  upward or contextualising 198

Feedback
  loop 5, 6, 14, 84, 85, 173
  negative 172f
  process of 200
  process of multiloop 243
  socio-psychological feed-back loop 274
  systems of 173
Forecasting
  methods of economic 240
  non-Markovian time-series 243f
  and sequences 223
  and systems 245f
  technological 241
Frequency
  of occurrence 162, 168
  of occurrence of pairs 161
  transitional 145, 156, 160
Function(s)
  continuous 242
  mathematical 273
  variable and time-dependent 252
Functionalism 202, 273

Game
  'imitation game' 39
  matrix games 39
  model of 121
  structure of 12
  theory of 12, 13, 173, 242
Genetics 172
Genotypes 197f
Grammar
  of behaviour 20, 116, 133, 203, 242, 263

  of behavioural system 260f
  context-free 263
  context-sensitive 263
  of conversation 117, 157, 169
  finite state 145, 161, 263
  generative 106, 114, 129, 219
  generative 'grammatical' 33
  for mirror-image languages 192f
  of natural language 107
  paradigmatical structure of 184
  of performance 25
  phrase-structure 219
  of sentences 117
  of social behaviour 260
  syntagmatic structure of 184
  of the taxonomic tree 224ff
  transformational 107, 128, 175, 219, 263f
  tree-like 113
  of type 0 175
  of type 1 175
  of type 2 175
  of type 3 175

Hierarchy(ies)
  of clusters 155
  cognitive 125
  of control 275
  of language 54, 107
  of means-end 232
  and social interaction 136
History
  and autobiography 253f
  and conversation 98
  of events 8, 132, 193, 204
  of experimentation 268
  'history grammars' 242
  and influence 65–74, 84
  of life 274
  and order of approximations 65–74
  and sequences 233
  and social meanings 108
  of speech and silence 41
  and system 'states' 246
  and variables 205ff
Hypothetical
  constructs 118
  objects or forces 4
Hypothetico-deductive
  argument 4
  method 132, 239, 266ff
  methodology 169
  research 115

Icon 202f
Illocutions 125

Influence
  additive   119
  circumstantial   195
  and history   65–74, 84
  intra-sentence   71
  matrix of   205
  non-interactive   119
  and process   273
  social   195
  of speech acts   67
  syntactic   71
  utterances and chain of   90
Information
  class of   98
  predictors of   98
  relevant and irrelevant   97
Input–output   6, 7, 8, 39, 45, 173, 200f,
    272
Instantiation   156f
Interaction
  in classroom   25, 247ff
  dyadic   9, 42, 193
  'grammatical' modelling of   117
  and history   65
  of personality and situation   260
  of process analysis   20
  and problem-solving groups   33
  sequences of   39
  structure of   34, 136
  social   (*see* Social Interaction)
  verbal   36, 39
Introspective mentalism   4, 118
Isomorphism, in language, discourse and
    interaction   106

Lag   173, 252
Language   3, 6, 17, 18
  and communication   30
  and conversation rules   18
  diachronic patterns in   109
  functional classification of   140
  grammar of natural   107
  hierarchy of   54, 107
  like discourse   106
  natural   37f
  program for natural   109
  and sequence   12
  and social behaviour   (*see* Social
    Behaviour)
  and social context (SPEAKING)   31
  and social interaction   20, 243f
  social use of   159
  structural study of   197
  and structure   9, 15
  syntax of   155
  of type 0–1–2–3   171

Langue
  as abstract language system   109
  and parole   110
Law(s)   10, 197
  causal   197
  natural   177
  physical   11, 16, 17, 240
  'Zipf's'   163
Linguistic
  analogy   50, 106, 117
  analysis   (*see* Analysis, linguistic)
  analysis of conversation   33
  competence   24, 31
  inquiry   3
  meaning   108
  methodology   31
  model   118
  structuralism   15, 121
  system of Chomsky   174
  technique   3, 16, 30
Linguistics   172
  and behaviour sequences   106, 137
  and discourse analysis   33
  generative   115, 177
  and linguistic pragmatics   33
  and structural models   119
  transformational   109
Locution(s)   3
  syntactic structure of   190
Logic
  of discovery   4, 239
  mathematical   119
Log-survivor curve   135, 162, 163
Loop
  closed   239
  open   239
  structure of   90–96

Map
  actor's mental   193
  analogy   (*see* Analogy)
  and generative model   237
  of goals   232
  of goals and means   243ff
  and rules   237f
  of transitions   (*see* Transitions map
    of)
Marker(s)   17
  of growing point   171
  semantic   107, 115
Markov
  analysis   66, 248
  chain   8, 28, 67, 72, 84, 113, 160ff, 171
  first-order system   189
  mathematics of   174
  methods of   174

model   60, 113, 161, 180
principles   41
process   170ff
stochastic series   85
structure   35
theory   173
Mathematics   241
  and linguistic structuralism   121
  mathematical logic   119
  mathematical representations   240
  and models   20, 274
Matrix
  asymmetrical   185
  of Bales   62
  of finite order   161
  of first-order conditional dependency
    203
  of influence   205
  of interchangeable utterances   149
  proactive   180ff
  reactive   180ff
  of reactive contingency   80
  of reactive tendencies   56
  of similarity   185
  social   198
  target m.   147
  of transitional frequencies   143, 160,
    165ff
  of transitional probabilities   7f, 34, 56,
    61, 84, 132, 248
Meaning
  behavioural   116
  dimensions of   107
  and everyday life   201
  and experimental method   201
  interactional   107, 124
  linguistic   108
  propositional   107, 124
  referential   107, 116
  social   108
  structural   116
  and symbol   109, 115
Means-end   232, 244
Method(s)
  categorical   141
  of consolidation   197f
  of control   243
  of conversational analysis   31
  data-driven method of analysis   132,
    263f
  of data-driven 'code breaking'   167
  emic   16, 19, 109
  ethological   122
  etic   16, 109
  and events   243
  experimental   4, 16, 200f
  of experimentation   20

extensive   199
forecasting m.   242
game-theory   241
generative   15
hypothetico-deductive   132, 239,
  266ff
of idiographic research   200
inductive   239, 266ff
intensive   199
of interaction process analysis   20, 33f
linguistic   16
of linguistic analysis   20
of Markov analysis   174
modelling   261
of naturalistic observation and recording
  20
observational   30
and paradigms   265
parametric   133
quantitative   133
of role playing   219ff, 245f
scientific   268
of sequence analysis   246, 261
of simulation   20, 241
stages of scientific   238f
structural   15, 121
syntactic   133
synthetic   15
theory-driven method of analysis   132,
  263f
Methodology
  and analogy   202
  and behaviour/conversation sequences
    238f
  of case-study   199f
  emic   60
  etic   19
  hypothetico-deductive   169
  idiographic   199f
  inductive   238
  linguistic   31
  of sequence analysis   242
  of social science   3
Mind
  as a complex control system   275
  nature of   270ff
  process of   4
Minkowsky coefficient   257
Model
  action structure m.   265
  anthropomorphic   2, 195
  behavioural   229f
  coherent   197
  combinatorial   204
  criticism of linguistic   118
  cybernetic   173
  dimensional   141

of discourse structure 178
discrete-state 241
of economic forecasting 240
finite state 112f
game 121
generative 127, 169, 199, 263
generative forecasting 265
of generative process 260
of global systems dynamics 240
hierarchical 217
higher order of linear stochastic 113
linear stochastic 22, 112
map and generative 237
Markov (*see* Markov, model)
mathematical 20, 274
of motor skill 173
non-stochastic 84
of pure research 241
and realist theory 228
retrograde m. and prior history 206ff
of rule 117, 195, 264
of sequence analysis of behaviour 241
of sequential structure 160
of social skills (*see* Social skills)
speculative 202ff
stochastic 115
structural 119, 264
of system dynamics 205ff
and theory 230
and theory-testing 229
Morphemes 11, 12, 83, 85, 105, 106, 107,
147, 263
Morphology, of complex events 3
Motor-skill, model of 5, 45

Non-verbal communication (NVC) 6, 9,
107, 137

Occurrence
conditions of 207
of events of discrete types 206f
formula of 206
frequency of 162, 168
probability of (*see* Probability)
of speech and pauses 41
Operations Research 173, 240, 243
Organization(s) 241
of behaviour 260
theory of behavioural 217
social 198

Pair
adjacency 21–22, 23, 25, 66, 143,
155

of events 218
frequency of occurrence of 161
proactive 47, 53
of question and answer 85
reactive 53
Paradigm(s) 159, 197
social psychology, 'new' and 'old'
201, 265ff
Paradigmatic
relation (*see* Relation, paradigmatic)
structure (*see* Structure, paradigmatic)
Parole
and langue 110
as observed language use 109
Parsing 3, 39, 50, 113, 247f, 265
of natural language 176
of surface structure 95
Path analysis 185
minimum 188, 260
Pattern(s)
of behaviour 4, 201
of events 197, 242
of human action 198
of movements 16
musical 10
reproduction of behavioural 238
sequential 20
of sound 16
temporal 11
Performance 118, 140, 203, 265
communicative 49
vs. competence 64, 106, 110–111,
120–121, 123
and conversation 60, 61
and parole 109
Perlocutions 125
Permutation(s) 242
Phenomena
language and social 20
surface 266ff, 271
Phenotypes 197f
Phoneme(s) 12
combination of 107
Phonology 115
Physics 4, 119, 252
theoretical 177, 197f
Plausibility
of dialogue 99
of loop structure 91ff
ratings for 183
Positivism 5
Proactive
behaviour 217
pair 47, 53
relation 165, 178
rules 180, 181
score 47

structure   74, 84
tendency   8, 35, 66
transition   34
Probability
first-order transitional   162
matrix of transitional   7–8, 34
of occurrence   87, 109, 110, 162, 242
transformational   22
transitional   54, 57, 60, 63, 64, 113, 173
transitional error   50, 96, 134
Problem-behaviour graph (PBG)   177
Problem-solving
and analysis of sequences   240
groups   33f
Process(es)
action regulating   201
analysis of temporal   160
biological   107
description of psychological   238
generative   4, 123, 127, 170, 193
linear stochastic   161, 171
mental process   1, 4
of mind   4
and phenomena   269
and product   201f, 238f, 243, 266ff
psychological   230, 272, 274
real behavioural   216
real generative   203
Program
computer   7, 11, 44, 118
natural language   109
Property
combinatorial   14
of discourse systems   16–18
semantic   106
structural   261
syntactic   106
Proposition(s)
aggregate   199
general   199
Psycholinguists   6
Psychology   4
cognitive   274
common-sense   (see Common-sense, psychology)
and ethogenics   201f
of faculties   198
functionalist version of   202
individual   198
as 'science of the possible'   274
scientific and common-sense   272
scientific micro-   241
Push-down
stack   192, 263
tree   192, 203

Quintuples   174f

Reactive
behaviour   217
contingencies   56, 60, 72
pair   53
relation   165
rules   180f
scores   47, 50, 53
sentence   178
structure   74, 85
tendency   8, 35, 54, 66
transition   34
Reality
individual and social   274
psychological   95
social   10, 64
Recipient
and caller   23
recipient design   23
'Recycling group'   248
Reflex arc   3
Reinterpretation
retrospective   75
Relation(s)
equivalence   147
morphological   135
paradigmatic   17, 30, 33f, 111ff, 116, 122, 125f
proactive   165, 178
reactive   165
semantic   115, 145, 147
structural   36
syntactic   116, 147, 234
syntagmatic   17, 30, 33, 122, 126
utterances and logical   38
Representation(s)
of actor's mental processes   195
canonical generative   254
cognitive   24, 193
of conversation   51
impaired   241
of 'interaction meaning'   107
mathematical   240
mis-   246
semantic   7, 16, 24, 54, 128, 129
social   128, 132
of social structure   189
syntactic   129
verbal   145
Response
accuracy of   169
latency of   169
Rule(s)
of alternation   33, 138
archetype for generative   170

artificial 126
behavioural 176
and classroom interaction 25, 246ff
complex 172
constitutive 22, 112, 125, 138, 155f,
  231
content of 33
context-dependent 171
context-free 113, 147, 171
context-sensitive 23, 113
of convergent substitution 172
of conversation 42
of co-occurrence 33, 138
and deviant cases 24
for discourse analysis 27–28
distributional 23
of ellipsis 28
essential 32
and function indicating device 32
generative 11, 36, 169, 263
generative behavioural 218
hierarchical 189
and history 260
and inference 190
'instrumentalist' 120, 189
interlocking bracketing 216f
left to right 172
and maps 237f
matrices of proactive and reactive 185
model of 117, 195
operations for generative 170ff
preparatory 32
of priority 192
proactive 180, 181
and propositional content 32
pseudo-Markovian 216f
reactive 180, 181
'realist' 120
recursive and non- 114, 171
regulative 32, 112, 122, 125, 138,
  147, 231
schemes of 183
second-order 178
semantic 18, 32
of semiotic competence 51
of sequence 188
sequencing 33, 138
set of 210ff
of sincerity 32
social 23
and social action 106
and speech-act 106, 125
and strategies 12
structural 50
and symbols 17
syntactic 18, 128
systems of first-order 183

of taxonomic tree 222
transformational 113, 198
'trivial' 222

Schemata
  and cognitive structure 127
  conceptual 177
  functional 140
Science(s)
  of action 2f, 20
  behavioural 3f, 121, 268
  causal 197
  and consolidation 197
  natural 2ff, 15, 197f, 241, 264, 268ff
  and paradigms 265f
  parametric 119
  physical 121, 268f
  of policy 3
  social 2ff, 15, 121, 268
  social science-making 2
  structural 119, 197
  theoretical 15
  and theory 270
Scores
  proactive 47, 50, 53
  reactive 47, 50, 53
  slot 47, 53
Segments 3
Semantics 14, 124
  of behaviour 16, 115
  meta-semantics in the analysis of dis-
    course 109
Semantic
  analysis 145, 147
  classification 264
  components 109
  content 21, 31, 54
  deep structure 109
  property 106
  relations 115
  representation 7, 16, 24
  rules 18
  theory 17
Sentence
  grammar of 117
  'response sentence' 51
  and sequence 11
  'sequence sentences' 51
  'situation sentences' 51
  structure of 12, 30, 67, 71, 105, 107,
    114, 191
  surface form of 109
Sequence(s)
  analysis of 9, 35, 37, 43, 60, 85,
    122, 124, 137, 143, 155, 157, 173,
    179, 244, 252, 250, 263

artificial 179
of behaviour 7f, 10, 12, 16, 36, 56,
106, 107, 111, 112, 114, 116, 118,
123, 173, 175, 177, 231, 233, 241,
262
behaviour and analysis of 133, 139
closing 143
of conversation 14, 20, 59, 63, 67, 75,
191
cross nested 85–90
of discrete events 205f, 264
of events 252
and history 233
ideal (see observed)
insertion 22
of interaction 39
of interactive behaviour 7
linear 85–90
nested 36, 85–90, 104, 193
'not hearing' 22
observed 222, 227, 234, 264, 267
preclosing 143
predictable 64f, 83
of question and answer 191f
reactive 178
reproduction of sets of 203
rule governed 19
sanctions and remedial 23
self embedded 36
and sentences 11
set of 203ff
of social action 106
of social behaviour 204ff, 264
sociometric 41
of speech acts 11, 21, 42f, 106
summons-answer 24, 66
of symbols 109
of utterances 52
zero and higher order 66–74
Similarity 165
between items 185
matrix of 185
syntagmatic 187
Simulation 39
computer 172, 177, 188
and conversation 39
of dialogue 72
of discourse structure 37, 38, 39
of interpersonal and intercultural differences 189
of natural language 37
of question and answer patterns 190
and speech acts 39
Situations 232f, 260, 263
Social behaviour 3, 5, 7f, 11, 14, 262
deep structure of 16
and explanations 201f

grammar of 260
hierarchical structure of 135
and language 20, 54, 108, 116, 264
non-verbal 139
and physical variables 40
structural analysis of 141
syntax and meta-syntax of 108f
verbal 139
verbal representations of 145
Social interaction 5, 7f, 10, 12f, 20,
37, 43, 51, 106, 111, 114, 122,
127, 130f, 135f
and deep/surface structure 193
like a discourse 106
and language 20, 243f
'process' of 271
and 'secondary' experiments 261
and synchronic/diachronic patterns
108
Social psychology 4f, 10, 265ff
alternative approaches to 110
and behaviour sequences 106
experimental 109
and individual psychology 198
'new and old paradigms' 201, 265ff
and parametric sciences 119
scientific approaches to 197ff
and structure of conversation 44
and surface phenomena 266
Social reality 10, 64
and deep structure 130
map of 196ff
Social Science (see Science, social)
Social skills, model of 5, 7, 173, 260
Social world 197ff
conversation and control of 26
and 'jigsaw theories' 231
macro- 178
micro- 178
structures of physical and social worlds
198
Sociality
everyday theory of 202f
Sociolinguistics 6, 31
Speaker
change of 41
characteristics of 101ff
and hearer 6, 12, 32, 37, 40, 45, 114,
125, 128
Speaking circuit 6
Speech
as action 124
amplitude of 40
codes of 6
pattern of 41
as social action 125
Speech-act(s) 11ff, 31, 51, 146, 190

categories of   78, 143f, 157, 180
and conversations   21, 113
families of   144
illocutionary force of   96
and meaning   107, 132
as performative utterances   54
and proactive relations   178
and rules   33, 107, 114
logical structure of   190
sequences of   106, 157, 162
and sequence analysis   60
and simulation   39
and social act classifications   142
temporally predictable sequences   64f
theory of   3
State(s)
absorbing   174
explanations and mental   231
finite-   112ff
grammar, finite-   145, 161, 263
models, discrete-   241
models, finite-   (*see* Model, finite-
state)
Stimulus-Response (S-R)   3, 5, 7, 8, 14
stimuli and cause   201
Stochastic
analysis of sequences   26
higher orders of stochastic series   189
linear stochastic model   22, 112, 113
linear stochastic process   161
linear stochastic series   83−84, 85−90,
113
model   115
process   113
series   8
transitions   243
Strategic Analysis   172
Strategy   12, 13
calculus of   242
nomethetic   199
Stream
of accounts   203
of behaviour   7, 12, 16, 106, 122, 133ff,
139, 142, 262
of social behaviour   8
Structuralism
French structuralist school   20
linguistic   15, 121
Structure
of action   9, 10
of act/action   16, 112
analysis of   15, 71
behavioural   123, 218f, 264
cognitive   127
complex   95
of conversation   (*see* Conversation,
structure of)

deep   16, 24, 106, 109, 126ff, 172, 189,
193, 222, 264
definition of deep   126
description of   44
diachronic   10, 13, 14, 197f
of dialogue   66, 83, 90
of discourse   (*see* Discourse, structure
of)
of game   12
grammatical   3
hierarchical   112, 169, 219
of interaction   34, 136
'jigsaw theory' of   228
of language   9, 15
linearity of   72
loop   (*see* Loop, structure of)
Markovian   178
mental   4
meta-semantic   159
meta-syntactic   159
molecular   13
nested   161, 172
paradigmatic   138, 141, 145f, 147, 155,
184
performative   54
permutable   228
phrase   50, 135
proactive   74
reactive   74
semantic   109
of sentences   (*see* Sentences, structure
of)
sequential   11, 50, 53, 60, 112, 160,
162, 188, 246
surface   24, 50, 95, 106, 111, 122,
129ff, 133, 172, 190, 193, 222
symbolic   112
synchronic   10, 13f, 197f, 231
syntactic   41
syntagmatic   138, 141f, 145f, 147, 184
of a system   197
transitional   246
tree structure   134, 171, 192
Symbols   16
arrangement of   108
and meaning   109, 114
and rules   17
and sequences   109
symbol combinations   108
Symmetry
of Bales's categories   35
and sciences of structure   177
Synchronic
patterns in social interaction   108
physical structures   13
structures   (*see* Structure, synchronic)
templates   198

Syntagms   157, 159
Syntagmatic
    relation   (*see* Relation, syntagmatic)
    structure   (*see* Structure, syntagmatic)
Syntax   13, 14
    of action   3
    of conversation   51, 179
    generative   122, 197
    of language   155 ·
    meta-syntax and analysis of discourse
        109
    and meta-syntax of social behaviour
        108–109
    syntactic form   54
    theory of   128
System(s)
    behavioural   5
    behaviour of the   20ff, 205, 272
    of belief   203
    and chemistry   13
    closed   6, 7, 14, 200
    complex behavioural   265
    of complex discrete-state   244
    and configurations   10
    configuration and relativistic   18
    continuous   243
    creative   17
    of discourse   (*see* Discourse, system of)
    dynamics   205, 243, 264
    and elements   10, 17
    ergodic   249
    experimental   229
    explanatory   231
    and forecasting   242
    instrumental   16
    interactive behaviour of the   246
    life as a closed   259
    linguistic   111
    of mind/world   273
    open   6, 7, 14, 200
    physical   5
    proactive   178
    real and analogical   202f
    relativistic   119
    representational   18
    rule   179, 189, 217
    social   1
    social action   20
    signalling   108
    of symbolic logic   11
    and structure   10, 246
    theory of   14
Summons-answer   (*see* Sequence)

Taxonomy
    behavioural   112

construction of *a priori*   158, 162
    of events   138ff
    numerical   119
    and social behaviour   138
Technique(s)
    content analytic   142
    ethological   169
    factor analytic   141
    'Gödel-numbering'   121
    linguistic   3, 16, 30
    of log-survivor analysis   162
    for the negotiations of accounts   120
    observational   30, 33
    practical problems and scientific   241
    psychological   16
    quantitative taxonomic   265
    of scaling   253
    of systems dynamics   243
    time-series analysis   252f
    for writing behaviour grammars   242
Technology   3
Templates   197
    diachronic   198, 231
    and social action   198
    synchronic   198
Tendency   (*see* Proactive and Reactive)
'Tesserae', of artificial behaviour   133f, 139
Theory
    of action   2f, 15
    of associative chains   161
    automata   20, 119, 174, 242
    of behaviour   269
    of behavioural organization   217
    of control   14
    of conversation   3, 15
    of data   238f
    of decisions   242
    of endogenous structure   231
    of endogenous templates   228
    of entities   230f
    everyday   202
    exchange   42
    and experimental methods   200
    of finite automata   65
    game   12f, 173, 242
    General Systems   172, 241, 252
    of grammar   107
    group and set   119
    of human behaviour   107
    of infinite groups   119
    of information   39
    'Jigsaw theory'   228, 231
    of language   95
    magnetic   129
    mathematical logic   119
    and models   228ff
    and natural science   230

of personality   260
of process   229
and prediction   239
realist   231
semantic   17
of semantic interaction   146
of sociality   202f
speech-act   3
of structures   141
of syntax   128
of systems   14
Time
    objective   76−83
    subjective   76−83
Trajectory
    of behaviour   172
    and fields   252
    of growth   172
    of life   255ff
Transfer function   7, 14, 200f
Transition(s)
    map of   177, 246
    negative   248
    stochastic   243
    transitional relevance place   21, 41
    utterance   63
    within animal   1, 66
Translation   7
    and language   44f
    mechanisms and precedence of   197
    process   7, 260
    translators of categories to sentences
        180
Tree
    Chomskian   96
    'convergent' and 'divergent' nodes in a
        246
    'push-down tree'   192, 203
    structure of the sentence   96
    taxonomic   221ff
    tree diagram   247
    tree structure   134, 171, 192
Turing
    automata   263
    -like criterion   68
    -machine   129, 174ff
Turn
    allocation component   21
    constructional component   21

Unit(s)   134

class of   157
embedded sub-   169
hypothetical   169
and speech acts   137
suitability of   133
units of behaviour   133ff, 139, 264
Utterance(s)   138
    blocks of   102
    class of   26, 38, 56, 59f, 148, 150, 155,
        263
    constative   124
    and context   155
    and conversation structure   52
    description of   51
    information for selection of   96ff
    performative   54, 124, 125, 143
    and reconstruction of conversation   45
    sequence of   52
    and social function   54
    strings of   83, 179
    and structure   44
    structure of   71
    and syntactic forms   51ff
    and transitional probability   54
    transitions   62
    typologies of   64
    and verbal context   49

Validity
    external   104, 200
    internal   104
    of methods   20
    of models   16
Variable(s)
    content   43
    continuous   160, 242
    and construction of models   205f
    dependent   4, 96
    endogenous   229
    exogenous   229
    and generalization   199f
    independent   4, 18, 200
    and parametric sciences   119
    personality   43
    physical   40
    process   43
    role vs. individual   101
    scalar   243
    sociological   6
Vector   252ff